Handbook of Systems Analysis

Overview of Uses, Procedures, Applications, and Practice

Handbook of Systems Analysis
Hugh J. Miser and Edward S. Quade

- Overview of Uses, Procedures, Applications, and Practice
- Craft Issues and Procedural Choices
- Cases

Handbook of Systems Analysis

Overview of Uses, Procedures, Applications, and Practice

Edited by
Hugh J. Miser
Edward S. Quade

JOHN WILEY & SONS
Chichester · New York · Brisbane · Toronto · Singapore

Copyright © 1985 Hugh J. Miser and the Edward S. Quade Estate
First published in the United States by Elsevier Science Publishing Company, Inc.
First published in the United Kingdom by John Wiley & Sons Ltd,
Baffins Lane, Chichester,
West Sussex PO19 1UD, England

National   01243 779777
International   (+44) 1243 779777

Reprinted November 1995
All rights reserved.

No part of this book may be reproduced by any means,
or transmitted, or translated into a machine language
without the written permission of the publisher.

Other Wiley Editorial Offices

John Wiley & Sons, Inc., 605 Third Avenue,
New York, NY 10158-0012, USA

Jacaranda Wiley Ltd, 33 Park Road, Milton,
Queensland 4064, Australia

John Wiley & Sons (Canada) Ltd, 22 Worcester Road,
Rexdale, Ontario M9W 1L1, Canada

John Wiley & Sons (SEA) Pte Ltd, 37 Jalan Pemimpin #05-04,
Block B, Union Industrial Building, Singapore 2057

British Library Cataloguing in Publication Data

A catalogue record for this book is available from the British Library

ISBN 0-471-90743-X

Printed and bound in Great Britain by Antony Rowe Ltd, Chippenham, Wiltshire

Contents

Preface   xi

Acknowledgments   xv

Chapter 1. The Context, Nature, and Use of Systems Analysis   1
Edward S. Quade and Hugh J. Miser

1.1. Introduction	1
1.2. The Context	2
Improving Blood Availability and Utilization	2
Improving Fire Protection	4
Protecting an Estuary from Flooding	6
Achieving Adequate Amounts of Energy for the Long-Range Future	7
Providing Housing for Low-Income Families	8
Controlling a Forest Pest in Canada	11
1.3. The Nature of the Problems	12
1.4. The Characteristics of Systems Analysis	15
1.5. Science and Systems Analysis	18
1.6. Related Forms of Analysis	21
1.7. Applications	22
1.8. The Value of Systems Analysis	24
1.9. The Craft of Analysis	29
1.10. Conclusion	30
References	31

Chapter 2. Systems Analysis: A Genetic Approach — 33
Giandomenico Majone

2.1. Change and Continuity — 33
2.2. From Operations Research to Systems Analysis — 35
2.3. From Systems Analysis to Policy Analysis — 44
2.4. ... and Back to Operations Research — 49
2.5. The Social Side of Systems Analysis: Professional and Institutional Developments — 52
2.6. The Evolution of Criteria of Quality and Effectiveness — 57
2.7. Conclusion: The Language of Systems Analysis — 62
References — 64

Chapter 3. Examples of Systems Analysis — 67
Edward S. Quade

3.1. Introduction — 67
3.2. Improving Blood Availability and Utilization — 68
    Background — 68
    Approach — 70
    Analysis — 71
    Implementation — 75
    Computer Modules — 78
    Impact — 78
3.3. Improving Fire Protection — 79
    Background — 79
    Origin of the Project — 80
    Analysis — 81
    Recommendations of the Project Team — 85
    History of the Implementation — 86
    Evaluation — 88
3.4. Protecting an Estuary from Flooding — 89
    Background — 89
    The Analytic Approach — 92
    Methods for Synthesizing and Presenting Results — 96
    Study Results — 99
    Conclusions — 104
    The Decision — 108
3.5. Providing Energy for the Future — 109
    Demand — 112
    Supply — 112
    System Properties — 113
References — 115

Chapter 4. The Methodology of Systems Analysis: An Introduction and Overview — 117
Władysław Findeisen and Edward S. Quade

- 4.1. Introduction — 117
- 4.2. A Framework for Systems Analysis — 121
  - Objectives, Alternatives, and Ranking — 121
  - A Framework for Analysis — 122
  - Iteration and Feedback — 123
  - Communication — 125
  - Phases of Analysis — 126
  - Partial Analysis — 126
- 4.3. Problem Formulation — 127
  - Purposes — 127
  - Objectives — 128
  - Values and Criteria — 130
  - Constraints — 131
- 4.4. Generating and Selecting Alternatives — 132
- 4.5. Forecasting Future States of the World — 133
  - The Future and Uncertainty — 133
  - Forecasting in Systems Analysis — 133
  - Forecasting Approaches — 134
- 4.6. Identifying the Consequences — 135
  - Predictive Models — 136
  - Limitations on Predictive Modeling; Experiments — 137
  - Using Models — 138
  - Summary Remarks — 139
- 4.7. Comparing and Ranking Alternatives — 140
  - Difficulties of Ranking — 140
  - Judgmental Comparison and Ranking — 141
  - Cost-Effectiveness and Cost-Benefit Criteria — 141
  - Value and Utility Approaches — 142
  - General Remarks — 144
- 4.8. Documentation — 145
- 4.9. Summary — 145
- References — 147

Chapter 5. Formulating Problems for Systems Analysis — 151
Peter B. Checkland

- 5.1. Introduction — 151
- 5.2. Formulating the Problem: The Concepts — 153
  - Problems and Problem Solving — 153
  - Exploring the Problem Area — 156
- 5.3. The Problem Environment — 159

5.4. Formulating the Problem: The Activities	161
5.5. Conclusion	165
Appendix A. A Workbook Outline to Aid Documenting the Problem-Content and Problem-Solving Systems	167
Appendix B. A Format for Issue Papers	168
References	169

Chapter 6. Objectives, Constraints, and Alternatives 171
Edward S. Quade

6.1. Objectives	171
Measuring Effectiveness	176
Multiple Objectives	178
6.2. Constraints	180
6.3. Alternatives	182
References	188

Chapter 7. Predicting the Consequences: Models and Modeling 191
Edward S. Quade

7.1. Introduction	191
7.2. The Need for Models	192
7.3. Modeling Techniques	194
Analytic Models	195
Simulation	196
Gaming	197
Judgmental Models	199
7.4. Model Building	203
Developing a Simple Model	203
General Remarks	205
Improving a Model	206
7.5. Predicting the Consequences	208
Establishing the Context	208
Establishing the Consequences	210
Sensitivity Analysis	211
7.6. Social Experimentation	212
7.7. What Do Models Give Us?	213
References	216

Chapter 8. Guidance for Decision 219
Brita Schwarz, Kenneth C. Bowen, István Kiss, and Edward S. Quade

8.1. Introduction	219
8.2. Criteria	220
8.3. Satisficing	222

8.4.	Suboptimization	223
8.5.	Cost–Benefit Analysis and the Cost–Benefit Criterion	224
8.6.	Cost-Effectiveness Analysis	227
8.7.	Decision Analysis	229
8.8.	Dealing with the Criterion Problem	230
8.9.	Value Analysis and Political Feasibility	234
8.10.	Uncertainties	239
8.11.	Risk Evaluation	241
8.12.	Decision Processes, Planning, and Policies	241
8.13.	Guidance from the Analyst	243
	References	245

Chapter 9. Implementation 249

Rolfe Tomlinson, Edward S. Quade, and Hugh J. Miser

9.1.	Background	250
9.2.	Implementation Concerns Early in a Systems Study	253
9.3.	The Role of the Systems Analyst in Implementation	255
	An Example: Improved Methods of Calculation	257
	An Example: An Organizational Computer System	259
	Implementation Involving Multiple Organizations	265
	Concluding Remarks	267
9.4.	Some Additional Issues and Difficulties	268
9.5.	Coping with Implementation Prior to Decision	271
	Matters of Good Practice	271
	Implementation Scenarios	273.
	Implementation Analysis	274
	Social Experiments	274
9.6.	Coping with Implementation After Decision	275
	Mediation and Persuasion	276
	Using the Power of the Mandate	276
9.7.	Concluding Remarks	277
	References	277

Chapter 10. The Practice of Systems Analysis 281

Hugh J. Miser

10.1.	Introduction	281
10.2.	The Organizational Context	282
10.3.	Developing a Professional Philosophy for Systems Analysis	286
10.4.	Awareness of the Problem Situation	290
10.5.	Formulating the Problem	293
10.6.	Gathering Information	297
10.7.	Formulating Alternatives	298

10.8. Choosing Modes of Analysis	299
10.9. Carrying out the Analysis	301
10.10. Formulating the Findings	302
10.11. Preparing the Communication Instruments	303
The Systems Analysis Report	304
Oral Presentation	307
Concluding Remarks	310
10.12. Additional Analysis	311
10.13. The Communication Campaign	311
An Example: Space Surveillance	312
An Example: Providing Energy for the Future	314
Concluding Remarks	314
10.14. Systems Analysis as an Agent of Change	315
10.15. Guidelines for Professional Behavior	316
Internal Evaluation	316
External Evaluation	317
Relations with Society	317
10.16. Conclusion	325
References	325
A Selected Bibliography	327
Author Index	333
Subject Index	337

Preface

Since the dawn of human history people have been facing problems arising from the operations of systems in which they themselves are important parts. However, the idea that systematic scrutiny in the spirit of science—and using its tools—can help solve them became widespread only in this century. Before 1935 the inquiries into such problems—and therefore into the systems from which the problems emerged—were few, scattered, and limited in scope. However, since 1935 the studies aimed at solving such problems by understanding the operations of their underlying systems have undergone rapid growth, encouraged by the successful work that took place just before and during the second World War.

This work has developed scientific knowledge of the behavior of man–machine operating systems, a technology to put such knowledge to work to solve their problems, a group of professionals with the relevant skills, and a body of successful problem-solving experience.

The success of this work—often called operations research—led to a significant expansion of its scope, so that by the middle 1950s it was not uncommon for the problems of very large operating systems to be investigated, or for knowledge from such work to be employed to design new operating systems. This enlarged purview necessitated bringing into the work specialists from many disciplines; thus it was not unnatural for the enlarged community doing the work to adopt a name for it: systems analysis—to emphasize the fact that, associated with each of the problems then being investigated, there was an existing operating system, or one being planned. The ensuing quarter century has seen growth in both the scope and diversity of systems analysis, including its extension to problems arising in situations for which no system had yet been defined.

Systems analysis is now applied to a wide range of highly diverse problems, and the patterns of analysis exhibit a corresponding diversity, depending on the context, the possible courses of action, the information needed, the accompanying constraints and uncertainties, and the positions and responsibilities of the persons who may use its results. In a rare case, a problem may fall within the sphere of responsibility of a single policy maker; however, it is far more usual for the relevant responsibilities to be diffused among many persons, often with significant portions of the problem lying outside existing authorities.

This diversity of activity has spawned a variety of names other than systems analysis under which work that can be described this way is done, depending on the professional, institutional, and geographical backgrounds of the analysts involved: operational research, operations analysis, policy analysis, policy science, systems research, and others. Thus, choosing a title for this handbook presented some difficulties; as a compromise, we chose the name associated with a stream of thought and activity that began over three decades ago in the United States and that has had an important influence on developing the activity throughout the world.

For a field exhibiting such rapid growth and diversity—even in its basic nomenclature—is the concept of a handbook a meaningful one? With so many ramifications, and so many extensions going on in so many new directions, is it possible to take a snapshot of the state of the art that will have enduring value? If the answer is "yes," what should a handbook be?

The key to arriving at positive answers to these questions is twofold: to restrict the attention in the handbook to the central core of the field as it now exists based on extensive experience, avoiding the temptation to stray into the many attractive and promising new branches; and to provide a challenging perspective of the future opportunities as yet unexplored, while at the same time offering normative standards of quality and substance where experience warrants.

Thus, we have centered the attention in this *Handbook of Systems Analysis* on the type of problem that has mainly concerned systems analysts in the past: those relatively easy to structure and in which some important aspect is dominated by technology. Although there were early exceptions, it is only within the past decade or so that the people-dominated problems—such as those found in the influences of government and industrial operations on the public and the environment—began to be explored in a major way by systems analysts; thus, it is still too early in this experience to warrant a handbook synthesis.

We have found that, for this context of problems dominated by technology and the analytic work that has investigated them, it is possible to compile a summary of the main currents of knowledge and practice, accompanied by a view of the future potential of the field. This handbook is the result.

Since systems analysis as it is currently practiced—and is likely to be for the foreseeable future—combines both old and new knowledge to evolve solutions to problems of operations, policies, and planning, the audience that needs information about it is extremely varied, ranging from technical specialists to intelligent nontechnical citizens with public concerns. Thus, we have divided the handbook into three volumes, depending on their purposes, contents, and audiences; although the three are intimately interconnected, each is a logical whole that is useful to its audience without reference to the others.

The first volume, *Overview of Uses, Procedures, Applications, and Practice,* is aimed at a widely varied audience of producers and users of systems analysis—government officials, legislators, business executives, scientists and technologists in other fields, public-interest groups, and concerned citizens, as well as students and practitioners; to keep systems analysis accessible to this broad audience, this book avoids technical details as much as possible. This volume provides a central description of the systems analysis process from the first appreciation that a problem situation exists through analysis and implementation to assessing the results. Several successful applications of the systems-analysis approach are described early in the book and used throughout to clarify the concepts and illustrate the nature of the work and its results.

The second volume, *Craft Issues and Procedural Choices,* consists of essays on these subjects by experienced systems analysts. While systems analysis is an interdisciplinary activity that borrows extensively from its contributing disciplines, this book is not devoted to their commonly used tools, methods, and techniques; rather, it directs its attention to matters of particular importance for systems analysis: selecting an analytic strategy, making the analysis feasible (by screening alternatives or satisficing, for example), special problems (such as forecasting, political feasibility, and cost), and professional issues (such as validation, equity, making an analysis team effective, and ethics). Thus, it avoids treating methods that, although useful from time to time in systems analysis, are adequately treated in other central sources such as, for operations research, Wagner's *Principles of Operations Research* (Englewood Cliffs, New Jersey: Prentice-Hall, 2nd ed., 1975) or the Moder and Elmaghraby *Handbook of Operations Research* (New York: Van Nostrand Reinhold, 1978). The essays in this book are therefore useful for systems analysts, professional workers in other fields who may be cooperating in a systems study, students of systems analysis, and persons interested in how work in this field proceeds.

The third volume, *Cases,* contains extended descriptions of actual cases in which systems analysis was used; thus, it illustrates the diversity of problems and approaches encountered in systems analysis. While some attention is paid to technical details, so that an analyst has a view of how the results were arrived at, as well as what they were, the descriptions are written so as to be accessible also to nontechnical readers who may want to skip the technical details. Insofar as possible, the descriptions view the cases from the point of view of the client as well as the analyst.

The focus of the first volume of this handbook is on systems analysis as a process accompanied by a substantial body of craft knowledge, a process involving substantial and continuing interaction between the analysts and their clients. Thus, the overview offered by the first volume cannot present hard and fast rules about how the analysis should be done; rather, it must proffer advice and counsel supported by examples exhibiting good practices as a basis for analysts and their clients developing their own approaches through practical experience with the craft of systems analysis. That is why, as pointed out above, this overview volume uses examples throughout to illustrate important points.

However, selecting and developing these cases presented us with many cruel dilemmas: rich examples showing the full gamut of systems-analysis properties and difficulties would have demanded more space than would have been reasonable, while cases simple and intuitive enough to be set forth economically were frequently too simple to be seen as true examples of the systems analysis art. Thus, most of the cases used in this book are something of a compromise, chosen, however, primarily on the basis of their ability to highlight the relevant points about the craft of systems analysis, and, wherever possible, suggest additional insights. In each case the background literature referred to in the text gives a great deal more detail that is well worth exploring further. And the third volume of this handbook offers a number of cases discussed in considerable depth.

The work of preparing this handbook has shown us that there is a great deal of existing knowledge, that there is a substantial body of practice, and that, in spite of its promise, the prospects for the field and its potential value for society are only dimly perceived in many quarters. Thus, at this relatively early stage in the development of systems analysis, a handbook has an important opportunity to bring the central core of knowledge and professional experience together in systematic form, to establish foundations for the further growth of systems analysis, to map its potentials, to indicate open questions and challenges, to offer guidelines for future development, and to provide a source of valuable information for actual and potential clients for systems analysis studies.

This handbook has been aimed at these purposes, and was prepared in the hope that it would serve them well enough to contribute significantly to the growth of systems analysis. If this goal is met, the Editors and contributors will be more than amply rewarded; they have worked in the belief that systems analysis, properly developed and skillfully pursued, can make important contributions to solving problems that the world will face in the future.

Hugh J. Miser
Edward S. Quade

Acknowledgments

The concept of a *Handbook of Systems Analysis* and a project aimed at creating such a work were originated at the International Institute for Applied Systems Analysis (IIASA), which owed its existence to the growth of systems analysis, particularly in the United States, and the perception that many problems of international and global scope could usefully be addressed by extending this approach appropriately.

IIASA is a nongovernmental interdisciplinary research institution located in Laxenburg, Austria, that was founded in October 1972 on the initiative of the academies of science or equivalent institutions of 12 nations (by 1978 these National Member Organizations numbered 17 and included countries from both East and West). In 1974 the National Member Organization from the USSR proposed that IIASA undertake to prepare a *Handbook of Systems Analysis,* and this project was supported by the Institute from 1974 through 1982. In 1974 and 1975, Roger Levien, later Director of the Institute from November 1975 until November 1981, conducted, together with Vil Z. Rakhmankulov, an initial survey of interests, needs, and possible contents. Edward S. Quade led the project from 1976 through 1978, Hugh J. Miser from 1979 on; Vil Z. Rakhmankulov, Władysław Findeisen, Giandomenico Majone, and Alexander P. Iastrebov participated in the project for various periods between 1974 and 1982. A conference held at IIASA in September 1978 devised the three-volume format in which the handbook now appears. The Institute's support for the project is hereby gratefully acknowledged.

In addition to the institutional support from IIASA and its 17 National Member Organizations, a great many individuals have contributed to the work of preparing the handbook, too many to make it feasible to recognize all of them in these acknowledgments. Some 160 persons responded to the survey that began the work leading to the handbook, 38 scientists submitted written comments on the manuscript of a preliminary version of the work as a whole, and 25 scientists from 14 National Member Organizations attended the 1978 planning conference that gave the handbook the three-volume design that it has today. To all of these people we are grateful for their support and for their contributions to the concept and details of the work.

With respect to the first volume, there are many additional persons to whom we owe debts of gratitude:

> Howard Raiffa, the founding Director of IIASA, and his successor, Roger Levien, both gave the handbook project enthusiastic support, the former from 1974 through 1975, the latter from 1975 through 1981.

> A large number of people, not known to us by name because they worked through the IIASA National Member Organizations and communicated with us through these organizations, reviewed preliminary versions of the chapters of the first volume as they were issued, as well as early versions of the book as a whole.

> Much of the substance of the book was supplied by the contributors: Brita Schwarz from Sweden; Władysław Findeisen from Poland; István Kiss from Hungary; Giandomenico Majone from Italy; Peter Checkland, K. C. Bowen, and Rolfe Tomlinson from England. Their contributions are indicated roughly in the chapter attributions; however, to make the book a unified and closely interconnected whole, the Editors have been at pains to blend the entire text together, so that for the most part it is now impossible to identify individual contributions uniquely. Each of these contributors also aided the project by giving the Editors their views on the volume as a whole.

> These scientists supplied the Editors with written comments on a semifinal version of the manuscript: H. L. Klaasen, C. J. Ruppert, J. W. Weehuizen, Th. L. M. Wortel, J. M. L. Janssen, and Gerard de Zeeuw from the Netherlands; Fehér Márta, Kocsondi Andras, and Tibor Engländer from Hungary; Johannes Dathe, Dietrich Fischer, and Thilo Wedlich from the Federal Republic of Germany; M. Peschel, Klaus Bellman, and Peter Sudau from the German Democratic Republic; Salah E. Elmaghraby, B. F. Goeller, Harold A. Linstone, and Alexander M. Mood from the United States; Kiyoshi Nagata and Hayao Teshima from Japan; L. Peter Jennergren from Denmark; Louis Vagianos from Canada; and Gregory Prastacos from Greece.

> Seven scientists provided cover-to-cover reviews of the text of the semifinal version: Yehezkel Dror from Israel; K. B. Haley and K. C. Bowen from the United Kingdom; G. D. Kaye from Canada; and Gene H. Fisher, Robert D. Specht, and Warren E. Walker from the United States.

All of these persons contributed significantly to the first volume of the handbook by raising questions, challenging statements, pointing out omissions, and making suggestions; we are indebted to them all. The seven re-

Acknowledgments

viewers, all of whom read the manuscript with great care, played an especially important role in improving it; one in particular—Yehezkel Dror—gave us searching comments in such detail and depth as almost to qualify him as a co-editor of the book, for which our appreciation is particularly heartfelt.

All of this, however, is not to say that the Editors accepted all of the suggestions and criticisms; indeed, many offered challenges to extension that would have greatly lengthened the text. Rather, we used the ideas that would, in our judgment, strengthen the arguments without making them unduly long and complicated, and that accorded with our own experience and knowledge, as checked against the literature as we knew it. Thus, the appearance of names on the preceding lists should not be construed as saying that any of these persons necessarily agrees in detail with what is presented in this book.

Nevertheless, if one were to compare early drafts with what is published here, he would see immediately how important the role of the commentators and reviewers has been in making the text of this volume of the handbook representative—as it should be—of the professional community whose work it describes.

No project of this duration and complexity can proceed without a great deal of day-to-day help, and this one is no exception; it was aided by many persons. To all we express gratitude. However, we would like to single out five members of the project staff who were particularly helpful: Karen Brown, Brigitte Gromus, Carolyn Lathrop, Jeannette Lindsay, and Michael Pearson.

We are indebted to a number of individuals and organizations for permission to quote material to which they hold the rights: to the *Administrative Science Quarterly* for the quotation from Herbert Simon in Section 6.2; to the Ballinger Publishing Company for the quotation from Henry S. Rowen in Section 1.8; to Basic Books for the quotations from Olaf Helmer in Sections 1.9 and 7.3, from C. E. Lindblom in Section 2.3, and from Donald A. Schön in Section 10.3; to the Elsevier Science Publishing Company and the authors for the quotations from K. A. Archibald in Section 9.1 and from Yehezkel Dror in Section 10.15; to Hamish Hamilton and Harper and Row for the quotation from Solly Zuckermann in Section 5.5; to Holt, Rinehart, and Winston for the quotation from John Dewey in Section 5.4; to *Interfaces* for the quotations and paraphrase of material from Gregory Prastacos in Section 3.2 and for the quotation from W. C. Giauque and R. E. D. Woolsey in Section 9.2; to the International Institute for Applied Systems Analysis for the quotations from the Energy Systems Program Group in Sections 6.3, 7.3, and 10.13, for the quotations from C. S. Holling in Sections 7.1, 7.4, and 8.8, for the quotation from Jermen Gvishiani at the beginning of Chapter 9, for the quotations from Eugene Bardach in Sections 9.1, 9.4, and 9.5, for the quotations from Howard Raiffa in Sections 10.8 and 10.10, and for the quotation from Giandomenico Majone in Section 10.15, as well as Tables 3.7 and 8.1, and Figures 3.9, 3.10, 8.2, 8.3, 8.4, and 8.5; to Milton Katz for the quotation in Section 10.15; to Donella Meadows for the quotation in Section 7.2; to Giandomenico Majone for the quotation in Section 6.2; to *Minerva* for the quotation from Hugh J. Miser in Section 10.15; to The MIT Press for the quotation from J. W. Forrester in Section 5.4, from Herbert Simon in Section 8.3, and from Eugene Bardach in Section 9.5; to Costanza Blackett for the quotations from P. M. S. Blackett in Section 2.2; to *Operations Research* for the quotation from H. P. Hatry in Section 6.1 and the quotations from Charles J. Hitch in Sections 7.7 and 8.1; to the Oxford University Press for the quotations from Robert Sugden and Alan Williams in Sections 2.3, 6.3, and 10.15; to the *Policy Studies Journal* and the author for the quotation from Yehezkel Dror in Section 8.9; to the *Public Administration Review* and the author for the quotation from Yehezkel Dror in Section 2.3; to the Princeton University Press for the quotation from Herman Kahn in Section 5.2; to The Rand Corporation for the paraphrase from Ira S. Lowry in Section 1.2, for the quotation from Charles J. Hitch and Roland N. McKean in Section 2.5, for the paraphrase from Warren E. Walker, David W. Singleton, and Bruce Smith in Section 3.3, for the paraphrase from B. F. Goeller et al. in Section 3.4, for the quotations from Charles J. Hitch in Sections 5.2 and 8.4, for the quotation from Albert Wohlstetter in Section 6.1, for the quotations from E. S. Quade in Sections 7.3, 8.4, and 10.15, for the quotation from Warren E. Walker, Jan M. Chaiken, and Edward J. Ignall in Section 7.4, for the quotation from Garry D. Brewer in Section 9.5, for the quotations from R. W. Archibald in Section 10.2, and the quotation from B. F. Goeller in Section 7.7, as well as Tables 3.1–3.6 and Figures 3.4–3.8 and 7.1; to *Science* and the author for the quotation from Alvin M. Weinberg in Section 10.15; to Stephen Toulmin for a quotation in Section 2.5; to the Regents of the University of California for quotations from Arnold J. Meltsner in Sections 9.1 and 10.15 and from Paul Sabatier and Daniel Mazmanian in Section 9.5; and to Van Nostrand Reinhold for the quotations from John G. Kemeny in Section 1.5 and Norman I. Agin in Section 10.4.

The Editors

Chapter 1
The Context, Nature, and Use of Systems Analysis

Edward S. Quade and Hugh J. Miser

1.1. Introduction

Many of society's problems emerge from processes associated with structures that combine people and the natural environment with various artifacts of man and his technology; these structures can be thought of as systems. Such problems, and the systems of which they are aspects, abound in modern society. The human and economic costs of road crashes arise in the operations of the highway traffic system, which combines drivers (and their drinking habits), passengers, pedestrians, highways, vehicles, the customs and rules of the road, the weather, and the surrounding environment. The problems of meeting the world's energy demands involve the energy system, which combines sources of energy, the means for converting these sources to usable forms, the distribution devices and procedures, the using community and the ways it employs energy, and the surrounding natural and economic environment—an environment that affects energy use and that is, in turn, affected by the energy system. Myriad urban problems are aspects of human aspirations and reactions to urban settlements, which combine in a natural environment people and their dwellings, their enterprises, their social services, their means of transportation and entertainment, their economic means for exchanging labor for products, the laws and customs that govern the system's behavior, and the organizational structures that make the whole work. Business problems emerge from business enterprises, which bring together capital, labor, management, and specialized knowledge to create products desired by the society in which the enterprises are embedded. And governmental problems often involve large governmental structures, with their purposes, constituencies, services, funding needs, and relations to the public.

Many elements of such systems exhibit forms of regular behavior, and scientific scrutiny has yielded much knowledge about these regularities. Thus, many of the problems that arise in these systems can be addressed by focusing such knowledge appropriately by means of the logical, quantitative, and structural tools of modern science and technology. The craft that does this is called *systems analysis* in this handbook; it brings to bear the knowledge and methods of modern science and technology, in combination with concepts of social goals and equities, elements of judgment and taste, and appropriate consideration of the larger contexts and uncertainties that inevitably attend such problems.

The central purpose of systems analysis is to help public and private decision- and policymakers to ameliorate the problems and manage the policy issues that they face. It does this by improving the basis for their judgment by generating information and marshaling evidence bearing on their problems and, in particular, on possible actions that may be suggested to alleviate them. Thus, a systems analysis commonly focuses on a problem arising from interactions among elements in society, enterprises, and the environment; considers various responses to this problem; and supplies evidence about the consequences—good, bad, and indifferent—of these responses.

Since its purpose is to provide an introductory description of systems analysis, this chapter contains discussions of the kinds of issues and problems that systems analysis addresses, the kinds of complexities and difficulties that arise, the central characteristics of a systems analysis, the role that science and technology play in it, what it does, where it finds application, the value that it has for society and those responsible for solving society's problems, and the art of carrying it through. The later chapters extend the discussions of these points.

1.2. The Context

Systems analysis can be applied to a wide range of highly diverse problems, and the patterns of analysis exhibit a corresponding diversity according to the context, the nature of the problem, the possible courses of action, the information needed and available, the accompanying constraints and uncertainties, and the persons who may use its results.

To illustrate this diversity, this section describes several problems to which systems analysis has been applied: improving blood availability and utilization, improving fire protection, protecting an estuary from floods, achieving adequate amounts of energy for the long-range future, providing housing for low-income families in the United States, and controlling a forest pest in Canada.

Improving Blood Availability and Utilization

Human blood, a living tissue of unique medical value, is a perishable product: in the United States it has a fixed lifetime during which it can legally be used

Section 1.2. The Context

for transfusion to a patient of the proper type and after which it has to be discarded; when the study about to be described was done, this lifetime was 21 days (it has since been extended to 35 days). The blood is collected in units of one pint from volunteer donors at various collection sites such as a regional blood center (RBC), and after a series of typing and screening tests it is shipped to hospital blood banks (HBBs) in the region of the RBC. The units are then stored at the HBB, where they are available to satisfy the random daily demand for transfusions to patients. Since in general not all units demanded and assigned to a patient are used, a unit can be assigned several times during its lifetime before it is transfused or outdated and discarded.

The efficient management of blood resources in a region is a difficult task. The blood distribution problem is complex, owing to blood's perishability, to the uncertainties involved in its availability to the RBC, and to the random nature of the demands and usages at each of the HBBs. Superimposed on these complexities are the large variations in the sizes of the hospitals—and therefore the HBBs—to be supplied, in the relative occurrences of the eight different blood groups, and in the mixes of whole blood and red blood cells called for. Finally, on the one hand there is the imperative of having blood available when and where needed (although elective surgery can be postponed because of a blood shortage, this act incurs additional costs for all concerned), while on the other hand there is the desire to operate efficiently and economically.

The two most common performance measures for an HBB are the *shortage rate* (that is, the proportion of days when supplementary unscheduled deliveries have to be made to satisfy the hospital's demand) and the *outdate rate* (that is, the proportion of the hospital's blood supply that is discarded owing to its becoming outdated). Suitable calculations convert these measures for individual hospitals to similar ones for a region.

In 1979 two systems analysts in the United States reported a study that went most of the way toward solving this problem of managing blood supplies efficiently. After studying the patterns of demand and supply, they were able to characterize the situation with relatively simple models, on the basis of which they were able to devise a decision support system for an RBC that addresses these questions: What are the minimum achievable outdate and shortage rates that can be set for the region? What distribution policy will achieve these targets? What levels of supply are needed to achieve alternative targets?

The blood management system they devised was characterized by centralized management at the RBC, prescheduled deliveries to the HBBs supplemented by emergency deliveries when needed, and a distribution policy according to which some blood is rotated among the hospitals. The operation of this system is based on a mathematical programming model whose objective is to optimize the allocation of the regional blood resources while observing policy constraints.

The final step was to implement this programmed blood distribution system (PBDS) in a trial region on Long Island, near New York City. Before PBDS came into effect, the RBC made an average of 7.8 blood deliveries per week to each hospital in the region, all unscheduled, and the outdate rate was 0.20. After PBDS was implemented, the average number of deliveries dropped to 4.2, of which only 1.4 were unscheduled, and the average outdate rate fell to 0.04, which appears to be about the lowest possible for this situation (some wastage being an inevitable consequence of the random demand and limited supply). These management improvements represented substantial cost savings.

The analysts designed the PBDS so that it can easily be adapted to new regions. Such adaptations have in fact been made.

Section 3.2 describes this outstandingly successful example of systems analysis in more detail.

Improving Fire Protection

Fire protection is a basic municipal service. In the face of significant increases in the demand for firefighting services, the size of the firefighting force and its distribution throughout a city impose important policy decisions on a city government: how many fire companies to support, where to locate them, and how to dispatch them. (A fire company is the basic firefighting unit; it consists of one or more motor vehicles, such as pumpers or ladder trucks, the associated equipment, and a complement of firefighters led by an officer. Such a unit usually has a firehouse, or fire station, of its own.) A policy that leads to rapid response with appropriate firefighting resources can save lives and reduce property loss significantly.

The trouble is that there is little agreement on just what is "appropriate." In order to evaluate alternative deployment policies, performance measures are needed together with models for use in calculating them. Fortunately, in the 1970s a team of systems analysts in New York City developed the required measures and models, which have now been applied there and elsewhere. A fundamental difficulty faced by the analysts was that for this context no direct performance measures were available, such as the observable shortage and outdate rates for the case of blood management.

A fire department's primary objectives are to protect lives and safeguard property, which can be measured by the numbers of fatalities and injuries and the value of property lost. However, it is not possible to use these as measures to evaluate different deployment policies because there is as yet no reliable way to estimate the practical effects that a change in policy would have on them. For example, if the number of fire companies on duty were doubled, no one can say with a satisfactory degree of confidence what effects

Section 1.2. The Context

the change would have on the number of casualties or property losses. The directions of the effects may be predictable for such a large change in deployment, but the amounts of the changes cannot be predicted with any reasonable accuracy. Moreover, for smaller—and thus more realistic—changes in deployment policy, it may be difficult to predict even the directions, let alone the sizes, of the changes in casualties and losses.

Therefore, in order to evaluate alternative firehouse configurations, the analysts developed three substitute, or *proxy*, measures, the first two of which are directly related to loss of life and property damage: (1) travel time to individual locations, (2) average travel time in a region, and (3) company workload. Changes in the number of firehouses and their locations yield changes in the values of these measures. These changes can be evaluated against the background of other considerations, such as hazards, fire incidence, costs, and political constraints.

The analysis team put an approach developed for New York City to work in an assessment of the firefighting deployment in the City of Wilmington, Delaware, USA. In 1973 Wilmington had eight firehouses, all but one antedating 1910. Thus, the city's growth and evolution suggested a fundamental reexamination of its firefighting deployment.

In conducting such a study, a great deal of data must be collected about the city and its fire and firefighting experience, but, for the analysis team's purposes, the two chief categories of input data were travel times from one location to another in the city and the demands for firefighting services (fire alarms and actual fires).

With this information in hand the analysts proceeded to their analysis, using three principal tools that they had already developed.

1. A *simple formula* for the relation between travel time and distance.
2. A *parametric allocation model* to determine fire company allocations satisfying a wide range of objectives and permitting them to be evaluated in terms of average regional travel times, average citywide travel times, and company workload. This model incorporates a simple formula that specifies the number of companies that should be allocated to each region, given the total number of companies to be deployed in the city and a parameter that reflects the desired objective.
3. A *firehouse site evaluation model* dealing with the question: Given a particular number of engine and ladder companies to be deployed in a region, where should they be located?

These models alone do not allow the analysts to retire to an ivory tower to select the optimal configuration for the city. Rather, they must be used cooperatively with the city officials who specify the objectives to be met and who judge the importance, not only of each of the proxy output measures calculated by the analysts for the options explored, but also of the many other relevant factors that are not embodied in the models.

For Wilmington, the results of the analysis suggested that the number of engine companies could be reduced by one or two and the remainder repositioned with little effect on fire protection. The final recommendation was that one company be eliminated and five of the remaining seven be relocated.

City officials adopted this recommendation. After lengthy negotiations with the firemen, it was implemented successfully. The result is a firefighting force as effective as before but with the costs significantly reduced.

Section 3.3 discusses this case in more detail.

Protecting an Estuary from Flooding

In 1953 a severe storm on the North Sea flooded much of the delta region of the Netherlands, killing several thousand people. Determined not to allow this to happen again, the government started a program to increase protection from floods by constructing a new system of dams and dikes. By the mid-1970s this system was complete except for the protection of the largest estuary, the Oosterschelde. Three alternatives for this task were under consideration: building an impermeable dam to close off the estuary from the sea, building a flow-through dam with gates that could be closed during a storm, and building large new dikes around the estuary.

In 1975 the Netherlands Rijkswaterstaat (the government agency responsible for water control and public works) and The Rand Corporation of Santa Monica, California, began a joint systems-analysis project with a view to helping decide what should be done. It set out to determine the major consequences that would follow from implementing each of the three alternatives for protecting the estuary. These consequences were grouped into categories including financial costs; security from flooding; effects on jobs and profits in the fishing industry; changes in recreational opportunities; savings to carriers and customers of the inland shipping industry; changes in production, jobs, and imports for the 35 industrial sectors of the national economy; changes in the populations of the species that make up the ecology of the region; and, finally, the social impacts—displacement of households and activities and significant effects on the regional economies. A major uncertainty was the severity and frequency of the super-storms that make the provisions for protection necessary.

By intention, the study did not conclude by recommending a particular alternative. Rather, it clarified the issues by comparing, in a common framework, the many different impacts of the alternatives. The choice among the alternatives was left to the political process, where the responsibility properly resides. (To go further by trying to rank the alternatives was inappropriate—as it usually is in a complex study of policy). There was no dominant alternative; rather, each was found to have a major disadvantage that might be considered serious enough to render it politically unacceptable: The storm-surge barrier alternative (that is, the flow-through dam) was by far the most

Section 1.2. The Context 7

costly, the impermeable dam was the worst for the ecology, and the open case, with new dikes around the estuary, lacked security.

The Rijkswaterstaat supplemented this work with several special studies of its own and submitted a report to the Cabinet recommending the more costly storm-surge barrier plan to the Parliament. It was adopted in 1976 and construction is now (1984) under way.

Section 3.4 offers a more extended discussion of this work.

Achieving Adequate Amounts of Energy for the Long-Range Future

The goal of systems analysis is to be as comprehensively relevant as necessary to produce useful results, and to produce findings that are as completely specified as the practical need dictates. However, such precision is possible only when the analysts have scientific knowledge that is sufficiently comprehensive to supply a strong foundation for the analysis and its results. Regrettably, all too often such knowledge is partial, sketchy, or even nonexistent, especially in cases looking far into the future or where the system of concern depends on the actions of individuals or social groups whose behavior is not well understood. In such cases, the portion of reality a model can encompass is severely restricted, but, systems analysis can still make important contributions to knowledge and policy. One approach to the problems of a sociotechnical system whose complexities are far from fully understood is shown by this example.

An interdisciplinary team at the International Institute for Applied Systems Analysis in Laxenburg, Austria, has completed an inquiry into the long-range energy strategies that the world might be able to pursue successfully (Energy Systems Program Group, 1981). Rather than attempt to design a global energy policy, the more modest aim was to provide information on energy to the world's nations, so that through their actions, alone or in concert, an equitable and far-sighted policy would evolve. Here, in place of the relatively simple blood-supply system of a previous example, we are confronted with complex interactions among the technologies, economies, environments, resources, people, social attitudes, and ambitions of many nations. Instead of a relatively homogeneous region, we have the full globe. And, in place of relatively few decisionmakers, we have a very large number of independent policymakers in public and private enterprises and in international companies and organizations.

The role of systems analysis in this setting is not to determine a single, best policy for a single decisionmaker, but to provide a broad perspective for autonomous decisionmakers to use in making their choices. The analytic approach is to identify and improve our understanding of the important interactions among energy-system components, among the policies of nations and industries, and among energy choices over time for the next 50 years or more. Many models are involved, and the work demands much data collection and many analyses.

Rather than construct a single comprehensive computational model of the world's energy system—impossible because of lack of knowledge, the sheer size and complexity of this system, and the widely differing questions facing decisionmakers concerned with it—the analysis team carried out an overlapping, interlinked series of investigations of such subquestions as these:

What will the evolving pattern of demand for energy be?
What resources will be available to satisfy the demand?
What technological options will be feasible?
What constraints will limit selections among the options?

To address these questions, the analysis team identified a spectrum of strategies responsive to different possible national, international, and industrial goals. As in many analyses, the analysts sought a synthesis—the invention and design of new alternatives: courses of action that would satisfy specified demands and constraints and achieve the given goals as nearly as possible. The hope is that, armed with this knowledge and the new alternatives emerging from the work, many decisionmakers will choose improved policies, supplementing short-term parochial outlooks with broader views encompassing a systemic understanding. Additional collective decision arrangements to address shared global interests may also be prompted by comprehensive understanding.

Section 3.5 gives a brief account of this study of the future of the world's energy system.

Providing Housing for Low-Income Families

Still other approaches may be necessary in certain problems. For instance, a policymaker may feel a need to intervene in a social situation but must avoid introducing extraordinary disruption or creating a costly program that, if it fails to achieve its purpose, may become politically impossible to discontinue. For such a situation, a social experiment may be the technique to apply, since controlled experiments allow strong inferences about causality. Social experiments, however, are expensive, and are not without methodological problems (for instance, transferring the results to different and larger contexts).

As an example, consider the carefully planned experiment conducted by The Rand Corporation between 1974 and 1980 in two metropolitan housing markets; it was part of a broader effort by the U.S. Department of Housing and Urban Development (HUD) to test the concept of housing allowances as a way of delivering housing assistance to low-income households. The purpose of the experiment was to learn how this form of assistance would affect the housing markets and communities in which it operated, and thus

Section 1.2. The Context

to judge the results that might be achieved by a larger and longer-range program.

For more than 40 years U.S. policymakers have sought to find ways of providing housing assistance to low-income families that would be cost effective, efficient, and equitable. Rental housing built and operated by local authorities, privately owned housing leased by public authorities, mortgage-interest subsidies to private landlords on behalf of their tenants, interest subsidies to low-income home purchasers, and other schemes have been suggested, argued about, analyzed, and, in some cases, even tried out, with results that have not warranted their large-scale adoption. In the early 1970s the idea of direct cash payments became prominent. It looked good on paper, but there was considerable opposition, based on disparate predictions of how it would affect the housing markets and the communities in which it would operate. Many feared rent escalation, real estate speculation, rapid turnover of neighborhoods, and hostility from those who would not be allowed to benefit from the program. Some foresaw that it would lead to deteriorating neighborhoods, some were afraid it would hasten racial integration, others that it would reinforce segregation.

The two sites chosen for the experiment contrasted in market structure and condition: one was undivided by racial segregation and had a "tight" market (that is, vacancy rates were low); the other had a "loose" housing market with a large, segregated minority population and a considerable number of older, poorly maintained dwellings.

In each experimental area a ten-year allowance program was operated by a nonprofit housing-allowance office under contract to HUD and the local housing authority. During the first five years (the experimental period) enrollment was open to all eligible households in the area. To qualify for payments, enrollees had to find decent, safe, and sanitary dwellings on the private market and maintain them to specified standards. The payments were intended to enable the enrollees to increase their housing expenditures and thus to obtain adequate housing, either by underwriting the costs of repairs or moving to new locations. Once the housing met the standards of adequacy, the remainder of the allowance could offset part of the housing expense. Housing quality was checked by periodic inspections.

Throughout the experiment the housing-allowance office dealt only with the participating households, who were responsible for finding qualified housing, negotiating rents and conditions of occupancy, and meeting obligations to landlords, mortgage lenders, and other parties to their transactions, as well as maintaining housing standards. This dependence on the initiatives of the households themselves is one of the key factors distinguishing this approach.

During the five-year experimental period a total of 25,000 households enrolled, and 20,000 received one or more payments. The Rand analysis team that monitored the program observed these results (among many others):

During the period when the experiment was mature, about a third of those eligible for payments were receiving them. About half of those enrolling did not live in dwellings meeting the program's quality standards at the time of enrollment; of these, about one-third dropped out, and the remainder met the requirements by moving or by repairing their existing homes.

Participation in the program increased the likelihood of occupying housing meeting the quality standards from about 50 to about 80 percent and reduced the preenrollment housing expense burden from about 50 to about 30 percent of gross income.

Enrollees were able to meet program standards without major expense because their housing defects were mostly minor health and safety hazards, rather than major structural defects or lack of basic domestic equipment. Only about a fifth of the extra money was spent on housing.

A full-scale open-enrollment allowance program had no perceptible effect on rents or property values at either site, one reason being that the program increased the aggregate housing demand by less than 2 percent.

The program had little effect on the physical appearance or social composition of the residential neighborhoods.

After three years of experience with the program, a majority of all heads of household and 90 percent of all participants though it was a "good idea."

After reflecting on the experimental evidence and consulting the available U.S. national data, the analysis team offered the following judgments about a national program that would follow the design of the experimental one:

First, budgetary relief for low-income households is probably a higher priority than better housing.

Second, the public cost per assisted household would be far below that entailed in programs that build new housing for the poor. Furthermore, about 85 cents of each program dollar would benefit the participants directly. Comparable estimates were 57 cents for an existing housing program and 34 cents for a public housing construction program. However, for an income-maintenance program with no housing requirements the estimate was 89 cents.

Third, at most 10 percent of all households (half of those eligible) would participate in a permanent national program, at an average public annual cost, including administration, of $1100 per recipient household (in 1976 dollars). About 30 percent of the participants would as a result occupy safer and more sanitary dwellings, and all would be able to spend more for nonhousing consumption.

Finally, a national housing-allowance program would affect only the participants and their housing; for good or ill, the broader community would remain unaffected.

Section 1.2. The Context
11

This account of the experiment and its findings, as well as the judgments about a national program, have been condensed from Lowry (1982).

Controlling a Forest Pest in Canada

Some systems problems are characterized, not only by limited knowledge, but also by short time horizons over which reliable predictions can be made and by conflicting interests that cannot be resolved by bringing them under a common administrative framework. A forest-pest management problem studied by C. S. Holling and a team of analysts from the International Institute for Applied Systems Analysis and the University of British Columbia provides an example.

The boreal forests of eastern North America are devastated periodically by a defoliating insect called the spruce budworm. An outbreak can kill a large proportion of the mature softwood forest, with major consequences to employment and the economy of the region. Extensive spraying of insecticides has succeeded in reducing tree mortality, but at the expense of maintaining incipient outbreak conditions over a considerably more extensive area. Thus, the problem was to aid the decisionmakers with relevant responsibilities to choose courses of action that would yield desirable consequences over the long run.

The objective of the analysis work, as originally conceived, was to examine the constraints on and consequences of several actions then obvious to all concerned (such as continuing spraying, stopping spraying, harvesting trees threatened by the budworm, and so on). However, the analysis group soon widened its objective, eventually gaining the client's acceptance of a broader inquiry. The group designed and characterized a range of alternative strategic policies and described their consequences by means of a variety of socio-economic, resource, and environmental indicators. Thus, the analysis group provided the desionmakers with information enabling them to consider policies, both singly and in combination, that could be judged in a variety of ways on the basis of the values of indicators developed by the analysis. (See Section 8.8 for a discussion of these indicators and how they would respond to alternative courses of action.)

These policies, which involve decisions about tree planting, cutting, and spraying, are difficult to formulate, because any change in them yields a new pattern of budworm infestation and tree growth and a changed harvest, affecting economic costs and benefits for individuals, business, and government. There are also social and recreational impacts.

Without systems analysis, the decisionmakers would have had to rely on their intuitions and previous experiences—perhaps supplemented by opinions from specialized experts—to design policies, evaluate their likely consequences, and select the most promising for implementation. But intuition, experience, and specialist opinion by themselves are severely limited when systems have complex interactions spread widely in distance and in time, as is the case in the budworm-forest system.

Systems analysis is able to provide help in the budworm case because biologists, foresters, and ecologists have learned enough about the spruce forest and the budworm to be able, under most conditions, to predict their responses to changes in the environment. Holling and his colleagues have used this knowledge to construct an interrelated set of models that enable computer calculations to stimulate with acceptable accuracy the behavior of the forest and the budworm under a broad range of changing conditions. These models make it possible to try out, by means of computer simulation, many policies that could be proposed. There is no guarantee that the model's results for a policy are what would occur were the policy to be implemented in the real forest, but checking sample predictions with historical data has given the model's users confidence in its predictions. With the information provided by this analysis, the decisionmakers are in a better position to understand the available options and to structure the process of choice accordingly.

Recently, drawing on the analogies that this work offers with other pest-control and environmental problems, Holling and his colleagues have described an approach to environmental management in general. However, because of the uncertainties and knowledge gaps that have attended this broadened inquiry, their emphasis has moved beyond predetermined and well-described policies toward more flexible "adaptive policies," as described in Holling (1978).

In carrying out this work, Holling and his team have devised a workshop approach in which representatives of key interests interact with the analysts and their models over a period of up to a year in order to evolve a common understandings—and both preferred and acceptable courses of feasible action leading to desirable objectives (Holling, 1978, especially Ch. 4).

Checkland (1981), working mainly with business firms, has used a similar approach to problems that cannot be reduced to evaluating predetermined alternative means.

Both of these developments are harbingers of the day when systems analysis will have extended its frontiers well beyond its presently well-understood arena to problems in which human behavior and other hard-to-understand elements are more dominant than in the ones usually studied today—and which are the central focus of this handbook.

1.3. The Nature of the Problems

These examples all deal with problems in which many elements interact as part of what, by definition, is conceived to be the system associated with the problem. For example, the problem of reducing the amount of blood that is discarded owing to its being outdated arises from the operations of the Greater

Section 1.3. The Nature of the Problems

New York Blood Program, a system that consists of the human donors, the regional blood centers, the hospital blood banks, the hospitals and patients using the blood, and the medical and administrative staffs who manage these activities, as well as the blood itself and the rules for its use.

The problems all involve numerous interrelated but disparate elements. For example, the forest-pest problem involves a system consisting of, among other elements, the forest, the insect pest, the lumber industry, the planting, cutting, and spraying policies, the economy and society of the region, and the environment in which they are embedded.

All of the cases exhibit phenomena widely distributed in both space and time. The pest-control study considered an area of 4.5 million hectares and, because the intervals between outbreaks of the forest pest range from 30 to 45 years, a time period of from 80 to 160 years. The energy study considered the entire world's production and consumption of energy between now and 50 years hence.

In each case many variables had to be considered—so many, indeed, that it is neither feasible nor desirable to attempt to set forth even an abridged list here. Chapter 3, where four of these examples are discussed more fully, gives an idea of the principal issues and variables considered.

From these cases, as one considers what may appear to be a simple problem, one can also imagine how the aspects that need to be considered proliferate. For example, the spruce budworm is a damaging forest pest, and the "obvious" way to reduce the damage it causes is to attack it. However, a spraying program against the pest, although successful in reducing its damage to the forest in the sprayed areas, was found to have a number of negative side-effects: the area of incipient outbreak widened significantly, and the spray posed threats to the environment and to human health. Thus, it became necessary to consider the budworm cycle in its forest habitat in some detail, which involved the analysts in the forest's natural cycle. Then, since an important reason to preserve the forest is to enable the lumber industry to remain healthy and productive, one must consider its operations, and hence the economy of the region to which it is an important contributor, particularly since the cost of any forest-management program must be levied against the resources of the region through taxes or otherwise. And so on.

The complexities of each of these problems, and the large numbers of people concerned with how they are solved, make it clear that many decisionmakers are involved, many people's interests are affected, and many constituencies may have competing objectives (for example, environmentalists may want to preserve the beauty and integrity of the forests, while lumbermen want to have its timber available for cutting). Moreover, all the problems are attended by many uncertainties: Weather patterns affect the sea's threat to the coastline regions of the Netherlands as well as the spruce budworm cycle, and unforeseen political and technical developments will almost certainly impact the world's energy situation in the future. Indeed, uncertainties are often present, and frequently irremovable, particularly when they arise from the natural environment or the goals of individuals, social groups, and countries.

Against this background of complications, the analyst seeking a successful application of systems analysis may have to overcome one or more of these difficulties:

Inadequate knowledge and data. Sometimes, even though the problem may be of long standing, data may be lacking or incorrect, cause-and-effect relations may be obscure, and no relevant literature or even theory from which to start may exist. Those with responsibilities for resolving the problem may have no mental model of the processes involved and thus lack an intuitive feeling as to the outcome. Well-known "facts" may be wrong. As Holling (1978, p. 97) observed, "The [budworm] model predicted that the forest would decline independently of insect damage, while it was 'common knowledge' that volume was high and would remain so if insects were controlled. We spent 2 months checking the model for errors when we should have been spending 2 days looking at the available raw data on forest volume. When we belatedly took this obvious step, the model was vindicated."

Many disciplines involved. Most system problems require scientific and technical knowledge from many different specialties. A multidisciplinary team is needed, a situation fraught with difficulties, for true interdisciplinary work is hard to carry out. For example, the forest-pest analysis and the ensuing work of applying its findings required inputs from biology, forestry, mathematics, operations research, ecology, business, economics, and public administration, among others—and professionals in all these fields participated in the work.

Inadequate existing approaches. If adequate methods do not exist, they have to be invented, developed, and tested. Existing approaches have frequently been developed within a single discipline by borrowing ideas from other disciplines without truly integrating them. A trial-and-error approach may be available theoretically, but, as a practical matter, it may be prohibitively costly or too risky.

Unclear goals and shifting objectives. To help decision- and policymakers, it is crucial to know what they want. While they usually have an idea of what is desirable, their statements of goals are often too vague to serve as useful guides to systems analysis, or as criteria to guide one's judgments of how well actions and programs serve the goals. Indeed, politicians may find an advantage in keeping their true goals concealed or so general that they have no operational significance. (There are other antinomies between systems analysis and political processes, but this is an important one.) In general, goals are a subject people find difficult to think about and make explicit.

Thus, one of the early tasks of a systems analysis is often to evolve with those concerned reasonably explicit statements of goals—even though the light shed on them as the systems analysis proceeds may suggest their revision, particularly since a decisionmaker frequently cannot decide what he wants to do until he has some idea of what can be done and what it will cost.

Pluralistic responsibilities. It almost always happens that, for a problem sufficiently complicated to call for a systems-analysis approach, there are many persons and organizational units with relevent responsibilities and authorities (and consequently with multiple, often conflicting, goals and objectives). All six examples illustrate this point.

Resistance to change in social systems. Resistance to change is so common a property of social systems as to hardly call for comment. Tradition is an important factor, but it is worth noting that many forms of institutional structure and government are deliberately designed to be so resistant to change as to survive even fairly strong perturbations intact. This is important for the systems analyst to consider, and his results—usually urging changes in response to the problems that prompted the analysis in the first place—must take careful account of this resistance if they are to be accepted and used.

Complexity. The examples we have so far considered all illustrate the complexity of systems problems. Indeed, it is this complexity that calls for systems analysis. Because complexity is characteristic of the typical problem for which systems analysis is an appropriate approach, the analysis will itself be complex.

This listing of difficult properties is not intended to discourage; rather, it is meant to underscore the importance of having an approach of proven usefulness. The history of systems analysis offers many cases where it has helped decision- and policymakers with their problems—and, unfortunately, some cases where the hoped-for benefits have not accrued. It is the purpose of this handbook to capture the lessons of this history, and thus offer its readers information about ways to approach such problems successfully, techniques that can help solve them, procedures for seeing the solutions into practice, and pitfalls that should be avoided. Indeed, it is the difficulties that this section has sketched that provide the rationale for and potential usefulness of this handbook.

1.4. The Characteristics of Systems Analysis

Systems analysis is the multidisciplinary problem-solving activity that has evolved to deal with the complex problems that arise in public and private enterprises and organizations. It did not emerge easily in response to an appreciation of the importance of such problems. Rather, as Chapter 2 shows, it grew on the foundations built by many specialties that dealt with simpler and less taxing aspects of systems.

It is neither possible nor desirable to define systems analysis in concise and comprehensive terms. Since systems analysis deals with diverse problems and different contexts, it assumes many forms adapted to the problems, the systems, and their contexts. To achieve its full growth and usefulness, it must continue this process of adaptation and extension, which should not be inhibited by too narrow a conception of what it is or how it fits into the social process of problem solving.

On the other hand, it is useful to describe common features that characterize systems analysis:

context—complex problems arising in public and private enterprises and organizations and (usually) involving their interactions with society and the environment;

method—a synthesis of understanding, invention, analysis, design, intuition, judgment, and a scientific approach;

tools—those of logic, statistics, mathematics, technology, and the sciences, employed by multidisciplinary teams;

aim—to assist in finding ameliorative responses to problems through designing and evaluating programs, decisions, and actions;

clients—those with responsibilities for or interests in these ameliorative responses;

relation—a continuing interaction between the analysis team and the clients throughout the work.

A complete systems analysis may involve as many as nine activities; they may have only hazy borders and some may occur in parallel, or in an order other than the one listed, and some may be repeated.

Systems analysis (Miser, 1980):

1. Marshals the evidence relating to the problem and the experience and scientific knowledge bearing on it (when necessary the analysis gathers new evidence and develops new knowledge).
2. Examines the social purposes relating to the problem, and helps persons and institutions to reconsider these purposes.
3. Explores alternative ways of achieving these purposes, which often include designing or inventing new possibilities.
4. Reconsiders the problem—and its possible reformulation—in the light of the knowledge accumulating during the analysis.
5. Estimates the impacts of various possible courses of action, taking into consideration both the uncertain future and the organizational structures that must carry forward these courses of action.
6. Compares the alternatives by applying a variety of criteria to their consequences.

Section 1.4. The Characteristics of Systems Analysis

7. Presents the results of the study in a framework suitable for choice.
8. Assists in following up the actions chosen.
9. Evaluates the results of implementing the chosen courses of action.

The first example discussed in this chapter, improving blood availability and utilization, exhibits all nine steps; to complete this long chain, the analysts took several years in cooperation with officials at many levels in the organizations with which they dealt. The fire-protection example exhibits all but the last step, which is not mentioned in the description. The estuary-protection example similarly follows this outline of steps; while the last two steps are not apparent from the short description here, the analysis team did assist in following up the actions chosen, but of course the evaluation of the results of the final implementation must await completion of the engineering works, as well as how they operate in practice.

On the other hand, the other three examples deviate considerably from this outline. The long-range future energy study was forced by the myriad complications of its context to narrow its future to two principal scenarios (with some variants) projecting a world without major surprises or political upheavals; thus only further work by national and regional teams can translate its findings into frameworks suitable for choice. The low-income housing experiment was designed to get enough reliable knowledge to permit further analysis and support reasonable short-term decisions. And the forest-pest work must await the slow processes of nature to yield the evaluations that will be the bases for the next steps in the work.

Indeed, although the list of steps refers repeatedly to the "problem," only a rather broad view of what this word can mean allows a discussion to cover the currently available experience with systems analysis. For the blood-supply case, we may perhaps say that the problem was to reduce the shortage and outdate rates—a rather sharply defined problem. However, for the study of the world's future energy supply, the situation was a great deal more complex. Originally the analysis team felt that 50 years would be enough to allow the world to effect a transition from reliance on exhaustible fossil fuels for much of its energy needs to renewable sources such as sunlight. However, the study itself showed that this was far too sanguine an expectation, so that the problem was changed to read something like this: Is there a path we can travel over the next 50 years that will lead us successfully toward a sustainable energy future at some later time? But one notices immediately that this is a very broad and general statement, lacking the precision of the one for the blood-supply case. Thus, it is common for a systems analysis to arise from a problem area or nexus of problems rather than a well-defined problem; if the context is sufficiently complicated, it may never get much beyond this without a major effort. Consequently, for "problem," in many cases, we must understand "problem situation," a very important fact for the reader to bear in mind in what follows, even though we shall usually speak of "the problem" to avoid complications in the discussion.

The lesson to be learned from these contrasts is that systems analysis cannot conform to an accepted, predetermined outline, but must respond to the conditions in the problem context and exploit such opportunities for assistance to decisionmakers as it may offer. Similarly, the disciplines involved, the methods used, the forms of communication adopted, and the schedule for the work must all respond sympathetically to the needs of the context and the officials with roles to play in it. Good systems analysis can be short and concise or long and arduous; it can employ no more than clear thinking, or very complicated mathematics.

It would be unfair to the reader to leave the impression, from the six examples we have described, that all systems analyses have happy results. For instance, a major study aimed at choosing a location for a third London airport considered a great many aspects of its problem, cost one million pounds, lasted more than two years, and employed an elaborate computer model; however, its recommendation was rejected for a variety of reasons, in part because it was not adequately comprehensive: important environmental considerations were not taken into account.

While it is possible to conceive of a large-scale system problem that lies in the hands of a single decision- or policymaker, the case of multiple responsibilities and interests is so much more usual as to be virtually characteristic. Thus, the findings of a systems analysis must, *a fortiori*, be aimed at, and be communicated to, a varied community. This provides systems analysis with another important role: unifying the knowledge base, logical framework, and overall perceptions of this community.

Indeed, there is a case to be made that, in many situations, a systems analysis is part of a social process of problem solving in which many people take part. In this conception, the analysts affect the social and operational environment of which they are a part, which in turn affects the problems that they are asked to work on, and how they go about the analysis. The argument for this point of view has been developed by a number of advanced thinkers in the field as being an important aspect of the future of systems analysis; Hildebrandt (1979; see also Schön, 1983) provides an introduction to this point of view and the literature that supports it.

1.5. Science and Systems Analysis

Scientific knowledge and the scientific approach are the cornerstones of systems analysis, but systems analysis itself is not science. The purposes of this section, therefore, are to clarify the relations between science and systems analysis and to show how systems analysis depends on science for its strength.

The domain of science is the phenomena of nature, including not only the phenomena described in such classic fields as astronomy, physics, chemistry,

Section 1.5. Science and Systems Analysis

and biology, but also the less-well-understood phenomena of social and sociotechnical systems.

Kemeny (1959, pp. 85–86) describes the method of science in this way:

> As Einstein has repeatedly emphasized, Science must start with facts and end with facts, no matter what theoretical structures it builds in between. First of all the scientist is an observer. Next he tries to describe in complete generality what he saw, and what he expects to see in the future. Next he makes predictions on the basis of his theories, which he checks against facts again.
>
> The most characteristic feature of the method is its cyclic nature. It starts with facts, ends in facts, and the facts ending one cycle are the beginning of the next cycle. A scientist holds his theories tentatively, always prepared to abandon them if the facts do not bear out the predictions. If a series of observations, designed to verify certain predictions, force us to abandon our theory, then we look for a new or improved theory. Thus these facts form the fourth stage for the old theory as well as the first stage of the new theory. Since we expect that Science consists of an endless chain of progress, we may expect this cyclic process to continue indefinitely.

As a matter of practice, the systems analyst (and many of the scientists who contribute knowledge to his work) speak of their theories as *models*—but the terms are really synonymous.

We then define science as the body of knowledge (or collection of facts and models) assembled by the method of science. The individual sciences are distinguished by the portions of nature they seek explanations for, rather than by their techniques, tools, or methodological approaches, although these may have somewhat characteristic associations with particular sciences.

The reader should understand that this very brief overview of the scientific method and how it yields the body of belief called scientific knowledge is intended only as a basic framework; it does not describe the order in which the steps are always taken, the day-to-day activity of scientists, or the interactive social process involved. For example, theories are often developed before observations are made to support or challenge them (as in the case of relativity theory), scientists often hold strongly to their beliefs in the face of challenging evidence, groups holding divergent theoretical beliefs debate with great vigor, and so on. For the scope and purposes of this book, however, we need not look beyond this basic framework.

Workers setting out to use the knowledge gained by science may find that the way is simple and direct. However, it is more usual for them to have to invent some sort of practical device to exploit their knowledge. In fact, for all but quite simple problems, much knowledge and many inventions must be brought together in a synthesis, as illustrated by almost any of today's high-technology artifacts (such as airliners).

These invention and design activities aimed at applying the knowledge of the physical sciences are what are usually meant by the term *engineering*.

Over recent decades there has been a tendency for the various classic branches of engineering to remain closely tied to the sciences on which they depend for the knowledge they use. It is also important to note that many engineering artifacts are involved in the problems that systems analysis is concerned with.

However, there are newer scientific activities investigating systemic phenomena that have not been incorporated in older sciences; the operations-research exploration of man–machine operating systems is a notable example.

Analysts looking over the scientific knowledge available during the last quarter century and the efforts to use it to design solutions to large-scale operating and policy problems saw the need for the classic and newer fields of science and technology to work together to solve these larger problems; this impetus led to systems analysis, as Chapter 2 describes.

Against the background of this discussion, systems analysis can now be described as the invention-and-design (or engineering) art of applying scientific methods and knowledge to complex problems arising in public and private enterprises and organizations and involving their interactions with society and the environment.

Thus, while systems analysis contains many scientific components, it is not itself a science; rather, it more nearly resembles engineering, for it is concerned, not only with theorizing, but also with choosing and acting, and its professionals work in close cooperation with those responsible for choice and action. However, while systems analysis involves many aspects of a craft, it uses the methods and knowledge of science insofar as possible and strives to uphold similar traditions; for instance, good practice holds that:

> Results should emerge from processes that can be duplicated by others to obtain the same results.
>
> Calculations, assumptions, data, and judgments should be reported explicitly; should not be influenced by personalities, reputations, or vested interests; and thus should be subject to checking, criticism, and disagreement.

Certain sciences—economics, sociology, and physics, to name a few—are particularly relevant to the problems that systems analysis addresses. Other disciplines—logic, mathematics, engineering, and computer science, for instance—provide the tools. Among the latter, operations (or operational) research is particularly significant because it is the discipline from which modern systems analysis emerged and because it shares a set of tools with systems analysis.

Systems analysis, as a name, may be relatively new, but it is not a new concept or activity. History records a number of past analytic efforts that, if carried out today, we would call systems analysis. The genesis of systems analysis as we mean it in this book (at least in the United States, where it became widespread in the defense and aerospace industries in the 1950s and then throughout the Federal government in the 1960s) took place in the late

1940s. The term was adopted in 1947 to distinguish research then being done for the U.S. Air Force on future weapon systems from operations research. The work was not operations research (as it was then understood), because both the objectives of the systems and their resource requirements had to be determined and the environment in which they would operate predicted. These inquiries were called systems analyses because they were concerned with decisions about well-defined systems. That an analysis dealt with a system, however, was important neither to its structure nor to the way in which it differed from operations research. Part of the difference lay in the need to introduce long-term economic factors and to consider interactions between means and objectives, activities not then considered within the scope of operations research. Today, however, operations research has broadened to take these considerations into account and, along with systems analysis, to treat considerations of equity and other political and social concerns.

In fact, systems analysis as it is characterized in this handbook, and operations research, as some define it broadly today, can be essentially the same. Cost–benefit analysis, systems engineering, and prescriptive modeling are also forms that systems analysis can take, but, as ordinarily practiced, they are more limited in scope. All these activities follow the same general approach to problem solving. Like systems analysis, they make use of many of the same disciplines, particularly economics, statistics, and probability theory; draw upon the same stockpile of tools (linear programming, queueing theory, and the computer, to name a few); and, when the need arises, employ procedures such as predictive modeling, sensitivity testing, optimization, and decision analysis. Hence, where we speak of systems analysis in the following chapters, others might use a different name; in the United States it could be policy analysis, in the United Kingdom perhaps operational research.

However, this handbook focuses its attention on problems of large-scale systems, and does not attempt to cover the smaller-scale problems also treated by operations research.

1.6. Related Forms of Analysis

One way to help make clear what systems analysis means in the sense of this handbook (and thus in the sense in which it developed) is to describe what it is not. First, it has nothing to do with classifying systems or with discovering properties common to categories of systems; these are subjects one might investigate in general systems theory or in a systems science. Nor does systems analysis concern itself with specifying the distinction between social and cultural systems. This does not mean, of course, that general systems theory or a systems science may not be useful in a particular study. In fact, systems analysis need have nothing whatsoever to do with any system other than the system defined by the activity itself and made up of the things, concepts, and relations involved in the investigation.

Second, modeling is not systems analysis. A system analysis is an attempt to discern and answer questions of importance in the choice of a decision or policy; a model is merely one of a number of useful devices for helping to obtain answers to such questions.

Further, systems analysis is not research for knowledge alone, nor is it causal analysis, concerned with discovering the nature and causes of social or environmental problems or the explanations of behavior, although such research may be necessary to a systems study. Systems analysis, in contrast, is concerned with analyzing and resolving issues arising in specific institutional contexts. Systems analysis thus is often a bridge between decisionmakers and the research community. If the latter, for example, is investigating the effects of economic incentives on work behavior, then a systems analyst helping to design an income maintenance program may use this research and make it known to policymakers.

Systems analysis is not a branch of applied mathematics, such as constrained optimization, or a branch of logic, such as the pure logic of choice. Finally, it does not claim to be identical with what is sometimes called rational decision making or rational problem solving, although the differences may not always be apparent.

The term "systems analysis," unfortunately, has several other interpretations. Although the words "systems" and "analysis" are clearly defined and have about the same meaning in all languages, when they are put together to form "systems analysis" uniformity disappears. Many scientists interpret systems analysis as the analysis of systems—an attempt to explain the behavior of complex systems—that is, as the act or process of studying a system (such as a business, a manufacturing plant, a telephone network, or a physiological function) in order to define its purposes and discover how it works. For others, it means general systems theory or a systems science. A few scientists even define systems analysis as systematic analysis; it is hard, however, to think of any analysis as being other than systematic. In certain other fields, such as business, computers, or psychology, systems analysis has even more specialized meanings. Most commonly, however, for most of the policy research community systems analysis is interpreted as a guide to decision—a study carried out to help bring about a better outcome than would have occurred without it.

1.7. Applications

Systems analysis has been applied with varying success to a wide spectrum of problems, both in type and area. In the field of education, the work ranges from efforts to increase efficiency in the use of space by using computer programs to allocate classrooms for school activities to analyses of the fundamental objectives of education; in the area of environmental protection, it ranges from setting the length of the salmon fishing season to designing a wildlife impact reporting system or to choosing among alternative methods of controlling pollution. In concept, systems analysis can be applied in any situation in which decisions are to be made or policy set, although, of course, there are situations (for instance, when an almost immediate decision is required) in which another approach might be more appropriate.

Systems analysis can be put to many uses, routine (such as optimizing a system for assigning police patrols) or nonroutine (such as working out the main feature of a housing maintenance plan). It can be used to raise questions about, and explore the consistency among, the objectives of different programs (say, whether a petroleum company should look to further profits from an increase in exploration or from diversifying into other areas). It can identify promising areas in which to seek new knowledge (using solar energy, for instance) and discover new uses for old products (for example, adding a chemical to water to decrease friction in its flow through fire hoses). Systems analysis provides this help by bringing knowledge, methods, ideas, and procedures from the academic, scientific, and research communities to bear on problems faced by political, business, and industrial decisionmakers.

Systems analysis often works well in a planning or programming context. The first studies to which the name was applied were military cost-effectiveness analyses. That is, they were studies that sought to determine a course of action that, for a fixed budget, would most nearly achieve some desired objective or, conversely, the alternative that would achieve a given goal for the least cost. Such decisions typically involve choices among good things; the problem is to find out which choices are better. Actually, many questions, both public and private, that require analytic help are of this type—as, for example, those involved in an attempt by a city fire department to provide an improved level of protection within its budget. A few such questions may require for their answers little more than careful data collection and the skillful application of standard techniques from operations research and economics.

Systems analysis has often been successful in helping with issues in which science and engineering dominate, as in many industrial and military applications. Such problems have usually arisen in completely man-made and directed enterprises—a manufacturing process, a weapons system, or an airline—something that was, or can be, designed with a clear purpose and has a structure following known laws of engineering, physical science, and economics, features that make it possible to discover and model the underlying relations. Authority in such areas is clear-cut and cooperative, ordinarily believing that analysis can help rather than hinder the situation.

In contrast, when political, organizational, and social factors dominate, as they do in most public problems—as for example, in designing a welfare system, setting standards for pollution control, or defining an urban renewal policy—goals may be political in nature (with their attainment hard to measure), authority diffuse and overlapping (with no confidence that analysis can help with the solution). Dalkey (1967) suggests that, because the underlying structure may have grown without conscious design, to discover the underlying model may require the same sort of profound digging that is required to determine the role of hormones in regulating body functions.

In addition, efficiency and effectiveness may have no clear meaning in such problems; questions of equity, or "who benefits" and "who pays," may be more critical to the acceptance of a proposed solution than any question of which policy generates the greater surplus of benefits over costs. The difficulties of deciding what ought to be done are likely to dwarf those of finding out how to do it. Nevertheless, systems analysis has helped here, even though it may not have offered a complete solution, by providing information, by isolating alternatives, and by yielding insights that have enabled decisionmakers to intuit better solutions. Systems analysis of this latter type is now being called *policy analysis,* particularly in the United States, partly to avoid confusion with the specialized use of the term "systems analysis" in the office management and computer fields.

1.8. The Value of Systems Analysis

The purpose of systems analysis, as stated earlier, is to help (and possibly to influence) a decisionmaker to choose a better course of action in a particular problem situation than he might otherwise be able to select. To be useful, however, the analysis does not have to provide a complete prescription as to what should be done in every conceivable contingency. In truth, it cannot; the uncertainties are usually such that, while the analyst may aim to produce facts and proofs, the results are merely evidence and arguments. But analysis can almost always eliminate the really bad alternatives, leaving the decisionmaker a choice among the relatively good ones.

Assistance to a decisionmaker can take a number of forms. For him, to decide is not enough; decisions must be accepted by other decisionmakers (a group that often includes some who must change as a consequence of the decision), and then be carried out. Systems analysis can help with both acceptance and implementation.

So far, systems analysts have mostly limited their work to trying to see that better actions are taken through discovering what these better actions might be, but sometimes, unfortunately, with "better" defined solely according to the analysts' standards; they have seldom tried to help by marshaling arguments and using systems analysis as a tool of advocacy for the better actions. However, some of the most significant uses of systems analysis may be obscured if we regard it simply as a means of producing information for the intellectual task of problem solving. Certainly, this is its most important function, but, particularly in the political arena, problem solving requires more than discovery of a good solution; it requires winning acceptance for this solution and seeing that its effect is not nullified during the implementation

Section 1.8. The Value of Systems Analysis

process. Systems analysis can be used to convert perceived problems into political issues, to legitimize decisions, and to assemble support for proposed actions.

Analysis before a decision, even though it is never adequate to prescribe the decision in every detail, has a number of virtues. Among other things, it can

- introduce a certain amount of objectivity into a subjective process;
- bring uncertainties to the decisionmakers' attention, and, when possible, take them into account explicitly;
- consider specific issues in larger contexts and determine interactions and side effects;
- shift debate from means to consequences;
- reveal unanticipated consequences of policies and actions;
- compare alternatives in a consistent and systematic way;
- provide new insight into issues;
- suggest better alternatives and eliminate inferior ones; and
- reveal some of the linkages between objectives and feasible results.

Nevertheless, it must also be admitted that there are potential ways to misuse systems analysis. For instance, whatever the analyst may be told is the purpose of a study, a decisionmaker may commission it to provide himself with an "expert" facade for promoting preconceived ideas or policies, an excuse for inaction and delay, or a shield for actions that are hard to penetrate or challenge without rival analysis. Then, too, systems analysis, unless properly carried out and communicated, may be misunderstood or produce misleading information—for example, by implying an unwarranted degree of confidence in oversimplified or partial results, or by overemphasizing the readily treated (but often less important) quantitative aspects of problems, while neglecting other attributes and values that are difficult to quantify and hence can be treated only by judgment. Canons of good practice enjoin the analyst from such pitfalls.

On the other hand, done properly and properly understood and acted upon, systems analysis can, in the opinion of most of those who have had some experience with it, bring the following beneficial consequences:

- policies and actions that may more effectively (and/or efficiently) achieve the decisionmakers' desired objectives, with fewer undesirable side-effects;
- explicit consideration of assumptions, uncertainties, costs, consequences, spillovers, etc.;
- an objective framework and common base for part of the political process through a separation and clarification of objective components;

improved understanding of the issues and hence better intuition on the part of the decisionmakers;

a logical framework for considering and setting policy goals;

improved managerial capabilities for planning and administration;

better means—economic, political, organizational, or technological—for setting and effecting national, regional, or institutional objectives;

new options, new goals, and new horizons that expand people's perceptions of what might be and that offer them the chance of improving their lives.

There are also adverse features that may follow from dependence on analytic methods. To minimize them, specific consideration must be given in systems analysis to the possibility that they may occur. Here are some examples:

unwanted delays in making decisions;

undesirable centralization and concentration of decisionmaking in top-level staff;

an increased dependence on complex processes (for example, computerized information systems) that require continuing attention by expensive talent in order to work well; or

elimination of inefficiency and redundancy that, while costly, may have served to meet unexpected contingencies. (Such paring, sometimes called "streamlining," often results in greater dependence on processes and policies that, while finely tuned to specific situations, may not be robust or reliable under changing or "dirty" conditions.)

However, adverse consequences of these types are the results of defective analysis or of its improper use; good analysts will see to it that such pitfalls are avoided. If, for instance, redundancy in a system is of value in spite of its additional cost, the analysis, when done properly, should show this to be the case.

Systems analysis, like every other human endeavor, has its limitations. One of these is that it is of necessity incomplete; time, money, and other costs place severe limitations on how thoroughly any topic can be studied. But even without such restrictions, the analysis is incomplete: It simply cannot treat all considerations that may be relevant. Problems tend to proliferate, as mentioned earlier, and there is no "stage at which we know all there is to know. We may stop because the return for effort is becoming vanishingly small, but there still will remain research that could be done" (Quade, 1982).

Since systems analysts are human, and since science presents us at best only with partial knowledge of the world's phenomena, it is too much to expect systems analysis to make recommendations that are rigidly objective, totally free from arbitrary judgment, and completely based on science, even

Section 1.8. The Value of Systems Analysis

about issues that are scientific in character. Faced with the problem of giving advice about such things as the effects on stratospheric oxygen of the nitric oxide in the exhaust of supersonic transports, the health hazards of low-level radiation, or the risk of failure of the emergency core-cooling system of a reactor, systems analysis is not in a position to provide unambiguous answers. This is due in part to inadequacies in today's scientific knowledge. Consider environmental standards: They have significant distributional aspects, for they affect people in different locations and walks of life in different ways, and questions of distributional equity cannot be settled on purely scientific principles.

Since it is the nature of systems analysis to explore the difficult problems on the frontiers of our understanding of the workings of complex systems, the history of the subject (as Chapter 2 brings out) has been strewn with difficulties, and failures as well as successes have occurred. Thus, systems analysis is not without its critics; they say that it is too complicated, that analysts are more interested in research than in solving real-world problems, that there is too much emphasis on narrowly defined costs, that it is a waste of money. Undoubtedly the results have sometimes been unusable and misleading; Hoos (1972) cites a number of examples. Important criticisms have been expressed by Dror (1971), Majone (1977), Tribe (1972), and Lynn (1980). Tribe's criticisms, as stated by Rowen (1976, p. 144), are that policy analysis (systems analysis, in our terms)

(1) Concentrates on tangible, quantifiable factors and ignores or depreciates the importance of intangible, unquantifiable ones;
(2) Leaves out of consideration altogether certain "fragile" values—e.g., ecological or aesthetic concerns;
(3) Focuses on results and, in its search for common measures, ignores both the processes by which preferences and decisions are formed and significant qualitative differences among outcomes;
(4) Tends to operate within limits set by the interests and values of the clients;
(5) In the effort to be objective, employs deceptively neutral and detached language in dealing with intensely moral issues;
(6) Artificially separates facts from values; and
(7) Tends to overlook distributional objectives in favor of efficiency objectives.

However, these criticisms of past practice must not be viewed as intrinsic to systems analysis; rather, they are pitfalls to be avoided. More recent practice, as illustrated, for instance, by the estuary protection example discussed in Section 1.2 and later in Section 3.4, shows that systems analysis can be free of many of these problems.

It is crucial for an analysis to be documented—clearly, concisely, completely, with the assumptions made explicit (to the extent that the analyst recognizes them), the constraints listed, the criteria spelled out, the structures of the models explained, and so on. One aim is to help others, another is quality control. Writing up the work will not ensure that the analysts are competent and fully honest, but it certainly increases the likelihood, and full documentation is the major piece of evidence from which reviewers may determine the quality of the work.

There are, of course, means other than systems analysis for helping a decisionmaker. The policy advisor is the traditional source of advice. He may be a generalist experienced in political and other matters or a specialist, an expert in economics, physics, sociology, or another field. Policy advisors are often well informed on the issues and the decisionmakers' preferences, but unless the advisors' assumptions and chain of logic are made explicit so that others can use the information and reasoning to form their own considered opinion, biases and omissions may go undetected. The opinion of the advisor can, in fact, be very helpful, particularly if it results from a carefully reasoned and impartial examination of the problem situation with due allowance for the costs and risks. In other words, if the advisor bases his opinion on whatever analysis is possible with resources and time available to him, the advice is likely to be superior to what he might give based on intuition alone. However, such an advisor is limited to what he can do acting alone.

Committees are a second alternative. The assumption in this case is that an advisor's knowledge and opinions are likely to be more valuable if they can be joined with the knowledge and opinions of other advisors and experts to reach a consensus. Unfortunately, the findings of many committees are obtained by bargaining rather than by reasoning, and, on a committee, personality and prestige often outrank logic.

A third alternative is "muddling through," a sort of trial-and-error process in which feedback from what actually happens is supplemented by limited analysis. Administrators and policymakers have long gone about making decisions in this way—using analysis on parts of their problems, taking remedial steps rather than innovative ones, moving away from ills rather than toward definite objectives, and seeking vague goals sequentially.

If systems analysis, however incomplete, is to be preferred to the intuition of an expert or the bargaining of a committee, it is because the results are better, that is, that the decisionmaker prefers the results from the analysis to the advice available without it. We cannot prove that analysis will produce better results; sensible decisions are clearly possible without systems analysis, and many have been made. Also, it is clear that the practice of systems analysis involves a cost, and the cost of analysis may be greater than the cost of error. However, the lessons of the history of systems analysis, and the magnitude of the problems the world faces in its sociotechnical systems, argue that, properly carried out and suitably applied, systems analysis can make important—even essential—contributions to solving these problems.

1.9. The Craft of Analysis

The difficulty in telling a would-be practitioner of systems analysis how to practice, as we try to do in this handbook, is that systems analysis, like scientific research and engineering practice, is to a large extent a craft activity in which skilled persons draw upon the knowledge and tools of many different sciences and technologies to create a product responsive to the needs of the eventual users. Unlike much of engineering, the work of the systems analyst (and of the scientist as well) is guided and controlled by methods that are mainly informal, *ad hoc,* and tacit rather than formal, public, and explicit. It is desirable for any presentation of the methods of systems analysis to make these guiding ideas as explicit as possible, but this may be impossible to do in written form alone. Case studies that illustrate how an experienced analyst goes about his craft may help, but such studies are not easily formulated and are no substitute for on-the-job training in an art or craft.

The way to carry out a systems analysis of a given problem or issue cannot be described by an unquestioned set of rules. There is no set of steps for the analyst to follow by the numbers that will lead the decisionmakers, without exception, to the correct decision. The primary decision—what action to take—is the responsibility of the decisionmakers. The path to the primary decision, however, depends on a host of what White (1972) calls "secondary decisions" by the analyst, made more or less subjectively, based on intuition and experience. These secondary decisions include the many simplifying assumptions that must be made if a complex issue is to be made tractable: the choice of what aspects of the primary problem to leave out, the selection of an analytic approach, the extent of the sensitivity testing, and many others. Proficiency in making these methodological and procedural decisions is part of the craft of systems analysis, as discussed at various places throughout this handbook, but especially in Chapter 10. A detailed examination of the work sketched in the examples at the beginning of this chapter would show many instances of the application of craft knowledge; for example, several successful simplifications were critical in enabling the models in the blood-supply example to yield easily computable results.

In systems analysis, artistry and craftmanship are nowhere more in demand than during model building. Often in constructing a model systems analysts may find themselves at the frontier of the state of the art. They may then have to rely heavily on judgment and intuition about whatever expertise may be available, for solid theory may be nonexistent. The demands of problems in the real world require that, even if the current state of science provides no theory, well established or otherwise, of the phenomena to be dealt with, the analyst [as Helmer (1966, pp. 5–6) states]

> must nevertheless construct a model as best he can, where both the structure of the model and its numerical inputs have an *ad hoc* quality, representing

merely the best insight and information that the analyst happens to have available. As further insights accrue and more experimental data become available, the [systems] analyst has to be prepared to discard his first model and replace it with an improved one. The tentative procedure, dictated by pragmatic considerations, is thus essentially one of successive approximation.

A good craftsman makes this process converge to a useful model within the relevant time period.

In time the profession of systems analysis will develop an epistemology of practice that will give it a mature and tested basic philosophy (perhaps along the lines suggested in Section 10.3), together with widely accepted and useful principles to guide its craft. This handbook is intended to contribute to this goal.

1.10. Conclusion

The notion has been around for a long time that numbers and logic ought, if not to rule the world, at least to play a larger role in that rule. Until recently, however, only a few philosophers have had much faith that this might actually come to pass. For the rest of us, quantitative scientific analysis admittedly had a place in engineering and in science itself, but for determining decisions and policy in the world of affairs it had very limited applications; that world would continue to be governed by tradition, judgment, and intuition; wisdom, insight, perseverance, and constructive politics, not calculation, made our leaders great.

Systems analysis presents a challenge to this point of view. It offers a way to bring scientists, including those in economics and the behavioral disciplines, and their knowledge and methods into domains where decisions have been almost the exclusive prerogative of politicians, lawyers, and entrepreneurs. To date—although not without some criticism—systems analysis has found many applications, with results at least promising enough to generate a desire for more.

Systems analysis, as we have argued, is not a method or technique, nor is it a fixed set of techniques; rather it is an approach, a way of looking at a problem and bringing scientific knowledge and thought to bear on it. That is, it is a way to investigate how to best aid a decision- or policymaker faced with complex problems of choice under uncertainty, a practical philosophy for carrying out decision-oriented multidisciplinary research, and a perspective on the proper use of the available tools. We have also in this chapter discussed the type of problem with which systems analysis can deal, given an idea of its value for policymakers and the public, and contrasted it with alternative sources of advice.

What this chapter has not done is provide advice on how to carry out a systems study, how to overcome or avoid the problems and difficulties so that desired outcomes are attained. Except for the more technical and mathematical tools, which are left to other volumes, this advice is contained in the remainder of this handbook.

One more point should be made here. For success, systems analysis requires not only a competent producer, but also a knowledgeable and sophisticated consumer or user. To get full benefit, the user needs to understand the character of policy-level research; he must, for instance, understand that finding out what needs to be studied is a crucial part of the process of applying systems analysis to almost every problem. For this reason, the chapters that follow in this volume are written both for the producer and the user of systems analysis.

References

Brooks, Harvey (1976). Environmental decision making: Analysis and values. In *When Values Conflict* (L. H. Tribe, C. S. Schelling, and John Voss, eds.). Cambridge, Massachusetts: Ballinger.

Checkland, Peter (1981). *Systems Thinking, Systems Practice.* Chichester, England: Wiley.

Dalkey, Norman C. (1967). Operations research, P-3705. Santa Monica, California: The Rand Corporation.

Dror, Y. (1971). *Ventures in Policy Sciences.* New York: Elsevier.

Energy Systems Program Group of IIASA, Wolf Haefele, Program Leader (1981). *Energy in a Finite World.* Volume 1: *Paths to a Sustainable Future;* Volume 2: *A Global Systems Analysis.* Cambridge, Massachusetts: Ballinger. [See also *Energy in a Finite World: Executive Summary.* Laxenburg, Austria: International Institute for Applied Systems Analysis.]

Helmer, O. (1966). *Social Technology.* New York: Basic Books.

Hildebrant, Steen (1979). From manipulation to participation in the operations research process. In *OR '78* (K.B. Haley, ed.). Amsterdam, The Netherlands: North-Holland.

Holling, C. S., ed. (1978). *Adaptive Environmental Assessment and Management.* Chichester, England: Wiley.

Hoos, Ida R. (1972). *Systems Analysis in Public Policy: A Critique.* Berkeley, California: University of California Press

Kemeny, John G. (1959). *A Philosopher Looks at Science.* New York: Van Nostrand Reinhold.

Lowry, Ira S. (1982). Experimenting with housing allowances, R-2880-HUD. Santa Monica, California: The Rand Corporation.

Lynn, Laurence E. (1980). The user's perspective. In *Pitfalls of Analysis* (G. Majone and E. S. Quade, eds.). Chichester, England: Wiley.

Majone, Giandomenico (1977). The uses of policy analysis. In *Annual Report.* New York: The Russell Sage Foundation.

Miser, Hugh J. (1980). Operations research and systems analysis. *Science* 209, 136–146.

Quade, E. S. (1982). *Analysis for Public Decisions, 2nd ed.* New York: North-Holland.

Rowen, Henry S. (1976). Policy analysis as heuristic aid: The design of means, ends, and institutions. In *When Values Conflict* (L. H. Tribe, C. S. Schelling, and John Voss, eds.). Cambridge, Massachusetts: Ballinger.

Schön, Donald A. (1983). *The Reflective Practitioner: How Professionals Think in Action.* New York: Basic Books.

Tribe, Laurence (1972) Policy science: Analysis or ideology? *Philosophy and Public Affairs* 2, 88–93.

White, D. J. (1972). *Decision Methodology.* Chichester, England: Wiley.

Chapter 2
Systems Analysis: A Genetic Approach

Giandomenico Majone

2.1. Change and Continuity

An adequate account of a field of inquiry should be capable of explaining its continuities as well as its changes—possibly in terms of the same underlying process. Considered over a sufficiently long period of time, a discipline like physics changes quite radically in its objects of inquiry, its methods, and its aims. Yet, despite such changes, the discipline maintains a recognizable continuity, less because of a common professional commitment to a central core of principles or key questions than because the problems on which successive generations of physicists have focused their attention are connected by recognizable lines of descent. These problems form, as Toulmin (1972, pp. 134–144) has put it, a "genealogy" of issues and of related concepts and tools.

Similarly, the development of systems analysis over the last 40 or so years reveals considerable changes in intellectual content, methods, and aims. The tactical problems that formed the main objects of inquiry of operations research (OR) during World War II were followed by the strategic problems investigated by defense analysts in the 1950s and 1960s. Today's policy analysts focus on social and economic problems: regulation and pollution control, energy and education, housing and health care. The accompanying changes in methods have been equally striking, from the relatively simple data analyses and differential equations of the early military applications to the static and dynamic optimization models of contemporary OR, to the econometric models of policy analysis. Aims have also changed. If the goal of the first analysts of military operations was essentially empirical—to give a scientific explanation of the facts and to make successful predictions of the effectiveness of new weapons and new tactics, that of the systems and policy analysts is primarily prescriptive—to assist the decisionmaker in choosing among alternative courses of action. And we are now beginning to recognize a third legitimate function or aim for systems analysis, that of a vehicle for persuasion and argumentation in the policy debate.

The question immediately facing the historian of systems analysis is whether an underlying continuity can be detected below these changes in problems, methods, and disciplinary aims. Or should one rather speak of mutations that have altered the original enterprise in fundamental ways? A good argument could be made in favor of the mutation hypothesis, yet the weight of the evidence favors the hypothesis of continuity, as I shall show. The difficulties of the proof should not be underestimated, however. In mature disciplines like physics or mathematics, essential continuity is maintained by the joint operation of a dual process of intellectual innovation and critical evaluation and selection. The pool of available theories and methods is continually enriched by intellectual novelties, but only a few of the novelties survive the severe tests to which they are exposed. In this way disciplinary identity can be maintained over considerable periods of time. But, in order for this dual process of innovation and selection to work satisfactorily, there must be professional "forums of competition" (Toulmin, 1972, ch. 1) within which new ideas can survive long enough to show their merits and defects, but in which they are also criticized and eliminated with enough severity to maintain the coherence of the discipline.

By contrast, systems analysis is still a maturing field in which the rate of intellectual innovation is much greater than the rate of critical selection. Hence a proliferation of approaches and "schools" that seem to have little in common. And, because of the fragility of the existing mechanisms of quality control, the survival or rejection of intellectual novelties seems to depend more on academic fashion and external support than on a sober assessment of their potentialities—as shown by the examples of game theory, value theory, and program budgeting.

The example of program budgeting suggests another important reason why the evolutionary model of "conjectures and refutations" is so much more complex in the case of systems analysis than in the traditional academic disciplines. Systems analysis is a form of articulate intervention into ongoing action programs (Boothroyd, 1978; see also Majone, 1980b). This means that the conceptual innovations proposed by systems analysts will be evaluated, not only by the canons of disciplinary criticism, but also according to criteria of social effectiveness. New proposals must fit into a certain intellectual tradition or research program (like all conceptual novelties) and must also be adapted to, and adopted by, an ongoing social process or action program (a problem that theoretical innovations do not have to face). Depending on time and circumstances, one or the other criterion—professional quality or social effectiveness—may prevail; but, in the long run, it is doubtful that an analytic proposal can survive without meeting some minimal standards of adequacy along both dimensions.

Toulmin's "genealogy of problems" is the element by which a field of intellectual inquiry preserves its disciplinary identity. However, in the case of systems analysis we should speak rather of a lattice of descendent problems,[1] to signify the fact that the problems of systems analysis do not develop just along disciplinary (or even interdisciplinary) lines, but also inevitably mix with issues derived from political, social, and institutional sources.

In our reconstruction we shall also have to bear constantly in mind that, like any other historically developing intellectual enterprise, systems analysis has two aspects. We can think of it as a (composite) discipline comprising, at any given time, a stock of theories, conceptual frameworks, and techniques for dealing with theoretical and practical problems; or we can view it as a profession comprising a set of institutions, roles, and people whose business it is to apply and improve these methods and techniques. Hence our account of the evolution of systems analysis falls into two parts, one dealing with disciplinary developments (Sections 2.2–2.4), the other with institutional and professional developments (Sections 2.5 and 2.6). Each part, by itself, gives an inadequate and distorted view of the field. A purely intellectual history of methodological developments cannot explain, for example, why, after World War II, OR developed along quite different lines in the United States, Britain, and Canada (or why, for that matter, industrial engineering had not developed in the 1930s into something like operations research). On the other hand, a study of professional organizations, roles (in industry, government, and the universities), and institutional mechanisms of evaluation and control (journals, conferences, policy research institutes) has more than sociological interest only if it is related to the historically developing cognitive basis of systems analysis.

2.2. From Operations Research to Systems Analysis

P. M. S. Blackett, the Nobel prize winning British physicist who was a leader of the early OR work, wrote two short but influential memoranda toward the end of 1941: "Scientists at the operational level" (written in order to inform the Admiralty of developments that had taken place in the operational research sections already established at different commands of the Royal Air Force), and "A note on certain aspects of the methodology of operational research" ("an attempt to set out, for the benefit of new scientific recruits to the operational research sections, some of the principles that had been found to underlie the work of the first two years of the war").[2] Together with another paper written by the same author a few years after the end of the war, "The scope of operational research" (Blackett, 1950), these notes rep-

---

[1] I borrow this expression from Ravetz (1973, especially pp. 191–199).
[2] These two memoranda, the second reproduced from a later version dated May 1943, appear in a collection of Blackett's papers on war (Blackett, 1962, pp. 171–176, and 176–198). They had also appeared in the April 1948 issue of *The Advancement of Science.*

resent not only some of the earliest, but also some of the clearest and most insightful discussions of the principles of OR as practiced during the 1940s.

The first step in establishing a sphere of professional autonomy is a claim to "cognitive exclusiveness" over some portion of reality (Larson, 1977). Consequently, Blackett takes great pains to differentiate the functions of the operations analysts from those of their closest potential competitors, technical services on the one hand, and operational staffs on the other:

> The object of having scientists in close touch with operations is to enable operational staffs to obtain scientific advice on those matters which are not handled by the service technical establishments.
>
> Operational staffs provide the scientists with the operational outlook and data. The scientists apply scientific methods of analysis to these data, and are thus able to give useful advice.
>
> The main field of their activity is clearly the analysis of actual operations, using as data the material to be found in an operation room. . . .
>
> It will be noted that these data are not, and on secrecy grounds cannot, in general, be made available to the technical establishments. Thus such scientific analysis, if done at all, must be done in or near operation rooms [Blackett, 1962, p. 171].

For example, weapon A is calculated by the technical department of a service to be 50 percent more efficient than weapon B. In actual operations, over a given period of time, B scores four successes, while A scores only two. Is this sufficient evidence to reject the estimates of the technical department and proceed as if B were the better weapon? Here the role of the operations analyst is similar to that of the statistician facing a standard problem in statistical inference. The task is to try to reject the null hypothesis—represented by the estimates of the technical department.

As another typical example of operations analysis, Blackett considers the problem of discovering the best use, under actual operating conditions, of a new device. Operations researchers can perform a useful function here by interpreting the "operational facts of life" to technical people, and technical possibilities to the operational staff; that is, by operating in a liaison capacity between the operational staff, the technical department that produced the device, and the development unit.

Particularly in times of war, the demand for new weapons and technical gadgets tends to become overwhelming. But, Blackett points out, relatively too much scientific effort is expended in the production of new devices and too little in the proper use of what is already available. Hence, another important task of operations research consists in providing numerical estimates of the value of changing over from one device to another, by investigation of the actual performance of existing systems, and by analysis of the likely performance of new ones. Incidentally, it will be noted how clearly Blackett prefigures here the future development of cost–benefit and cost-effectiveness analysis, which was to play such a large role in systems analysis in the 1950s and 1960s.

Having established a sphere of autonomy for a problem-solving approach that is neither purely technical, nor exclusively operational, but partakes of both functions, Blackett goes on to raise three methodological questions about OR: Is it scientific? Is it new? If so, in what ways?

Now, if one accepts the usual characterization of operations research as the application of the scientific method to the study of operations, then the answer to the first question must be "yes"—by definition. The trouble with this characterization is that there is no unique scientific method, least of all in the sense of a set of mechanical rules that would allow one to move safely from data to conclusions. It is true that the pioneers of operations research, men like P. M. S. Blackett, C. H. Waddington, P. M. Morse, G. E. Kimball, and B. O. Koopman were scientists—physicists, biologists, and mathematicans of high caliber. But what they brought to the new field was not a particular method, or even advanced scientific knowledge, but a new perspective and a set of superb craft skills in examining the available evidence, considering what conclusions could be drawn from it, deciding what other information was required, and how it could be obtained.[3]

This distinction is important because the view of science as craftsman's work (and it is precisely in this sense that operations research or systems analysis may be considered scientific, as I have argued at some length elsewhere (Majone, 1980a)) leads to quite different methodological positions from those suggested by a vulgar-positivistic view of science. A dogmatic interpretation of the nature of scientific method can easily lead to an attitude which Tukey (1979) has recently expressed in an aphorism: "We don't want to try to measure anything where we cannot be proud of the measurement process." The craftsman, on the other hand, tries to do his best with the materials and tools at his disposal—always keeping in mind Aristotle's dictum that "precision is not to be sought for alike in all discussion, any more than in all products of the crafts." See, for example, what Blackett (1962, p. 185) has to say about the use of rough data in operations research:

> No pregnant problem should be left unattended for lack of *exact* numerical data, for often it is found on doing the analysis that *some* significant conclusions recommending concrete action can be drawn even with very rough data. In other cases this is, of course, not so. But till the problem is worked out, one cannot tell.
>
> It often happens that when the problem has been worked through in a very rough form, it is found that data which were thought to be important

---

[3] There is an interesting analogy with the takeover in the late 1940s of theoretical biology by men originally trained in physics. The development of molecular biology is essentially due to these "emigré physicists," but as Szilard has emphasized, what these men brought to biology was "not any skills acquired in physics, but rather an attitude: the conviction, which few biologists had at the time, that mysteries can be solved" (see Toulmin, 1972, p. 234).

are actually unimportant, and vice versa.... It must always be remembered that the object of the analysis is practical—that is, that it should lead to action. Attempts at undue and unnecessary precision are to be avoided. [Emphasis in original.]

Incidentally, the problem of making effective use of rough data is still very much with the policy analyst of today, as shown for example by a recent insightful paper on "assessing unknown numbers: order of magnitude estimation" by Mosteller (1977).

Concerning the second and third questions, Blackett argues that operations research has a considerable degree of novelty, but this relative novelty lies "not so much in the material to which the scientific method is applied as in the level at which work is done, in the comparative freedom of the investigators to seek out their own problems, and in the direct relation of the work to the possibilities of executive action" (Blackett, 1962, p. 201).

Of these three distinctive features of original OR work, the second—the comparative freedom of the investigators to seek out their own problems—seems to be the most important. "In fact," Blackett adds, "the most fertile tasks are often found by the [operational research] group themselves rather than given to them. That this is so is only to be expected, since any problem which is clearly recognized by the executives is likely, in an efficient organization, to be already a matter of study."

If this is so, it is wrong to argue, as Mood does, that industrial engineers, quality control experts, time-and-motion experts, investment counselors, product packagers, and personnel managers (!) have been doing operations research in industry "for at least a couple of generations."[4]

In fact, it seems very doubtful that any of these alleged precursors of OR would meet all three criteria set down by Blackett. Before the large-scale introduction of operations research methods, most analyses of industrial operations were largely empirical in character. Certainly, they were not carried out in that atmosphere of a "first-class pure scientific research institution," which, according to Blackett, is necessary to the effectiveness of an OR team. It is also doubtful that the early analysts of industrial operations had the freedom to seek out their own problems, being usually constrained by the specific research tasks assigned to them by management. As already noted, social and institutional factors were probably responsible for the fact that industrial engineering and "scientific management" did not actually evolve into genuine OR work, as the term is understood today—despite some remarkable initial successes and the efforts of people like Frederick Taylor and

---

[4] See Mood (1953) for his critical review of Morse and Kimball's *Methods of Operations Research*. Probably in response to this criticism, Morse too began to see precursors of operations research everywhere: "Though the term is new, this sort of research is not new, of course. Taylor and his followers, with their time and motion studies, investigated a small part of the field; traffic engineers have been struggling with another part; systems engineering is closely related; and so on" (Cf. Morse, 1956, p. 5).

his favorite disciple, Morris Cooke, to pull the industrial engineer "out of his present status of being a hired servant" (as quoted by Larson, 1977, p. 140).

Space does not permit going into the details of Blackett's memorandum on the methodology of operations research. I should like, however, to mention briefly two notions that, introduced there for the first time into the OR literature, were to become standard approaches in the subsequent development of systems analysis. My main reason for mentioning them is to point out an interesting strand of continuity in the evolution of systems analysis. Under the name "variational method" Blackett introduced a type of analysis closely analogous to the economist's marginal reasoning. According to the variational method, each new tactical situation is to be treated as a variation of some old one—about which some data are always available. The problem is to find out how a given system would be altered if some of the variables that determine its effectiveness were varied. The practical applicability of the method depends on the fact that technical devices cannot change very rapidly because of the time required by development and production; even tactical operations do not usually change very fast, if for no other reason than the necessary duration of training. Thus, even if a new system B is not very similar to the old system A (so that the differentials of the input variables, dX_1, dX_2, ..., by which the effectiveness of B can be derived from that of A, are not very small) the results may be fairly reliable, "provided common sense and judgment are used."[5]

A second interesting idea discussed in the memorandum is a method for comparing alternative systems under uncertainty that later came to be known as *a fortiori analysis*. Sometimes lower or upper bounds on the possible effectiveness of a system are known more accurately than the actual values. Thus, to compare a new system B with an existing system A whose effectiveness Y_A is known, assume upper limits (i.e., most favorable to B) for the relevant input variables. Let Y'_B be the estimated upper bound on the effectiveness of B. If $Y'_B < Y_A$, then system B is certainly inferior (if $Y'_B > Y_A$, no meaningful conclusion can be derived without more calculations). If there is a lower bound Y''_B (most unfavorable case for B), and if $Y''_B > Y_A$, B is certainly superior. Some 15 years after Blackett's original memorandum, two well-known analysts from The Rand Corporation were to write that "more than any other single thing, the skilled use of *a fortiori* and break-

---

[5] In more modern language, Blackett (1962, pp. 180–182) is assuming that the effectiveness or yield of a system, denoted by Y, is determined by n inputs $X_1, X_2, \ldots, X_n$: $Y = F(X_1, X_2, \ldots, X_n)$. The partial derivative $\partial Y/\partial X_i$ is then the marginal rate of change of the yield Y with respect to the input X_i. If these partial derivatives can be estimated (and Blackett discusses some statistical and analytical methods for estimating them), then the operational effect of changes in input variables (weapons, tactics, training, etc.) can be estimated by means of the total differential: $Y' = Y + (\partial Y/\partial X_1)dX_1 + (\partial Y/\partial X_2)dX_2 + \cdots + (\partial Y/\partial X_n)dX_n$, where Y' is the effectiveness of the new system. The interested reader should compare Blackett's original memorandum with Alain C. Enthoven's "The simple mathematics of optimization," published as an appendix to Hitch and McKean (1960, pp. 361–405).

even analyses separates the professionals from the amateurs" (Kahn and Mann, 1956).

Thus, before the end of World War II, operations researchers had already developed a number of concepts and approaches whose usefulness would be fully revealed in subsequent decades. However, it is worth pointing out again that, with the notable exception of search theory developed by B. O. Koopman and others in the U. S. Navy's Operations Research Group, successful wartime applications of operations research were not based on new theories or advanced technical tools, but on a sophisticated use of craft skills, learned in the scientific laboratories, in recording, analyzing, and evaluating data, in establishing quantitative relationships, and in setting up testable hypotheses. The first textbook on operations research, Philip M. Morse and George E. Kimball's *Methods of Operations Research,* contains no more advanced mathematics than multiple integration, differential equations, and continuous probabilities.[6]

The mathematical and statistical theories that form the technical core of OR today—queuing theory, mathematical programming, inventory theory, network flows, applied stochastic processes, control theory—were developed (and sometimes rediscovered) after World War II, with the introduction of OR in industry and as a subject for teaching and research in universities. An excellent example of OR as practiced in the early 1950s is Edie's work on traffic delays at toll booths (Edie, 1954)—first winner of the Lanchester Prize, awarded annually for a book or paper making a significant contribution to the advancement of the state of the art of OR.

Probably the most significant methodological development of the first decade after the Second World War was the creation of a set of efficient techniques for programming several activities sharing limited resources. The general problem is to determine the level of each activity that optimizes the output of all activities without violating the given resource constraints. There are several reasons for the practical and conceptual significance of this development, especially the linear programming models developed by G. B. Dantzig and other researchers. First, the mathematical problem of maximizing an objective function subject to various constraints covers a very wide range of situations occurring in production and inventory control, in military planning, in agriculture, transportation, financial management, and so on. In the important special case of a linear (or piecewise linear) objective function and linear constraints, the solution algorithm (simplex) developed by Dantzig can be implemented efficiently with the help of a digital computer, thus allowing

---

[6] The 1951 Morse and Kimball volume was first published in 1946 as a classified technical report under the auspices of the U.S. Office of Scientific Research and Development and the National Defense Research Committee. Similarly, the work on search theory was also issued as a classified report in 1946 under the same auspices. However, Koopman (1980) combines the text of this early report with newer material; for an illuminating review that also traces the growth of the subsequent literature, see Stone (1982).

the explicit solution of quite large programming problems. Second, the programming viewpoint opened up a number of important connections with economic theory—particularly with the neoclassical theory of production and the "new welfare economics." In this respect, great economic significance attaches to the fact that a direct by-product of the solution of a mathematical programming problem is a set of shadow prices, or Lagrange multipliers, representing the effects on the objective function of marginal changes in one or more constraints. Finally, the linear programming approach turned out to be significantly, and often surprisingly, related to other methods of importance for operations research, such as game theory, input–output analysis, and network flow theory. These different connections are discussed at great length in two landmark publications of this period: *Activity Analysis of Production and Allocation* (Koopmans, 1951) and *Linear Programming and Economic Analysis* (Dorfman, Samuelson, Solow, 1958).

As these developments (and others in inventory theory, waiting-time and replacement models, and applied stochastic processes) suggest, important changes were taking place between 1945 and 1955 in personnel, disciplinary aims, and, consequently, in the implicit standards of evaluation and criticism. While people like Blackett, Waddington, and Morse were returning to their laboratories and university departments, a new generation of analysts was entering the OR scene—people primarily interested in the more formal aspects of scientific methodology and proficient in mathematical manipulations, but often lacking the craft skills and the mature critical judgment of the old masters. The goal of operations research, as the early practitioners saw it, was "to find a scientific explanation of the facts (Waddington, 1973, p. 26). The phases of investigation followed the pattern prevalent in the science laboratory: "past operations are studied to determine the facts; theories are elaborated to explain the facts; and finally the facts and theories are used to make predictions about future operations" (Blackett, 1962, p. 177).

Given this paradigm, the relevant standards of criticism were those of the natural sciences. In fact, the situations investigated by operations researchers during World War II were particularly well suited to such an approach. Typically, military operations could be regarded, without serious distortion, as being representative of a class of repetitive situations "where theories built up in response to earlier examples of the situation could be checked out against later examples, monitored while proposals for improved action were in use, and used to detect their own dwindling validity as the situations changed" (Boothroyd, 1978, p. 13). The industrial applications of the late 1940s presented many of the same features; for example, work like that of L. C. Edie (1954) on traffic delays at toll booths and that of C. W. Thornthwaite (1953 and 1954) on agricultural operations still followed the classical pattern and appealed explicitly to the established criteria of validation.

However, by 1955 the focus of professional interests had clearly shifted away from military operations, while the scope and methods of OR work had changed sufficiently to raise serious questions about the relevance of the traditional standards of evaluation and criticism to contemporary professional practice. The increasing popularity of computer-based models (with the attendant serious problems of validation) made the need for new criteria of criticism even more obvious. A consecutive reading of the recommendations of the Lanchester Prize Committee, starting with the first report in 1954, gives a good indication of the difficulties experienced by the profession in finding agreement on a set of relevant criteria of evaluation.

Let us return to the changes in the disciplinary composition of operations research. In the early stages of development, the part played by economists in OR activities, compared to that of natural scientists and mathematicians, had been quite modest. With the expansion of the scope of operations research in the post-war years, particularly in the United States, to include military strategy as well as a growing number of public policy problems in health, education, transportation, housing, and the social services, the role of the economist was bound to become increasingly important—as shown by the election of Rand economist C. J. Hitch to the presidency of the Operations Research Society of America in 1959. As a group, economists have made two basic contributions to the development of the field: first, a penetrating critique of certain conceptual inadequacies (e.g., in the selection of criteria and in the treatment of time) of early OR applications; second, the proposal of an intellectual framework derived from decision theory and the microeconomic logic of choice as the most appropriate paradigm for operations research.

A good example of the new critical attitude is Hitch's (1953) paper on "Sub-optimization in operations problems." The validity and usefulness of operations research, Hitch argues, depend to a large extent on the ability to choose the correct criterion or objective function for the problem under discussion. "Unless operations research develops methods of evaluating criteria and choosing good ones, its quantitative methods may prove worse than useless to its clients in its new applications in government and industry" (Hitch, 1953, p. 87). The main criterion for judging whether the objective function chosen for a given level of analysis is the correct one is consistency with the relevant objective function at a higher level. Unfortunately, too many OR studies in the past have failed to meet this criterion. For example, in devising a suitable strategy for the defense of naval convoys against attacks by enemy submarines, one should keep in mind that the relevant higher-level objective is winning the war. The criterion of effectiveness chosen at the operational level should be consistent with it, but the criterion actually used during World War II—which amounted to maximizing the "exchange ratio" of enemy losses to one's own losses—is not necessarily compatible with the higher-level goal. As a matter of fact, the decision to increase the size of the convoys so as to improve the exchange ratio disregarded a number of factors (congestion of port facilities, reduced operating efficiency of ships in large convoys, longer turnaround times, redirection of enemy effort) that were obviously important for the general strategy of the war.

The examples of improper suboptimization given by Hitch are mostly of a military nature, but the phenomenon is quite general. Thus, the sales department of a profit-maximizing firm is not supposed to suboptimize (for example, to maximize the sales minus selling costs), but to choose actions that maximize the total profits of the firm. Similarly, the correct goal of the production department (in terms of the profit targets of the entire organization) is not, in general, the minimization of cost per unit of output, nor the maximization of productivity per man–hour but, again, a mode of operation that is conducive to the maximization of total profits.[7]

Similar criticisms have been voiced by other economists in different contexts. Feldstein (1963, p. 21), for example, writes that "quantitative methods in government management decisions can be extremely fruitful, but in the absence of an appropriate framework they can be empty algorithms which hide misleading advice in a mass of reassuring calculations." He then goes on to argue that operations research achieves maximum usefulness only if it is considered in a framework of economic analysis of the appropriate benefits and costs of alternative actions. Feldstein draws his examples from the experience of the British National Health Service. He shows that it is a mistake to approach health-service decisions as problems of meeting specific community "needs." Rather, they should be approached as problems of allocating scarce health resources among competing uses. For example, operations researchers have made elaborate calculations of the number of hospital beds needed to meet doctors' requests in a given region, without raising probing questions about the optimal number of beds, weighing the benefits of hospitalization and longer stay against alternative uses of scarce health resources.

In part, these criticisms reflect the traditional opposition between the economic viewpoint, which is concerned with finding the best allocation of given resources among *competing* ends, and the technical viewpoint, which is concerned with finding the best way of using given resources to achieve a *single* end. However, in a deeper sense what is at issue is the appropriate conceptualization of the system under investigation. The economist's recommendation for avoiding the pitfalls of suboptimization is the "golden rule" of allocative efficiency: scarce resources having alternative uses should be allocated so as to make each resource equally scarce (i.e., equally valuable at the margin) in all uses. But allocative efficiency can be achieved only if resources can be freely combined and substituted for each other according to their

---

[7] What came to be known as "the criterion problem" is discussed at great length in two early classics of systems analysis: *Efficiency in Government through Systems Analysis*, by R. N. McKean (1958), and *The Economics of Defense in the Nuclear* Age, by C. J. Hitch and R. N. McKean (1960).

relative prices or scarcities—fewer hospital beds and more outpatient services, less air support and more ground forces. In this logic, the internal organization of the system is irrelevant, if not positively misleading, since it tempts the analyst to make the scope of the analysis coincide with the boundaries of administrative units and decisionmaking authority.

Thus it is only a slight overstatement to say that the difference between the traditional operations researcher and the economist turned systems analyst is that the traditional operations researcher first establishes what the system to be studied is, and then inquires about the problems of that system, whereas the systems analyst first determines what the real problem is and only then inquires about the appropriate system or systems within which this problem must be considered if it is to be solved fruitfully (Hoag, 1957). The emphasis on system design (as opposed to the static analysis of given alternatives), characteristic of so much early writing on systems analysis, fits quite naturally the new decisionmaking paradigm, although, paradoxically, it implicitly reintroduces many of the institutional and political factors whose influence the microeconomic paradigm of allocative efficiency had attempted to minimize. As we shall see, policy analysis emerged in the late 1960s as an attempt to reconcile the opposing logics of "economic rationality" and "political rationality"—broadly understood. But in the period we are considering now (from the early 1950s to mid-1960s) the success of the economic paradigm in transforming early-vintage operations research into a more ambitious and intellectually, if not technically, more sophisticated systems analysis is almost complete. Cost-effectiveness analysis, modeling, optimal timing of projects, gaming, grand strategy—everything seems now to fall into its proper conceptual place.

It is true that microeconomic logic does not deal adequately with decisionmaking under uncertainty. However, economists were quick to close the gap by appropriating decision theory—an approach to the problem of choice under uncertainty originally developed by probabilists but so general in scope that it could claim, with some justification, to include operations research as well as wide areas of economics and statistics. Thus, the new paradigm seemed to have an answer for all problems of choice, at least in principle (Arrow, 1957). Systems analysis came to be widely regarded as a decision technology, concerned not just with how systems behave, but also with how they should behave. A prescriptive approach to decisionmaking was the new symbol of rationality in industry and in government, displacing the earlier emphasis on prediction and the "scientific explanation of the facts."

2.3. From Systems Analysis to Policy Analysis

Cost–benefit analysis (CBA) is simply a method of setting out the factors that have to be taken into account in making economic choices, particularly in the case of investment projects, for the purpose of maximizing the present

Section 2.3. From Systems Analysis to Policy Analysis

value of all benefits minus that of all costs, subject to given constraints. This technique of economic calculation had been given special attention in one of the early and most influential discussions of systems analysis, McKean's *Efficiency in Government Through Systems Analysis* (1958), which was primarily concerned with water resources development. Perhaps for this reason, CBA became almost identified with systems analysis in the mind of many people, professionals as well as laymen—despite the warning by two well-known economists that CBA is "only a technique for taking decisions within a framework which has to be decided upon in advance and which involves a wide range of considerations, many of them of a political or social character" (Prest and Turvey, 1965, p. 685). Although the claim made by some advocates that CBA is "a natural and logical extension" of systems analysis and operations research seems in retrospect rather exaggerated, there is some truth in the statement that it is "more ambitious than them in evaluative scope and in technique" (Williams, 1972, p. 200). Hence, by examining, however briefly, the underlying purpose of CBA and the type of relation between analyst and decisionmaker that it implies, we can gain a better understanding of the strengths and weaknesses of the economist's approach, and its significance for the development of systems analysis.[8]

Since CBA is used in relation to a decision problem—how to choose between two or more alternative courses of action or social states—it assumes a well-defined decision-maker or group of decisionmakers. Since it is typically, thought exclusively, applied to public decisions involving the welfare of the community as a whole, the decisionmaker is supposed to act in the public interest. Analytic technicalities aside (choice of a discount rate, treatment of uncertainty, estimation of consumers' and producers' surplus, distributional weights, and so on), the distinguishing features of CBA are explicitness and consistency. CBA is explicit in the sense that, in principle, all assumptions are clearly stated, evidence is presented, calculations and conclusions are reproducible. It is explicit also in the sense that it must state clearly not only the decisionmaker's objective function, but also the alternatives that have been examined and the constraints that have been used. In short, the analyst attempts to translate into a well-defined decision problem what was initially, in many cases, only a problem situation—a feeling that things are not as they should be, but without a clear idea of how they might be put right.

The second feature, consistency, is of crucial importance not only for CBA but also for the entire prescriptive, or normative, approach to the analysis of decisions. We have already met the problem in our discussion of suboptimization: How does one make sure that lower-level decisions are consistent with higher-level ones? The answer given there—the "golden rule" of allocative efficiency—presupposes a centralized and fully informed decisionmaker ca-

---

[8] For a more complete treatment, see Sugden and Williams (1978). The last chapter is particularly relevant to this discussion.

pable of estimating the marginal utilities of the available resources in all their possible uses. Similarly, the utility-maximization rule of decision theory is a way of making sure that the decisionmaker's choice (under uncertainty) is consistent with his subjective estimates of the probability of different contingencies and with the utilities he attaches to various conditional outcomes. These meanings of consistency are all relevant to the practice of CBA, but in addition to the efficiency and logical aspects there is a political and ethical problem that no serious analyst can evade. To quote Sugden and Williams (1978, pp. 233-234):

> If decision-makers were able to specify a different set of objectives for each decision that they had to make, cost-benefit analysis would be, as opponents of the decision-making approach have alleged, little more than window-dressing. To ensure that a pet project received the sanction of cost-benefit analysis, a decision-maker would need only to revise his objectives in the appropriate way. If the analyst is to escape the charge of window-dressing he must be prepared, in the report that he makes of his analysis, to discuss the wider implications of the objectives that he has used. If, for example, he has been asked to use in a cost-benefit analysis of a particular medical treatment a valuation of the prolonging of life that is clearly inconsistent with current policy towards medical care in general, he ought to make this inconsistency clear when he reports. Otherwise the result of his work may be to mislead more than to enlighten.

Thus the analyst should practice explicitness and preach consistency. This is a reasonable prescription if we assume a unique decisionmaker or a group whose members share common objectives and disagree only about questions of fact. But, the political scientist objects, this is not at all the situation prevailing in public policymaking. Health, education, and housing policies are the outcomes not of the choices of a unitary decisionmaking body, however powerful, but of political processes involving different interest groups, a variety of political and bureaucratic institutions, pressure groups, and, in our technological society, the analysts themselves.

The normative approach breaks down, our critic continues, because it rests on the fiction of a benevolent dictator with complete information about the preferences and interests of all members of the community, with no preferences of his own, and capable of implementing his decisions fully. Not surprisingly, in the microeconomic paradigm, politics and human nature belong to the institutional or behavioral givens and are taken to lie outside the scope of analysis. In fact, normative analysis, being a generalized logic of choice, terminates at the moment a decision is taken, leaving aside questions of policy implementation, evaluation, and termination (as distinct from *model* evaluation and implementation).

Ironically, the political scientist's critique of the economist's approach to systems analysis is, in a sense, quite similar to the critical stance taken by economists, a decade earlier, with respect to operations research. Both crit-

Section 2.3. From Systems Analysis to Policy Analysis

icisms revolve around the notion of suboptimization—in one case with respect to economic rationality, in the other, with respect to political rationality. The difference is that, while the notion of economic rationality can be explicated precisely in terms of economic efficiency (either in the general Pareto sense, or in the more special sense of allocative efficiency), no generally accepted explication of "political rationality" seems to exist. Consequently, attempts to differentiate policy analysis from systems analysis have moved along different lines. We can distinguish two main directions. According to one school of thought, policy analysis is systems analysis writ large—in the sense that it includes, in addition to the technical and economic aspects of a policy problem, also the political aspects that systems analysis is supposed to have overlooked (whether or to what extent the charge is correct is an empirical question that cannot be discussed here). Dror's (1967) manifesto is typical of this position. In policy analysis:

1) Much attention would be paid to the political aspects of decisionmaking and public policy making (instead of ignoring or condescendingly disregarding political aspects). . . .
2) A broad conception of decisionmaking and policy making would be involved (instead of viewing all decisionmaking as mainly a resources allocation). . . .
3) A main emphasis would be on creativity and search for new policy alternatives, with explicit attention to encouragement of innovative thinking. . . .
4) There would be extensive reliance on . . . qualitative methods. . . .
5) There would be much more emphasis on futuristic thinking. . . .
6) The approach would be looser and less rigid, but nevertheless systematic, one which would recognize the complexity of means–ends interdependence, the multiplicity of relevant criteria of decision, and the partial and tentative nature of every analysis.[9]

The immediate practical question is how political and institutional considerations can be handled with the same professional competence as the more familiar technical and economic factors. One possibility is suggested by "political feasibility," a notion that is used frequently, if loosely, in policy discussions. To take political feasibility seriously means to be prepared to list the specific political and institutional constraints that limit the freedom of choice of the policymakers (Majone, 1975b). Once these constraints have been made explicit, it will often be possible to estimate the consequences of small variations on the cost of achieving the policy objectives. In this way, a rough estimate of the opportunity costs of a political constraint can be obtained (Majone, 1975a; Williams, 1972). Suppose, for example, that a publicly owned oil company is considering where to locate a new refinery. If government

---

[9] This manifesto is quoted by Wildavsky (1969) in a paper that, together with an earlier one (Wildavsky, 1966), probably represents the most influential criticism of systems analysis by a political scientist.

policy forces the company to build the plant in a part of the country in need of special economic assistance, the implied cost of this political constraint can be evaluated by reference to a situation in which the constraint is not present.

As long as policy analysis is conceived as systems analysis writ large, the role of the political analyst is entirely analogous to that of the economist or of the technical expert: He translates his assessment of the political situation into a set of constraints and, together with other specialists, estimates the consequences of those constraints for the expected level of achievement of the policy objectives.

The second direction in which a differentiation between systems analysis and policy analysis has been sought is quite different, since it emphasizes the process rather than the outputs or outcomes of policy making. Here the analyst is viewed less as a problem solver or advisor than as designer of procedures for group decisionmaking, and as a catalyst in the implementation process. The advocates of this process-oriented view of analysis are impressed by the enormous complexity of policymaking, and by the cognitive and information-processing limitations of the human mind. This lack of match between intellectual capacity and the complexity of social processes dooms to failure any attempt to find complete and explicit solutions to policy problems. Policy problems are never solved, but only shifted and (sometimes) ameliorated—or, rather, to the extent that a policy problem is temporarily resolved (i.e., removed from the agenda of issues under current debate), this usually happens because a consensus has been reached by the participants in the policy process, not because a solution, in the sense of normative analysis, has been found. But, if policy problems are resolved by social interactions (bargaining, decentralized markets, voting, persuasion, and so on), what role is left for policy analysts?

Lindblom, whose writings represent the most articulate and influential expression of the process-oriented approach, recognizes three distinct forms of adaptation of analysis to interaction (Lindblom, 1977, p. 316; see also Braybrooke and Lindblom, 1963):

> One is analysis by any participant of how he can play his interactive role better to get what he wants—frankly partisan analysis asking "What shall I buy?" or "How shall I vote?" or (for a businessman) "How can I increase sales?" or (for a legislator) "How can I get this bill through the House?" The second is analysis of how to enter into existing interactions most successfully to achieve some public purpose which one, as a public official, has a responsibility to pursue. "Should taxes be cut to stimulate employment?" "Should criminal penalties for street crime be increased?" The third is analysis of possible changes in the basic structure of the interaction processes themselves. "Should markets be made more competitive by breaking up big business?" "Should the criminal justice system be revamped?" "What changes are required in parliamentary organizations?"

Notice how the three kinds of adaptation roughly correspond to the historical development of systems analysis, from the early applications of operations research to specific problems of tactics and logistics, through the broader concerns of systems analysis, to the preoccupation with institutional reform that characterizes contemporary policy analysis. Probably the most important insight to emerge from a serious reflection on this development is the recognition that analysis has a procedural as well as a substantive function. It provides not only evidence and arguments, but also an intellectual structure for the policy process. Even when its conclusions are not accepted, its categories and language, its rational ordering of general ideas affect—even condition—the policy debate. The importance of this procedural function is directly related to the basic lack of certainty of policy determinations. When the correctness of a decision can be established unambiguously, the manner in which it is reached is largely immaterial; only results count. But when the factual and value premises are uncertain and controversial, when objective criteria of success or failure are lacking, the formal characteristics of the decision process—its procedure—become significant. Brooks (1976, p. 115) draws a revealing analogy between analysis and legal procedures:

> The usefulness of systems analysis depends on the fact that its conclusions purport to be based on a set of neutral principles that command a wider consensus than those conclusions themselves would be likely to command without a demonstration that they are logically deducible from such principles. In this sense, policy or systems analysis perform a function with respect to political-technological decisions similar to that performed by a judicial process with respect to conflicts between individuals. A court decision is accepted by the disputing parties largely because it is based on a set of rules both parties accept applied through a procedure which both parties are prepared, before knowing its outcome, to accept as unbiased.

One does not have to agree with Brooks that analytical conclusions can be formally deduced, *more geometrico*, from a set of neutral principles to recognize the importance of his observations. In our societies the rationality and legitimacy of public policies depend on procedural, even more than on substantive, considerations. For analysis to perform a quasi-judicial function with respect to policy decisions, its own rules of evidence and procedure must be spelled out in great detail. As I shall argue in the second part of this chapter, this calls for a determined effort by the systems analysis profession to develop standards of adequacy and suitable mechanisms of quality control.

2.4. ... and Back to Operations Research

I shall summarize the preceding discussion by exhibiting in tabular form the distinguishing features and characterisitic problems of the three stages of systems analysis as shown in Table 2.1[10]

---

[10] This table expands an analogous classification proposed by Levien (1980).

Table 2.1. Distinguishing Features and Characteristic Problems at Three Stages of Systems Analysis

	Operations research (1940s)	Systems analysis (1950s)	Policy analysis (1960s–1970s)
Disciplinary aims	Discovery of empirical regularities in operations; operational design; prediction and testing	Resource allocation; analysis of conflicting systems; system design; systems engineering	Problem formulation; analysis of distributional consequences and institutional constraints; design of decisionmaking procedures
Evaluation criteria	Technical efficiency; cost minimization; output maximization	Economic (allocative) efficiency	Political and administrative feasibility; consensus on policy
Characteristic features and methods	Unitary decisionmaking; system, policy, and goals given; statistical inference; differential equations; search theory; queuing and inventory models; control theory	Group decisionmaking; policy and goals often not given; operations embedded in larger sociotechnical systems; microeconomics; constrained optimization; decision and game theory; simulation; econometrics	Public policymaking; ill-defined goals; institutional framework given; public finance and political economy; organization theory; data analysis and large-scale social experimentation
Typical applications	Tactical operations; logistics; production scheduling; waiting lines; inventory control; programming	Choice among weapon systems; strategic studies; resource allocation in a national health system; development of water resources	Policy planning; reform of existing national systems of health, education, or social security; pollution control; program evaluation; program implementation

Section 2.4. ... and Back to Operations Research

At this point, two clarifications are necessary to avoid misunderstandings. First, the terminological distinctions among operations research, systems analysis, and policy analysis, while fairly common in English-speaking countries (but not without some ambiguities even there: Where, for instance, do management science and systems engineering fit in the series?) are by no means universally accepted or used. In many countries a single label like "operations research" applies to all three stages or forms of analysis that have been distinguished here. In such a case, "operations research" assumes exactly the same meaning as "systems analysis," as the term is used in this handbook.

Second, it is important to realize that a classification like the one suggested by Table 2.1 is only a cross section or time slice of the entire process of disciplinary evolution. To obtain a complete evolutionary representation one would have to combine a cross-sectional description with longitudinal study. Such a cross-sectional and longitudinal study of operations research, for example, would show, not only the successive changes in the pool of concepts and techniques available at different points in time, but also a continuous evolution in aims, methods, and evaluative criteria (in short, in the self-image of the discipline) reflecting, at least in part, analogous developments in systems and policy analysis. Instead of a linear development, in which systems analysis follows operations research and is followed by policy analysis—a linear order has been adopted here only for expository reasons—what we have is a dialectical sequence in which different modes of analysis coexist in more or less close mutual interaction. Thus, in recent issues of journals like *Operations Research* and *Management Science* one finds articles on air-pollution control and water-quality management, on majority voting and distributional constraints on public expenditure planning, on evaluating the quality of social services and implementing new ideas in bureaucracies, on decision analysis and medical malpractice, even on the design of electoral districts—topics and papers that could have appeared also in *Policy Sciences, Policy Analysis,* or some economics journal.

It has already been noted that the most important factor tying the different specializations and approaches of systems analysis together is the way in which an initial problem develops and mixes with other issues to form a lattice of descendent problems. Energy policy modeling is a good example of this phenomenon. The first energy models developed in the early 1970s dealt largely with technical and economic issues that could be handled by standard OR methods. There were short- and medium-term linear programming models of energy supplies, and econometric models of energy demands; quadratic programming models of price-responsive oil demands and supplies, and the resulting international equilibrium; year-by-year simulations of electric utilities pricing and equipment-ordering policies, and so on.[11] The omission of social, political, and institutional considerations—health and environmental effects

---

[11] For a useful recent survey, see Manne, Richels, and Weyant (1979).

of different modes of energy production, safety problems, the risk of nuclear proliferation, issues of scale and of the political implications of alternative energy paths—did not appear to be too serious in the early stages of the policy debate. But, as opinions have become polarized and public appreciation of the more remote implications of policy choices has increased, the need to deal explicitly with the broader social and political issues has been generally accepted by the modeling community. After years of rather fruitless debate, even the most technically minded analysts have been forced to recognize that technology and economics can play only a limited role in the ongoing energy controversy, and that energy policy is inherently as interdisciplinary field. "It involves economics, law, politics, engineering, resource geology, biomedical impacts, and environmental risk assessment—along with the methodologies that are already familiar to the operations researcher: optimization algorithms, simulations, decision analysis and econometric estimation" (Manne et al., 1979, p. 1).

The case of energy policy modeling raises another issue of the utmost importance today for all systems analysts: the role and effectiveness of formal analysis in the policy process. It takes us beyond the strictly disciplinary aspects of the evolution of systems analysis and into the professional and socio-institutional dimensions, to which we now turn.

2.5. The Social Side of Systems Analysis: Professional and Institutional Developments

The preceding sections have largely dealt with the internal history of systems analysis—the development of concepts, methods, and techniques in response to the changing nature of the objects of inquiry, and to intellectual challenges arising within the profession. This intellectual development must now be related to the larger social context in which analysts operate. The question to be investigated now is how the historical development of institutions and roles, publications and incentive systems both reflect and influence the intellectual concerns and aspirations of the systems analysis profession.

It has already been suggested that neither approach—internal, intellectual history on the one hand, external, social history, on the other—is by itself sufficient to give an adequate account of the entire development of the field. Social or institutional factors do not explain, for example, the cycles of expansion and depression experienced by certain areas of research and application, such as game theory. On the other hand, national differences in style and aims of systems analysis activity cannot be explained only, or even primarily, on intellectual grounds. Thus, the fact that industrial operations research in the United States adopted a systems approach quite early has been attributed to the high degree of specialization and professionalization of applied industrial research there. At the time the operations researchers arrived on the scene (the first public meeting between operations researchers

Section 2.5. The Social Side of Systems Analysis

and industrial managers took place in Cleveland only in 1951), industrial engineering, statistical quality control, systems engineering, marketing, and personnel and financial management were already recognized fields of professional specialization. Hence, according to this theory, in order to define a field of cognitive exclusiveness, American operations researchers had to focus on the interactions of specific industrial functions and the organization as a whole (Ackoff, 1957). One need not agree fully with the explanation to recognize that the factors involved are institutional rather than disciplinary. Similarly, the relatively late development of academic operations research in Europe, as well as the difficulty of establishing academic curricula in policy analysis, are largely due to institutional and sociological differences existing between European and American university systems.

At this point some chronology may be helpful. The first OR professional society was formed in the United Kingdom in 1948 as the Operational Research Society (initially, Operational Research Club). The Operations Research Society of America followed in 1952, with Philip M. Morse as its first president. The initial membership of both societies included many scientists who had taken part in the development of military OR during World War II. However, the focus of professional interest was rapidly shifting to industrial applications. One sign of this redirection of professional interests is the foundation in 1953 of The Institute of Management Sciences—an international society, but with most of its members in the United States. In 1957 the first International Conference on Operational Research was held at Oxford University. It was attended by 250 delegates from 21 countries. One important outcome of this conference was the International Federation of Operational Research Societies (IFORS), formally constituted on 1 January 1959, with three initial members: Operational Research Society, Operations Research Society of America, and Société Française de Recherche Opérationnelle (founded in 1956). Between 1959 and 1975, 24 additional national societies were founded in Western and Eastern Europe, Asia, Latin America, Australia, and South Africa, and soon joined IFORS.[12]

Operations research journals follow closely the developmental pattern of professional societies, starting with the *Operational Research Quarterly* (now the *Journal of the Operational Research Society*), founded in 1950 and published by the U.K. Operational Society, and *Operations Research* (1952), published by the Operations Research Society of America. In all fields of learning, scholarly periodicals are among the most powerful institutions of science, and systems analysis is no exception in this respect. In fact, if it is true that even in the older natural sciences "the very raison d'être of many scientific societies lies primarily in the journals they sponsor, only secondarily in their formal meetings" (Toulmin, 1972, p. 270), in the case of systems analysis professional journals sometimes take the place of professional soci-

---

[12] For additional information and bibliographical references, see Miser (1978).

eties. For instance, while no professional societies focusing on the field of policy analysis existed until 1980 policy analysts in government, universities, and research institutes tended to gravitate intellectually toward publications like *Policy Sciences*, founded in 1970, and *Policy Analysis*, founded in 1975. In these cases, the lack of a sponsoring professional organization was compensated, to a limited extent, by the presence of very large (by usual standards) editorial boards.

Communication between analysts and decisionmakers is one of the crucial practical problems of systems analysis. Since the increasing specialization of the field creates serious language barriers, publications have begun to appear whose primary goal is to encourage interaction between producers and consumers of analysis, as well as among the various divisions and professional groups within the systems analysis community. Perhaps the best known exemplar of this literature is *Interfaces*, published jointly since 1974 by The Institute of Management Sciences and the Operations Research Society of America (this journal originated in 1971 as *The Bulletin* of TIMS).

Having stressed the role played by journals in the disciplinary and professional development of systems analysis, we should also note some of their problems and limitations. The first problem, mentioned here only briefly, since it will be discussed in the next section, is that of the critical criteria used in the refereeing process. How to reconcile rigor with relevance is the crucial difficulty. The desire for rigor, especially in the highly specialized sense of formal or axiomatic rigor in which the term is often used, may (and often does) prevail over the requirements of relevance. In the trend toward greater formalization some critics see the possibility that systems analysis may lose its identity and be assimilated into other fields of inquiry.[13]

A second difficulty in assessing the state of systems analysis through professional publications is that journals and research reports tend to give a distorted picture of the field—a picture strongly biased in the direction of theoretical developments. For security, proprietary, or other reasons many actual applications are not published or appear in print with a delay of years. Thus, one of the most famous studies in military systems analysis, the Strategic Bases Study conducted by Albert Wohlstetter and other Rand analysts, was initiated in 1951, completed in 1954, declassified in 1962, and discussed in a professional journal only in 1964 (Smith, 1966, pp. 195–240). Even when actual case studies are reported, the necessity of concealing the identity of the sponsor and the true nature of the problem investigated often induces a stylized presentation in which many of the details that are so important for understanding the craft aspects of systems analysis are completely lost.

Next to journals, standard textbooks represent an important locus of scientific authority and are the main channel by which the intellectual advances of a discipline become the collective property of a profession.

---

[13] For a recent expression of this view, see Bonder (1979).

Section 2.5. The Social Side of Systems Analysis

> Whereas the "micro-evolution" of scientific ideas is manifested in the most up-to-date research discussions . . . its "macro-evolution" is embodied in the standard texts accepted as authoritative in each successive generation . . . These standard works define the successive bodies of doctrine that form the accepted starting-points for the next generation. By digesting the specialized literature of the preceding generation, indeed, these comprehensive expositions create a "conceptual platform" on which the next generation of budding scientists can stand firm, in defining and attacking their own disciplinary problems [Toulmin, 1972, pp. 277–278].

The successive stages of development of systems analysis are clearly marked by a series of distinguished texts, starting with *Methods of Operations Research* (Morse and Kimball, 1951), issued as a classified technical report in 1946 and published commercially five years later. A comparison of the table of contents of this text with that of the influential *Introduction to Operations Research* by Churchman, Ackoff, and Arnoff (1957) reveals graphically the shift of professional interests from military to industrial problems, as well as the emergence of new (or rediscovered) analytic methods like queuing and inventory theory, linear programming, and game theory.

This first textbook dealing with nonmilitary matters has been followed by scores of texts, treatises, and reference works now appearing with increasing frequency in all industrialized countries. The award in 1969 of the Lanchester Prize of the Operations Research Society of America to the first edition of Wagner's *Principles of Operations Research* is another indication of the professional significance of an outstanding didactic work. The sheer size of Wagner's book—almost 1100 pages—is evidence of the number of ideas and methods that were sufficiently well developed and tested by the end of the 1960s to be expounded in an introductory presentation of basic principles. Yet the differences from earlier works like the Churchman, Ackoff, and Arnoff *Introduction* are not merely quantitative. As an interesting example of the process of conceptual selection referred to previously, I may mention the fact that game theory, which received chapter-length treatment in the *Introduction*, is omitted in Wagner's *Principles*, except for the minimax theorem of two-person, zero-sum games—and it is relegated to an exercise in the chapter on duality.[14]

Again, whereas the earlier *Introduction* grew from lecture material prepared for short courses in operations research, Wagner's text reflects a stage of development in which undergraduate and graduate courses in operations research form a well-established component of academic curricula in business, economics, engineering, and public administration.

---

[14] This omission corresponds to the judgment often, if not so caustically, expressed in professional circles that "in practicing operations research, we have found that game theory does not contribute any *managerial insights* to real competitive and cooperative decisionmaking behavior that are not *already* familiar to church-going poker players who regularly read the *Wall Street Journal*" (Wagner 1975, p. xi). This should be compared with the opinion expressed some 20 years earlier by Churchman, Ackoff, and Arnoff (1957, p. 519) that game theory "started a new way of thinking about competitive decisions."

Although no comparable standard textbooks of systems analysis exist, a series of five volumes appearing over two decades did much to give the field a well-recognized structure. The first of these volumes, Hitch and McKean's *The Economics of Defense in the Nuclear Age*, published in 1960, represents a milestone in its evolution. While the title and many of the examples in the text refer to military applications, the underlying philosophy is completely general:

> In this book we will be concerned with economics in its most general sense. Economics is not exclusively concerned . . . with certain types of activities (industrial) rather than others (military), or with the traditional points of view of budgeteers and comptrollers. Being truly economical does not mean scrimping—reducing expenditures no matter how important the things to be bought. Nor does it mean implementing some stated doctrine regardless of cost. Rather economics is concerned with allocating resources—choosing doctrines and techniques—so as to get the most out of available resources [Hitch and McKean, 1960, pp. 1–2].

The ensuing four volumes had a widening influence as their contexts widened. *Analysis for Military Decisions*, a collection of essays edited by E. S. Quade, appeared in 1964; while it was an appreciation of systems analysis aimed principally at military users, it laid down valuable structural principles and concepts of wide relevance and value for analysts facing nonmilitary problems. *Systems Analysis and Policy Planning: Applications in Defense*, edited by Quade and W. I. Boucher, appeared in 1968; it extended the appreciation of the 1964 volume and brought it up to date. Quade's *Analysis for Public Decisions* (first edition 1975, second edition 1982) provides a broad overview with wide relevance for both users and producers of systems analysis.

The Economics of Defense and the Quade volumes are intellectual products of an institution, The Rand Corporation, whose name stands for one of the most influential "schools" of systems analysis; its organization and style of work have been imitated throughout the world. The history of the institution in its most creative period is well documented (Smith, 1966) and need not be retold here. However, the history of Rand raises an issue of organizational design for policy research institutes that is too central to our discussion to be ignored. Why was the nongovernmental nonprofit form of organization chosen for Rand and for other policy research institutes, including Resources for the Future, the Stanford Research Institute, The Brookings Institution, and, more recently, the International Institute for Applied Systems Analysis? Other institutional solutions were, after all, possible—as part of a government staff, or of a university, or as a (for-profit) consulting firm. But each of these alternatives presents serious disadvantages for the kind of work—medium- to long-range, multidisciplinary, independent, and objective—that a high-level policy research institute is supposed to do (cf. Gorham, 1975, and Smith, 1966, Ch. 2). Research carried out by government agencies tends to be narrow and short-run in nature because the problems immediately facing such agencies are typically narrow and short-run. Also, the incentive structure of large bureaucracies does not favor independent opinions and serious efforts at deep understanding. Blackett (1962, p. 175), it may be recalled, argued that the atmosphere required for an operations research group "is that of a first-class pure scientific research institution, and the caliber of the personnel should match this." This seems to suggest the university as a suitable environment for systems analysis activities. Unfortunately, universities are structured largely along disciplinary lines, and the cost of breaking down these lines in order to attack policy problems (which by their very nature cut across disciplinary boundaries) can be prohibitively high. Again, the incentive system of the university, with its emphasis on publication in specialized journals and on peer recognition, is not conducive to policy-relevant research. Finally, an organization operating for profit depends on the financial support of its clients and consequently tends to concentrate on short-run and limited problems, like in-house government policy research. Since a consulting firm must show "concrete results" to justify its fee, it will tend to look at the more easily quantifiable aspects of policy problems, where standard tools and techniques can be applied directly.

The nongovernmental, nonprofit form of organization has emerged as a response to the failure of other institutional arrangements to provide a congenial atmosphere for carrying out fundamental, independent, multidisciplinary policy research. This is not to say that the results have been uniformly good. In fact, nonprofit institutions present their own characteristic problems and dangers. To a large extent, these are related to the lack of generally accepted criteria for evaluating their performance, and to the ever-present possibility of conflict between professional excellence and practical effectiveness. These issues will be discussed in the next section.

2.6 The Evolution of Criteria of Quality and Effectiveness

The existence of suitable mechanisms of quality control is one of the distinguishing features of a well-established profession. Professional quality controls fulfill a double function: an internal one, to ensure adherence to group expectations about performance by members of the profession; and an external one, to ensure that the users of professional services can rely on their being of an acceptable quality. Ideally, the two functions, and the corresponding criteria, should integrate and support each other. In practice conflicts can and do arise, especially in the case of young professions like systems analysis, and then it is not clear which function should prevail. General prescriptions are useless, and only a detailed knowledge of the current stage and historical development of the profession can suggest sensible compromises.

Naturally, the importance of quality standards has been recognized since the beginning. Some of the citations given in previous sections from Blackett's early memoranda show this quite clearly; and the charter of the Operations

Research Society of America states as one of the purposes of the society "the establishment and maintenance of professional standards of competence for work known as operations research." But for many years the issue of quality standards remained dormant, only to explode in the early 1970s in a form for which the analytic profession was intellectually unprepared. Knowledge of these developments is helpful for understanding the nature and evolution of systems analysis as an intellectual craft.

The first practitioners of operations research had little doubt that what they were doing was scientific in character, despite the differences in the objects of inquiry—military operations or, more generally, man–machine systems—from those of traditional scientific research. The main goal of operations research was "to find a scientific explanation of the facts." For, as Waddington (1973, p. 26) explains, "only when this is done can the two main objects of operational research be attained. These are the prediction of the effects of new weapons and of new tactics." According to Blackett's crisp formulation (1962, p. 171) "operational staff provide the scientists with the operational outlook and data. The scientists apply scientific methods of analysis to these data, and are thus able to give useful advice."

Similarly, in the definition of OR adopted by the Operational Research Society of Britain, the word "science" or "scientific" occurs three times. Operations research is proclaimed to be the application of the methods of science to complex problems, a discipline whose distinctive approach is the development of a scientific model of the system being analyzed and whose purpose is to help management determine its policy and actions scientifically.

Given this paradigm, the relevant standards of quality are those of the natural sciences, as we saw in Section 2.2. The situations investigated by operations researchers during the Second World War and the early post-war period fit the paradigm quite well, and appeal explicitly to the same scientific criteria of evaluation and criticism.

Another important characteristic that early industrial OR shared with military OR was a reasonable clarity in the definition of the roles of analysts and decisionmakers. Whether the users of analysis were high-level officers or high-level managers, analysis was done primarily, and often (because of the requirements of military or industrial secrecy) exclusively, for them. The analyst did not have to address himself to an audience other than the decisionmaker or a small group of decisionmakers who had commissioned the study. Problems of implementation could be safely assumed to be the responsibility of a well-defined hierarchical authority, and the same authority could establish, if not standards of quality, at least criteria of effectiveness.

By the early 1950s all this was changing, at an increasingly rapid rate. Changes in personnel were accompanied by changes in the nature of the problems analysts were investigating, and in the institutional context in which analysis was done. We noted in Section 2.2 that, as natural scientists like Blackett, Waddington, and Morse were returning to their university departments and laboratories, the new generation of analysts entering the profession—mathematicians, logicians, statisticians, and control theorists—was more interested in the formal aspects of scientific research and often lacked the craft skills and the maturity of critical judgement of the old masters.[15] At the same time, the problems claiming analytic attention were becoming more abstract and complex. Strategic issues, whether in business or government, loomed increasingly important on the frontier of professional thinking and practice. Subjective uncertainty was seen to be much more crucial than statistical regularities or deterministic models. Moreover, the increasing role played by systems analysis in the public sector meant that analysts—no longer discreet advisors to the prince, but actors in a political process in which advocacy and persuasion could not be neatly separated from objective analysis—had to pay attention to questions of equity and institutional feasibility. The high uncertainty surrounding strategic problems and the long times needed to implement a proposed solution meant that direct empirical verification of analytic conclusions was often impossible. If in 1953 Kimball (1953) could still say of operations research that

> it is based on the conviction that the factors affecting . . . operations can be measured quantitatively and that there exist common laws obeyed by the basic variables. . . . the main problems concerning operations research today are the discovery of such laws and the development of techniques . . . for rapid, simple application . . . ,

his younger colleagues were increasingly skeptical about the possibility of discovering "laws of operations," and whether, indeed, the discovery of laws was a meaningful professional aim. At the time Kimball was writing, the move away from description (and generalization) to prescription as the hallmark of the systems analyst was already clearly discernible.

The implications of these developments for the search for professional standards of quality are quite far-reaching. If it is no longer possible to believe in the objective validity of the conclusions of an analytic study, and if even the criteria of success of the decision it supports are ambiguous, then evaluation by results becomes meaningless and must be replaced by such process-oriented criteria as internal consistency and professional (or even political) consensus.

The shift toward process-oriented evaluation is quite visible in the list of 13 criteria worked out by the Lanchester prize committee (1957) in order to supplement the broad, but not very operational, guidelines adopted by the preceding committees. However, the issue of professional standards came

---

[15] "By now a new generation of officers and analysts has come on the scene, many of whom have never had the sobering experience of seeing their optimistic predictions disproved by deaths on the battlefield. They too often are willing to take the assumptions given them by designers and by 'intelligence' as gospel truth, and to base their calculations on them without adding any correction factors for 'the fog of war' " (Morse 1972, p. 240).

truly alive only in 1971, with the publication of "Guidelines for the practice of operations research" prepared by an ad hoc committee of the Operations Research Society of America (ORSA Ad Hoc Committee on Professional Standards, 1971). The particular controversy that led to the formation of the ad hoc committee does not concern us here, except for the fact that in that controversy well-known analysts, applying standard technical tools to the same policy issues, had come to opposite conclusions and recommendations. The primary concern of the committee was, in the words of the president of the Society, "the professional conduct of the debate, the quality of the argumentation, the adherence to established study procedures in operations research and systems analysis" (loc. cit., p. 1123).

Unfortunately, most comments on the report of the ad hoc committee were directed at an appendix where the behavior of some of the participants in the substantive debate was severely castigated. With a few notable exceptions (Wagner, 1972; Mitroff, 1972), the Guidelines themselves received little attention, aside from some cursory remarks on their innocuous, if laudable, character. This is indeed a pity, for the profession could have greatly benefited from a critical examination of the specific standards proposed, and of the outdated philosophy of science on which they rested. The philosophy of the report gives great emphasis to two dichotomies: "pure" and "applied" science on the one hand, and "analysis" versus "advocacy" on the other. However, these distinctions are irrelevant, if not positively misleading, for evaluating the quality of professional practice.[16]

To begin with, the most significant similarities between science and systems analysis are to be found not in the *outcome* but in the *process* of research—more precisely, in the craft aspects common to all forms of disciplined intellectual inquiry. The actual work of the scientist requires knowledge that is acquired only through practice and precept and that therefore is not scientific in character. This craft knowledge is a repertoire of procedures and judgments that are partly personal, partly social. Thus, to decide whether data are of acceptable quality, scientists apply standards that derive not only from their own experience, but also reflect the professional norms of teachers and colleagues, as well as culturally determined criteria of adequacy. Personal and social judgments are also involved in data manipulation, in the choice of tools and models, in the selection of evidence, and in the construction of an argument.

The importance of craft knowledge and experience is even greater in systems analysis. Because the conclusions of a systems study cannot be proved in the sense in which a theorem is proved, or even in the manner in which propositions of natural science are established, they must satisfy generally accepted criteria of adequacy. Such criteria are derived not from abstract logical canons

---

[16] For more detailed arguments, see Majone (1980a; 1980b, pp. 151–162), as well as Wagner (1972) and Mitroff (1972).

Section 2.6. The Evolution of Criteria of Quality and Effectiveness

(the rules of a mythical standard scientific method) but from craft experience, depending as they do on the special features of the problem, on the quality of the data and limitations of the available tools, on the time constraints imposed on the analysts, and on the requirements of the sponsor and/or decisionmaker.

In short, craft knowledge—less explicit than formalized theoretical knowledge, but more objective than pure intuition—is essential for doing systems analysis as well as for evaluating it. Not artificial distinctions between pure and applied science, between analysis and advocacy, but close attention to the fine structure of the analyst's task is what is required for serious evaluation. This structure can be described in terms of categories like data, information, tools, evidence, and argument that are applicable to any type and style of analysis, retrospective as well as prospective, descriptive as well as prescriptive, argumentative as well as "scientific." Take, for example, the category *evidence*. Evidence is not synonymous with data or information; it is information selected from the available stock and introduced at a specific point in the argument in order to persuade a particular audience of the truth or falsity of a statement. Selecting inappropriate data or models, placing them at the wrong point in an argument, or choosing a style of presentation which is not appropriate for the intended audience can destroy the effectiveness of information used as evidence, regardless of its intrinsic cognitive value. Hence, criteria for assessing evidence must be different from those for assessing facts. Facts can be evaluated in terms of standard scientific criteria, but evidence must be evaluated in accordance with a number of factors peculiar to a given situation, such as the specific nature of the case, the type of audience, the prevailing rules of evidence (including, of course all relevant scientific rules), and even the persuasiveness of the analyst. Thus the assessment of the quality of the evidence presented in an analytic study is a microcosm of the complex social process of evaluation in which scientific and extrascientific, objective and advocacy elements are inextricably intertwined.

Analogous problems arise in evaluating the practical effectiveness of some studies. Unlike the analyses of military operations conducted in wartime, and some small-scale industrial applications, it is extremely difficult, as already mentioned, to evaluate the usefulness of large-scale policy studies in terms of actual results produced. This is due to a number of reasons. First, there is usually a long time lag between the adoption of a policy recommendation and its actual implementation. Second, it is difficult to sort out the effects of a particular decision from among a multitude of confounding factors. Third, and most important, the social and institutional context in which systems analysis is done has changed dramatically in the last two decades. In the early days the relationship between decisionmaker and advisor, between producer and user of analysis was much clearer than it is today. This is still reflected in the ORSA Guidelines, though the description given there of the client–analyst relationship was probably already outdated at the time the

Guidelines were published. Now it is quite common for policy research to be sponsored by one organization, carried out by another, used by a third organization, and perhaps evaluated by yet another agency (which, in turn, may commission the evaluation to an independent research group). Clearly, the sponsor's criteria of effectiveness are not the same as those of the user, or the controller. Thus the analyst must attempt to satisfy a number of different, sometimes conflicting, expectations. The best he can do is to achieve some acceptable level of adequacy in each direction: he must *satisfice* rather than maximize any one particular criterion. Actually, the situation is even more complex than this, for many policy studies in fields like energy, risk assessment, or education are "designed to influence congressional debates and to affect the climate of public opinion, not to guide decisions within individual corporations" (Manne, Richels, and Weyant, 1979, pp. 1–2). The effectiveness of such analyses can only be measured in terms of their impact on the ongoing policy debate: their success in clarifying issues, in introducing new concepts and viewpoints, even in modifying people's perceptions of the problem. Here analysis is no longer separable as a problem-solving device from social interaction but becomes an integral part of the process by which public issues are raised, debated, and resolved.[17] In fact, the historical development of systems analysis provides additional evidence for the truth of the statement that the "creation of a *thing*, and creation plus full understanding of a *correct idea* of the thing, are very often parts of one and the same indivisible process and cannot be separated without bringing the process to a stop" (Feyerabend, 1975, p. 26; emphasis in the original).

The concluding section of this chapter argues that the unavoidable complexity of the language of systems analysis reflects the fundamental difficulty of separating ideas from action.

2.7. Conclusion: The Language of Systems Analysis

As the preceding pages show, the question of how scientific systems analysis (or operations research or management science) is keeps recurring throughout the field's history. Traditional claims for its scientific status have always been faced by what appears to be an insoluble contradiction: If systems analysis is scientific, its task is not to prescribe or suggest a course of action, but to provide scientific explanations and predictions; if, on the other hand, it aspires to guide action it must be prescriptive and persuasive, and hence it cannot be scientific—not, at any rate, according to the received view of scientific method. Some writers have attempted to solve the dilemma by arguing that systems analysis offers "scientifically based" advice. This argument however,

---

[17] On social interaction as a mode of problem solving, see Lindblom (1977). Whereas Lindblom treats analysis and social interaction as alternative ways of solving social problems, I stress the difficulty of separating the two in practice.

Section 2.7. Conclusion: The Language of Systems Analysis

is basically unsound since, as Hume showed two centuries ago, there is no logical bridge between "ought" and "is."

Why do methodologically conscious systems analysts keep raising the question about the scientific status of their subject, despite repeated failures to answer it satisfactorily? The reason, I suggest, is that behind it loom two issues that analysts rightly feel to be of crucial importance for an understanding of what they are trying to do. First, what is the language of systems analysis? That is, what is the logical status of the different propositions analysts produce in the course of their work? Second, what standards of quality and rules of methodological criticism are applicable to the different kinds of propositions?

The historical evolution of the second issue has been outlined in the preceding section. In discussing the first issue, I make use of the concept of systems analysis as a craft. The systems analyst as craftsman is a producer of data, information, and arguments, but also a social change agent. Analysts must influence some people to accept their proposals and other people to carry them out; they are expected to take some responsibility for implementation. "Experienced practitioners realize that such implementation depends not only on factual analysis, but also on the client's organizational structure, the capabilities and biases of the client's personnel, and the client's management style" (Wagner, 1972, p. B-611). In particular, successful implementation depends on the ability to persuade people that a proposed course of action is not only good for the organization, but also compatible with the self-interest of its members. A well-designed incentive system is a very effective form of persuasive analysis.

Often the analyst must even persuade the decisionmaker. For example, one of the important functions of systematic analysis is to point out what cannot be done rather than what can; in other words, it is the duty of the analyst to make decisionmakers aware of constraints that they would rather ignore. But aside from straightforward physical and resource constraints, it is not usually possible to give a logically tight proof that a certain factor is an actual constraint rather than simply a "problem." Hence the decisionmaker must be persuaded to accept some limitations on his freedom of choice on the basis of something less than a full proof. [For a more detailed argument and some examples, see Majone, (1975a, pp. 49–69).]

Perhaps we can see now why the long-drawn-out debate over whether systems analysis is descriptive (like "pure science") or prescriptive (like technology) has been so fruitless. Systems analysis is concerned with theorizing, choosing, and acting. Hence, its character is threefold: descriptive (scientific), prescriptive (advisory), and persuasive (argumentative–interactive). In fact, if we look at the fine structure of analytic arguments we see a complex blend of factual statements, methodological choices, evaluations, recommendations, and persuasive definitions and communications. An even more complex structure emerges when we look at the interactions taking place between analysts and different audiences of sponsors, policy makers, evaluators, and interested publics. Moreover, descriptive propositions, prescriptions, and persuasion are intertwined in a way that rules out the possibility of applying a unique set of evaluative criteria, let alone proving or refuting an argument conclusively. The historical pattern of the development of systems analysis can be interpreted as the progressive realization of the complexity of the language of policy advice and the slow evolution of appropriate forms of criticism.

References

Ackoff, Russell L. (1957). A comparison of operational research in the U.S.A. and Great Britain. *Operational Research Quarterly* 8, 88–100.

Arrow, Kenneth J. (1957). Decision theory and operations research. *Operations Research* 5, 765–774.

Blackett, P. M. S., (1950). Operational research. *Operational Research Quarterly* 1, 3–6; also in Blackett (1962, pp. 199–204).

_____(1962). *Studies of War*. New York: Hill and Wang.

Bonder, Seth (1979). Changing the future of operations research. *Operations Research* 27, 209–224.

Boothroyd, Hylton (1978). *Articulate Intervention*. London: Taylor and Francis.

Braybrooke, D., and C.E. Lindblom (1963). *A Strategy of Decision*. New York: Free Press.

Brooks, Harvey (1976). Environmental decision making: Analysis and values. In *When Values Conflict* (L. H. Tribe, C. S. Schelling and John Voss, eds.). Cambridge, Massachusetts: Ballinger, pp. 115–136.

Churchman, C. West, Russell L. Ackoff, and E. Leonard Arnoff (1957). *Introduction to Operations Research*. New York: Wiley.

Dorfman, Robert, Paul A. Samuelson, and Robert Solow (1958). *Linear Programming and Economic Analysis*. New York: McGraw-Hill.

Dror, Yehezkel (1967). Policy analysts: A new professional role in government service. *Public Administration Review* 27, 200–201.

Edie, Leslie C. (1954). Traffic delays at toll booths. *Operations Research* 2, 107–138.

Fairley, W. B., and Frederick Mosteller, eds. (1977). *Statistics and Public Policy*. Reading, Massachusetts: Addison-Wesley.

Feldstein, Martin S. (1963). Economic analysis, operational research, and the National Health Service. *Oxford Economic Papers,* March 1963, 19–31.

Feyerabend, Paul (1975). *Against Method*. London: NLB.

Gorham, William (1975). *Why Policy Research Institutes?* RM 75-56. Laxenberg, Austria: International Institute for Applied Systems Analysis.

Hitch, Charles J. (1953). Sub-optimization in operations problems. *Operations Research* 1, 87–99.

_____and Roland N. McKean (1960). *The Economics of Defense in the Nuclear Age*. Cambridge, Massachusetts: Harvard University Press.

Hoag, Malcolm W. (1957). What is a system? *Operations Research* 5, 445–447.

References

Kahn, Herman, and Irwin Mann (1956). Techniques of systems analysis, RM-1829. Santa Monica, California: The Rand Corporation.

Kimball, George E. (1953). A philosophy of operations research (abstract). *Operations Research* 1, 145.

Koopman, B. O. (1980). *Search and Screening: General Principles with Historical Applications.* New York: Pergamon Press.

Koopmans, Tjalling C. (1951). *Activity Analysis of Production and Allocation.* New York: Wiley.

Lanchester Prize Committee (1957). Report. *Operations Research* 5, 575–578.

Larson, Magali Sarfatti (1977). *The Rise of Professionalism.* Berkeley and Los Angeles: University of California Press.

Levien, Roger E. (1980). Outcome measurement: A US viewpoint. Unpublished manuscript. Laxenburg, Austria: International Institute for Applied Systems Analysis.

Lindblom, Charles E. (1977). *Politics and Markets.* New York: Basic Books.

Majone, Giandomenico (1975a). The feasibility of social policies. *Policy Sciences* 6, 49–69.

_____(1975b). On the notion of political feasibility. *European Journal of Political Research* 3, 259–274; also in Nagel (1977).

_____(1980a). *The Craft of Applied Systems Analysis,* WP-80-73. Laxenburg, Austria: International Institute for Applied Systems Analysis.

_____(1980b). Policies as theories. *Omega* 8, 151–162.

Manne, Alan S., Richard G. Richels, and John P. Weyant (1979). Energy policy modeling: A survey. *Operations Research* 27, 1–36.

McCloskey, Joseph F., and Florence N. Trefethen, eds. (1954). *Operations Research for Management.* Baltimore, Maryland: The Johns Hopkins Press.

McKean, Roland N. (1958). *Efficiency in Government Through Systems Analysis.* New York: Wiley.

Miser, Hugh J. (1978). The history, nature, and use of operations research. In Moder and Elmaghraby (1978), 3–24.

Mitroff, Ian I. (1972). The myth of objectivity, or why science needs a new psychology of science. *Management Science* 18, B-613–B-618.

Moder, Joseph J., and Salah E. Elmaghraby, eds. (1978). *Handbook of Operations Research,* Vol. 1. New York: Van Nostrand Reinhold.

Mood, A. M. (1953). Review of Morse and Kimball's *Methods of Operations Research. Operations Research* 1, 306–308.

Morse, Philip M. (1956). Statistics and operations research. *Operations Research* 4, 2–19.

_____(1972). Letter to the editor. *Operations Research* 20, 239–242.

_____and George E. Kimball (1951). *Methods of Operations Research.* New York: Wiley.

Mosteller, Frederick (1977). Assessing unknown numbers: Order of magnitude estimation. In *Statistics and Public Policy* (W. B. Fairley and F. Mosteller, eds.). Reading, Massachusetts: Addison-Wesley, pp. 163–184.

Nagel, Stuart S., ed. (1977). *Policy Studies Review Annual,* Vol. 1. Beverly Hills and London: Sage.

ORSA Ad Hoc Committee on Professional Standards (1971). Guidelines for the practice of operations research. *Operations Research* 19, 1123–1148.

Prest, A. R., and R. Turvey (1965). Cost–benefit analysis: A survey. *Economic Journal* 75, 683–735.

Quade, E. S., ed. (1964). *Analysis for Military Decisions.* Chicago: Rand McNally.

_____(1982). *Analysis for Public Decisions,* 2nd ed. (1st ed.: 1975) New York: North-Holland.

_____and W. I. Boucher, eds. (1968). *Systems Analysis and Policy Planning: Applications in Defense.* New York: Elsevier.

Ravetz, J. R. (1973). *Scientific Knowledge and its Social Problems.* Harmondsworth, England: Penguin.

Smith, Bruce L. R. (1966). *The Rand Corporation.* Cambridge, Massachusetts: Harvard University Press.

Stone, Lawrence D. (1982). Review of Koopman's *Search and Screening. SIAM Review* 23, 533–539.

Sugden, Robert, and Alan Williams (1978). *The Principles of Practical Cost–Benefit Analysis.* Oxford, England: Oxford University Press.

Thornwaite, C. W. (1953). Operations research in agriculture. *Operations Research* 1, 1, 33–38.

_____(1954). Operations research in agriculture. In *Operations Research for Management* (J. F. McCloskey and F. N. Trefethen eds.). Baltimore Maryland: The Johns Hopkins Press, pp. 368–380.

Toulmin, Stephen (1972). *Human Understanding,* Vol. 1. Princeton, New Jersey: Princeton University Press.

Tribe, L. H., C. S. Schelling, and J. Voss, eds. (1976). *When Values Conflict.* Cambridge, Massachusetts: Ballinger.

Tukey, John W. (1979). Methodology and the statistician's responsibility for BOTH accuracy AND relevance. *Journal of the American Statistical Association* 74, 786–793.

Waddington, C. H. (1973). *OR in World War 2: Operational Research against the U-boat.* London: Elek Science.

Wagner, Harvey M. (1971). The ABCs of OR. *Operations Research* 19, 1259–1281.

_____(1972) Commentary on ORSA guidelines. *Management Science* 18, B-609-B-613.

_____(1975). *Principles of Operations Research,* 2nd ed. Englewood Cliffs, New Jersey: Prentice-Hall. (1st ed.: 1969.)

Wildavsky, Aaron (1966). The political economy of efficiency: Cost–benefit analysis, systems analysis, and program budgeting. *Public Administration Review* 26, 292–310.

_____(1969). Rescuing policy analysis from PPBS. *Public Administration Review* 29, 189–202.

Williams, Alan (1972). Cost–benefit analysis: Bastard science? And/or insidious poison in the body politick? *Journal of Public Economics* 1, 199–226.

Chapter 3
Examples of Systems Analysis

Edward S. Quade

3.1. Introduction

Systems analysis, while not a completely new idea, has been practiced for a relatively short time. Many people are not aware of the kinds of issues to which it might be applied, the results that can be expected, or the resistance its most logical results can meet. Examples and case histories can clarify the advantages and drawbacks of a systems approach to decisionmaking, particularly in applications to public decisions outside a military or industrial context.

Analysts as well as lay readers may also profit from reviewing examples. The craft of systems analysis is not easy to master. Often analysts must take actions important to the success of their study that do not appear to be a step in any systematic way of describing the process of carrying out such a study—the sort of thing that comes from practical experience. The review of examples and case studies is to a limited extent a substitute for practice, although not an adequate one. Examining cases can also help to make clear some of the compromises with mathematical and scientific exactitude that are often needed to make progress—compromises forced not only by the pressure of time or the need to win acceptance for the work, but also because without them the mathematics might be beyond our capabilities.

Each of the examples presented in this chapter emphasizes different aspects of the analytic process. The arrangement is roughly in the order of increasing difficulty.

In the first case—improving blood availability and utilization—the problem was narrow and clearly defined, and an adequate measure of effectiveness was available, one that the decisionmakers, a small group of professionals, relatively free from political influence and sympathetic to the use of analysis, did not question. The approach, although it required imagination to design, made use of well-established mathematical models. Our attention here is on the means to obtain a demonstrably superior solution and its smooth implementation.

The second case—improving fire protection—deals with a situation in which the process of converting the results of analysis into changes in operations was more difficult and time consuming than the process of performing the analysis. Here the decision as to what action to take had to be made on the basis of a proxy or surrogate measure of effectiveness, using crude models of recent design, thus leaving room for debate and disagreement by those whose special interests were threatened.

The third case—protecting an estuary from flooding—involves a major decision, affecting an entire country, in which a choice had to be made among strategies, no one of which was clearly superior to any of the others in all respects. Here the major attention is to the method by which the results were presented to the decisionmakers, Cabinet officials and legislators—most without analytic training, representing constituencies with widely varied interests—who had to choose and act in an intensely political situation. This case typifies problems in which there can be no direct empirical verification that the choices made are best, or even adequate.

The fourth case—providing energy for the future—concerns a critical global problem, i.e., one whose issues cut across national boundaries and for which no solution can be successfully implemented without cooperative joint action. In contrast to the previous cases, while the analysis demonstrated that solutions exist, owing to the nature of the decisonmaking situation it was unable to provide more than general guidelines for obtaining good decisions. The study findings offer a body of information that can inform the hundreds of decisions, possibly otherwise uncoordinated, that will be required during the next few years to work toward the goal of achieving a globally sustainable solution.

In preparing the descriptions of the case studies that follow we have made no effort to distinguish between material written by the analysts and that inserted or modified by the author of this chapter. Most of the material is, in fact, taken almost verbatim from the original reports and other publications.

3.2. Improving Blood Availability and Utilization

Background

Blood is a living tissue of unique medical value. It is the vehicle that carries oxygen, nutrients, and chemicals to all parts of the body and carries away waste products. It appears in eight major blood types in the human population, and it has several components (red cells, white cells, platelets, and plasma), all of which can be extracted from whole blood. Each component serves a separate function in the human organism and has a different use in medical

Section 3.2. Improving Blood Availability and Utilization

treatment. All of the components are perishable, with periods of usefulness (at the time of this study) varying from 24 hours (for platelets) to 21 days (for red cells). Whole blood and red cells, both of which then had a usefulness of 21 days, together account for more than 95 percent of the transfusions that take place in the United States today. When the work to be discussed was done, blood's legally defined lifetime in the United States was 21 days, after which it had to be discarded; its lifetime has since been extended to 35 days.

Blood is collected in units of one pint per donor at collection sites such as regional blood centers (RBCs), hospital blood banks (HBBs), or mobile units. After collection it undergoes a series of typing and screening tests and, once processed (i.e., frozen or separated into components), it is shipped, as needed, to hospital blood banks, where it is stored and then made available to patients for transfusions.

A hospital blood bank operates as a storage and issuing agency. During the course of a day the blood bank receives a random number of transfusion requests for each blood type, each request for a random number of units. Once a request—always for a specific patient—is received, the requested number of units of the appropriate type are removed from free inventory and, after a successful crossmatch, they are placed on reserve for the patient. Units that are not transfused are returned to the free inventory. Units that are not used within their legal lifetimes are considered *outdated* and are discarded from inventory.

Historically, HBBs have generally maintained high inventories of most of the eight different types of each blood product in order to make sure of satisfying patient needs, and have accepted the low utilization resulting from spoilage. In 1974 the national utilization rate of whole blood and red blood cells prior to expiration was estimated to be only 80 percent. At that time, the U.S. Federal government adopted a national blood policy calling for an all-volunteer blood supply to be accessible to all segments of the public. The blood supply was to be efficiently administered through forming regional associations of blood service units in each of which an RBC and the HBBs that it serves would collaborate.

Each year over two million hospitalized Americans depend on the timely availability of the right type of blood products at 6000 HBBs. If the right blood products are not available at the HBB when required, medical complications or postponements of elective surgery can result, which translate into extra days of hospitalization and expenses or to potentially serious medical consequences. On the other hand, since most blood products may only be administered to a patient of the same blood type within 21 days of collection, overstocking leads to low utilization, which increases costs and is wasteful of the scarce blood resource. Or, as Johanna Pindyck, Director of the Greater New York Blood Program (GNYBP), the largest in the world, puts it, "We face the major problem of how to maximize the availability of blood to each of . . . 262 hospitals . . . while effectively discharging our implicit covenant to our donors to see that their gift is efficiently utilized" (Brodheim and Prastacos, 1979).

In 1979, Eric Brodheim of the New York Blood Center and Gregory P. Prastacos of the University of Pennsylvania reported a study that goes a long way toward providing a solution to many problems of blood distribution and utilization. (The existing blood transfusion practices were taken as given, and thus were not studied as part of the work.) The description of their study that follows, together with the background above, is taken almost verbatim from their reports (Brodheim and Prastacos, 1979; Prastacos, 1984). Management science and operations research techniques had previously been the basis of much work on blood management: Prastacos (1984) cites 99 references.

Approach

The complexity of the blood distribution problem is primarily due to blood's perishability, the uncertainties involved in its availability to the RBC, and the variabilities in demand and usage at each of the HBBs. Superimposed on these complications are the large variations in the sizes of the HBBs to be supplied, in the relative occurrences of the different blood groups, and in the mix of whole blood and red blood cells.

Since blood, by U.S. national policy, is derived from volunteer donors, its availability is uncertain and is a function of factors that cannot be controlled by the RBC. The demand and usage of blood at HBBs are also uncertain and vary from day to day among hospital facilities. The HBBs within a region may range from those transfusing a few hundred units to those transfusing tens of thousands of units per year. The most frequently occurring blood type (O positive) occurs in approximately 39 percent of the population, while the least frequently occurring blood type (AB negative) occurs in only about 0.5 percent of the population. Although most medical authorities agree that at least 90 percent of all blood transfusions could be in the form of red blood cells, some hospitals continue to transfuse whole blood almost exclusively; however, the number transfusing red blood cells is changing as transfusion practices change.

The national blood transfusion service is characterized by diversity. Each RBC has independently evolved its own philosophy and techniques for blood distribution. Each region strives for self-sufficiency in supplying the blood needs of the hospitals in its region from donors who also reside in approximately the same area. Because of these factors, it is essential that any strategy devised be defensible from the point of view of both the RBC and each of the wide range of HBBs that it serves. Furthermore, any strategy that involves interactions among RBCs must provide clearly defined benefits for all participants. Some objectives conflict (e.g., availability versus utilization of blood

Section 3.2. Improving Blood Availability and Utilization

at an HBB), and the costs involved are difficult to estimate (e.g., the cost of unavailability).

As a result of this complexity, regional blood management systems have historically been decentralized and reactive in nature, characterized by HBBs that place daily orders to bring their inventories to what each considers a safe value and an RBC that tries to fill these orders as they come, while keeping a necessary buffer in the stock. This has created a feeling of uncertainty, resulting in low utilization and much spoilage.

After becoming thoroughly familiar with the practical operations of the Long Island blood distribution system, which was to be the test bed for their analysis, Brodheim and Prastacos reasoned that three important management concepts should be introduced. First, instead of individual ordering from the RBC by every HBB, a regional management system should be developed to allocate most of the available regional resources among the HBBs so that they are utilized efficiently. This calls for some form of centralized decisionmaking at the RBC, which is to operate under objectives of overall regional efficiency, as opposed to the existing mode of decentralized decisionmaking with the objective of local (i.e., HBB) efficiency.

Second, any regional strategy that allocates blood products that are to be retained until transfused or outdated will result in low utilization, especially by small-usage HBBs, which, in aggregate, account for the largest part of overall blood usage. Consequently, some form of blood rotation is required whereby freshly processed blood is sent to an HBB from which it may be returned, some time later, for distribution according to the regional strategy.

Third, it is desirable that a significant portion of the periodic deliveries to the HBBs be prescheduled. The uncertainty of supply faced by the HBB can thus be reduced, with a resulting improvement in planning operations and utilizing resources.

Analysis

The blood needs of an HBB can be expressed in terms of the *demand* for blood (i.e., the number of units required to be on hand for possible transfusion) and the *usage* of blood (i.e., the number of units transfused). A model is required that translates demand and usage to availability and utilization as functions of the RBC blood distribution policy and the HBBs' blood stocking policy. Such a model was established by a combination of statistical analysis and Markov chain modeling; it was then used to derive regional allocation strategies with desirable properties regarding availability and utilization.

The availability rate (i.e., the fraction of days when the inventory of a given blood type is sufficient to meet the demand) at an HBB depends only on the statistical pattern of demand and the total inventory level. To establish this relation, data were collected on the daily demands for each blood type at a number of HBBs. These data, together with comparable information published by other researchers, provided a total of 49 data sets, each set containing the daily demands for one blood type at one HBB over a period of at least six months.

Statistical analysis established a smoothed "universal" relation between inventory level and mean daily demand, with availability rate as a parameter, shown in Figure 3.1. Additional tests showed that this model could predict the availability rate to within approximately 10 percent of actual experience for availability rates in the range of 80–99 percent.

The acceptable range of availability rates for HBBs was then established by requesting a number of HBBs to provide concurrent estimates of their mean daily demand and the inventory levels in each of the eight blood types that they considered adequate. In almost all cases the levels that the HBBs considered adequate turned out to correspond to availability rates between 90 and 95 percent.

Analysis also established that the daily usage could be modeled as a mixture of a Poisson and a triangular-type distribution whose parameter is related to the mean daily usage. This analysis showed that the parameters for the models of demand and usage could be readily estimated from records maintained by HBBs and that the availability rate could be estimated reliably by the model.

The utilization rate (i.e., the fraction of the supply that is transfused)

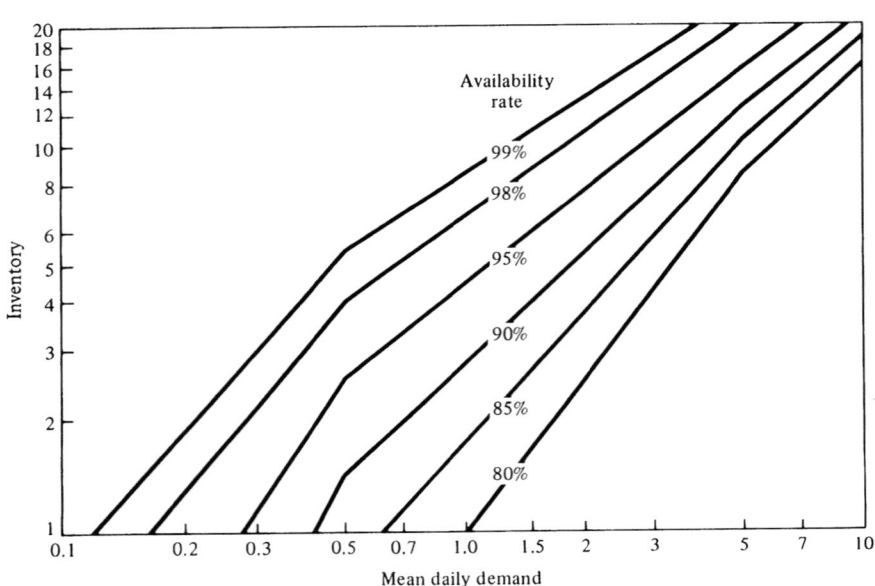

Figure 3.1. Inventories and mean daily demands for blood units for given availability rates at hospital blood banks. (*From Brodheim and Prastacos, 1979.*)

Section 3.2. Improving Blood Availability and Utilization

depends on the distribution strategy (size, age mix, and frequency) of the blood supply in an HBB, as well as on the demand. After consultations with the HBBs, and in agreement with the management concepts outlined here, the following class of policies was chosen for analysis. Each HBB receives periodic shipments at intervals between one and four days long (to be determined from the analysis, depending on the size of the HBB and other considerations). Each periodic shipment to the HBB includes a number of fresh (or, long-dated: from one to two days old) rotation units and a number of older (or, stock-dated: from six to seven days old) retention units. The latter are retained until transfused or discarded, but the rotation units that are in excess of a fixed desired inventory level at the end of the period are returned to the RBC for redistribution. Modeling this situation called for a finite-state Markov chain analysis.

The utilization rate model is illustrated for a fixed utilization rate of 98 percent by the family of broken lines in Figure 3.2, where the scheduling factor ρ is the fraction of mean daily usage that is replaced by retention shipments. As an example, if an HBB's mean daily usage for a given blood

Figure 3.2. For various mean daily usages U, the combinations of inventory level I and scheduling factor ρ (the fraction of mean daily usage that is replaced by retention shipments) that will achieve a utilization rate of 98%. (Heavy curve: trend; light solid lines: calculated optimal solutions; dashed curves: feasible solutions.) (*From Brodheim and Prastacos, 1979.*)

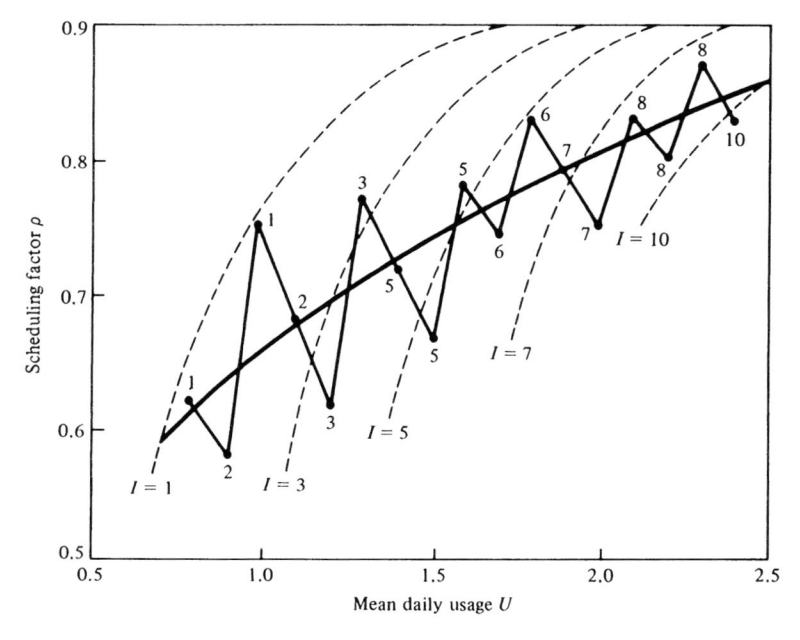

product is 1.5, then the HBB can achieve a utilization rate of 98 percent by any of the following combinations: desired inventory $I = 1$ and $\rho = 0.89$, or $I = 3$ and $\rho = 0.82$, or $I = 5$ and $\rho = 0.70$.

It was shown that this stocking procedure maintains the mean inventory close to this desired inventory level most of the time. It was also shown that adding additional stages of returns and redistribution would make only slight improvements in the availability and utilization rates achieved. Since multiple redistributions introduce severe logistical problems and significant transportation costs, distribution strategies involving more than two stages of distribution were not investigated.

Having derived these models to predict the HBB availability and utilization rates for any policy implemented by the RBC, the analysts examined the regional allocation problem, assuming that there were fixed penalty costs associated with nonavailable and nonutilized units. They found that the policy minimizing the total expected one-period cost was

1. first to allocate all available retention units so as to equalize the utilization rates at all HBBs, and
2. then to allocate all available rotation units (which are not subject to spoilage while at the HBB) so as to equalize the availability rates at all HBBs.

It was also shown that this policy is independent of unit penalty costs, and that it maximizes both the availability and utilization of blood in the region simultaneously. That is, any deviation from the policy that would reduce utilization would also result in reduced availability for the next period, and vice versa.

In addition, the analysts found that this short-term policy had the same structural characteristics as the policy that was optimal over the long run, and even that the utilization and availability rates calculated for the short term corresponded very closely to the optimal values for the long run. Thus the analysts could return to the result showing that the foregoing distribution policy for the one-period case was optimal and establish the following principle:

> A distribution policy should seek to equalize utilization rates and availability rates among the HBBs in the region. This is also a policy that has the essential elements of "fairness" in spreading equally the nonavailability and nonutilization risks among hospitals regardless of their relative size; consequently, it is a highly defensible policy

Finally, it was shown that the highest possible regional availability and utilization rates are achieved when the desired inventory level for each blood type in each HBB is at the value that minimizes the total number of rotational units required to achieve these availability and utilization rates.

It is a straightforward effort by computer to calculate the combination of

Section 3.2. Improving Blood Availability and Utilization

inventory level and scheduling factor that requires the minimum number of rotational units. The minimum numbers of rotational units required to achieve a fixed utilization rate of 98 percent and an availability rate of 95 percent are indicated by the points connected by the straight-line segments in Figure 3.2. This solution appears irregular because inventory levels must be integer values and rounding occurs at very small values. As an example, the minimum rotational shipments required to an HBB with a mean usage of 1.5 units daily to obtain the target goals above occur when the desired inventory is 5 units, and the scheduling factor is set to 0.67. The trend line, the heavy line in Figure 3.2, indicates simultaneously the optimal values in inventory level and scheduling factor for given values of mean usage.

Next, various operational considerations were taken into account. One of these was the need to equalize the mix of fresh to older bloods among HBBs. Another was to standardize the delivery interval. It was determined that, for blood types where mean daily usage is small, the mean required number of units on rotation is independent of whether the delivery interval is one, two, or four delivery days. For higher values of mean daily usage, the difference between one- and two-day delivery intervals remains slight, but increasing the delivery interval to four days causes significant increases in the mean number of rotational units required to achieve the policy objectives.

As a result of these observations, HBBs that transfuse less than approximately 1500 units per year receive deliveries every four delivery days. Since analysis showed little distinction in the number of rotational units required between one-day and two-day intervals between deliveries, all larger HBBs were encouraged to adopt two-day intervals between shipments.

The final model was then formulated as a mathematical program. The decision variables determined by the program are the distribution parameters: the size of rotation and retention shipments, frequency of deliveries, and desired inventory levels for each HBB.

The objective of the program is to achieve the set target values for availability and utilization rates while conforming to the operational constraints, with the minimum possible amount of total fresh rotational blood needed in the region. Even though the model is highly nonlinear, its structure is decomposable, and the optimal solution is readily obtained by parametric enumeration.

Implementation

The analysts then turned to the task of implementation in their test region, the Long Island Blood Services (LIBS) distribution system. LIBS is approximately the median size of existing regional associations and processes approximately 100,000 units of blood per year. It serves a diverse area ranging from rural Suffolk County to parts of New York City, with 34 hospitals and a combined population of two million persons. LIBS is one of four divisions of the GNYBP, which serves approximately 18 million people in the greater New York area. The separation into divisions facilitates interaction among them for such purposes as smoothing out local short-term shortages and surpluses.

The implementation of the program was carried out in a series of planned stages. At first only four hospitals were invited to join the program. They were provided support to correct rapidly the start-up problems that occurred. Once the HBBs were working to the satisfaction of their supervisors, they described the system to supervisors of other HBBs at seminars where the operations research staff, wherever possible, played the passive role of providing information when requested to do so. Responding to this approach, all but four very small HBBs in Long Island voluntarily joined the program over a two-year period, and none have dropped out.

A major advantage of the programmed blood distribution system (PBDS), both to the RBC and to the HBBs, is the ability to preschedule most deliveries. Prior to PBDS being implemented, a number of delivery vehicles were dispatched as orders came in. For urgent orders, vehicles were dispatched immediately, while for more routine orders an attempt was made to hold vehicles back until several deliveries in the same geographical area could be combined. This procedure was expensive and, perhaps more importantly, resulted in situations where even urgent orders were delayed, since delivery vehicles were not always available during peak delivery hours.

With the PBDS most deliveries are prescheduled and take advantage of known traffic patterns in order to minimize delivery time. An interactive, computer-aided procedure was devised that assigns HBBs to delivery routes so as to meet their time and frequency-of-delivery requirements. The 12-delivery-day planning cycle is split into three groups of four delivery days, after which the delivery cycle repeats. In each four-delivery-day cycle each HBB receives either one, two, or four deliveries. The procedure tries to satisfy the delivery requirements without leaving gaps in consecutive time slots, since an empty time slot indicates idle time.

An opportunity to test the flexibility of this delivery scheme occurred when the LIBS blood center was moved from one location to another several miles away. It was found that the delivery routes could be adjusted rapidly, and the required reassignment of the HBBs was determined conveniently.

The resulting regional blood flow is illustrated in Figure 3.3 The aging of the RBC inventory is shown down the center with the scheduled movement of blood to HBBs to the left and the nonscheduled movement to the right. The long-dated, stock-dated, and short-dated RBC inventories refer to blood units that are suitable, respectively, for rotation shipments, for retention shipments, and solely for supplemental shipments, which are filled by the oldest available units. The arrows indicate a blood flow that is normalized to 1000 units collected.

On the basis of this anticipated regional blood flow, the RBC's inventory

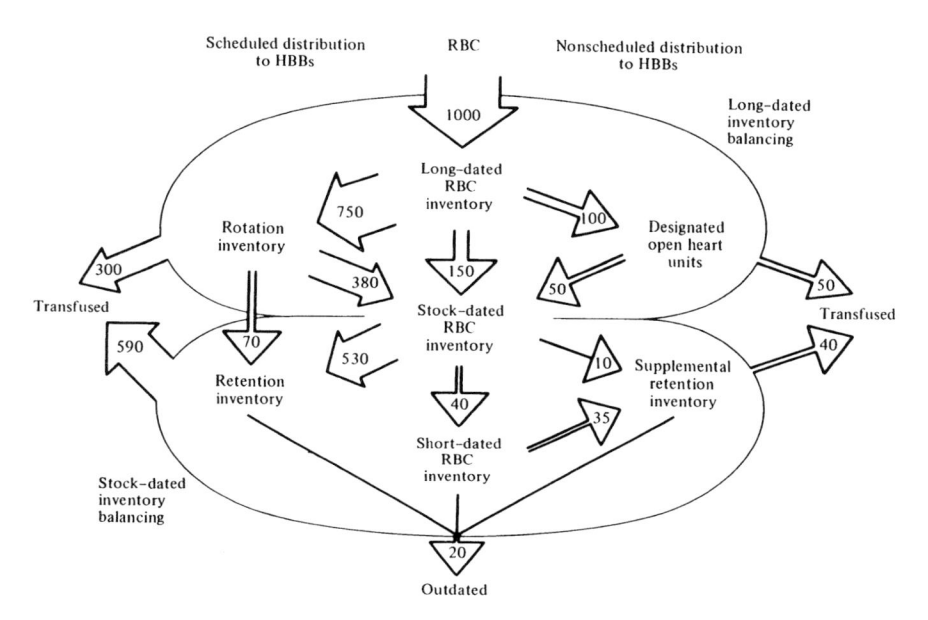

Section 3.2. Improving Blood Availability and Utilization

Figure 3.3. An illustration of a planned regional blood flow based on the presumption that 1000 units are collected and distributed. (*From Brodheim and Prastacos, 1979.*)

is evaluated and adjusted daily. Stock-dated inventory balancing is performed late each afternoon after all rotational returns have been received. It involves the part of the flow circled toward the bottom of Figure 3.3. The available stock-dated inventory is compared to the scheduled retention shipments and to the anticipated supplemental shipments, plus a small reserve for unusual circumstances (shown as becoming short-dated inventory). When the inventory for any product exceeds these requirements, the excess units are designated as surplus and transshipped to the New York Blood Services (NYBS) division of GNYBP. When stock-dated inventory is below requirements, then either surplus long-dated units (if available) are retained or, if possible, the shortage is made up from the other divisions of GNYBP.

Long-dated inventory balancing is performed each morning after the bulk of the blood collected the previous day has been typed. It involves the part of the flow circled at the top of Figure 3.3. The long-dated regional inventory that is expected to become available during the day is compared to the commitment of units for scheduled rotation shipments plus units required to meet open heart surgery needs (a specialized procedure where only fresh blood units are suitable). Any units in excess of these requirements are either retained to make up for shortages in stock-dated inventory, as has been discussed, or are made available for transshipment to other divisions of GNYBP. Since LIBS collects in excess of its needs, there is usually a surplus of rotation units, especially of the more common blood types.

Computer Modules

To improve its effectiveness and transportability, PBDS has been computer-coded in three basic modules, which together constitute a decision support system for managing blood in a region: policy selection, distribution schedule, and control procedure. Each of these modules has a special purpose in the implementation and operation of PBDS in a region, and each can be addressed interactively by the user (RBC director or distribution manager) in order to determine or evaluate strategic or tactical decisions in blood management.

The policy-selection module is run first. It uses the region's data on the demand and usage patterns of the HBBs, together with the models outlined earlier, to produce a policy-selection table. This table presents the decision-maker with alternative targets (shortage rate, outdate rate, scheduling factor) that can be obtained for different levels of blood supply in the region.

Once targets are selected, they are put into the second model, which handles distribution scheduling. The output of this module is a detailed schedule of the shipments of rotation and retention blood for each blood type that each HBB will receive on each delivery day. These schedules are communicated to the HBBs for comment and feedback. Once this phase is completed, the PBDS operation can begin.

Finally, in order to detect possible changes in the needs of the HBBs, a series of hypotheses tests are run every two weeks as a control procedure. If a change is detected, new estimates are made and new distribution schedules are computed. In this way the RBC keeps its data and operations an up-to-date reflection of the changing patterns of blood needs and usages in its region.

Impact

The impact of PBDS can be most directly measured in terms of improvement in blood utilization. Prior to the implementation of PBDS, the utilization rate in the LIBS region was 80 percent, which was also then the national average. Since the implementation of PBDS, the utilization rate for LIBS has improved to 96 percent, while the national average has improved little if at all. The improvement in utilization at LIBS translates to an 80 percent reduction in wastage, and therefore to an annual saving of $500,000 per year.

Of lesser economic impact is the reduction in the number of deliveries. Before PBDS was implemented, an average of 7.8 weekly deliveries were made to each hospital, all of which were unscheduled; after PBDS was implemented, the number of deliveries dropped to 4.2, but only 1.4 were unscheduled. By associating a cost of $10 to an unscheduled delivery to an HBB and a $5 cost to a scheduled delivery (which is part of a route), PBDS has achieved a 64 percent reduction in delivery costs. This translates to an annual cost saving of $100,000. Additional important, though less tangible, cost savings are achieved by implementing sounder blood banking practices to reduce discrepancies between actual and achievable performance for individual HBBs.

Probably the most important benefit from PBDS comes from improved blood availability to patients. Since deliveries to the hospitals are mostly prescheduled, elective surgeries can also be prescheduled so as to minimize the number of surgeries postponed for lack of the right blood products. However, the savings from this improved availability are extremely difficult to estimate and quantify.

3.3 Improving Fire Protection

Background

How many fire companies to support, where to locate them, and how to dispatch them are important questions for U.S. cities as fire incidence increases (Figure 3.4) and inflation shrinks their budgets. Between 1969 and 1975 many

Figure 3.4. The total number of fire alarms, Wilmington, Delaware, 1965–1974. (*From Walker, Singleton, and Smith, 1975.*)

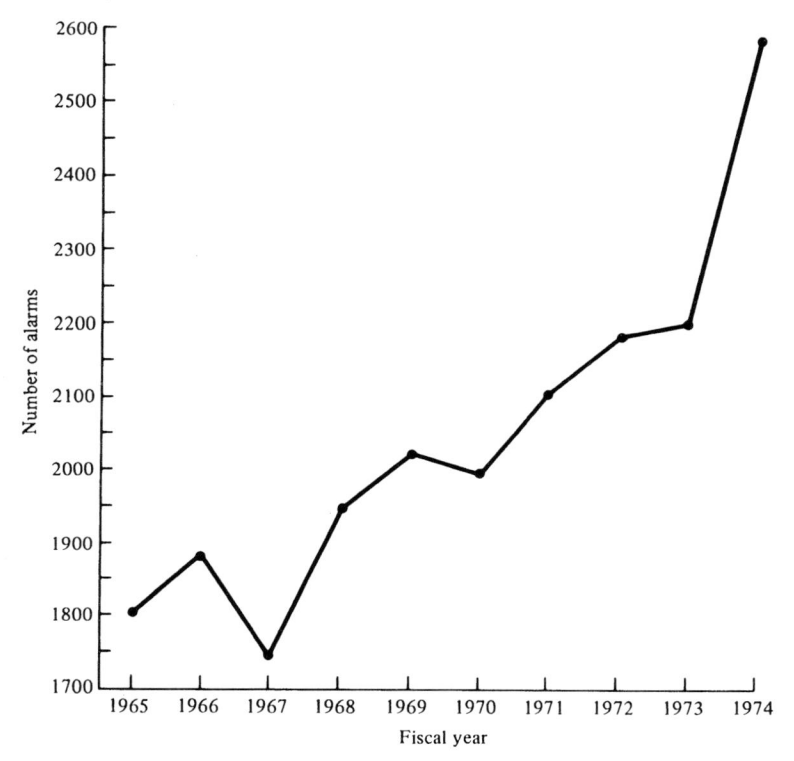

new techniques were developed at The New York City–Rand Institute to help resolve these questions (Walker, Chaiken, and Ignall, 1979). This case describes a fire department deployment study carried out in Wilmington, Delaware, by a local project team with technical assistance from The New York City–Rand Institute (Walker, Singleton, and Smith, 1975; Walker, 1978).

Wilmington is the largest city in Delaware. It has large concentrations of the poor (in 1969, 16 percent of all families had incomes below the poverty level), the aged, and minority groups (44 percent nonwhite), all with greater-than-average needs for public servies to be paid for from a declining tax base. Although a shipping and transportation center, Wilmington's economy has shifted away from manufacturing to executive offices and service industries. Its operating budget for fiscal 1978 (excluding education) was $27,796,641, or $346 per capita.

The Wilmington Bureau of Fire (the official name of the department) is administered by a chief, who reports to the Commissioner of Public Safety. The chief is appointed by the mayor, usually from within the Bureau and on the basis of merit, tenure, and experience. The Bureau is the only fully paid fire department in Delaware.

Origin of the Project

Of the eight firehouses in Wilmington in February 1973, only one had been built after 1910. The exception was the result of a 1967 study conducted by the city's Department of Planning and Development, which concluded that not one, but seven new firehouses should be built and that one of the old houses should be renovated. After the first firehouse was built, however, the architect predicted a substantial overrun for the second one. (The 1967 study had projected $304,000 for the second fire-house, and $475,000 was actually allocated in the 1972 and 1973 capital budgets, but the new cost figure was more than $700,000.)

In addition, the new mayor questioned the overall adequacy of the city's fire protection, and his newly appointed chief questioned the firehouse locations recommended by the 1967 study. Together, these considerations led to an administrative decision in August 1973 to suspend the construction of any new firehouses until a thorough analysis of the situation could be undertaken.

At this time Wilmington learned that The New York City–Rand Institute had a contract with the Office of Policy Development and Research of the U.S. Department of Housing and Urban Development (HUD) to assist a number of cities in using methods developed at the Institute for analyzing the deployment of emergency service vehicles. The HUD contract had, among its objectives, to determine the usefulness of the methods and the ease with which understanding and the ability to use them could be transferred to city personnel. Wilmington applied to the Institute for assistance in determining where to locate the previously budgeted replacement firehouses; it was later chosen as one of the cities to be assisted under the HUD contract.

The analysis, which began in February 1973, was conducted by a local project team led by the Director of Program Analysis in Wilmington's Department of Planning and Development, with guidance provided by The New York City–Rand Institute staff. The primary objective was to evaluate, and to revise if necessary, the deployment study of 1967.

Analysis

Fire protection is a basic municipal service. The size of the firefighting force and its deployment throughout a city impose important policy decisions on the city government. A policy that leads to rapid response with the appropriate firefighting resources can save lives and reduce property loss. The difficulty is that there is little agreement on just what is "appropriate." In order to evaluate alternative deployment policies, both performance measures and models to use in calculating the values of the measures under different policies are needed. It is these measures and models that The New York City–Rand Institute supplied (Walker, 1975).

Since a fire department's primary objectives are to protect lives and safeguard property, the most important measures of its performance are the number of fire fatalities and injuries and the amount of property loss. It is not possible, however, to use these measures to evaluate different deployment policies because there are as yet no reliable ways to estimate the effects that different policies have on them. For example, if the number of fire companies on duty were doubled (or halved), no one can say with a satisfactory degree of confidence what effects the changes would have on the numbers of casualties or property losses. The direction of these effects may be predictable for large changes, such as doubling or halving, but the quantitative (practical) consequences are not—and in the case of more realistic small changes in deployment policy, neither the directions nor the sizes of the changes in casualties or damage are predictable.

Therefore, in order to evaluate alternative firehouse configurations, three substitute, or *proxy*, measures were used, the first two of which are directly related to loss of life and property damage: (1) travel time to individual locations, (2) average travel time in a region, and (3) company workload. With these measures, the consequences of changes in firehouse location can be evaluated against the background of other considerations, such as hazards, fire incidence, costs, and political constraints.

Before the proxy measures can be calculated, certain data must be collected and analyzed.

Most of the time fire companies, just by being present, provide insurance against fire losses rather than engage in actual firefighting. However, if a fire occurs, the department wants companies both available and close by in order to reach the scene of the fire as quickly as possible. The degree of coverage given a location may therefore be measured by the expected travel time to the location from the nearest firehouse. Areas close to firehouses are considered well covered, those far away poorly covered. Thus, one measure of regional coverage is the maximum travel time (or distance) from the nearest firehouse to any point in the region.

Actually, several travel-time measures were considered in the test-city analyses. For example, because engine and ladder companies perform different tasks at a fire, it was important to separate travel times by type of company. In addition, since two units of the same type working together may be able to make some action that neither could perform alone, the travel time of each arriving apparatus was considered. Therefore, one way to evaluate alternative deployments of fire companies was to consider the set of travel times for the engine and ladder companies assigned to respond to each potential incident location.

It is rare for one deployment policy to produce travel times that are superior to those of another policy for each and every incident location, and consideration of the changes in travel time to all incident locations would be an overwhelming task. Consequently, the comparison of alternative policies usually involves summary statistics, such as travel times to groups of incident locations. The groups may be formed in several different ways—by region of the city or by company response area, for example. In Wilmington, these measures were used:

> The average travel time to all locations in the group, with each location having equal weight. (This is a useful measure of the general coverge that a department provides for any type of incident.)
>
> The expected travel time to a *structural fire* (that is, one involving a structure), taking into account that some locations experience more *structural alarms* than others. (This measure estimates the travel times that a department can expect to achieve to fires that have the greatest potential for life and property loss.)
>
> The maximum travel time to any incident location in the group.

In order to analyze alternative deployment policies, a way is needed to estimate travel times from firehouse to incident locations. There are several possibilities. For example, one could develop a matrix containing the estimated travel times between all pairs of firehouse and incident locations. The method used in this study employs empirical data to develop a general relation between travel distance and travel time. Then, given the travel distance between any two points (which can be easily estimated from their grid coordinates), the travel time can be estimated.

Figure 3.5 shows the results of an experiment to gather the data needed to estimate travel time in Wilmington, Delaware. Five fire companies (two engines, two ladders, and a rescue squad) recorded the distance traveled and

Section 3.3. Improving Fire Protection

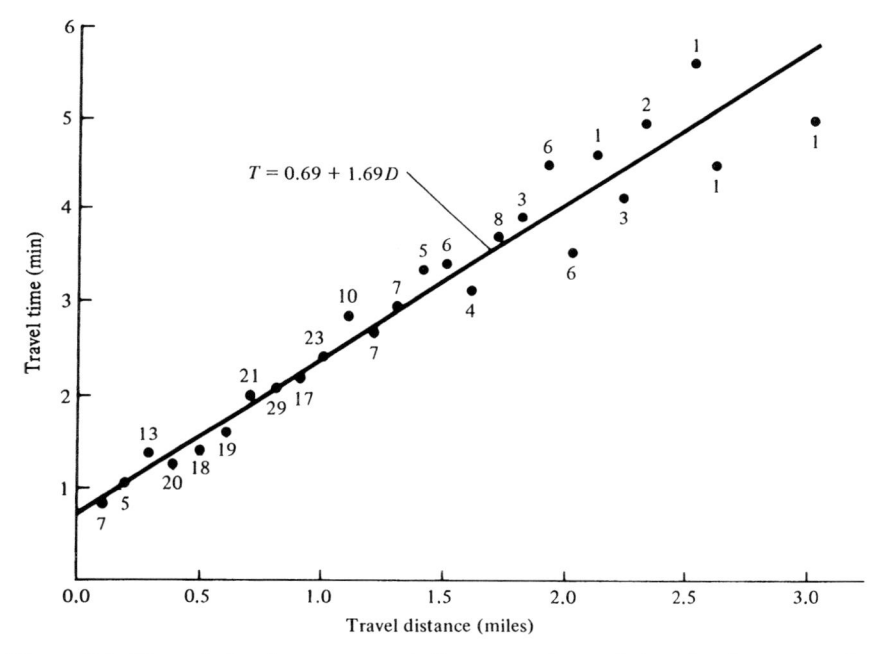

Figure 3.5. The relation between travel distance and travel time for fire companies in Wilmington, Delaware. (Points show the average of n observations, where n is the number immediately above.) (*From Walker, Singleton, and Smith, 1975.*)

the travel time for 243 responses. The best estimates of travel time T (in minutes) were obtained by using the relation

$$T = 0.69 + 1.69 D,$$

where D is the travel distance in miles.

This model was used in a subsequent analysis of the deployment of Wilmington's fire companies. After the distance between a firehouse and an alarm box was estimated (using another model), the time required to travel this distance was estimated using the model. For example, if a travel distance was estimated to be one mile, the model predicts the travel time to be 2.38 minutes $(0.69 + 1.69 = 2.38)$, or 2 minutes, 23 seconds.

A second model, the theoretically derived *square-root law* [see (Walker, Chaiken, and Ignall, 1979) and Section 7.4] was used to estimate the average travel distance $\bar{D}$ (in miles) in a region for the first-arriving company using the equation

$$\bar{D} = const. \cdot \sqrt{A/\bar{N}}.$$

The constant depends on street configuration and on how companies are distributed in the region; A is the area of the region (in square miles), and $\overline{N}$ is the average number of companies available in the region (the average number available is the number of companies located in the region less the average number that are busy). For cities like Wilmington, a value of 0.55 for the constant was found to give good estimates. Thus the average travel time for the first-arriving engine company in a region in Wilmington with area A and an average of $\overline{N}$ companies available was estimated as

$$\overline{T} = 0.69 + 1.69\,(0.55)\sqrt{A/\overline{N}}.$$

It is possible to answer some deployment questions using this simple model. For example, it can be used to determine how the average travel time in a region would change if the number of companies were changed.

A model known as the *parametric allocation model* (Walker, Chaiken, and Ignall, 1979) was also employed in the study. This model was developed to determine fire company allocations that would satisfy a wide range of objectives and to permit them to be evaluated in terms of average regional travel times, average citywide travel times, and company workload. The model incorporates a simple formula that specifies the number of companies that should be allocated to each region, given the total number of companies to be deployed in the city and a parameter that reflects the desired objective.

The formula first makes sure that enough companies are allocated to each region to meet the region's average firefighting workload. The remaining companies are then allocated in proportion to a combination of each region's realized and potential demand. Realized demand is related to the alarm rate in a region. Potential (or latent) demand is related both to the risk of fire and the magnitude of possible loss if a fire occurs. A run-down residential area might have a large realized demand because of a high structural alarm rate, but a moderate potential demand because the buildings are all brick. An industrial area, on the other hand, might have a low alarm rate but a high potential demand. The formula incorporates a trade-off parameter that allows the user to determine how much emphasis to place on either type of demand.

The model is constructed in such a way that there are values of the trade-off parameter that give allocations satisfying three specific objectives. One parameter value will equalize workloads in all regions, another will minimize the average citywide travel time, and a third will equalize average travel times for all regions.

The user is free to choose one of these three parameter values to obtain an allocation that satisfies one of the three explicit objectives, or he can choose an intermediate value in order to effect a compromise among the objectives. Thus, without specifically embracing a given objective, the manager can generate a variety of allocations and choose the ones that he likes best based on his intuition, experience, and the resulting measures of performance in

Section 3.3. Improving Fire Protection

each region. The model ensures that each allocation is the best obtainable for each compromise.

Since, in this case, the administration was interested in the possibility of phasing out one or more engine companies, the model was used to make a gross determination of which regions in the city should lose companies (if companies were to be eliminated) and how the remaining companies should be allocated.

The question then remained, Given a particular number of engine and ladder companies to be deployed in each region, where should they be located in the regions? To answer this question, a second model, the *firehouse site evaluation model* (the siting model) was used (Walker, Chaiken, and Ignall, 1979, Ch. 10) to evaluate specific locations. Over 100 different fire company arrangements were compared.

The siting model is not an optimization model. It will not specify the "best" arrangement of fire companies. It is an informative model that, for each configuration that the user suggests, predicts the resulting values of a large number of performance measures. A subset of the performance measures may be tabulated for comparison with the results from other configurations. The results for several configurations that seem most promising must be evaluated by someone with suitable qualifications, whose responsibility it is to interpret the numbers in the light of factors that the model does not incorporate—community and union reactions, costs, and other political realities, to name a few. As this is not an optimization model, a policymaker who understands the entire operational and political context of the department must ultimately decide which of the alternative configurations is best. If none is considered good enough, then still others must be analyzed.

Recommendations of the Project Team

In late 1973, results from the siting model and fire-incidence data on overlapping alarms (that is, alarms in simultaneous progress) suggested that the number of engine companies in Wilmington could be reduced by one or two companies, and that the remainder could be repositioned with very little effect on fire protection. In particular, the siting model estimated that with eight engine companies (instead of nine) the citywide average first-due engine travel time would increase by 1.2 seconds (a 1 percent increase). This model also estimated that the average first-due engine travel time to structural fires would increase by 3.6 seconds (2.5 percent). And, according to the model, the maximum first-due engine travel time would not change.

The project team's proposals for redeployment are shown in Figure 3.6, a map of Wilmington showing the specific moves and the one elimination recommended. The company to be eliminated was engine company 7 in region 1, which shared a firehouse with ladder company 3. By eliminating engine company 7, and assigning its stationmate ladder company 3 and the nearby

86   Chapter 3. Examples of Systems Analysis

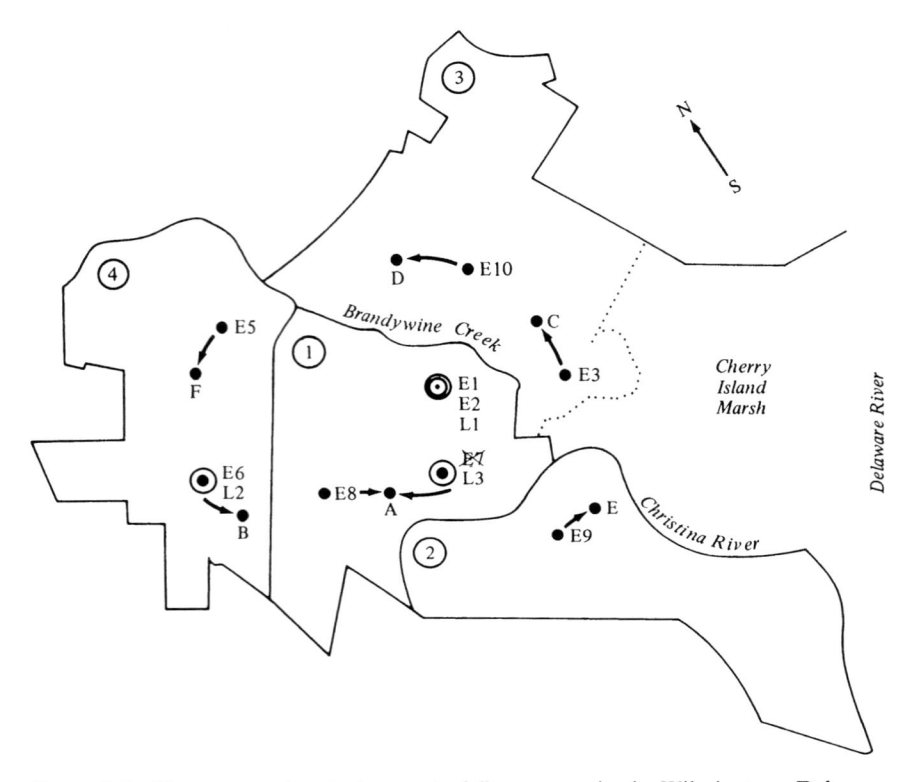

Figure 3.6. The proposed redeployment of fire companies in Wilmington, Delaware (E, engine company; L, ladder company; demand region numbers are circled). (*From Walker, Singleton, and Smith, 1975.*)

engine company 8 to a new house at location A, two things would be achieved. First, the old house occupied by engine company 7 and ladder company 3 could be closed permanently. Second, engine company 8 would move to a position where it could handle much of engine company 7's workload.

In addition to the recommendations affecting engine companies 7 and 8 and ladder company 3, the project team further recommended that five of the seven other engine companies be moved to new houses, as they were built, at the locations indicated by letters in Figure 3.6. Only one of the two other ladder companies, ladder company 2 in region 4, was to be moved. Ladder company 1, and the two engines housed with it in the new (1971) center city firehouse, were to remain in place.

History of the Implementation

The mayor accepted the recommendations and directed that negotiations with the firefighters' union proceed with the objective of eliminating at least one

Section 3.3. Improving Fire Protection   87

company. In preparation for the negotiations, numerous meetings of the project team and interested city officials were held to identify potential issues and strategies and to gauge union reaction to the proposed cuts. In addition to the cuts, wages and a number of fairly routine issues were also to be negotiated.

Negotiations began in April 1974 and continued until a settlement was finally approved by the union membership in October of that year (Singleton, 1975). The city's proposals were offered as a package (a given salary increase, contract language changes, manning cuts, etc.) to be accepted or rejected as a unit. These proposals, including the immediate cut of two engine companies, were presented in detail in the first negotiating session. The union responded a few weeks later with a detailed reply opposing any cuts. The city attempted to stimulate movement by proposing a compromise of an immediate one-company cut and another possible cut after a 15-month study to examine the effects of cutting the first. This proposal was rejected by the union.

On June 30 the existing contract expired. Although no specific agreement was made, the city continued all of the provisions of the expired contract. However, with no contract, the city had the right to act unilaterally on matters formerly governed by the contract—including the proposed cuts in manpower requirements.

Early in July the city chose to adopt the position of a "last, best, and final" offer to the firefighters' union. The proposal included a one-company cut. The union negotiating committee agreed to put it to a membership vote, which defeated it overwhelmingly.

In August a settlement with the union representatives was reached calling for continued pay parity with the police, the elimination of one engine company, and changes in contract language. While base pay parity was preserved, the firefighters accepted a $100 annual "uniform maintenance allowance" increase (from $50 to $150) as a type of productivity increase. The contract was submitted to the membership and, once again, was defeated, though by a narrow vote. The reasons for the rejection appear to have been the explicit acceptance of the company cut in the contract and a general feeling that the firefighters had been unduly pressured.

The city's response to the negative vote was a strongly worded statement and unilateral elimination of one engine company (Engine Company 7) at 8:00 A.M. the following morning. This unilateral action speeded the final settlement by removing the issue of cutting one company from the negotiations; it was no longer necessary for the firefighters to agree to it, since it was already done.

Within two weeks the firefighters ratified a new contract, which contained no significant differences from the one previously rejected, other than elimination of the specific agreement to the one-company cut. It is estimated that eliminating engine company 7 has saved the city at least $240,000 per year, a figure that does not include accrued pension liability.

The elimination of engine company 7 was viewed with alarm by many in Wilmington, especially the firefighters. However, the Commissioner of Public Safety, the Fire Chief, and most firefighters agree that the cut has produced no identifiable reduction in safety either to life or property since it was made. In addition, from January to March 1976 the University of Delaware's College of Urban Affairs studied public perception of municipal service delivery in Wilmington. Fire protection was regarded by those interviewed as one of the best of the city's services. No change relative to the protection prior to the cut was noticed. No one in the city has complained of negative effects since the cut, not even the firefighters' union.

Other progress has been made in implementing the recommendations. In April 1977, engine company 3 moved into a new firehouse built six blocks northwest of its old house and approximately at the location recommended. In May 1977, engine company 8, ladder company 3, and battalion 2 moved to a new firehouse on the site recommended by the project team. Both new firehouses were dedicated on June 17.

An interesting development in the construction of the two new houses was the creation of standardized plans for building them, resulting in substantial savings in money and time. The other firehouses scheduled to be built in the next few years will be constructed using the same standardized plans. While this is not a direct outcome of the analysis, it is, in the opinion of Wilmington officials, an outgrowth of the team approach and analytical thinking about fire problems.

Wilmington is following the project team's original recommendations in rebuilding and resiting its firehouses, with some minor modifications. Detailed plans for a new firehouse for engine company 9, to be located immediately behind the existing house, are being drafted. Most of the funding for the new house is expected to come from the Federal government.

The city has also budgeted some of its own capital for firehouse construction. A firehouse for engine company 5 and one for engine company 6 and ladder company 2 will be funded locally. Construction of a new firehouse for engine company 10 would complete the original set of recommendations made by the project team. The reduction in manpower costs from the elimination of one engine company will more than cover the increased debt service engendered by building the new firehouses.

Evaluation

The analytic work performed in Wilmington led to two broad, successful results: the implementation of effective changes in the deployment of firefighting resources, and the creation of an internal ability to perform further analyses as needed. While many influences combined to achieve these results, several major themes can be identified as largely responsible:

1. A well-constituted, well-informed project team, capable of applying analytic thinking and the output of computer models to problem solving.

Section 3.4. Protecting an Estuary from Flooding 89

2. Timely assistance from outside consultants with experience in using and transferring directly applicable technology.
3. Skillful labor negotiation, based on both analytic results and a clear understanding of the interests of all parties.
4. Support from and decisive action by the chief executive.

Further information on implementation and evaluation is given by Singleton (1975) and Walker, Singleton, and Smith (1975).

3.4 Protecting an Estuary from Flooding
Background
In 1953 a severe storm flooded much of the Delta region of the Netherlands, killing several thousand people and inundating 130,000 hectares of land. The possibility of such a catastrophe had often been discussed in the Dutch Parliament, but not much had been done to prevent it. As a consequence, in 1954 the Dutch government—possibly overreacting—embarked on a massive construction program for flood protection. By 1975 the new dams, dikes, and other works were nearly complete for all Delta estuaries except the largest, the Oosterschelde (Figure 3.7). There the program was interrupted by controversy, as goals other than security began to seem important.

The original plan had been to dam the mouth of the Oosterschelde, completely closing it off from the sea. This threatened the estuary's ecology and its oyster and mussel industries. Opposition developed and the Dutch Cabinet directed the Rijkswaterstaat, the agency responsible for water control and public works, to investigate alternative approaches. In April 1975 this agency set up a joint research project with The Rand Corporation to help with the work. The project, named the *Policy Analysis of the Oosterschelde* (POLANO) is summarized in detail in a series of reports (Abrahamse et al., 1977; Bigelow and DeHaven, 1977; Bigelow, Bolten, and DeHaven, 1977 a, b; de Ferranti, Heuer, and Weehuizen, 1977; Goeller et al., 1977). These publications offer something not usually found in the literature of systems analysis: a detailed report on the approach and results of a study that contributed in an important way to the outcome of a highly controversial public policy decision. The description below is taken, with minor changes in wording, from the summary volume (Goeller et al., 1977) of the report prepared for the Rijkswaterstaat (RWS).

Environmentalists objected that an impermeable dam across the mouth of the estuary, turning it into a fresh water lake, would destroy its rare ecology. They were joined by the oyster and mussel fishing industry. On the other hand, those primarily concerned with safety strongly supported the plan for closing off the estuary. As an alternative, the Cabinet proposed the construction of a storm-surge barrier (SSB) at the mouth of the Oosterschelde. The barrier was to be a flow-through dam with large gates that would be closed

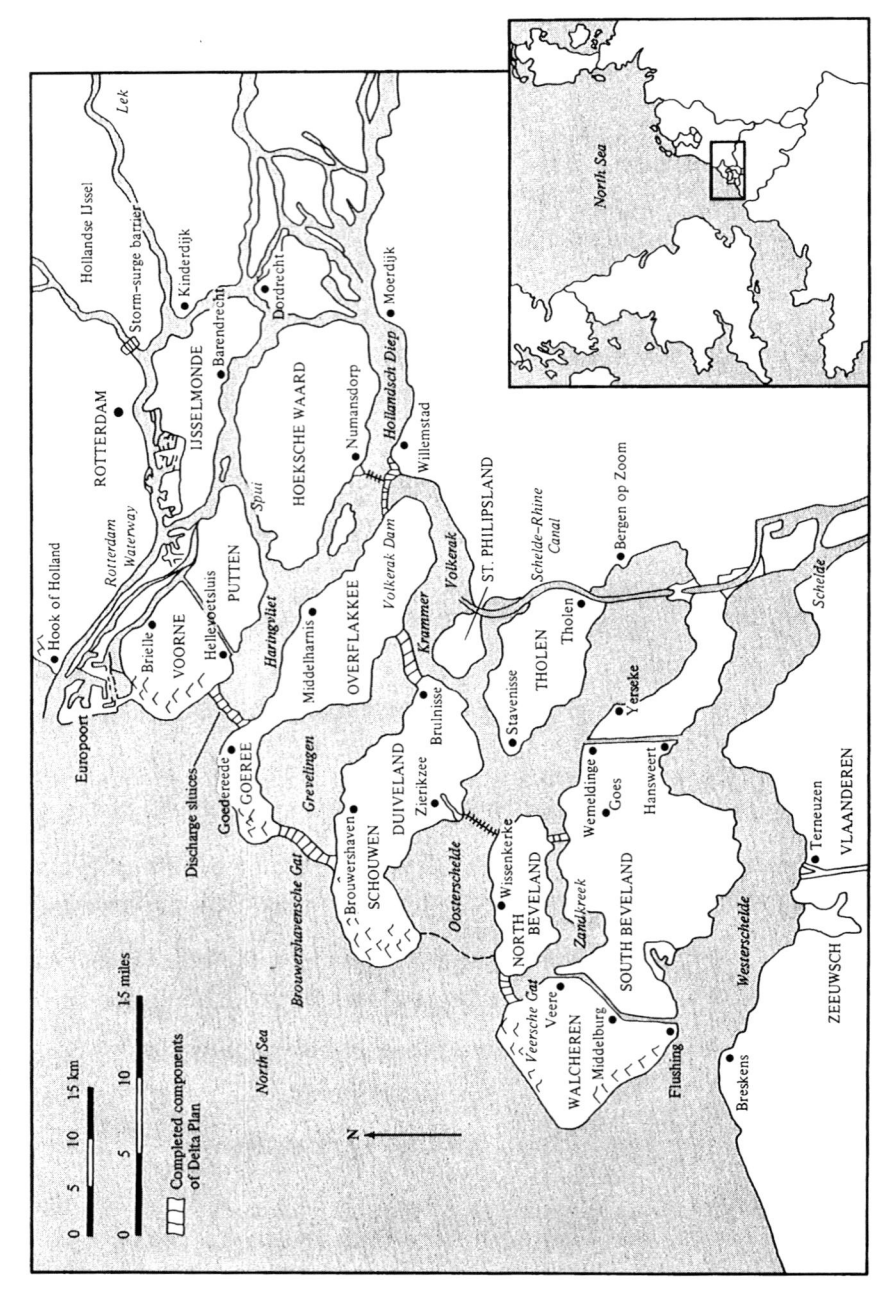

Figure 3.7. The Delta region of the southwest Netherlands, showing the Delta plan components completed by 1975. (*From Goeller et al., 1977.*)

Section 3.4. Protecting an Estuary from Flooding 91

during severe storms. Under normal conditions, the gates would be open to allow a reduced tide to pass into the basin, the size of the tide being governed by the size of the aperture in the barrier. The Cabinet specified that the barrier had to be complete by 1985 and had to provide protection against a storm so severe that it might be expected to occur only once in 4000 years.

There were still some who feared that the barrier, with its reduced tide, might seriously damage fishing and the ecology. They pressed for yet another alternative: leaving the mouth of the Oosterschelde open to maintain the original tide and constructing a system of large dikes around the estuary's perimeter.

Implicitly rejected at this stage was an obvious fourth alternative of a completely different character: Do nothing at all—or at least almost nothing in terms of the total public expenditures required relative to the costs of the three main alternatives. For example, one version of this alternative might be to

- do no rebuilding of the coastal defenses against flooding in the Oosterschelde vicinity (except routine maintenance of the current dikes) and
- limit further action to measures such as enhancing storm prediction capabilities, improving evacuation procedures, and establishing an indemnification fund for compensating future property losses.

In the context of prevailing Dutch public opinion, options of this kind were not realistic and were accordingly expressly excluded from the scope of the study mandate. Had they been included, the main argument on their behalf would be that the funds currently intended for rebuilding coastal defenses might be more beneficially spent on other needs (e.g., on automobile safety, which also affects both lives and property).

Thus, there were three main strategies to consider for protecting the southwestern Netherlands against North Sea flooding: the closed dam, the storm-surge barrier, and leaving the mouth of the estuary open (with higher dikes around the perimeter). Further, two compartmented dams were included in each case to separate the Oosterschelde into three basins: a western basin, located close to the mouth of the estuary; an eastern basin, located close to the opposite end; and a northern basin, located in the Krammer/Volkerak. (The purposes of this separation were to aid water management and to provide tide-free navigation, as required by treaty with Belgium, for the ship canal passing through the rear of the Oosterschelde.) Of these basins, the western basin would remain salt water, while the eastern and northern ones would become fresh water. The location of the dam creating the northern basin was to be the same in all three strategies, but the location for the dam separating the eastern and western basins was undecided. Different locations for this dam would produce basins of different sizes, and hence different strategies.

Each strategy involved a number of variations: the size of the aperature in the storm-surge barrier approach, for instance. The possible consequences of each approach (and its variations) on the environs of the Oosterschelde and on the Netherlands as a whole had to be estimated. These consequences, or *impacts* as they were called, are numerous. They include the *security* of people and property from flooding; the *financial costs* to the government from the construction and operation of the works; the changes in the kinds and populations of biological species that constitute the *ecology* of the region; the additional employment and other *economic* effects that occur not only in industries directly involved in building the barrier but also indirectly in other, interrelated industries; the quantity and quality of water available in various locations (called *water management* impacts by the Dutch); and various *social* effects, including the displacement of households and special ramifications on local residents.

A dominant aspect of this type of problem is that most of the consequences cannot be expressed naturally in the same units and some (e.g., aesthetic qualities) cannot be satisfactorily quantified at all. Further, different groups perceive and value particular consequences differently.

In the joint research effort each organization concentrated on different, but complementary, tasks. Rand's primary task was to develop and apply a methodological framework for predicting and comparing the many possible consequences. The RWS's primary tasks were, on the basis of special engineering and scientific studies, to develop a specific design for each alternative approach, to analyze the consequences of the designs in which it had special expertise (e.g., the effects on salinity), and to provide data, as well as assistance, for the methodology being developed with Rand.

The Analytic Approach

Figure 3.8 portrays the analytic approach, indicating the stages of the analysis.

Screening alternatives. Each approach to protecting the Oosterschelde has many variations; for example, several different types of storm-surge barrier are possible and several different apertures could be considered for each type. The possible alternatives are so numerous that it becomes impractical to evaluate all of them in terms of detailed impacts. One is thus compelled to identify a manageable number of the more promising alternatives for subsequent evaluation. *Screening* reduces the number of alternatives that merit further evaluation—that is, one identifies the promising alternatives (and rejects the inferior ones). The criteria for screening include security, ecology, and construction costs; for example, an alternative that would not clearly provide the desired level of security or would provide it with a higher cost and a less desirable ecology than some other alternative was to be ruled out.

The RWS did the final screening, with the help of studies by several special committees and its own investigations.

Section 3.4. Protecting an Estuary from Flooding

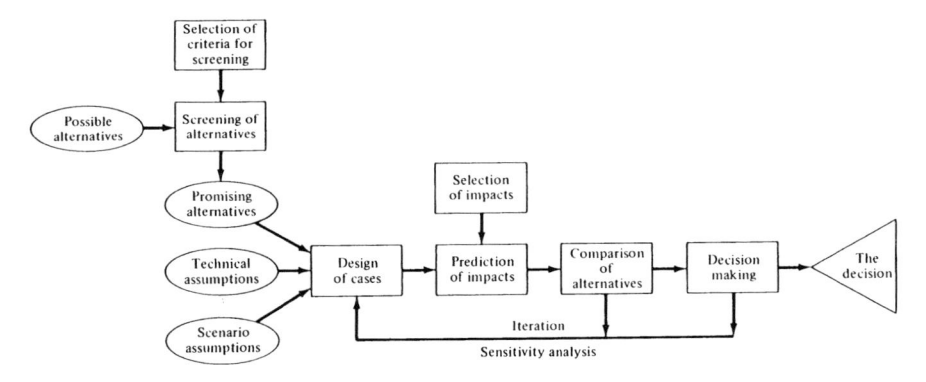

Figure 3.8. The stages of the Oosterschelde analysis. (*From Goeller et al., 1977.*)

Designing cases. Screening identifies promising alternatives to use in designing cases. These *cases* include a scenario (e.g., about the economic future) and a set of technical assumptions. The *technical assumptions* are merely assumed values—explicitly stated—for the most uncertain factors in the system, such as the excess water level associated with a storm occurring not more than once in 4000 years or how much wave overtopping will cause dike failure.

Comparing alternatives and decisionmaking. For each case the many impacts of the various alternatives are estimated using appropriate models and are then presented to the decisionmakers for them to compare alternatives. In most systems analyses the different impacts associated with a given alternative have been combined into a single measure of performance, but this approach generally loses information and may substitute the analyst's values for those of the decisionmakers. However, in the approach used in this case, Rand displayed the various impacts in a table (such as Tables 3.1, 3.2, and 3.3), called a *scorecard*, that also shows, by shading or a color code, each alternative's ranking for a particular impact. To this information the decisionmakers can then add their value judgments about the relative importance to be assigned to the different impacts, thereby to select a preferred alternative—that is, to make a decision. In POLANO the decisionmakers were the Dutch Cabinet and Parliament, the elected representatives of the people.

Iterating the analysis On the basis of an initital comparison of alternatives, the analysts identified as desirable a number of sensitivity analyses. Additional comparisons were then designed that involved changing the alternatives, the technical assumptions, the scenario, or combinations of all three. Evaluations of the alternatives in these additional comparisons, or the expressed concerns of the decisionmakers in response, yielded yet another set of changes for investigation. This process continued iteratively until the decision was made.

Table 3.1. Financial Costs Scorecard for POLANO[a]

Item	Closed case	SSB case	Open case
Construction cost from 1 January 1976	2135	4645	3620
Annual maintenance and operations	10	25	15
Peak year expenditures	420	690	410
Peak year	1980	1980	1980

Source: Goeller et al. (1977, p. 26).

[a] Rankings: ☐ best case; ▨ intermediate case; ■ worst case.
All costs are in million DFL.

On account of the intensely political nature of the problem, it was recognized that during, and even after, the time a choice among the three alternative approaches was made, there would be a need to satisfy the desires and allay the fears of the many interested parties. This could not be done by comparing benefit–cost ratios or other single indices associated with the individual alternatives. Instead, environmentalists, fisherman, shippers, vacationers, and

Table 3.2. Security Scorecard for POLANO[a]

Item	Closed case	SSB case	Open case
Long run:			
Land flooded (ha) in a once-in-4000-years storm, $L(90)$[b]	0	0	400
Technical uncertainty	none	scour[c]	dikes
Transition period expected damage:			
Land area flooded (ha)	430	200	530
Value of real property flooded (million DFL)	50	20	60
Number of people at risk	800	360	970

Source: Goeller et al. (1977, p. 51).

[a] Rankings: ☐ best case; ▨ intermediate case; ■ worst case.
[b] For such a storm, there is a 90 percent probability that the amount of land area flooded will be no more than the indicated value.
[c] Refers to the possibility that a current-caused hole may develop in the bottom and weaken the barrier.

Table 3.3. Ecology Scorecard for POLANO[a]

Item	Alternatives Closed case	Alternatives SSB case	Alternatives Open case	Present Oosterschelde
Key inputs:				
Salt basin area (km^2)[b]	202	365	370	476
Tidal range at Zierikzee (m)	0	2	3	3
Primary production (tons/day)	200	350	350	450
Detritus import (tons/day)	0	990	550	700
Percent of present primary food available[c]	17	116	78	100
Total biomass:				
Amount (tons afdw[d])	5,200	29,700	21,300	28,500
Percent of present amount	18	104	75	100
Potential abundance of birds:				
Benthos eaters (tons afdw)	1	9	7	10
Fish eaters (tons afdw)	4	0.06	0.03	0.05
Plant eaters (tons afdw)	more	same	same	
Potential shellfish culture:				
Mussels (percent of present)	13	90	100	100
Oysters (percent of present)	0	90	100	100
Nursery function:				
Shrimp (percent of present)	0	400	50	100
Fish (percent of present)	0	133	73	100
Transients:				
Rapid kill of benthic biomass (tons afdw)	11,500	4,500	4,200	
Rapid kill (percent of present benthic biomass)	68	27	25	
Change in average density of benthic biomass from present (g/m^2)	−25	22	−1	
Number of years to stabilize	6.5	6	0	

Source: Goeller et al. (1977, p. 81).

[a] Rankings: ☐ best case; ▦ intermediate case; ■ worst case.
[b] The closed case has a smaller salt basin because, without tidal flow, it was impossible to keep a large basin sufficiently saline. The other cases use a large basin to preserve the existing environment better.
[c] Primary food available = primary production rate + detritus import rate.
[d] Ash-free dry weight.

others would want to know as precisely as possible how their area of special interest would be affected by whatever actions were contemplated. These considerations implied two things—the need for very many relatively small models that could answer specific questions about particular aspects, rather than for one or a few large models, and the need for a scheme that would enable not only the primary decisionmakers (the Cabinet) but also the Dutch people to apply their own judgments to the impacts they considered significant.

Space limitations preclude describing the many models by which the various impacts were estimated. They are summarized by Goeller et al. (1977) and discussed by Abrahamse et al. (1977), Bigelow and DeHaven (1977), Bigelow, Bolten, and DeHaven (1977a,b), and de Ferranti, Heuer, and Weehuizen (1977). Many were relatively standard, such as those used by the RWS to estimate dam and dike construction costs, developed through long experience with similar construction projects. Other models, such as those used to assess long-run and transient changes in ecology and flood security, required developing new methods (with results considerably more uncertain). The development of these models was handicapped by lack of either experimental data or a scientific theory. Nevertheless, rather than omit these components, the analysts modeled them using whatever data were available in combination with the opinions of experts. The decision to proceed reflects a widely held belief, perhaps best stated by Forrester (1969, p. 114):

> Much of the behavior of systems rests on relationships and interactions that are believed, and probably correctly so, to be important but that for a long time will evade quantitative measure. Unless we take our best estimates of these relationships and include them in a system model, we are in effect saying that they make no difference and can be omitted. It is far more serious to omit a relationship that is believed to be important than to include it at a low level accuracy that fits the plausible range of uncertainty.

If a relation is believed to be important, one acts accordingly and makes the best possible use of the information available.

Methods for Synthesizing and Presenting Results

Once the impacts of the alternatives had been assessed, a major difficulty still remained: synthesizing the numerous and diverse impacts of each alternative and presenting these impacts to the decisionmakers as the basis for comparing alternatives. In the usual aggregate approach to synthesis, each impact is weighed by its relative importance and combined into some single, commensurate unit such as money, worth, or utility. The decisionmakers use this aggregate measure to compare alternatives. Of the several aggregate techniques, perhaps the best known is cost–benefit analysis, which converts

Section 3.4. Protecting an Estuary from Flooding

as many impacts as possible to monetary terms and sums the results. (See Chapter 8 for further discussion.)

The aggregate approach had several major disadvantages for POLANO. First, the aggregation process loses considerable information. For example, it might suppress the fact that the major disadvantages associated with one alternative arise from environmental problems, whereas those associated with a second alternative are financial problems.

Second, any single measure of worth depends strongly on the weights given to different impacts when they are combined and on the assumptions used to get them into commensurate units. Unfortunately, these crucial weights and assumptions are often implicit or highly speculative. They may impose a value scheme bearing little relation to the decisionmakers' concerns. For example, cost–benefit analysis assumes implicitly that a dollar's worth of one kind of benefit has the same value as a dollar's worth of another; yet, in many public decisions, monetarily equivalent but otherwise dissimilar benefits would be valued differently by different elements in society. Also, in converting disparate impacts to monetary values, cost–benefit analysis must sometimes make speculative assumptions, such as, how much money is one red-necked grebe worth? Are a million grebes worth a million times one grebe?

Third, the aggregate techniques are intended to help an individual decisionmaker or a closely knit group choose the preferred alternative, the one that best reflects their values (importance weights). Serious theoretical and practical problems arise when, as in POLANO, there are multiple decisionmakers: Whose values are used (the issue of interpersonal comparision of values), and what relative weight does the group give to the preferences of different individuals (the issue of equity)?

It has been proved that there is no rational procedure for combining individual rankings into a group ranking that does not explicitly include interpersonal comparison of preferences (Sen, 1970). To make this comparision and to address the issue of equity, full consideration of the original impacts appears essential.

Finally, to be theoretically valid, the aggregate techniques (other than cost–benefit analysis) require that the importance (value) of each impact be independent of the size of all other impacts. In the real world, however, this condition is not always satisfied. Each impact that violates this condition must be suppressed, either by eliminating it or by treating it at the next level of aggregation.

In POLANO the analysts chose a disaggregate approach that presents a column of impacts for each alternative, with each impact expressed in units natural to it. In comparing the alternatives, the decisionmaker could then assign whatever weight he deemed appropriate to each impact. Explicit consideration of weighting thus became central to the decision process itself, as we believe it should be. The analysis could therefore consider the full range of possible effects, using the most natural description for each effect. Some effects were decribed in monetary terms and others in physical units; some were assessed with quantitative estimates (e.g., "100 jobs would be created"), others with qualitative comparisons ("recreation opportunities would increase slightly"), and still others with statements of nonordinal facts ("an attractive tourist site would be destroyed"). A disadvantage of this approach is that the amount of detail makes it difficult for the decisionmaker to see patterns or draw conclusions.

To aid the decisionmaker in recognizing patterns and trading off disparate impacts, POLANO used a display device called a *scorecard*, as illustrated by Tables 3.1–3.3. [This device had been used earlier by the project leader, Bruce Goeller, as part of a transportation study conducted by Rand for the U.S. Department of Transportation; for a discussion, see Chesler and Goeller, (1973).] Impact values are summarized (in natural units) in a table, each row representing one impact and each column representing an alternative. The scorecard adds shading to the table of impacts to indicate each alternative's ranking for a particular impact. An entire column shows all the impacts of a single alternative; an entire row shows each alternative's value for a single impact. Numbers or words appear in each cell of the scorecard to convey what is known about the size and direction of the impact in *absolute* terms— without comparison between cells. When shading is added to highlight differences in ranking among the alternatives, each impact must be considered separately. (That is, impact values are ranked across columns for each row, independently of all other rows. The ranking assignments do *not* involve comparisons among rows.) Sometimes a row receives no shading, either because the impacts are comparable in size for all cases or because they are highly correlated with some other row that has already been shaded.

The scheme used in Tables 3.1–3.6 for contrasting the best, intermediate, and worst cases is one easily handled in print media. However, an analyst presenting such tables to a group of clients will find that color is a much more striking and useful form of differentiation. In fact, the Rand analysts who did the study we are discussing used blue shading for the best case, gray for the intermediate case, and yellow for the worst case.

The scorecard has several advantages, as POLANO shows. It presents a wide range of impacts and permits a decisionmaker to give each impact whatever weight he deems appropriate. It helps him to see the comparative strengths and weaknesses of various alternatives, to consider impacts that cannot be expressed in numerical terms, and to change his subjective weightings, and to note the effect this would have on his final choice. When there are multiple decisionmakers, the scorecard has the additional advantage of not requiring explicit agreement on weights for different social values: It is generally much easier for a group of decisionmakers to determine which alternative they prefer (perhaps for different reasons) than what weights to assign the various impacts.

The ranking assigned reflects certain assumptions about what is "best" or "worst" for each impact. To derive maximum benefit from scorecards, these

Section 3.4. Protecting an Estuary from Flooding 99

assumptions must be made explicit, because different assumptions (and hence different rankings) might be appropriate in some circumstances and for some interest groups. For example, in times of a slack economy, an increase in employment would be a favorable impact. In that circumstance, the alternative with the largest stimulus to employment would be designated "best" and the one with the least stimulus would be designated "worst." When the economy is straining at full capacity, additional impetus to employment would only result in increased wage and price inflation and would have the opposite ranking.

As this example demonstrates, the assumptions underlying shading assignments can be crucial. Generally, there is little doubt as to which assumptions should be adopted. Sometimes, however, two different sets of assumptions are equally plausible; for example, recreational growth near the Oosterschelde might be encouraged or prohibited. This quandary can be resolved by presenting parallel but separate scorecards for each set of assumptions.

Even apart from the ranking assumptions, scorecards can occasionally impose more of the analyst's value scheme on the findings than appears at first glance. The analyst chooses the impacts to display, their order of presentation, and their units of expression. These choices can, of course, influence the impressions conveyed. To be effective, therefore, scorecards must be carefully designed and interpreted. Other techniques for synthesizing multiple impacts require similar caution but suffer from the additional disadvantages mentioned earlier.

POLANO prepared separate scorecards to summarize each impact category and the entire study. (Examples appear in Tables 3.1–3.6.)

Study Results

The Rand/Rijkswaterstaat POLANO team analyzed and compared many different consequences, called *impacts* in its work. In addition, a number of sensitivity analyses were performed to learn how the impacts, or consequences, would change with variations in the design of the alternatives and in the assumptions made for several uncertain factors. The most significant impacts—and their major uncertainties—will now be summarized.[1]

Costs. In comparing the financial costs for the alternatives, estimated by Rijkswaterstaat engineers, the study concluded that the storm-surge barrier case would require an investment of nearly 4,700 million DFL,[2] a quarter

---

[1] Except for ecology, the storm-surge barrier impacts are for a barrier with an 11,500-square-meter aperture, the Rijkswaterstraat's nominal design. This aperture would reduce the tide to about two-thirds of its present value. For ecology, although the storm-surge barrier impacts in the scorecards are based on this aperture, the conclusions are based on a sensitivity analysis of aperture size and other relevant factors.

more than the open case and double the closed case. After construction, the annual costs for maintenance and operation would be small, ranging from 10 million DFL for the closed case to 25 million DFL for the storm-surge barrier case. (See Table 3.1.)

Security. To assess the security from flooding, the POLANO study developed a method for estimating the likelihood and severity of potential flood damage to land, people, and property under each of the three alternatives. The alternatives were subjected to many simulated threats, expressed in terms of storm water levels, and the expected damage from flooding was then calculated. The performance of the method and its assumptions were evaluated by comparing its damage estimates of dike failures and flooding, section by section, with the actual damage values of the 1953 storm.

The degree of safety for each alternative was estimated for two time periods: the transition period, which occurs before the protective construction is complete, and the long run. Although the values of the safety impacts change with the designs and technical assumptions (for example, the water level produced by a once-in-4,000-years storm), it was shown that the safety rankings of the three alternatives remain unchanged for both the long run and the transition period. (See Table 3.2.)

Ecology. For assessing changes in long-run ecological balances, the study developed a method (Bigelow, Bolten, and DeHaven, 1977a) to predict the effects of the different cases on the average abundances of biological species found in the Oosterschelde. This estuary, with its tidal shoals and mud flats, is an ecologically rich natural reserve of international significance. It serves as a feeding area for resident and migratory birds, as a location for the commercial culturing of oysters and mussels, and as a nursery for the young fish and shrimp populations from the North Sea. It was feared that construction associated with the cases would seriously damage this ecology.

The study analyzed the many relevant factors influencing ecology that varied among the alternative cases—different apertures for the storm-surge barrier (which would produce different tides), different sizes for the salty Western Basin, and different rates for nutrient flows and fishing. For these factors, the method predicted changes in the long-run average abundances of 18 groups of similar species, such as oysters and mussels, fish-eating fish, and plant-eating birds. It considered such natural processes as predation, migration, and photosynthesis. By using mathematical concepts new to ecology and by concentrating on long-run rather than day-to-day changes, the

---

[2] In this study DFL is the symbol for Dutch guilders, the official monetary unit of the Netherlands. (The FL derives from florin, the historial unit.) The reader who wants to compare guilders with dollars can use a conversion factor of 2.5 DFL per dollar (40 cents per DFL). This factor was a rough approximation of the fluctuating exchange rate at the time the study was done.

Section 3.4. Protecting an Estuary from Flooding

method is considerably easier to apply than traditional models of the same ecosystem. To validate it, its estimates were compared with actual ecological observations made in the Grevelingen, an adjacent estuary recently transformed into a salt-water lake.

The study concluded that the closed case is by far the worst ecologically and that one's preference among the other alternatives depends on one's goal for the ecology. If the goal is to minimize the change from the present ecology, in terms of total amount of biological life (biomass) and relative species abundance, the preference will be either the open case or a storm-surge barrier case with a large aperture (20,000 square meters), but if the goal is solely to maximize total biomass,[3] a storm-surge barrier case with an aperture between 6500 and 11,500 square meters is preferable. However, the preference should not be firm, because of uncertainties concerning the amount of nutrients brought in from the North Sea in the storm-surge barrier case.[4] Thus, although ecological considerations may help one to reject the closed case, they do not distinguish strongly between the open case and the storm-surge barrier case in which the aperture exceeds 6,500 square meters. (See the ecology scorecard in Table 3.3, for which the storm-surge barrier has an aperture of 11,500 square meters.) The choice among these alternatives will thus depend strongly on other factors, such as cost and security.

Beside the long-run changes discussed above, the study considered three transient disturbances to the Oosterschelde ecology. First, after construction there would be a "rapid kill" of biomass where the reduced tide dries out the organisms or where the water becomes fresh. For the transient effect, the closed case, with the largest tidal reduction, is by far the worst. The open and storm-surge barrier cases have roughly one-third the kill, with the open case best by a small amount.

The second transient ecological disturbance considered was the possibility that oxygen-free (anaerobic) water would be created in the eastern basin of the Oosterschelde if it were converted from a salt-water to a fresh-water lake. This conversion would kill the existing flora and fauna, and their subsequent decomposition by bacteria might temporarily deplete the oxygen in the newly freshened water. The further decomposition of the dead organisms, occurring while the water remained oxygen free, would produce bad odors and murky water and prevent the growth of almost all organisms suited to a fresh-water environment.

---

[3] And if one is willing to accept the consequent shift of relative species abundance from the present situation toward one in which noncommercial bottom species such as snails and worms are more abundant.

[4] This nutrient import is in the form of dead organic matter (detritus). Rand recommended that the detritus import be measured directly. When this was done, the figure obtained, 670 tons per day, turned out to be remarkably close to the 700 tons per day predicted by the model (Table 3.3), which, because it greatly exceeded the import rate predicted by others, had been the subject of controversy.

The study concluded that anaerobic conditions (Bigelow and DeHaven, 1977) were not likely to occur in the eastern basin if a small fresh-water lake were created, regardless of its month of closure, although sustained below-average wind velocities could cause transient anaerobic conditions if this basin were to be desalinated in the summer. Anaerobic conditions are likely to be encountered if a large fresh-water lake is created and closed off during the months of June through September. (It is precisely these months when closure would probably take place, because calm weather is considered essential for constructing the final stages of the compartment dams.) By this criterion, alternatives that involve a small eastern basin were favored. (Anaerobic conditions appeared quite unlikely in the northern basin.)

The third transient ecological disturbance considered was algae blooms—population explosions of these organisms. When conditions are favorable to algae, as a consequence of construction activities in the Oosterschelde, the resulting bloom may poison the fish and plants, clog filters in water systems, or discolor the water. Or, when conditions become unfavorable, the bloom may suddenly die off, and the bacterial mineralization of the dead algae may then deplete the water of oxygen, which can cause the death of desirable fish.

The study developed a method (Bigelow, Bolten, and DeHaven, 1977b) to estimate the risk of algae blooms in salt water. Although there is little likelihood of basinwide fish-killing algae blooms in the unchanged Oosterschelde or in the western basin for any of the alternatives, local problem spots may occur on very sunny days in places with stagnant water and abundant nutrients from agricultural runoff or waste discharges. The study reached no conclusions about algae blooms in the eastern or northern basins of the future Oosterschelde because there were insufficient data about nutrient concentrations and insufficient time to extend the methodology to fresh water. It recommended research to remedy this, noting that algae blooms, unlike the other transient disturbances considered, could be a recurring threat, aggravated by future growth in regional activities.

Recreational impacts. Under the then current Dutch policy, endorsed by regional and national agencies, the Oosterschelde and most of the central Delta area were to be kept in as undeveloped a state as possible. Because this policy was seen as susceptible to change, the study examined the recreational impacts under two contrasting policy scenarios. The first assumed that the present policy of no investment in recreation would be retained; the second that an unrestrained investment policy would be adopted. The predicted impacts under the two policies are shown in Table 3.4. Note that in reading this table, the *best* designations for the no-investment case are assigned to the alternative that would do most to minimize recreational activity in the Oosterschilde vicinity. For the unrestrained-investment case, however, best is linked to maximizing benefits to recreational visitors.

Table 3.4. Recreational-Impact Scorecard for No-Investment and Unrestrained-Investment Policies for POLANO[a]

	No investment			Unrestrained investment		
	Closed case	SSB case	Open case	Closed case	SSB case	Open case
Sea beaches:						
Added shoreline (km)	8	0	0	8	0	0
Increase in attendance (annual visits, in thousands)	338	0	0	>338	0	0
Inland beaches:						
Added shoreline (km)	17	11	6	17	11	6
Increase in attendance (annual visits, in thousands)	108	88	68	>108	>88	>68
Boating:						
Sea access restricted for large boats?	yes	yes	no	yes	yes	no
Added moorings due to departure of fishing vessels	<160	0	0	<240	0	0
large boats	<900	<900	0	<900	<900	0
Sportfishing:						
Decrease in saltwater fish quantity (percent)	75	0	25	<75	0	25
Added shoreline (km)	17+	11+	6+	17+	11+	6+
Fresh-water fish available?	yes	no	no	yes	no	no
Touring:						
Decrease in attractiveness of areas around dikes	none	minor	major	none	minor	some
Major tourist site at mouth of Oosterschelde?	no	yes	no	no	yes	no

Source: Goeller et al. (1977, pp. 112, 113).
[a]Rankings: ☐ best case; ▨ intermediate case; ■ worst case.

Other economic and social impacts. The study examined the three alternatives in light of their effects on jobs and profits in the fishing industry; changes in recreational opportunities and demand; savings to the carriers and customers of the canal shipping industry; total (direct plus indirect) changes in production, jobs, and imports for the 35 industrial sectors of the national economy; and, finally, as social impacts, the displacement of households and activities and the effects on the regional economy.

Even before the POLANO study began, there had been extensive speculation in the Netherlands on the dire economic and social consequences of construction in the Oosterschelde; the potential shutdown of the local fishing industry, for example, was a major concern. A main conclusion of the study is that most economic and social effects would be minor—and some even beneficial. The most significant effects would be the gain in total employment due to construction and the losses to the fishing industry. (See Table 3.5.)

Conclusions

Unlike many analyses, POLANO did not conclude by recommending a particular alternative. Rather, it compared the alternatives in terms of their many impacts but left the choice to the political process, where the responsibility properly resides. POLANO contributed in a direct and substantial way to this process by clarifying the issues, assessing the consequences, showing the influence of uncertainty, and comparing the alternatives, as comprehensively as possible, in a common framework.

Table 3.6 presents the summary scorecard for the nominal cases. It displays most, but not all, the impacts considered. Some were omitted to make the comparison more manageable; most of these were small enough to seem politically unimportant, or were comparable in size for all cases, or were highly correlated with other impacts already displayed.

Certain general observations can be made. First, there was no dominant alternative, one that was best for all the impacts. Second, each case had a major disadvantage that might be considered sufficiently serious as to render it unacceptable to the decisionmakers: The storm-surge barrier case was by far the worst for cost, the closed case worst for ecology, and the open case worst for security.

Third, the alternatives differed in the sizes of the changes from the then existing situation. The closed case offered the most extreme changes, desirable and undesirable, for most impacts (cost being a notable exception); the open case offered the least change (except for displacement of houses); and the storm-surge barrier case was usually intermediate, although it had the largest values for total biomass, the national economy, and financial cost.

Finally, the alternatives showed their primary advantages and disadvantages

Table 3.5. The Commercial Fishing, Inland Shipping, National Economy, and Regional Effects Scorecards for POLANO[a]

Item	Closed case	SSB case	Open case
Commercial fishing scorecard			
Annual fishing losses:			
Jobs	**199**	7	0
Production (million DFL)	**30.3**	1.4	0
Value added (million DFL)	**13.7**	0.6	0
Export revenue (million DFL)	<2	<1	0
Domestic consumption (million DFL)	<1	<1	0
Inland shipping scorecard			
Impact measures:			
Cost savings to industries that ship goods (1976–1999, million DFL, undiscounted)	27.2	8.9	**0**
Separation of commercial and recreational traffic	much	some	**little**
Alternative routes always available?	**no**	yes	yes
National economy scorecard			
Total increases[b] in peak year:			
Jobs	5800	9000	**5700**
Imports (million DFL)	110	**200**	130
Percent stone imports	2	4.8	5
Production (million DFL)	**580**	940	560
Wages and profits (million DFL)	**250**	400	230
Regional effects scorecard			
Number of households displaced	0	0	**124**
Total (direct plus indirect) economic increases, peak year:			
Production (million DFL)	**−37**	13	38
Jobs	**−230**	90	290
Road travel:			
Improvements in opportunities	medium	minor	**slight**
Damage to rural environment	**medium**	**minor**	slight

Source: Goeller et al. (1977, pp. 100, 103, 120, 123).
[a] Rankings: ☐ best case; ▨ intermediate case; ■ worst case.
[b] Direct plus indirect increase.

Table 3.6. Summary Scorecard for the Nominal Cases for POLANO[a]

Item	Closed case	SSB case	Open case	Present Oosterschelde
Financial costs (million DFL)				
Construction cost from 1 January 1976	2,135	4,645	3,620	
Annual maintenance and operations	10	25	15	
Peak year expenditures	420	690	410	
Security				
Long run:				
Land flooded (ha) in 1/4000 storm[b]	0	0	400	
Technical uncertainty	none	scour	dikes	
Transition period expected damage:				
Land flooded (ha)	430	200	530	
Value of real property flooded (million DFL)	50	20	60	
Number of people at risk	800	360	970	
Ecology				
Transients:				
Rapid kill of benthic biomass[c]	11,500	4,500	4,200	none
Gradual loss of biomass[c]	5,050	−8,000	300	none
Long run:				
Time to stabilize (years)	6.5	6.0	0.0	
Total biomass (tons afdw)	5,200	29,700	21,300	28,500
Potential benthos-eating birds[c]	1	9	7	10
Potential fish-eating birds[c]	4	0.06	0.03	0.05
Potential mussels (percent of present)	13	90	100	100
Potential oysters (percent of present)	0	90	100	100
Fish nursery function percent of present	0	133	73	100

Source: Goeller et al. (1977, pp. 127, 128).

[a] Rankings: ☐ best case; ▨ intermediate case; ■ worst case.
[b] $L(90)$: For such a storm, there is a 90 percent probability that the amount of land area flooded will be no more than the indicated value.
[c] Tons afdw (ash-free dry weight).
[d] Annually, in thousands.
[e] Total (direct plus indirect) increase.

Table 3.6 (*continued*)

	Alternatives			
Item	Closed case	SSB case	Open case	Present Oosterschelde
Fishing				
Jobs lost	199	7	0	
Annual production loss (million DFL)	30.3	1.4	0	
Accumulated net loss (million DFL)	89	0	0	
Shipping				
Accumulated savings through 1999 (million DFL)	27.2	8.9	0	
Recreation				
No-investment policy:				
Added sea beach visits[d]	338	0	0	
Added inland beach visits[d]	108	88	68	
Percent decrease in salt-water fish quantity	75	0	25	
Number of moorings added	< 1,060	< 900	0	
National economy (peak year)				
Jobs[e]	5,800	9,000	5,700	
Imports[e] (million DFL)	110	200	130	
Production[e] (million DFL)	580	940	560	
Regional effects				
Number of households displaced	0	0	124	
Jobs[e], peak year	−230	90	290	
Production[e], peak year (million DFL)	−37	13	38	

in different impact categories. The closed case was by far the best for cost, near best for overall security, but very much the worst for ecology and fishing. The storm-surge barrier case was best for security (assuming the scour problem is solved) and employment, near best overall (depending on the goal) for ecology, but by far the worst for cost. The open case was perhaps best for ecology overall (depending on the goal), best for fishing, but worst for employment and certainly security.

As in all such studies, the impacts and conclusions presented in the POLANO report must be viewed with certain qualifications. First, strictly speaking, the results apply only for specific designs and design variations of considered in the sensitivity analyses. This qualification is important primarily for the storm-surge barrier, whose design was still in flux when the analysis was completed; indeed, its design was changed, after the analysis was done, from pillars-on-pits to a new concept called the *pillar solution*. Most conclusions of the study, however, are quite robust: A design modification may change the *value* of a particular impact, but usually not its *ranking* with respect to the other alternatives. For example, a new design for the storm-surge barrier is likely to have a different cost than the pillars-on-pits design, but the storm-surge barrier case will doubtless still be the most expensive and create the most employment.

Second, there are several major uncertainties underlying the results that are capable of altering the values for particular impacts and, in some instances, their rankings. There is one major uncertainty common to all three cases: If the recreational policy in the Oosterschelde region were to switch from the present no-investment policy, intended to discourage recreational growth, to an unrestrained-investment policy, then the recreational impact values shown in Table 3.4 would be changed and all the rankings would be reversed. Except for this, the closed case has no major uncertainties, and the open case has only one other—the risk of structural defects in the dike foundations, whose potential size and possible solutions are both unknown. The storm-surge barrier case, however, has several additional major uncertainties: Because it is a large-scale R&D project, its construction costs may be underestimated. It needs additional research to ensure that the risk of serious scour is in fact negligible and it needs measurements of detritus import and sedimentation to reduce the ecological uncertainties.

The Decision

On 5 April 1976, one year after POLANO began, Rand presented a summary report in the form of an all-day briefing at the Rijkswaterstaat headquarters; it described the methodological framework and summarized the results of the analysis. Rand then helped the Dutch members of the POLANO team to

Section 3.5. Providing Energy for the Future 109

combine the jointly obtained POLANO results with the results of several special Rijkswaterstaat studies. This work became the foundation of the Rijkswaterstaat's May 1976 report, *Analysis of Oosterschelde Alternatives* (Rijkswaterstaat, 1976), which was presented first to the Cabinet and then to Parliament, along with the Cabinet's recommendation for a decision.

The Cabinet recommended the storm-surge barrier plan, with a small eastern basin, to Parliament. This plan was adopted in June 1976, but no aperture size was specified for the barrier. Parliament requested additional analysis by the Rijkswaterstaat to help determine the best aperture size, in the range from 11,500 top 20,000 square meters. In September 1977, on the recommendation of an interdepartmental advisory committee, Parliament approved an aperture of 14,500 square meters. Construction is now (1984) underway.

Even before construction of the storm-surge barrier began, it was realized that more detailed attention had to be given to the control strategy for operating the barrier's many large gates. Such a strategy includes (1) the actions that govern the times and rates at which gates close and open, (2) the rules underlying the decisions for these actions, and (3) gathering and processing the required information. The strategy had implications that would affect the design of the barrier. To assist the Rijkswaterstaat in determining a control strategy, a Barrier Control (BARCON) Project was established in April 1977. The Rijkswaterstaat contracted with Rand for the study and set up a Dutch counterpart research team. This work has been completed (Catlett et al., 1979).

3.5. Providing Energy for the Future

Today's economies are run largely on fossil fuels—coal, natural gas, and especially oil—energy sources that in the next 40–100 years will be exhausted or at least too costly to exploit except for very specialized purposes. To provide the necessary energy the world's economies must soon begin to use renewable sources, and do so at an expanding rate. Whether the rate can be accelerated rapidly enough not to require radical changes in growth and consumption patterns throughout the world is a question that presents a host of problems, technical, social, and political.

In mid-1973, during the so-called energy crisis, the International Institute for Applied Systems Analysis (IIASA) began a program of study to provide insights into the long-term dimensions of various energy problems. It was clear—or at least it soon became clear—that the term "energy crisis" was misleading; difficulties in supplying and using energy were not temporary and were spread throughout society. They would continue, and the nations of the world would have to learn to deal with them. The objective of the study became more focused: to find a feasible way to provide sources of energy that could be sustained for the foreseeable future. The aim was not to find the optimal way, or even a politically acceptable way, but merely, given a few reasonable assumptions about political and social conditions, to find a technologically possible path to take us from the state of uncertainty that existed in the 1970s, and still exists today, to a state in which future energy sources appear secure and adequate for the entire world. The study is reported in a two-volume work (Energy Systems Program Group of IIASA, 1981), from which the summary of this section is taken.

A 50-year time frame, from 1980 to 2030, was selected for the work. One reason for such a long time period is that in the past it has taken roughly 50 years for a new type of primary energy to increase its market share from 10 to 50 percent of the total supply. It was also felt that at least two human generations (or 50 years) would be needed to accommodate changes in the social infrastructure that have to parallel the required changes in the technical infrastructure. Yet for certain aspects of the study 50 years is not long enough, particularly when one looks ahead to the time when inevitably no fossil resources will be available.

It also became clear that no long-term solution to the energy problem is possible within a single nation or region. One reason is that the impact of energy-related human activities on the environment can no longer be considered negligible. Another is that today roughly 25 percent of the world's energy comes from one place on the globe, the Middle East, thus creating a strong technical and political linkage between almost all parts of the world. On the demand side the situation is similar. It thus seems appropriate to treat the world as a whole, for otherwise more than one nation may plan to import the same barrel of oil, ton of coal, or uranium ore.

Many factors affect every path to an energy future. They include the current demand for energy and the changing rate of increase in demand, the absolute size of energy resources and their allocation through trade, the build-up rates of supply facilities, the rate at which new sources can be introduced, the total size and nature of environmental and ecological impacts, the management of these impacts, the societal and political acceptance of the required technical and economic changes, the relation between energy policy and social problems, and so on. A complete investigation would require that all these elements be handled adequately. Although three of the impacts were considered in the study—innovation rates, management of environmental and ecological impacts, and social and political acceptance of technoeconomic changes—the IIASA team felt that more complete research than it could provide was needed. The last factor, the relation between energy problems and policies and more general social problems, was not treated, although a number of relevant assumptions were made. First, constraints on possible solutions were limited to those that were physical or structural; political and social constraints were recognized but were not applied explicitly, allowing the entire range of tech-

Section 3.5. Providing Energy for the Future

nologically possible alternatives to be explored. Second, the study assumed a surprise-free future; no major catastrophes such as nuclear wars and no technological breakthroughs that cannot be anticipated today were assumed to occur. Third, population and economic growth were assumed to be modest (a world population of no more than 8×10^9 by 2030, for instance). Also assumed were major energy conservation and aggressive exploration for additional energy resources plus a functioning world trade in oil, gas, and coal, so that the interim needs of all parts of the world could be met. Fourth, in all cost evaluations, the dollar and other monetary units were assumed to have constant value, thus decoupling the terms of trade from the effects of inflation.

The project began by characterizing energy demands, supply opportunities, and constraints and then matching them. To manage the wide variety of resources, economic systems, and industrial structures found in the various nations and regions of the world, it was found possible to consider seven groupings homogeneous in the factors of interest. These groupings were selected for their economic and energy similarities rather than for geographic proximity. The study did not merely add up national energy projections but examined regional economic growth patterns and energy intensity trends that,

Figure 3.9. The estimate of the world's population growth used in the IIASA energy study. (*From Energy Systems Program Group of IIASA, 1981.*)

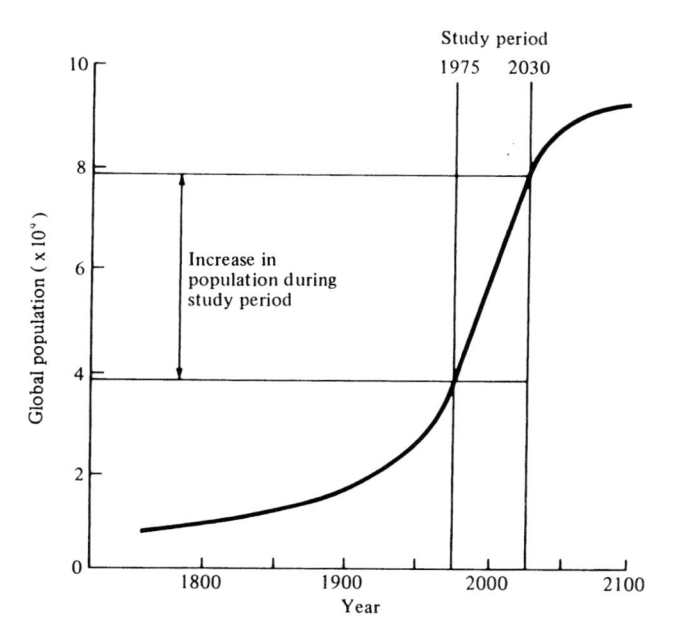

when coupled with population figures and prices, provided long-term estimates of energy demand.

Demand

Three major factors affect energy demand—population, economic, and technological growth. Demand is also affected by the associated changes in lifestyle and urbanization. To estimate these changes, a break down even finer than into regions was required. As derived by the IIASA studies, the expected number of people on earth is expected to increase from 4000 to 8000 million (4 to 8 $\times$ 10^9) by 2030. As illustrated in Figure 3.9, the flattening of the population growth curve that begins about 2030 would have largely taken place by 2100, making it possible to envisage population conditions as becoming relatively stable. Total primary energy demand was estimated to lie somewhere in the range of 16 to 40 TWyr/yr. (One terawatt-year, or 1 TWyr, is 10^{12} watt-years and is equivalent to 5.2 $\times$ 10^9 barrels of oil.) In 1975 global primary energy consumption was 8.2 TWyr/yr.

One other important factor in the demand for energy is the real cost of energy—that is, its cost relative to other goods and services. The use or nonuse of energy cannot be considered a principal goal; energy, along with other resources, is an input to lives and work. Depending on the costs, one exchanges the amounts of the various inputs to produce the results one wants. When the price of energy goes up, we use less of energy and more of other things.

Technological progress tends to increase efficiency and thus to decrease energy demand. Changes in lifestyle can either increase or decrease energy demand. Up to now the result has been a decrease in demand per unit of productive output, but an increase in per capita energy demand, one that is expected to continue.

Another factor affecting energy demand is urbanization; increased urbanization brings with it an increased per capita consumption of energy. By 2030 it is expected that 70 percent of the world population will live in urban areas, as compared to slightly over 40 percent today.

Supply

The study established that, in a purely physical sense, there is no energy supply problem. There are sources whose production rate and durability are virtually unlimited; this is true, for instance, for nuclear breeders and fusion reactors and for solar power. However, the world has not as yet invested the capital and prepared the facilities to make use of these sources. With additional large investments of capital and skill, the study demonstrated that environmental and ecological impacts can be almost totally eliminated. Strong conservation measures will largely take care of demand. Hence, in a technical sense, given adequate time to take the necessary measures, there should be no energy problem. But there is one, and it is getting worse. The problem thus becomes one of finding a path for doing what is necessary, one that is not only possible in principle but also one that humanity may be persuaded to take.

Such a path is beset by constraints—on water, land, materials, manpower, risk, market substitutability, and so on. Supply capabilities are constrained by whatever forces limit each particular technology—public approval for nuclear power, carbon dioxide for fossil fuel combustion, market penetration, and the economics of central station supply for solar power. Each potential source—nuclear, central-station solar power, individual small-scale installations, wind, biomass, ocean currents, and so on—had to be investigated in detail and its advantages and drawbacks taken in account.

Consider coal, as an illustration. The total amount of recoverable coal that might fall within reach of economically viable technical capabilities is tremendous. To exploit it, however, there are very large water, energy, land, material, and manpower requirements, coupled with the problem of building the mining and transportation capabilities for producing and handling it. Burning coal in the quantities required to substitute for oil and gas would violate any limit one might like to set on carbon dioxide emissions.

Consequently, coal use must be viewed differently than it has been in the past. It cannot be the dominant energy source in a high-energy-consuming world, but, as a large source of chemically reduced carbon, it can be used as a base from which to synthesize liquid fuels when oils become too expensive—as they eventually must. Since the demand for liquid fuel is the driving force behind the energy problem, the study devoted most of its work on coal to ways to convert the coal enterprise step by step into a liquid fuel synthesis industry, and to do it in a way that would minimize carbon dioxide emission. This implies allothermal liquefaction through the use of hydrogen produced exogenously from nuclear or solar sources, along with carbon from coal to produce methanol or other synthetic hydrocarbons. This method, as opposed to autothermal liquefaction, in which the process heat comes from coal itself, requires less coal and releases far less carbon dioxide.

System Properties

The energy problem exists in the context of the continuity of human institutions and the maintenance of a healthy environment. This context acts as an overall constraint on what can be done to alleviate the problem.

Demands, resources, technologies, and constraints must be integrated and balanced in order to find out if a feasible path to sustainable energy future can be established. In the study integration and balance were achieved iteratively by developing two scenarios plus a number of variations. The IIASA high scenario was chosen to be consistent with relatively high economic growth throughout the world, leading to a level of global primary energy consumption

Table 3.7. Global Primary Energy Demand by Source for the High and Low Scenarios[a]

Primary source	Base year (1975)	High scenario 2000	High scenario 2030	Low scenario 2000	Low scenario 2030
Oil	3.83	5.89	6.83	4.75	5.02
Gas	1.51	3.11	5.97	2.53	3.47
Coal	2.26	4.94	11.98	3.92	6.45
Light water reactor	0.12	1.70	3.21	1.27	1.89
Fast breeder reactor	0	0.04	4.88	0.02	3.28
Hydroelectricity	0.50	0.83	1.46	0.83	1.46
Solar	0	0.10	0.49	0.09	0.30
Other[b]	0	0.22		81	0.17
					0.52
Total[c]	8.21	16.84	35.65	13.59	22.39

[a] The figures in the table are in terawatt-years per year, where 1 terawatt = 10^{12} watts and 1 terawatt-year is the equivalent of 5.2×10^9 barrels of oil.
[b] Includes biogas, geothermal, and commercial wood use.
[c] Columns may not sum to totals owing to rounding.
Source: Energy Systems Program Group of IIASA (1981).

in 2030 equal to slightly more than four times the 1975 level. The IIASA low scenario assumed lower economic growth rates, leading in 2030 to a little less than three times the 1975 rate of primary energy consumption. Table 3.7 shows the energy demand developed from the two scenarios, and Figure 3.10 shows the proportionate shares (the growth of coal liquification being especially important).

These scenarios and the variations were prepared using a sequence of mathematical models, assisted by the judgment and intuition (i.e., by the various mental models) of the participants. Neither of the scenarios is intended as a prediction of what future energy development will be like; the future might develop like either of the two scenarios, but the possibility it would do so is extremely unlikely. Total energy consumption by 2030 might well fall somewhere in between, but large differences in how the sources are distributed between, say, nuclear and solar power might still exist.

The supply explorations and scenario constructions are, in a sense, the tangible products of the study. The first demonstrates that the required energy is physically present. The second indicates technically plausible and consistent ways in which new energy sources might first supplement and then, by 2030, begin to replace the current fossil sources.

The most important conclusion of the IIASA study is that it is technically feasible to meet the world's future energy needs. There are, of course, difficulties and expenses involved, but the world is not doomed because nature has not given us the necessary endowment for 8 billion people, or even for a larger number, such as 12 billion. There is thus a factual basis on which political and social issues, such as setting environmental standards or determining development policies for nuclear power, can be investigated and dealt with.

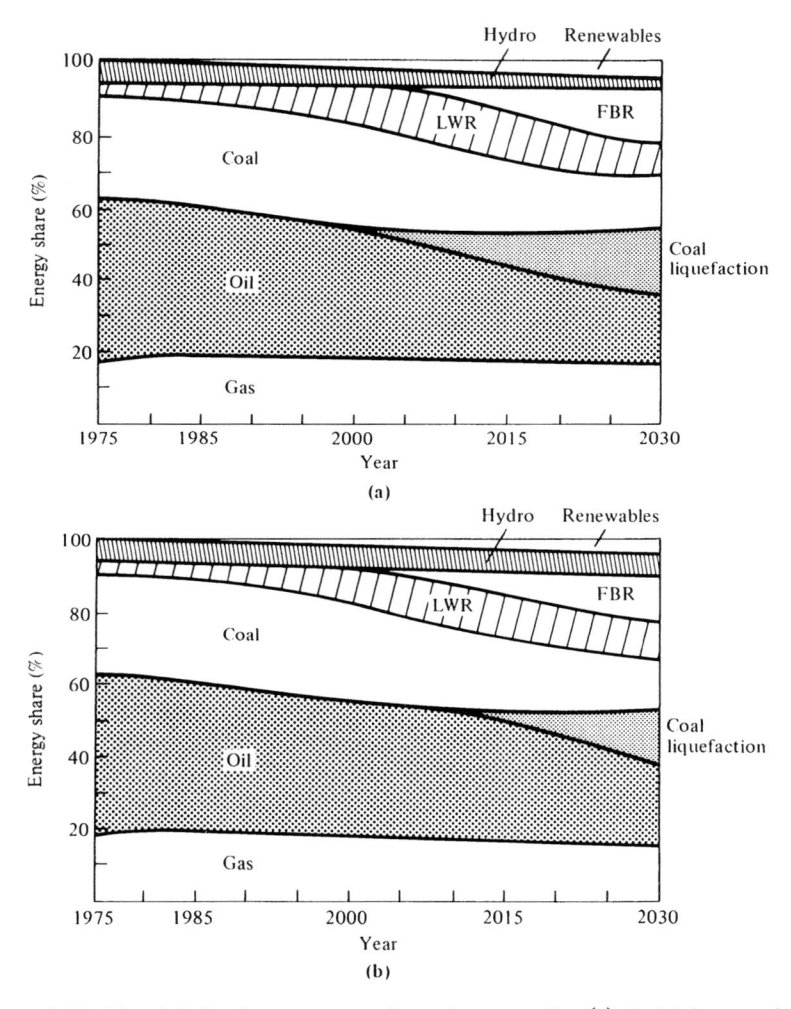

Figure 3.10 The global primary energy shares by source for (a) the high scenario and (b) the low scenario. (*From Energy Systems Program Group of IIASA, 1981.*)

References

Abrahamse, A. F., et al. (1977). *Protecting an Estuary from Floods—A Policy Analysis of the Oosterschelde. Vol. II: Assessment of Security from Flooding,* R-2121/2-NETH. Santa Monica, California: The Rand Corporation.

Bigelow, J. H., and J. C. DeHaven (1977). *Protecting an Estuary from Floods—A Policy Analysis of Oosterschelde. Vol. V: Anaerobic Conditions and Related Ecological Disturbances,* R-2121/5-NETH. Santa Monica, California: The Rand Corporation.

———, J. G. Bolten, and J. C. DeHaven (1977a). *Protecting an Estuary from Floods— A Policy Analysis of the Oosterschelde. Vol. III: Assessment of Long-Run Ecological Balances,* R-2121/3-NETH. Santa Monica, California: The Rand Corporation.

_____, _____, _____(1977b). *Protecting an Estuary from Floods—A Policy Analysis of the Oosterschelde. Vol. IV: Assessment of Algae Blooms, a Potential Ecological Disturbance,* R-2121/4-NETH. Santa Monica, California: The Rand Corporation.

Brodheim, E., and G. Prastacos (1979). The Long Island blood distribution system as a prototype for regional blood management. *Interfaces* 9, 3–20.

Catlett, L., et al. (1979). *Controlling the Oosterschelde Storm-Surge Barrier—A Policy Analysis of Alternative Strategies. Vol. I: Summary Report,* R-2444/1-NETH. Santa Monica, California: The Rand Corporation.

Chesler, L. G., and B. F. Goeller (1973). *The STAR Methodology for Short-Haul Transportation: Transportation Impact Assessment,* R-1359-DOT, Section II. Santa Monica, California: The Rand Corporation.

de Ferranti, D. M., F. J. P. Heuer, and J. W. Weehuizen (1977). *Protecting an Estuary from Floods—A Policy Analysis of the Oosterschelde. Vol. VI: Selected Social and Economic Aspects,* R-2121/6-NETH. Santa Monica, California: The Rand Corporation.

Energy Systems Program Group of the International Institute for Applied Systems Analysis, Wolf Haefele, Program Leader (1981). *Energy in a Finite World: Vol. 1. Paths to a Sustainable Future; Vol. 2. A Global Systems Analysis.* Cambridge, Massachusetts: Ballinger. [See also *Energy in a Finite World: Executive Summary.* Laxenburg, Austria: International Institute for Applied Systems Analysis.]

Forrester, J. W. (1969). *Urban Dynamics.* Cambridge, Massachusetts: The MIT Press.

Goeller, B. F., A. F. Abrahamse, J. H. Bigelow, J. G. Bolten, D. M. de Ferranti, J. C. DeHaven, T. F. Kirkwood, and R. L. Petruschell (1977). *Protecting an Estuary from Floods—A Policy Analysis of the Oosterschelde. Vol. I: Summary Report,* R-2121/1-NETH. Santa Monica, California: The Rand Corporation.

Prastacos, G. (1984). Blood inventory management: An overview of theory and practice. *Management Science* 30, 777–799.

_____, and E. Brodheim (1980). PBDS: A decision support system for regional blood management. *Management Science* 26, 451–463.

Rijkswaterstaat (1976). *Analysis of Oosterschelde Alternatives.* (An English translation is available: *Policy Analysis of Eastern Scheldt Alternatives,* Nota DDRF-77.158. The Hague, Netherlands: Rijkswaterstaat.)

Sen, A. K. (1970). *Collective Choice and Social Welfare.* San Francisco: Holden-Day.

Singleton, David W. (1975). Firefighting productivity in Wilmington: A case history. *Public Productivity Review* 1(2), 19–29.

Walker, Warren E. (1975). *The Development of Emergency Services: A Guide to Selected Methods and Models,* R-1867-HUD. Santa Monica, California: The Rand Corporation.

_____(1978). *Changing Fire Company Locations: Five Implementation Case Studies,* 023-000-00456-9. Washington, D.C.: Government Printing Office.

_____, Jan M. Chaiken, and Edward J. Ignall, eds. (1979). *Fire Department Deployment Analysis—A Public Policy Analysis Case Study (The Rand Fire Project).* New York: North-Holland.

_____, David W. Singleton, and Bruce Smith (1975). *An Analysis of the Deployment*

Chapter 4
The Methodology of Systems Analysis: An Introduction and Overview

Władysław Findeisen and Edward S. Quade

4.1. Introduction

For a systems analysis to be undertaken, someone must think there is a problem—or at least recognize the possibility that a problem exists. That is, he must be dissatisfied with the current or anticipated state of affairs and want help in discovering how to bring about a change for the better. Systems analysis can almost always provide help, even if it does no more than turn up relevant information or indicate that certain actions offer little hope of bringing about improvement. In most circumstances, the analysis may even discover a course of action that will bring about the desired change, a course that can be recognized as the most advantageous and implemented by those with authority to act.

Systems analysis can also be used to present factual arguments and reliable information to help win acceptance for a proposed course of action. In addition, it can help, both before and during the implementation process, to prevent the chosen course from being rendered ineffective by adverse interests, misinterpretations, or unanticipated problems. This chapter, however, is restricted to presenting the methodology of systems analysis insofar as it relates to discovering better solutions or information that may lead to them: advice as to how systems analysis can be used as an instrument of persuasion or an aid to implementation is postponed to Chapters 8–10. The difficulties in winning acceptance for a course of action and then implementing it must nevertheless be considered during the process of seeking and evaluating a possible solution. A course of action that is not acceptable to those who must approve it, or that cannot be implemented for political or other reasons, is not a solution.

Although a systems analysis may be carried out without a specific user or set of users in mind, such work is not likely to have much influence other than to inform public debate. This chapter therefore discusses the methodology as if the analysis were commissioned by, and carried out for, a single decisionmaker. He is assumed to be an individual who wants to make decisions as rationally as possible by taking into consideration the probable consequences of each available course of action—selecting the "best" action by balancing its cost against the extent to which it helps to achieve his objectives and possible other benefits. (As a simple extension, we can also consider the single decisionmaker to be replaced by a relatively small group with roughly similar preferences.) The analyst's basic procedure is to determine what the decisionmaker wants, search out his feasible alternatives, work out the consequences that would follow the decision to adopt each of the alternatives, and then, either rank the alternatives in terms of their consequences according to criteria specified by the decisionmaker, or present the alternatives with their consequences (in a framework suitable for comparison) to the decisionmaker for ranking and choice.

In reality, as the examples discussed in Chapters 1 and 3 show, the decisionmaking situation is rarely so uncomplicated. The person for whom a study is done is usually but one of many participants in a decisionmaking process, and he must use the results of the analysis as evidence and argument to bring the others to his point of view before acting. The decisionmaking model of the previous paragraph is not, therefore, an adequate model for decisionmaking in the public sector or for policy and strategy formulation when many decisionmakers are involved. In these cases the decisions cannot be separated from the managerial, organizational, and political situation in which they are made (Mintzberg and Shakun, 1978), and the model we are assuming for the decisionmaker [called the *rational actor model,* or model I by Allison (1971)] must be supplemented or modified by bringing in organizational and political considerations (Allison, 1971; Lynn, 1978; Rein and White, 1977). Nevertheless, as Allison (1971, p. 268) remarks, "For solving problems, a Model I–style analysis provides the best first cut. Indeed, for analyzing alternatives and distinguishing the preferred proposal, there is no clear alternative to this basic framework." Therefore, throughout this chapter, we stick to this basic, unsophisticated view of the decisionmaking situation.

As an example to illustrate the basic procedure, assume that a legislative committee wants to propose legislation to increase highway safety. It is willing to consider three alternatives: a requirement for devices to make the use of seat belts automatic, lowering the maximum speed limit and enforcing it more strictly, and establishing higher standards for issuing drivers' licenses. They ask the legislative analyst to carry out a systems analysis.

It is useful to consider a problem of this type in terms of these elements:

Objectives—what the decisionmaker desires to achieve. In the example, the objective is increased highway safety, a goal whose achievement the analysis must determine how to measure.

Alternatives—the means by which it may be possible to achieve the objectives. Depending on the problem, the alternatives may be policies, strategies,

Section 4.1. Introduction   119

designs, actions, or whatever it appears might attain the objective. In the example, although the alternatives are limited to three types, within each type there are many possibilities to consider.

Consequences—the results that would ensue were the alternative to be adopted and put into effect. In the highway safety example, if the alternative of a lower maximum speed limit with stricter enforcement were implemented, a positive consequence (a benefit) would be a lower rate of fatal highway accidents; a negative consequence (a cost) would be the need for more police officers to be hired or taken from other tasks. Other terms are often used instead of consequences: In environmental analysis, the consequences are called *impacts*; in decision theory, *attributes*; and elsewhere the terms may be *outcomes, effects,* or *results.*

Criteria—rules or standards that specify in terms of consequences (or some subset of them) how the alternatives are to be ranked in order of desirability. For the example, a possible—although not necessarily a sensible—criterion might be to rank the alternatives in decreasing order of the ratio of the reduction in the annual number of fatalities from implementing the alternative to the expenditure of public funds required.

Model—an abstraction, a set of assumptions about some aspect of the world, either real or imaginary, intended to clarify our view of an object, process, or problem by retaining only characteristics essential to the purpose we have in mind. It is a simplified conceptual or physical image that may be used to investigate the behavior of a system or the result of an action without altering the system or taking the action. The simple scrawl we might use to represent a road network in giving directions to a passing motorist is a model; it replaces the need to escort the motorist to his destination. Note that it is a simplification of the real world tailored to a specific purpose; it does not include information extraneous to the purpose in mind such as scenic highlights along the way, or where restaurants are located, or when parking is permitted. If the model's purpose were different, say, because the motorist wanted to use it as a guide to where to lunch along the way, then additional information would be included and the model changed.

A model is made up of factors relevant to the problem and the relations among them essential to the purpose in mind. A model may take many forms. Some common types are a set of tables, a series of mathematical equations, a computer program, a physical simulation (rare for systems analysis), or, most often in everyday life, merely a mental image of the situation held by someone contemplating an action. Such conceptual or mental models are, unfortunately, rarely made explicit with a sequence of logical arguments. Often they are no more than hunches, frequently provably wrong when made explicit. In one form or another models must be used throughout every analytic process. (For more discussion, see Chapter 7.)

In most systems analyses explicit models are normally used for predicting both the context or environment in which the alternatives are to be implemented and their associated consequences. This is necessary because the factors are usually so numerous and their interrelations so complex that intuition and mental models are not adequate to handle the large number of factors and their intricate relations. Some highway safety measures, for instance, have counterintuitive effects: Certain crash barriers reduce fatalities but increase some kinds of injuries. Other measures have interdependencies that strongly affect their joint performance: An energy-absorbing bumper, for instance, would save more lives if it were installed alone rather than in combination with a shoulder harness (Goeller, 1969a).

Predicting consequences is not the only, or even the first, use of models in a systems analysis. It is however, the most prominent use, for such models are likely to be elaborate and programmed for a computer, whereas many other models used in systems analysis may be no more than well-thought-through concepts. In our example many different models are needed to estimate the results for the alternatives, and their consequences are of different types. For instance, a model to estimate the monetary costs of doubling the strength of the highway patrol must differ from a model for predicting what effect the presence of an increased patrol force will have on traffic fatalities. [For a discussion of traffic safety models, see Goeller (1969b). For the mathematics underlying some models, see Mood (1982).]

In our example an early problem for the analyst is to find a way to turn the vague goal of increased highway safety into something of a more operational character—in other words, to settle on a way to measure it. One measure might be the reduction in the annual number of fatalities; another might be the reduction in the annual (monetary) cost of highway accidents to the victims. The full list of possibilities may be long, and finding suitable scales for some of them is often a problem in itself.

Unfortunately, the choice of measure may affect critically how the alternatives are ranked. For instance, while strict enforcement of the speed limit may reduce fatalities—a serious consequence of high-speed collisions—it may have little effect on the number and cost of "fender-bending" accidents—which are numerous and costly to the participants. More stringent requirements for a driver's license may reduce both significantly.

Another task for the analyst is to check the alternatives for feasibility. It may turn out, for example, that, in the current state of the art of automotive engineering, the alternative of automated seat belts is not feasible owing to, say, public unacceptability. Of course, if this alternative were far superior to all the others in increasing safety, the decisionmaker would probably want to investigate the cost and effectiveness of a campaign to change public opinion. This typifies how problems expand. Similarly, the analyst may find that the passage of legislation to lower the current maximum speed limit is not feasible. This alternative may then have to be replaced by stricter enforcement of traffic regulations.

The analyst will also want to search for and examine alternatives not on the original list—such things as better emergency ambulance service, eliminating unguarded railroad crossings, and changed car design—for these alternatives may promise increased highway safety at less cost than those on the original list, and, when presented with supporting calculations, may lead the decisionmakers to expand the list of possibilities they are willing to consider. Indeed, as will be emphasized in Chapter 6, the discovery, invention, or design of new and better alternatives is often the real payoff from systems analysis.

In predicting the results associated with the various alternatives, as we remarked earlier, the analyst may have to use radically differing models or methods. A model to show the effect of improved driving skills on the number fatalities can differ considerably from a model to predict the way a lower speed limit affects fatalities. On the other hand, predictions for both cases may be obtained statistically from experiences in other jurisdictions with similar driving conditions, although it may not be easy to define "similar". In comparing alternatives various future contexts may also have to be considered, with predictions or conjectures made about the effects of, for instance, a petroleum shortage on automobile traffic, changing car preferences, population movement, and other exogenous factors beyond the decisionmakers' control.

One run-through of the set of procedures is seldom enough. Several cycles or iterations are almost always necessary to refine the first models and assumptions, and thus increase one's confidence in the outcomes. For instance, it may be discovered that certain alternatives that restrict automobile drivers produce effects that spill over onto entirely different groups of people (say, those that ride public transportation) in ways that differ from alternative to alternative and that were not anticipated when the alternatives were first formulated. Additional emergency medical services for traffic accident victims, for instance, may increase the burden on the supply of doctors and hospital beds, and hence the analyst may have to enlarge the analysis to include aspects of the medical and public transportation systems and carry out additional calculations.

With this background, we now turn to a more detailed and thorough description of the procedures we have suggested.

4.2. A Framework for Systems Analysis

Objectives, Alternatives, and Ranking

Most problems [Ackoff (1957) argues all problems, but see Checkland (1981, p. 155)] ultimately reduce to evaluating the efficiency of alternative means for a designated set of objectives. Analysis to assist someone to discover his best course of action may thus be considered as an inquiry into three basic questions:

1. What are his objectives?
2. What are his alternatives for attaining these objectives?
3. How should the alternatives be ranked?

The three questions expand further when we consider these points:

To be able to identify the feasible alternatives, one must know not only the objectives but also the constraints within which the decisionmaker is free to act.

Before the consequences can be determined, one must consider the context in which the alternatives are to be implemented, but such future contexts are uncertain.

To determine the consequences, one needs models to predict what will happen if the decisionmaker chooses an alternative, given each particular contingency, context, or future state of the world being considered.

If the analyst is to rank the alternatives, it is necessary to investigate the decisionmaker's value system and that of any other parties whose opinions the decisionmaker may wish, or be forced, to consider.

A Framework for Analysis

Systems analysis, like science, is a craft (Majone, 1980). The way in which a study is organized and carried out depends on many choices made by the analyst that are often based on little more than professional experience and informed intuition. An approach that may produce valuable insights when used by one analyst may yield faulty or misleading conclusions when used by another. Nevertheless, every systems analysis will be composed of certain more or less typical activities that have to be linked to each other appropriately. From this point of view, we can present a first approximation to the systems-analysis process schematically, as in Figure 4.1, where the main components are represented (other breakdowns are, of course, possible, and the order in which one approaches a study may vary):

1. formulating the problem;
2. identifying, designing, and screening the possible alternatives;
3. forecasting future contexts or states of the world;
4. building and using models for predicting the results; and
5. comparing and ranking the alternatives.

These components encompass several additional activities, three of which are indicated in Figure 4.1: *determining the boundaries and constraints, identifying the objectives,* and *determining the decisionmaker's values and criteria.*

Section 4.2. A Framework for Systems Analysis 123

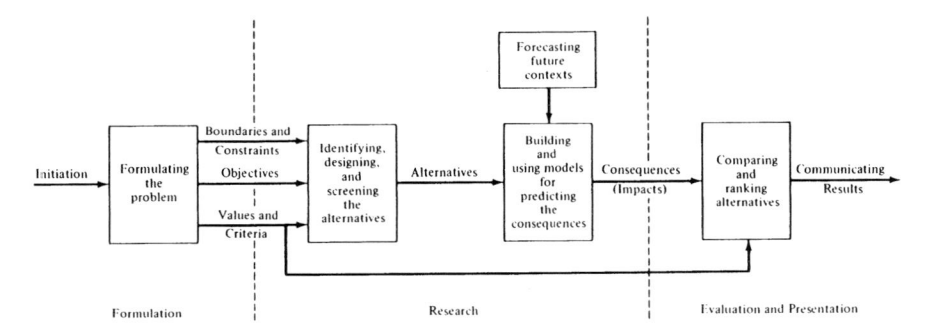

Figure 4.1. The systems-analysis procedure.

Among the activities omitted from Figure 4.1 but needed for every analysis are *data collection and analysis,* and *communication between analyst and decisionmaker.* Further, it does not show either the possible followup activities that may follow a systems analysis whose recommendations are adopted or the evaluation work that may accompany the implementation process.

The arrows in Figure 4.1 show the principal flows of information from activity to activity.

Iteration and Feedback

In most investigations, few of the component activities depicted in Figure 4.1 can be performed adequately in a single trial. Iteration is needed; that is, intermediate results, or even a preliminary version of the final result, may force the analyst to alter initial assumptions, revise earlier work, or collect more data. A decisionmaker, for instance, may not settle on a set of objectives until there is a good idea of what can be done, or the decisionmaker may want to impose additional constraints after discovering what some of the consequences are.

Figure 4.2 shows some of the typical iterations and feedback loops in a systems analysis study. However, the figure does not show the essential continuing interactions with the decisionmaker that accompany the analysis. These can easily affect its course, since they occur frequently and respond to the issues and preliminary findings that appear in the analysis, rather than follow a preset course.

One feedback loop is from the consequences to designing alternatives. For instance, the decisionmaker may become aware that the alternative he would like to select has certain features that may later present difficulties in implementation; he may then suggest changes in the alternative and want to know how they will affect its standing. By the feedback loop from consequences to designing alternatives, we modify or refine some of the alternatives (typically

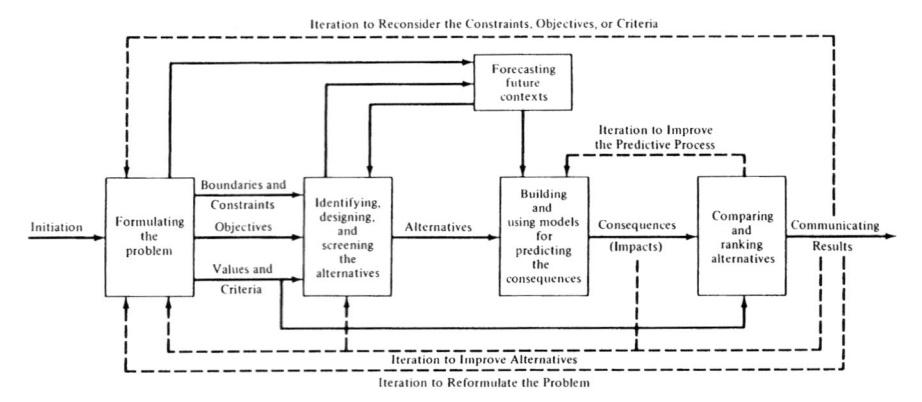

124   Chapter 4. The Methodology of Systems Analysis

Figure 4.2. The systems-analysis procedure with iteration loops. (The figure does not show the essential continuing interactions between the analysis team and the decisionmaker involved.)

by adjusting their parameters) after considering the consequences of doing so. The process of refinement through iteration may be done separately for each alternative; it is sometimes, although rarely, based on a formal optimization procedure.

Another typical loop is the one from the model results back to problem formulation. This iteration is necessary because it is usually impossible to set the objectives and determine the constraints with precision before knowing something about their implications. It may become clear, for instance, that more can be achieved than originally seemed possible. A first cut at comparing and ranking alternatives may also suggest a need for redefining them, since the characteristics that make certain alternatives superior may become obvious for the first time; in fact, it may be necessary to design an entirely new set of alternatives.

Furthermore, we—or the decisionmaker—may be dissatisfied with the results obtained under our current assumptions and constraints. Iterations may be needed and carried out to see what the "cost" of the constraint is, that is, how much more of the objective could be obtained or how much the monetary cost could be lowered if a constraint were weakened. We may eventually negotiate removing, or softening, some of the constraints. If this is not possible, the decisionmaker's objectives may have to be lowered. Iterative sensitivity investigations may also lead us to further efforts at refinement.

Another important purpose of iteration is to improve the models used for prediction. The process may result in simplification as elements and relations originally thought to be significant are found to have negligible effect.

Analysis does not necessarily end when iteration no longer brings significant improvement and the various courses of action open to the decisionmaker have been compared, ranked, and presented for his choice. As mentioned in Section 4.1, an analyst, although not necessarily the original one, may also be needed to provide assistance with additional tasks—to help resolve unanticipated problems arising during discussions with other decisionmakers or problems arising during implementation of the decision, and, even much later, to evaluate the results after the process of implementation has succeeded (or failed).

Although most of the infeasible alternatives should have been screened out during the earlier stages of the analysis, the implementability of a course of action may remain in question even after implementation is well under way. One reason is that the final decision may not have been presented in a way adequate to instruct and motivate those who have to execute it and who may have their own ideas as to how to interpret it. There may also be considerations that are important for implementation [such as the need to revamp the implementing institutions or resistance due to "traditions" (Shils, 1981)], but that were not important to the choice between alternatives. In order to keep the problem workable, these considerations may not have been investigated in detail.

Implementation may not start until long after the analysis is completed, so that changes in the state of the world different from those forecast in the analysis may require the implementation process to be modified. What was the future during the analysis may have now become the past, and an analyst may be needed once again to modify a program that is now partially inappropriate. Indeed, the need for a complete reanalysis can never be totally dismissed.

Finally, the analyst may be called on to assist the decisionmaker in evaluating the progress of the implementation, for, by virtue of the analyst's previous studies of the problem and knowledge of the cause–effect relations, he may be able to detect the reasons for discrepancies and deviations from the effects originally intended.

Communication

Communication is important for the success of systems analysis. Communication with the decisionmaker is vital, not only to discover his goals and the constraints under which he operates, but also because his advice and judgment are indispensable at all stages of the analysis—and he must not be surprised by an unexpected outcome (Walker, 1978). The results are much more likely to be accepted and used if the decisionmaker and his staff participate in producing them. Throughout the procedure there should therefore be a continuous dialogue between the analyst and the decisionmaker and his staff. This dialogue influences their attitude toward the problem even before the study is finished and helps to make sure that all important facets of the real situation are considered. The constant exchange of information also means that the results will not come to the decisionmaker or his staff as a shock— a circumstance that can alone lead them to reject the findings.

Another reason for continuing communication is that the initial problem formulation can never be complete and all-inclusive. As mentioned above, preliminary results of the analysis will modify the initial views, new questions will arise, and the preferences, constraints, and time horizons may change.

Phases of Analysis

There are many more linkages between the component activities of systems analysis than those shown in Figure 4.2. Despite this complex interdependence, it is convenient to discuss the procedure in three phases:

1. *formulation*;
2. *research*, comprising generating, investigating, and screening alternatives, forecasting the contexts, and determining the consequences; and
3. *presentation*, comprising comparison and documentation.

We shall characterize the phases of systems analysis, as well as the more important component activities, in more detail in the following sections.

Partial Analysis

Before doing so, however, we note that not every successful systems analysis study contains every phase or component. Here are some typical examples:

In forecasts of the future state of the world no immediate action may be contemplated (as in the econometric forecasts that analysts are asked to provide governments or large industrial companies).

Impact analysis consists in determining all the significant consequences, or merely a certain class of consequences, of a proposed action. For example, environmental impact studies, to determine the consequences of a particular technological development on the environment, may involve no comparison or ranking.

Decision analysis provides assistance in making a choice among a limited number of well-specified alternatives whose consequences are assumed to be known. Here the analysis merely provides a framework for ranking these alternatives. A typical instance is the choice of an industrial project from among several available alternatives or a decision to select equipment from competing suppliers.

Quick response analysis is carried out under crisis conditions or when time is very short. Here what we later describe as an issue paper (Chapter 5, Appendix B, gives an outline) may be the most that is possible with the available time and resources.

In these examples not all of the component activities of a complete systems analysis are carried out. On the other hand, there are cases where all the activities take place, but where some need to be emphasized more than others.

Whenever a partial analysis is commissioned, the assumption is that someone, usually the decisionmaker, will provide the missing aspects. The decisionmaker will generally do this by judgment or assumptions based on his experience and knowledge of the situation because, while some decisionmakers have the ability to carry out the required analysis, they rarely have the time.

4.3. Problem Formulation

Purposes

Generally speaking, problem formulation (the subject of Chapter 5) implies isolating the questions or issues involved, fixing the context within which the issues are to be resolved, clarifying the objectives and constraints, identifying the people who will be affected by the decision, discovering the major operative factors, and deciding on the initial approach. It is expected that problem formulation will provide, among other things,

- a preliminary statement of the objectives and ways to measure their achievement;
- a specification of some promising courses of action, i.e., alternatives;
- a definition of the constraints;
- an anticipation of the types of consequences to be expected, how to measure them, and possible criteria for ranking them; and
- a plan for the analysis.

Problem formulation should result in specifying the limits of the inquiry, the questions to be addressed, the aspects of the real world to be included, the time frame, and the analytic resources needed to carry out the work. The scope of the problem can be limited by limiting the number and type of alternative actions to be considered, but it is not possible to confine the effects of these actions within neat boundaries.

For many reasons, the problem-formulation stage can be seen as a small-scale systems analysis study in itself. It may involve a very broad range of inquiries into the hierarchies of objectives, the value systems, the various types of constraints, the alternatives available, the presumed consequences, how the people affected will react to the consequences, and so on. The models used for prediction, however, are still crude and may be entirely judgmental. A systematic approach to problem formulation through some fairly formal device such as an elementary form of issue paper may be desirable. (Chapter 5 describes this device and provides further information about problem formulation.)

As one aspect of problem formulation, the analyst must consider the analytic approach to be taken, which, of course, depends on the situation being confronted. For example, if the decisionmaker has been assigned a fixed budget, the analysis may attempt to discover an alternative that is attainable within the given budget and that will enable the decisionmaker to achieve, or most nearly achieve, his objective. Alternatively, it may be that progress is required in correcting some undesirable condition. The analytic objective may then become to discover the point at which the marginal benefits of corrective action become equal to the marginal costs. Another possibility is that the analysis be directed toward ascertaining whether some proposed course of action yields a sufficiently high rate of return on the required investment to make it attractive.

As the study progresses and more information becomes available, the analytic approach may have to be modified.

Formulation involves critical assumptions made by the analyst because alternative formulations leading to different outcomes may seem equally tenable. The decisionmaker's advice is important here in deciding which formulation to accept. Restating the problem in different ways, or in redefining it, can clarify whether it is spurious or trivial and may, indeed, point the way toward a solution. Until the problem is defined and the issues clarified, it may not be clear that the study effort will be worthwhile. The great pitfall is that the result depends on the underlying assumptions made by the formulator, and he and the decisionmaker may not be aware of what these assumptions are.

Problem formulation is a crucial aspect of systems analysis for good reason. As Ackoff (1974, p. 8), speaking of society in general, put it, "We fail more often because we solve the wrong problem than because we get the wrong solution to the right problem."

Objectives

An important part of the analyst's job is to determine what the decisionmaker's objectives actually are; Chapters 5, 6, and 8 give a more thorough discussion of the difficulties frequently encountered at this stage. The terms *goal* and *target* are often used interchangeably with *objective*. However, properly speaking, a goal is more broadly stated, less likely to be quantitative, and usually unspecified as to time; a target, on the other hand, is concrete, quantitative, specified as to time, and operational. An objective lies somewhere between.

In many situations there is a hierarchy of objectives with different levels to consider. Often the levels of objectives differ according to the time horizon. For example, in economic and corporate planning there is a hierarchy of short- and long-term objectives that have to be mutually consistent. The fear of setting objectives that may prove inconsistent with higher-level, more

Section 4.3. Problem Formulation

comprehensive, objectives may lead a decisionmaker to specify an objective at too high a level to be helpful in the analysis. One consequence may be that the choice of the courses of action required to attain the higher-level objective may not be the decisionmaker's to make.

Setting the objectives is a crucial step, since it is the objectives that suggest the possible alternatives. To be considered an alternative, a course of action must appear to offer some chance of attaining the objectives. Sometimes, even though the problem and the objectives are not clearly formulated, people propose a solution and support it strongly. The analyst may then have to work backward from the proposed solution to the assumptions in order to ascertain what problem the proposed solution is supposed to ameliorate and what objectives are being sought.

We would like to be able, for the sake of analysis, to measure the degree to which an objective will be attained by the course of action under consideration. For this reason, if the original objective cannot be satisfactorily quantified, one must often define a proxy objective: a substitute that points in the same direction as the original objective, but which can be measured. For example, income might be a proxy for quality of life. Sometimes the proxy is one dimension of a multidimensional objective, as when reduction in mean travel time is used as a proxy for improved transportation service. In such a case it may be better to use a weighted index in which all dimensions are represented (Raiffa, 1968).

If the degree to which the objective has been attained is measurable in some sense, one can set a target value; for example, an average travel time of 40 minutes. Often, to be more flexible, we prescribe an interval, for example, an average travel time of less than 45 minutes, which leaves more freedom for the choice of alternatives.

In many cases, the decisionmaker has multiple objectives. Sometimes these bear little relation to each other, while in other cases they contribute to a single higher-level objective. An example of the latter situation is the quality of urban life as a higher-level objective to which several component objectives, such as better housing, less air pollution, reduced travel times, less aesthetic discomfort, and others, contribute. If we cannot work out the relative contribution of each factor, we ordinarily seek alternatives that improve, in a measurable degree, all, or the majority, of the contributing component objectives, leaving the ultimate ranking to the decisionmaker.

Multiple objectives are usually competitive; that is, an alternative designed to bring about maximum improvement in one objective is associated with a deterioration in others, because of limited resources or other constraints. For example, a desire for a decrease in noise pollution may force undesirable constraints on the rapidity of urban transportation.

To reconcile multiple objectives may present a serious problem, as treated in Chapter 8 and numerous other publications (e.g., Raiffa, 1968; Keeney and Raiffa, 1977; Mood, 1982).

Values and Criteria

A course of action will have many consequences. Some will contribute to a particular objective, some will detract from it, and still others will act as side effects, that is, consequences that are neutral with respect to the objective, yet with possible productive or counterproductive implications. If we wish to say how good an alternative is, we need not only a measure of value for each of its relevant consequences, but also some way of combining their impacts into a total. If we want, moreover, to be able to rank the different alternatives in order to indicate a preference, we need a criterion. The values held by a decisionmaker, that is to say, the importance he attributes to the various consequences, determine the criterion; hence, if the analyst is to suggest the criterion, the decisionmaker's values must be investigated.

A decisionmaker is likely to be interested in ranking according to more than one criterion: For instance, in effectiveness, for which the alternatives are ranked according to the extent they achieve important outcomes, or in cost-effectiveness (see Section 8.6). The analyst can usually supply such rankings. Equity, the extent to which the benefits and costs are fairly distributed throughout society, is much more difficult for the analyst, although possibilities do exist for ranking according to certain definitions (Dunn, 1981). Adequacy, the extent to which the alternatives solve the problem, may have to be left to the decisionmaker. Sometimes, as in the Oosterschelde example, the entire criterion problem may be best left to the decisionmakers (see also Section 8.8).

Any measure of value is subjective. The same thing may be valued differently by different people. In practice the values of the decisionmaker override those of all other interested parties, because he will decide whether to take a given course of action. In all cases, however, the preferences of the persons or groups that the decisionmaker serves, or of those who will be affected by the decision, must be considered, for the decisionmaker may not only want to take these preferences into account, but may feel it necessary to do so in order to implement what he wants done.

For example, consider the air pollution to be caused by a future industrial plant. If no pollution standards or penalties exist, does this mean that the industrial manager can neglect pollution, although he knows the damage it will cause? Clearly, he cannot—even if moral considerations were not a factor—without considering the cost of the decision to do so. The people affected may (say, through their influence on future standards) affect the profitability of the plant. It is the duty of the analyst in such a case to indicate the impact of pollution on those who will be affected and somehow to transfer their subsequent dissatisfaction to the decisionmaker's balance sheet.

The aim of the systems analyst, especially when working for a client, is to make recommendations based on his analytic work and its assumptions. If the analyst lets his own goals and values override the results of the analysis, he abandons his role as an analyst and assumes that of an "expert" advisor.

This may be an appropriate and desirable role in some circumstances, but, if so, the analyst should make clear that he has assumed it and how it relates to his analysis.

Section 4.7 and Chapter 8 give more attention to criteria problems. Chapter 10 discusses the role of the analyst further.

Constraints

Constraints are restrictions on alternatives. Constraints may be physical properties of systems, natural limitations, or politically imposed boundaries that do not permit certain actions to be taken. Thus, constraints may imply that certain consequences cannot be obtained and that certain objectives cannot be achieved. The alternatives, consequences, and objectives that are not prohibited, directly or indirectly, by the constraints are referred to as *feasible*. Some examples of possible constraints are physical laws, natural-resource limitations, available manpower, existing legislation, accepted ethics, allocated investment money.

Some constraints are known initially or stated by the client. Others are discovered during the analysis. Still others are not discovered until the consequences are known. Some political or cultural constraints may not even exist until implementation has begun and opposition has had time to develop.

The question of feasibility is important, if not dominant, in systems analysis, and usually it is difficult to deal with. Finding a feasible alternative, *any* feasible alternative that offers a reasonable chance to improve the situation, may be a satisfactory result in some complex situations.

There are many different kinds of constraints. Some are permanent and can never be violated (physical laws or global resources, for example). Others are binding in the short run but may be changed by the passage of time or removed by invention or by improvement in the state of the art. Still others are man-made, set by the political situation, or merely by the decisionmaker's tastes. Thus, some constraints are firm, others less so.

There are constraints at all levels of decisionmaking. Usually, the lower the level of decision, the more constraints there will be to consider (although often they are not very firm). For example, an analysis of alternative urban transportation systems would have to consider a cost constraint, air and noise pollution standards, and perhaps an employment constraint. These are usually constraints imposed by higher decisions and not directly by total resources or by nature. Such decisions may be changed by another decision, if the analysis provides a good case for the change. The case may consist, for example, in showing how much more of the objective can be gained and how slight the increase in cost will be if the constraint is changed by various amounts. It may happen, for example, that a slight lowering of the standard of admissible pollution would cause a substantial reduction in the cost of producing an industrial product. Analysis of this type can thus determine the cost of the constraint. We should not forget, however, that by removing the constraint the benefit to the polluting party may be far less than the cost imposed on those being polluted.

As already said, it cannot be expected that all constraints, and much less so the set of feasible alternatives that results from considering the constraints, will be revealed during problem formulation. In any event, it is important for the analyst to record the constraints under which he feels he must work as they appear. With respect to those resulting from higher-level decisions, it is desirable to get some feel as to how firm these constraints are and, in particular, whether they are defined and definite for the whole time horizon. Otherwise, the analysis may investigate actions or alternatives that will be entirely inappropriate.

For a further discussion of constraints, see Chapter 6 and Majone (1978).

4.4. Generating and Selecting Alternatives

It can hardly be overstated that generating alternatives is, in systems analysis, an exercise of creativity and imagination, appropriately tempered by a thorough and broad knowledge of the issues. The alternatives considered in a particular case may be wide-ranging and need not be obvious substitutes for each other or perform the same spectrum of functions. Thus, for example, education, recreation, family subsidies, police surveillance, and low-income housing (either alone or in various combinations) may all have to be considered as possible alternatives for combating juvenile delinquency. In addition, the alternatives are not merely the options known to the decisionmaker and the analysts at the start; they include whatever additional options can be discovered or invented later.

The set of potential alternatives initially includes all courses of action that offer some chance of attaining or partially attaining the objectives. Whenever it is sensible to do so, the null alternative, the case of no action, sometimes treated as the base case, should be included for the purpose of comparison. Later, as the constraints are discovered or partial results obtained, the set is reduced.

In most cases a number of alternatives are explicitly suggested by the decisionmaker; that is, alternatives are defined by a more or less detailed enumeration of their specific characteristics. Others are discovered or invented by the analysts.

There are usually a number of characteristics (frequently unstated) that a decisionmaker expects or would like the alternative he selects to attain to a reasonably high degree: insensitivity, reliability, invulnerability, and flexibility (they are defined and discussed in Section 6.3).

The deliberate generation of a wide range of alternatives is an essential step in system analysis. One cannot investigate all of them thoroughly; it would be too costly and excessively time-consuming. Moreover, one could not then expect the client to look over the results. Some form of screening that reduces the set of alternatives to a manageable number is usually needed. Dominance or near dominance may get rid of a few. Eliminating those with some unfavorable consequence, such as excessively high cost, is another possibility. Elimination based on the analyst's judgment of a group of impacts is a further possibility; one can set up a set of standards based on five or six characteristics, and those that fail to meet these standards can be judged not good enough (Eilon, 1972; Walker and Veen, 1981).

The final few alternatives that survive this screening can then be examined in much greater detail. In fact, even after the selection is made, there may be aspects of the chosen alternative that need to be worked out in greater detail before the final program for implementation is prepared.

Strong alternatives make for easy analysis. An outstandingly good alternative may make further analysis unnecessary; it may simply look so superior that its acceptance is immediate.

4.5. Forecasting Future States of the World

The Future and Uncertainty

A necessary task in every systems analysis is to predict the consequences of each alternative that is being considered. As this prediction depends on the future context or state of the world during the period in which the alternative is to be implemented, the results are uncertain. To gain an idea of the nature of this uncertainty, predictions are usually made for several alternative futures.

Given a particular forecast or assumption about the future of the world, assessing the outcome of a course of action involves answering two questions:

What will happen as a result of this action?

What will happen without this action?

Neither question can ever be answered with certainty, because both involve a forecast of future conditions, i.e., of a future state of the world, or, at least, the segment of the world being investigated.

Forecasting in Systems Analysis

Thus forecasting is needed in every systems analysis. It is required even when we just want to discover if action is needed. Weather forecasting is one example, and econometric forecasts used to draw inferences about the future state of national economies are another. We should note that, although sophisticated models and extensive statistical data analyses are used in these two forecasts, we do not insist on knowing the cause–effect relations. The forecasting models show correlations but may fail to show dependencies. It is a common pitfall to neglect the difference and thus to draw false conclusions about what a deliberate action may bring about. For example, we cannot cause rainfall by forcing birds to fly at low altitudes, although the two occurrences are known to be strongly correlated in some climates (because both of them are effects of the same cause—air humidity).

A forecast of the future state of the world (in practice, just a very modest segment is all that is usually needed) is, of course, required in order to predict the consequences of an alternative, because the consequences depend on both the properties of the alternative and on the context in which it is implemented. If our confidence in the accuracy of the forecast is not extremely high (the usual case), we will want to carry out the analysis for several different projections of possible states of the world.

Forecasting Approaches

Forecasting future states of the world can be done in a variety of ways. Techniques range from scenario writing (i.e., preparing a set of assumptions about the future state of the world, generated by tracing out a hypothetical but plausible chain of events) to mathematical forecasting models. Whatever technique is used, a forecast is always based on past and current data, observations, or measurements, plus assumptions about connections to the future. When expert judgment alone is employed, it may to a large extent be carried out implicitly. For many of the broad problems to which systems analysis is applied, forecasting can make but very little use of quantitative models. Scenario writing, assisted by a wide range of forecasting methods, is then the main source of the required forecasts.

A forecasting technique should be chosen that is not too sophisticated for the available data. If data are scarce or inaccurate, simple judgmental forecasting models are often as good as the very complex ones. It may be impractical, in the early stages of analysis when more qualitative answers are sought, to attempt to use the more complex forecasting models.

It may be appropriate at this point to indicate that even the best forecasting technique determines the future only in a probabilistic way. For example, it may—in the best case—state the expected value and the variance, or the confidence interval within which the value can be contained with some probability. The variance, or the confidence interval just mentioned, is bound to increase as the future considered is more distant.

In some applications of systems analysis it is appropriate to replace a probabilistic forecast of the future or an impartial scenario by an active element. For example, when a plan for developing water resources is being considered, we may ask whether the water demands of all users will be satisfied under all possible circumstances if this plan is implemented. This question calls for an examination of the worst case of the weather and other conditions.

We can, for this purpose, treat the state of nature as acting against us. In the model we can assign the role of nature to an antagonistic player and thus make use of gaming. Needless to say, to get reasonable conclusions, the action possibilities available to the opponent will have to be bounded in some way; otherwise, no water system could withstand the test. In any case, the game may reveal what exogenous conditions are the most dangerous, and we can then try to determine whether these conditions are likely to happen.

In many analyses there is a need to consider infrequent contingencies, events or conditions that may happen whose probabilities are low or very low, but which—if they happen—have significant consequences. Usually, these consequences are of a detrimental nature, but, on occasion, the opposite can occur (as when a low-probability R&D investment succeeds).

4.6. Identifying the Consequences

A particular alternative will have a large number of consequences. Some of these are benefits, things that one would like to have and that may contribute positively to attaining the objectives. Others are costs or negative values, things that one would like to avoid or minimize. Some of the consequences associated with an alternative, although they may have so little influence on attaining the desired objective that they may appear at first to be negligible in the evaluation, may nevertheless spill over significantly onto the interests of other groups of people or other decisionmakers. These, in turn, may be able to affect the decision through pressure on the decisionmaker or by making their objections known during implementation. It may therefore become necessary to enlarge the study by introducing these spillover effects into the comparison of alternatives.

In the broad sense, costs are the opportunities foregone—all the things we cannot have or do once we have chosen a particular alternative. Many costs can be expressed adequately in money or other quantitative terms; others cannot. For example, if the goal of a decision is to lower automobile traffic fatalities, a delay imposed on motorists by schemes that force a lower speed in a relatively uncrowded and safe section of road will be considered by most drivers to be a cost that outweighs any benefits. Such delay not only has a negative value in itself, which may be expressed partially in monetary terms, but it may cause irritation and speeding elsewhere and thus lead to an increased accident rate or even to a contempt for law, a chain of negative consequences difficult to quantify.

An important question, and one of the analyst's important decisions, is to determine which consequences to consider. Which are the relevant ones? We cannot avoid some assessment of the magnitudes and values of the consequences at an early stage in the analysis. For practical reasons, analysis must be limited; if we consider too many phenomena in the physical, economic, and social environment as being related to the issue under investigation (too many consequences), then the analysis will become expensive, time-consuming, and ineffective. The important consequences are those that must be taken into account in decisionmaking, but the list may have to be enlarged, for the decisionmaker is an interested party and may stress beneficial outcomes while neglecting those implying costs irrelevant to him but detrimental to others.

Therefore, the major responsibility is with the analyst: What consequences to consider is one of the important secondary decisions in the study. Initial assessments based on experience, reasoned judgment, and an understanding of the issue are a starting point, but have to be augmented in the course of analysis and in response to requests for additional information when the results are presented.

There is one more question related to listing the relevant consequences. In considering them, how far into the future shall we look? Among the important factors influencing the answer are these: First, how far-reaching are the objectives (what is the decisionmakers' time horizon) and what lead time is required? Second, how long will the consequences (beneficial and detrimental) last? Third, how important is the future in comparison with the present (what is the discount rate)?

The first two factors are quite different and may conflict, in the sense than an action taken to achieve a short-term objective may have long-lasting consequences, making it harder to achieve an objective more remote in time. The time horizon of analysis has to be matched to both; the analyst is obliged to tell a short-sighted decisionmaker what the consequences of his actions will be in the more distant future.

The third factor may be overriding. If we are not concerned about the future (if our discount rate is high), then it is of little significance how long the consequences extend.

Predictive Models

The consequences of an action cannot be measured or observed before it is taken; They must be predicted (or estimated) from our present understanding of the context and of what the real relations between the contemplated action and its consequences are.

While models of many sorts may be used for prediction, the models most used, and often the only type even considered for this purpose by analysts, are mathematical models. A mathematical model consists of a set of equations and other formal relations, frequently in the form of computer programs, that represent the processes and circumstances determining the outcome of alternative actions. These models, as do any models, depend for their validity on the quality of the scientific information they represent. Our current capability to design mathematical models in whose predictions we have confidence is limited, particularly for questions of public policy, where social and political considerations tend to dominate. Here, what are often regarded as

Section 4.6. Identifying the Consequences

less satisfactory judgmental models, models that depend more, and more directly, on expertise and intuition and are not as precise and manageable, may have to be used.

It is convenient in predictive models to distinguish two sets of factors that simultaneously influence the consequences: the action and the context, or *state of the world*. The state of the world includes all exogenous factors, that is, all factors beyond control by action but that nevertheless influence the consequences or outcomes. The convenience of this approach is that the forecast of future conditions now contains most of the uncertainty. Furthermore, rather than assume that everything is related to and influences everything else, we draw a boundary enclosing everything that has an influence on the consequences under consideration. (That is, not all the outside world is considered to be the environment.) We then draw another boundary, containing the significant influences of an action (the consequences). The actual decision as to where to set these boundaries is made tentatively when the problem is first formulated. The decision is then revised, possibly several times, first when crude models are used to screen the alternatives, next when more refined models are designed to predict the consequences more precisely, and subsequently on iteration.

Limitations on Predictive Modeling; Experiments

Even in situations where the phenomena and relations required for prediction are quantifiable, the correctness (validity) of the models used for prediction is limited by many factors: restricted knowledge of the laws of system behavior, inadequate data, inability to deal effectively with very complex relations, and so on.

Two of the difficulties are that (1) the data from passive observations alone may not reveal the cause–effect relations and (2) human behavior is an important element of most problems addressed by systems analysts, and it is often highly unpredictable. Another difficulty arises when the system being modeled contains one or more decisionmakers whose decisions influence the outcome. Their behavior has to be incorporated into the model. To do this, individual "players" may be inserted into the model to represent, for instance, a manager, a legislative body, a political party, an element of society, or even a sector of the economy—entities which, with our present state of knowledge, cannot be modeled satisfactorily by a set of equations or a computer program. The player is then supposed to act as his real-life conterpart would. Such human activity is often called *role playing* and the model a *man–machine simulation*. Models of this kind, although not necessarily involving computers, have been known for a long time as operational games, war games, business games, etc., depending on the context.

If predictive models appear inadequate, say, because of the difficulties involved in predicting the actions of a relatively large number of people in a new situation, the model builders may suggest a social experiment. It might consist, for example, of testing a proposed course of action on a sample group and on a parallel control group, and then comparing the results to arrive at conclusions about the action or to build a model and modify the action before it is applied full-scale (Riecken, 1974). Such experiments are as yet too little understood, too new, and too expensive for widespread use.

An experiment can tell how the system reacts in the present, but not how it will react in the future under changed conditions that cannot be duplicated in the experiment. Because of these and other limitations, we should recognize that experimentation alone can hardly be a substitute for modeling, but should be considered a supplementary activity.

No model can be fully validated; that is, it can never be proved that its output will conform to reality. We can, however, increase our confidence in its predictions by working with it, checking it against other models and against historical data, and using it to predict the outcomes in known situations. Better yet is to subject the model to a range of tests and comparisons deliberately designed to reveal where it fails. Such tests are not designed to eliminate the uncertainty that is part of the dynamics of the relevant phenomena, but to give the user an understanding of the extent and limits of the model's predictive capabilities (See Section 7.4, on validation.)

Using Models

Using a model is simple in principle: We take the proposed action as an input to the model, take the assumed or predicted state of nature as another input, and work out the output, that is, the model-predicted consequences.

It is important to investigate the sensitivity of the consequences obtained from any model to the uncertainties or errors in our choices of parameters or assumptions. To do so, we need only make a series of changes in various aspects of the alternatives, the environment, or the model itself and observe how the results are changed. Sensitivity analysis helps to make explicit the types and degrees of uncertainty that exist in the outcome and to identify the dominant and controlling parameters. A similar investigation, but with respect to major changes in the exogenous factors or assumptions about the future state of the world, is sometimes referred to as *contingency analysis*. (See also Section 7.5.)

The actual techniques by which the consequences are predicted for given inputs depends on the kind of model used; for example, whether it is an analytic model (an explicit mathematical relation or formula) or a judgmental model. However, all kinds of useful models should permit assessing sensitivities.

We are well aware that the future can at best be determined only in a probabilistic way. It is therefore correct, at least in principle, to ask the model to predict the probabilistic features of the consequences. We may, for example,

Section 4.6. Identifying the Consequences   139

be interested in the range or interval within which a consequence will be contained with some given (and high) probability. Obtaining answers of this kind requires much information, which will seldom be found in systems analysis applications. In particular, adequate probabilistic data on the future state of nature, i.e., on future environmental inputs, would have to be available, but seldom are.

We should also mention that the techniques of estimating the probabilistic features of the outcomes may be quite complex and time-consuming. If an analytic model is not available, a stochastic computer simulation can be carried out. In this technique the computer model is subjected to a large number of suitably generated random inputs that imitate the stochastic environment. A statistical analysis of the outputs provides the required probabilistic data. This kind of analysis is important in some applications. In many cases, however, a computer simulation is the least desirable model. It is costly, except possibly in the model-building stage, and it has low insight, since it does not show how the observed outcomes are obtained. Nevertheless, it may be the only choice open (Section 7.3; Majone and Quade, 1979).

In most applications of systems analysis the scarcity of data and the inaccuracy of models do not permit or justify a precise probabilistic analysis. We should, however, always realize the probabilistic character of the problem and proceed cautiously. A common pitfall, for example, is to take the expected value of the environmental input as a basis for determining the expected value of the outcome. A simple example will explain what happens. Assume a crop increases with humidity but is more sensitive to drought than to above-average rainfall. Calculating the average crop on the basis of average rainfall would then be wrong, since the losses due to dry years will be more than the gains in the wet years.

Summary Remarks

It sometimes happens that, in a worthwhile application of systems analysis, in spite of all the effort put into model building and forecasting, the analysts cannot claim that the predicted consequences will happen with reasonably high probabilities. It should be understood from what has been said that this uncertainty in the answer cannot be entirely overcome. Is it, then, reasonable to spend money and time on systems analysis, to build and use models in cases where they cannot predict accurately?

The answer is yes. First, if the decisionmaker has to make a decision, imperfect assistance by analysis is likely to be better than that offered by off-the-cuff judgment and intuition. Second, analysis may permit comparing alternatives, even if absolute accuracy in predicting consequences is low. Contingency analysis (that is, investigating the sensitivity of the results to changes in environment or context) may demonstrate that a certain alternative is best, or at least very good in a wide range of situations. For example, suppose that there is no probabilistic forecast of the future but that there are several scenarios that cover the likely spectrum of possibilities. If we then detect, by a consistent analysis, that the consequences of action a_1 are better than those of action a_2 under all, or most, of the representative scenarios, this result is a useful indication of the superiority of a_1. Other useful indications that a model can provide are properties of sensitivity itself: A course of action that makes a system insensitive to exogenous factors, or makes it resilient (that is, able to recover from shocks) is advantageous even if we do not know its exact consequences.

4.7. Comparing and Ranking Alternatives

Difficulties of Ranking

Assume the consequences of each alternative have been determined for a number of contingencies. How can we compare the alternatives? An obvious method, which may not be easy to apply if the number of contingencies is large, is to display them and their consequences in a suitable framework so that the differences and similarities stand out. The analyst, however, may also be asked to do more: to rank the alternatives so that a choice may be made. This is equivalent to asking him to develop and apply a criterion.

Ranking can be difficult for several reasons.

In many cases one alternative may be superior to another in some aspects and inferior in others.

The diverse consequences of an alternative cannot in general be aggregated into a single index that bears a satisfactory relation to performance in attaining the objectives.

When outcomes are spread over time, the time preferences, and thus the rankings, may change as time changes.

There may exist consequences that can be quantified only subjectively.

The future conditions under which the proposed alternatives will have to function are uncertain. At the same time, the range of probable future conditions is wide and bears strongly on the presumed consequences.

Nevertheless, in spite of the difficulties, a choice may have to be made. We are concerned about the extent to which this choice can be assisted by the analyst; for example, about the extent and the means by which we can reduce the variety of consequences of each alternative into a few, but nevertheless reliable, indicators.

There is also a danger in overaggregation, i.e., in trying to merge too many entities into a single index value. One should not overlook the fact that the judgment of the decisionmaker on a set of displayed impacts may reflect his preferences more closely than any index arrived at by arbitrary quantification,

Section 4.7. Comparing and Ranking Alternatives 141

questionable arguments, and value estimates by the analysts. Direct judgment by someone informed about the situation may quite often lead to the right decision, as opposed to an index-based decision, even though the index may have been correctly determined on the basis of the available information. The study of ways of protecting the Oosterschelde estuary from floods (described in Sections 1.2 and 3.4) is an example in which the analysts wisely avoided any temptation to combine impacts into simple indices.

Judgmental Comparison and Ranking

The method used in the Oosterschelde study (see Section 3.4) is to display the consequences of the alternatives to the decisionmaker using color or shading to show the ranks. Such a display, the scorecard, aims to present the decisionmaker with the full spectrum of consequences, both good and bad, and, where appropriate, with an indication of who benefits and who pays the cost. The decisionmaker can superimpose on this relatively objective information his feelings for the values as well as incorporate the value judgments of the society he represents. This approach also makes it possible to show sensitivities, that is, to show how the impacts or ranks change when parameters and external conditions vary. To do this, one prepares a scorecard for the same alternatives under the changed conditions, and compares it with the previous one. For further discussion of the scorecard approach, see the third subsection of Section 3.4 and Sections 8.2–8.7 (cf. Mood, 1982, Ch. 20).

The scorecard is equally effective for multiple decisionmakers, for each individual may form his own opinion based on his preferences and prejudices, and a consensus can then be worked out through committee. The scorecard is also easily understood by the public at large.

Any evaluation and ranking of the alternatives by analysts or experts may ignore important factors known to the decisionmaker but never made explicit to the analysts and experts. Therefore, such ranking may be unsatisfactory to the decisionmaker. For this reason alone, he should always be presented with the major alternatives and their consequences. In other words, if we present a decisionmaker with the result of someone else's evaluation, we should produce the scorecard for all highly ranked alternatives.

The sheer mass of information, however, makes the use of indices of various sorts attractive.

Cost-Effectiveness and Cost–Benefit Criteria

For the purpose of comparing and ranking alternatives, one often tries to describe their relative merits by means of one, or at most a few, indicators (index value, figure of merit, or objective function). Any such approach has to sacrifice the details, the individual features of the alternatives, for the sake of making comparison easier.

Cost-effectiveness can be used to rank alternatives when there is a single dominant objective, and the effectiveness of the various alternatives in attaining the objective can be measured on a single scale that is directly related to the objective, or is a good proxy for it. Alternatives are ranked either in terms of decreasing effectiveness for equal cost or, less frequently, in terms of increasing cost for equal effectiveness. The ratio of cost to effectiveness is sometimes used, but ratios have many defects as criteria (Hitch and McKean, 1960).

The cost-effectiveness criterion is open to a number of objections. For one, even in the simplest cases, effectiveness may not measure value, which depends on the particular decisionmaker. For another, if the ranking is close, the decisionmaker may want secondary effects taken into account.

Another objection is that cost as used in cost-effectiveness criteria reflects only the costs that are inputs—the money, resources, time, and manpower required to implement and maintain an alternative. The penalties or losses that accompany an implemented alternative—it may, for instance, interfere with something else that is wanted or bring undesirable consequences to other people—are costs that must usually be taken into account in other ways.

Finally, even if cost and effectiveness are properly determined, the decisionmaker is still faced with the problem of what to do. He needs both a way to rule out or accept the alternative of doing nothing, and then a means to set the scale of effort—either a cost he must not exceed or an effectiveness level he needs to achieve. The ratio of cost to effectiveness is not a satisfactory guide (Hitch and McKean, 1960), even if he is totally uninterested in the scale of effort.

The cost–benefit criterion is the most commonly used in analysis for public decisions. In principle, it avoids the difficulties associated with cost-effectiveness. The costs and benefits that follow each choice of an alternative, taking account of the times and probabilities of their occurrence, are measured in the same units, usually monetary ones. The excess of the total benefits over total costs is then used to rank the alternatives. Whether such a transfer into monetary or other terms can properly include all, or an adequate number, of the relevant considerations, such as the differing times at which the costs and benefits are realized, is, however, a difficult question. For a more complete discussion, see Fischhoff (1977), Mishan (1971), Sugden and Williams (1978), and Section 8.5.

Value and Utility Approaches

If a scorecard approach is used, there will be as many scorecards for each alternative as there are scenarios of the future to be considered. On each

Section 4.7. Comparing and Ranking Alternatives

scorecard the number of entries is the number of consequences multiplied by the number of alternatives to be evaluated and compared. The result may be that the large amount of data makes it difficult for the decisionmaker, without some aggregation, to make a judgmental ranking and choice.

It is therefore understandable that there is a tendency to evaluate each alternative by a single indicator, such as effectiveness for fixed cost or net benefit in a cost–benefit analysis. We still have, of course, the various possible futures, and hence several different values of the chosen indicator for each alternative. Nevertheless, the display of alternatives is more lucid and transparent.

The theory behind using a single index to represent the many noncommensurable features of an object, in our case an assumed alternative, is well developed by decision analysts, who have formalized it in terms of the multiattribute value function (Keeney and Raiffa, 1977; Raiffa, 1968). In this approach one tries to build a function that models the decisionmaker's value system. It has to be established on the basis of his preferences, that is, of his individual judgments, and this is where the difficulties arise. It is, for many reasons, hard to obtain a value function that could replace the actual decisionmaker on complex and unique issues. It is possible, however, for multiattribute value functions to be used as a guide or directive in the initial selection, design, and fine tuning of alternatives or as one of the ranking criteria to be compared with rankings done by other means. The preferences of public officials may not always be the preferences of the people they represent, but it is through this association that the analyst can get an idea of the preferences of the decisionmaker.

One still faces the problem of uncertainty: Even if we agree on a single indicator and we can evaluate the alternatives by it for each of the possible states of nature, how should they be ranked, since we do not know which of these states of nature will occur? Let us assume that, from one source or another, the probabilities of the various future states of nature are known or can be estimated. It seems quite natural in this case, or at least simplest, to rank the alternatives on the basis of the mathematical expectation (expected value) of the outcome.

Using a multiattribute value function that assigns a single value indicator to a given alternative for each state of nature, one can calculate the average value for each alternative over all possible states of nature. The alternatives can be then ranked according to the average, i.e., expected, values.

It should be noted, however, that a straightforward average may not indicate the choice that a given decisionmaker would make. To take account of this, the notion of utility is used, a basic concept used in the theory of decision under uncertainty. This theory assigns utilities to consequences in such a way that ranking expected utilities of alternatives is the same as the decisionmaker's preference order for the same alternatives. Utilities are assigned to consequences by means of utility functions; a utility function describes the attitude of the given decisionmaker toward risk and is thus different for risk-averse and risk-prone decisionmakers (Keeney and Raiffa, 1977).

Direct use of utility theory, i.e., of utility functions and the expected utility principle, for ranking alternatives and, in particular, for making a final choice, cannot be recommended without reservation. Assigning utility by using utility functions involves a great deal of judgment by the analyst; several simplifying assumptions with respect to the form of these functions are also indispensable. Nevertheless, as in the case of multiattribute value functions, expected utility may be valuable as one of the means by which the alternatives can be screened and assigned a tentative ranking, even if it cannot be recommended as a unique and ultimate criterion for choice.

The theory can be extended to the case of multiple decisionmakers.

General Remarks

Relatively little can be added to what was said in the first paragraph of this section: Comparing alternatives is, in all practical cases, difficult. We should also remember that, although comparison and choice go together, the two parts are done by different people. It is the duty of the analyst to provide a comparison of alternatives and possibly a ranking, but it is the right and responsibility of the decisionmaker to make the choice.

It is therefore reasonable not to rely entirely on the rankings provided by cost–benefit criteria, multiattribute value functions, or utility functions. A scorecard of the alternatives, reduced, perhaps, to the most relevant attributes, should accompany any rank-ordered list of alternatives.

The analyst should not be upset if the choice of the decisionmaker is the third- or fourth-ranked alternative. Such a choice indicates only that there are additional aspects and values that the decisionmaker did not disclose or that were misunderstood by the analyst. The analysis at this stage may be considered a success if the decisionmaker has made an analysis-based decision in the sense that he has chosen a course of action taking into account consequences that have been duly and appropriately analyzed. We must remember, however, that the analyst's goal (unfortunately, seldom fully attained) is not merely to find the course of action best suited to achieve the decisionmaker's objectives and satisfy his constraints, but to find the course of action closest to this ideal that can be accepted by the other participants in the decisionmaking process and then implemented without undesirable modification, extra cost, or delay.

As mentioned in Section 4.2, the role of analysis does not necessarily end at the choice by the decisionmakers of a particular course of action. Analysts, although often not the original analysts, will be called on to assist with implementation, especially in the early part of this process when there may be a need to interpret aspects of the program, as well as for modifications due to circumstances impossible to anticipate earlier. Other analysts—who should not be the original analysts—will also play an important role when it comes to evaluating the results of the implemented action and the original analysis itself. This last is a step that should be—but rarely is—carried out after every systems analysis.

4.8. Documentation

One of the important hallmarks of professionalism in systems analysis is that, as a study proceeds, the analysts record their assumptions, data, parameter estimates and why they were chosen, model structure and details, steps in the analysis, relevant constraints, computer code and changes thereto, results, sensitivity tests, and so on. Thus, at completion, the analysis team has the basis for preparing a complete and conscientious documentation of the work that will be understandable to someone who is technically trained but who has not been a member of the project team (House and McLeod, 1977, pp. 76-87; Meadows and Robinson, 1984). House and McLeod suggest standards and formats for such documentation (see also Gass, 1984).

In the flurry of activity that brings the study to a conclusion and presents its findings to the client, there is a temptation to slight the final preparation of the documentation—or to forgo it altogether. There are compelling reasons for the analysts not to yield to this temptation.

First, if the study's findings are adopted by the client and implementation takes place, new questions will arise that will need further analysis, which must not be delayed while the analysts—either the original ones or new ones brought in for the implementation phase—try to puzzle out what was done originally in the face of the incomplete or inchoate documentation. Second, after a major study is completed, it is not unusual for new analysts to test the results in various ways—an important step in the process of gaining confidence in the analysis results; if analysts other than the original ones cannot understand the documentation, this confidence is seriously undermined right at the start. Third, clear and complete documentation buttresses confidence in the analysis; its absence inevitably carries with it the opposite effect.

Beyond these rather practical reasons, there is the overriding one stated at the beginning of this section: Clear documentation of a study's processes—as well as its results—is a hallmark of professionalism.

4.9. Summary

If readers compare what has been said in this chapter with the accounts of systems analyses set forth in Chapters 1 and 3, they will see some connections—but perhaps not as many as they would expect. The reason is a simple one: In published accounts of completed systems analyses the authors focus attention on the findings and the direct path that led to them, suppressing all the contributing activity that does not lead directly to the results. Thus, for the most part, one can only imagine the false starts, the approaches that did not work, the debates over objectives, the alternatives that proved to be uninteresting, the data that were inadequate, the interactions with the client in the process of developing the framework for the analysis, and so on, and so on. These matters could be discussed, but only by the analysts directly involved, and the resulting length would exceed what seems reasonable for a handbook—nor would most analysts want so much laundry hanging on the line.

Thus, this chapter distills from many experiences what many analysts have learned, in the hope that it will help future investigators, but with the warning that everything that is said here must be reconsidered carefully in the light of the case in hand. Experience in facing such issues is an essential part of an analyst's training, but, while some of this experience can be passed on in papers, books, and this handbook, much will have to be learned on the job. An apprenticeship under a wise and experienced systems analysis leader is the best way of learning the craft. Perhaps the best use of this handbook for the fledgling analyst is in connection with such an apprenticeship, to provide questions, contrasting experience, and an entry to the large literature that can extend his experience.

This chapter has discussed systems analysis as though a single decisionmaker were being served; indeed, it began with an argument that this was an appropriate focus. On the other hand, all the examples of systems analysis presented in Chapters 1 and 3 clearly involve more complicated administrative situations: For the simplest case—that dealing with improving blood availability and utilization—it would be fair to say that the head of the Greater New York Blood Program was the client, but this official's operations are hedged about by a very large number of administratively independent heads of hospital blood banks, all of whom had to agree to a cooperative arrangement of the sort proposed by the analysts before it could be brought into being and be effective. In fact, persuading the blood bank officials that the new cooperative system was in everyone's best interests was one of the key implementation tasks facing the analysts at the end of their analytic work.

Similarly, the Chief of the Wilmington Bureau of Fire can be considered the client for the fire-prevention case, but he too was enmeshed in a bureaucratic and political structure that constrained his choices, and had to be convinced of their value before they could become effective. Not the least of these influences came from the firemen's labor union.

While the Netherlands Rijkswaterstaat commissioned The Rand Corporation's systems analysis work (as an extension of their own work on protecting the Oosterschelde estuary from excessive flooding), the network of decisionmakers was very large, with the Netherlands Parliament playing an ultimately deciding role.

For the IIASA study of the world's energy future there was, of course, no world decisionmaker to commission the study or to report its findings to; rather, there were thousands of persons in national governments, energy enterprises, and the general public interested in the findings, and their potential influences on their own activities and attitudes. However, for a government or an energy enterprise to make decisions sympathetic to the IIASA study's findings would almost invariably involve the organization in making a complementary study of its own, focused sharply on its own concerns. In fact, the IIASA world-wide analysis has been followed by a number of such studies.

In view of the evidence of our examples that the decisionmaking situation is almost invariably complex, can we sustain the argument made at the beginning of this chapter that it is useful to begin the discussion with the presumption that there is a single decisionmaker being served by a systems analyst? We certainly cannot do so if we then try to carry this presumption into real life. However, we can accept this convention provided it is a useful device for thought and discussion, as we hope this chapter has established. It may be particularly useful if it serves to sharpen the analysts' appreciation of the complications of the actual decisionmaking situation they are facing, and forces them to think constructively and work effectively toward it. Otherwise, knowing that there is no decisionmaker for a global problem, analysts may fail to sharpen their findings enough to make them usable to decisionmakers with smaller purviews.

A final word. Success in systems analysis is a matter of degree. A result that uncovers a feasible alternative or leads to the rejection of bad but strongly advocated actions may be all that can be produced; even merely to identify the major uncertainties or the key factors can be considered a successful outcome. Moreover, factors other than extensive knowledge of the methodology may be equally important to success. Perception of what the real policy problem is, setting up the right project staff, communicating effectively and operating in harmony with the decisionmakers, and presenting the results in a clear and objective way are some of the factors leading to successful outcomes.

References

Ackoff, R. L. (1957). Towards a behavioral theory of communication. *Management Science* 4, 218–234. Also in *Modern Systems Research for the Behavioral Scientist* (W. Buckley, ed.). Chicago: Aldine, 1968.

———(1974). *Redesigning the Future: A Systems Approach to Societal Problems.* New York: Wiley.

Allison, Graham T. (1971). *Essence of Decision.* Boston: Little, Brown.

Checkland, P. (1981). *Systems Thinking, Systems Practice.* Chichester, England: Wiley.

Dunn, W. N. (1981). *Public Policy Analysis.* Englewood Cliffs, New Jersey: Prentice-Hall.

Eilon, S. (1972). Goals and constraints in decisionmaking. *Operational Research Quarterly* 23(1), 3–15.

Fischhoff, B. (1977). Cost–benefit analysis and the art of motorcycle maintenance. *Policy Sciences* 9, 177–202.

Gass, S. I. (1984). Documenting a computer-based model. *Interfaces* 14(3), 84–93.

Goeller, Bruce F. (1969a). *Methodology for Determining Traffic Safety Priorities: A Collision Prediction Model*. P-3962. Santa Monica, California: The Rand Corporation.

_____(1969b). Modeling the traffic-safety system. *Accident Analysis and Prevention* 1, 167–204.

Hitch, C. J., and R. McKean (1960). *The Economics of Defense in the Nuclear Age*. Cambridge, Massachusetts: Harvard University Press.

House, P. W., and John McLeod (1977). *Large Scale Models for Policy Evaluations*. New York: Wiley Interscience.

Keeney, R.L., and Howard Raiffa (1977). *Decisions with Multiple Objectives: Preferences and Value Tradeoffs*. New York: Wiley.

Lynn, Laurence E., Jr. (1978). The question of relevance. In *Knowledge and Policy: The Uncertain Connection* (L. E. Lynn, Jr., ed.). Washington, D.C.: National Research Council.

Majone, G. (1978). *The ABC's of Constraint Analysis*, Working paper No. 2. New York: The Russell Sage Foundation.

_____(1980). *The Craft of Applied Systems Analysis*. WP-80-73. Laxenburg, Austria: IIASA.

_____and E. S. Quade (1979). *Pitfalls of Analysis*. Chichester, England: Wiley.

Meadows, D., and J. M. Robinson (1984) *The Electronic Oracle: Computer Models and Social Decisions*. Chichester, England: Wiley.

Mintzberg, H., and M. F. Shakun, eds. (1978). Strategy formulation. *Management Science* 24, 920–972.

Mishan, E. J. (1971). *Cost Benefit Analysis*. New York: Praeger.

Mood, A. M. (1982). *Introduction to Policy Analysis*. New York: North-Holland.

Nelson, Richard R. (1974). Intellectualizing about the moon-ghetto metaphor: A study of the current malaise of rational analysis of social problems. *Policy Sciences* 5, 381.

Quade, E. S. (1968). Introduction. In *Systems Analysis and Policy Planning* (E. S. Quade and W. I. Boucher, eds.). New York: Elsevier.

_____(1982). *Analysis for Public Decisions*, 2nd ed. New York: North-Holland, pp. 30–67.

Raiffa, Howard (1968). *Decision Analysis*. Reading, Massachusetts: Addison–Wesley.

Rein, Martin, and Sheldon H. White (1977). Policy research: Belief and doubt. *Policy Analysis*, 3, 249.

Riecken, H. W. (1974). *Social Experimentation: A Model for Planning and Evaluating Social Interaction*. New York: Academic.

Shils, E. (1981). *Tradition*. London: Faber and Faber.

Stokey, Elizabeth, and Richard Zeckhauser (1978). *A Primer for Policy Analysis*. New York: Norton.

Sugden, R., and A. Williams (1978). *The Principles of Practical Cost–Benefit Analysis*. Oxford, England: Oxford University Press.

References

Walker, W. E. (1978). *Public Policy Analysis: A Partnership between Analysts and Policymakers*, P-6074. Santa Monica, California: The Rand Corporation.

―――― and M. A. Veen (1981). *Policy Analysis of Water Management for the Netherlands: Vol II. Screening of Technical and Managerial Tactics.* N-1500/2-NETH. Santa Monica, California: The Rand Corporation.

White, D. J. (1975). *Decision Methodology.* London: Wiley.

Chapter 5
Formulating Problems for Systems Analysis

Peter B. Checkland

5.1. Introduction

To begin a new study, a systems analyst can usefully write down, as his first contribution to the work, the sentence from science-fiction writer Poul Anderson that Koestler (1969) calls "my favorite motto": "I have yet to see any problem, however complicated, which, when . . . looked at . . . the right way, did not become still more complicated." This is not meant as a flippant opening remark, but rather as a useful reminder of the essential nature of a mode of inquiry that hopes to use rational means to help bring about change in the world's complex systems. Systems analysis aims at results that affect complex human operating systems, and the analyst should keep in mind that he is dealing, at least in part, with creatures who, in themselves and their interactions with each other and their surrounding environment, often exhibit a level of complexity far beyond what his intellectual tools can cope with. Thus, he must approach his task circumspectly, recognizing that his activity, while carried out in the spirit of science with a view to achieving testable results, is rather a form of—or an aid to—social architecture.

Because the systems analyst addresses problems of real-world systems, in considering how to formulate problems he must realize how this context differs from classical science and technology, where the laboratory is a natural domain (Checkland, 1977). In the laboratory a scientist reduces the variety of factors he must consider, and thus can define with some precision the problem he proposes to work on; he can decide with considerable arbitrariness which factors to vary and which to keep constant, and where to draw the boundary around his investigation.

The position of the systems analyst, however, is quite different. His problems exist in the real world; the phenomena he investigates cannot be taken into a laboratory, and they are usually so entangled with many factors as to appear inseparably linked with them. Thus, an apparently simple technical problem of transportation becomes a land-use problem, which is seen as part of an environment–conservation problem. Moreover all of these matters are now as much issues of political choice as they are of technical analysis. As the problem expands, do all the wider factors necessarily become part of the original problem? Can any boundary be drawn? Can the analyst justify the limits that practicality forces him to impose? An analyst trained in the methods of science who wishes to extend them as far as he can into the problems of sociotechnical systems thus faces an important challenge, one that Churchman (1968) calls the "challenge to reason."

In fact, the systems analyst, in seeking to contribute to real-world decisions, always finds himself facing, not a well-defined problem, but a problem area or situation; his problem is really a nexus of problems, what the French refer to as a "problématique," or what Ackoff (1974) calls "a mess."

The systems analyst's problem arises because someone feels that something in the real-world situation needs changing, and decisions need to be taken to move it away from an unsatisfactory position. But, whether the decisionmakers perceive and state the problem in precise terms ("Which vehicle design should be adopted?"), or merely indicate an area of concern ("How can we design a better health-care system?"), the analyst knows that he faces an expanding network of concerns, institutions, actors, and values.

While his mode of thought and discourse follows the pattern, as much as possible, of the public rational discourse of science, he should prudently avoid two pitfalls: In his initial task of problem formulation, he should avoid committing himself to a single point of view, and he should avoid thinking too quickly in terms of possible solutions.

At the end of the problem-formulation phase of the work, the study outline is clear in its first form. The problem area has been explored and the main issues defined. The client understands clearly what kind of work he can expect in subsequent phases, what kinds of alternatives will be examined, what kinds of criteria will be used to judge them, what major relations exist within his decisionmaking situation, what kinds of risks he is taking. All this has been made clear and, importantly, has been expressed in explicit issue papers and other documents.

Since the systems analyst is dealing with a problématique, he is not surprised when the eventual outcome of his work strays somewhat from what he anticipated in his initial problem formulation. His process of inquiry will itself educate, and thus possibly lead to changes in outlook or modified values, even changes in the situation itself. The situation may also be changed by new external factors emerging during the course of the work. However, if the analyst has made his initial formulation clear and explicit, then it will be possible to adjust both the problem boundaries and the crucial issues realistically and coherently. It is in the nature of systems analysis that its process continually enriches the perceptions of the problems, and iteration to previous

Section 5.2. Formulating the Problem: The Concepts 153

phases of the analysis occurs frequently, as Chapter 4 brings out. Thus, the analyst should formulate the problem so as to facilitate reformulation. This is an important point, because the work done at the beginning determines the shape and content of what is done later.

The next section discusses the concepts the analyst needs in order to formulate a problem, the third describes the problem's environment, and the fourth deals with organizing the formulation activities. The final section summarizes the conclusions reached.

5.2. Formulating the Problem: The Concepts

The systems analyst begins his work cautiously, because his initial aim must be to appreciate the context of his study without imposing a rigid structure on it. From the start he must have available a number of concepts relating to the idea of formulating a problem. Since awareness of these concepts must precede and inform any use of prescribed activities, this chapter describes them before discussing an operational sequence of activities appropriate to the problem-formulation phase of the systems analysis.

Problems and Problem Solving

Since systems analysis aims to generate and present information in order to improve the basis on which decisionmakers exercise their judgment, a setting in which this approach is used will have players with two different roles: a problem giver, the would-be decisionmaker who welcomes aid as he tackles his problem, and a problem solver, here the systems analyst, who aims to improve the basis for decisionmaking. It is possible, of course, for one individual to occupy both roles: a systems analyst may adopt the approach to his own problems; or a decisionmaker may carry out his own systems study. Nevertheless, it is important to distinguish between the two roles and to be aware of the relations between the problem itself and the effort to alleviate or solve it. Each affects the other. For example, the problem content implies the problem-solving resource requirements, which may be a factor affecting the boundaries chosen for the problem's formulation.

In any systems analysis, then, we may assume that there is a problem content and a related problem-solving activity. Since any real-world problem is a problématique, and since problem solving is a net of different but connected activities, we may refer to a problem-content system and a problem-solving system. These systems contain the roles of problem giver and problem solver, respectively.

With this general model for any systems analysis, the problem-formulation phase is an elaboration of it for a particular issue and a particular problem-solving activity. The problem-formulation phase defines the problem-content system (its boundaries and limits, what is inside and what is excluded) and the nature of the problem-solving system and its resources. Finally, the relations between the two have to be examined, in order to ensure that a reasonable balance exists between the task and the available resources. The problem-formulation phase will describe the problem and examine the implications of doing something about it. Only then can begin the task of resolving the issue, making the decision, or solving the problem.

This general model of systems analysis is the first concept appropriate to the analyst. The second is an awareness of different problem types and their characteristics; the problem spectrum stretches from well-defined problems, which I shall term "hard," to ill-structured problems which, following Rapoport (1970), I shall term "soft."

Systems analysis had its origins in relatively well-structured problems calling for expertise in economics and technology (as described in Chapter 2), but its aspirations are to help decisionmaking in a wide range of problems, including cases where, as Quade (1982) puts it, "a decision [is] made by society for itself . . . or for society by its elected representatives— . . . decisions that have material effects on members of the public other than those involved in making the decision." Indeed, the aspirations extend to making substantial contributions to problems on an international scale that are, in Raiffa's terms (1976), "politically sensitive." Analysis aimed at improving the basis for such public decisions will always involve soft problems. Therefore, the analyst must develop and retain a sense of the hard and soft elements in any study he undertakes, and avoid treating one set of elements as if it were the other.

Although the terms "hard" and "soft" are difficult to define precisely (and we probably ought to resist defining them too sharply, since their role is to remind the analyst of connotations, rather than to provide a formula) we can get an insight into them from the history of systems analysis. Examination of the literature of systems analysis as it emerged within The Rand Corporation, as well as the literature of the closely related systems engineering, shows that both activities were based on the same model of what constitutes a problem (Checkland, 1979, 1981). Both assume that problems may be posed as a matter of selecting an efficient means to achieve a defined end. Hence, problem solving becomes a matter of defining objectives and creating possible means of achieving them with criteria to measure cost and effectiveness. This is an exceptionally powerful idea, and it has supported most systems analysis successfully. But a systems analyst who aspires to tackle problems in the public arena—those of energy, health-care systems, or urban renewal, for example—will have to ask: What makes the objectives meaningful? What are the values they embody? Whose values are they? What other values may be expressed in other objectives? Work on the philosophy underlying systems analysis [such as Churchman's (1968, 1971)] and on its application in soft problems (e.g., Checkland, 1972, 1981) shows how quickly such questions arise even in studies that might at first seem well defined.

Hard problems are ones that may be posed as selecting a means to achieve

Section 5.2. Formulating the Problem: The Concepts

desired objectives, a formulation that leads to problems having relatively sharp boundaries and well-defined constraints. Appropriate information flows for the decision process are capable of clear definition, and, most important, what the analyst will recognize as "a solution" to the problem is clear. This contrasts with the content of soft problems, which may be defined as ones in which all these elements are themselves problematical. Here many objectives are unclear, some important variables are unquantifiable, and the analysis will necessarily have to include examining the value systems underlying the various possible objectives.

A given study is likely to contain both hard and soft aspects: real-world problems rarely fit entirely into any predefined category. But is is important for the analysts in the problem-solving system to keep the two concepts clear in their minds. Then they may formulate the hard aspects with precision, marshaling the proper intellectual tools (often quantitative ones), and proceed to make appropriately different kinds of explorations of the softer aspects. Doing this explicitly does not guarantee that the systems analysis is a good one, but it at least makes it possible to examine a significant piece of decisionmaking in the spirit of science, which is the aim of systems analysis.

The significance of this hard/soft separation is nicely illustrated by Kahn (1960, pp. 119–120) in an account of the development of the early thinking in The Rand Corporation:

> In the early days at Rand most studies involved an attempt to find the "optimum" system, given some reasonably definite set of circumstances, objectives and criteria.

But then occurred a technological breakthrough. A new viewpoint emerged, and softer considerations became paramount:

> We now tend to compare a rather small number of different systems under widely varying circumstances and objectives. No simple criteria of performance are used. The major attention is focused on the uncertainties. A system is preferred when it performs reasonably well under probable circumstances in terms of high-priority objectives, and yet hedges against less probable or even improbable situations, and does more than just pay lip service to medium- and low-priority objectives.

The conclusion is that it is important to realize that

> overall planners must design from the beginning for the complete range of plausible objectives.

An interesting illustration of the relevance of this important (but hard-to-follow) advice occurred when two analysts made a presentation to a decision-aiding group associated with high levels in the government of a Western European country, the kind of group frequently described as a think tank. They described how they would analyze an ill-structured problem and produce a report or make a presentation which analyzed several possible courses of action and the likely consequences of following them. Their lament was that, when a related government decision was taken some months later, it always turned out to be "for purely political reasons," rather than on the basis of their analysis of alternatives! In their striving for objectivity and, where possible, quantification, they had failed to notice that, in a study whose clients are professional politicians, Kahn's "complete range of plausible objectives" includes, high on the list, political objectives. The political consequences of their analyzed courses of action were a legitimate part of all of their problem-content systems—but one they had largely ignored.

Exploring the Problem Area

The distinctions between the problem-content and problem-solving systems and between the hard and soft problem types are important general ideas that should guide the investigations in the problem-formulation phase. At a more detailed level there are now a number of other considerations to be discussed; they concern the concepts that the investigation should weld into a coherent whole.

The map-making activity of problem formulation focuses on a problem situation in which there is a decisionmaker and a client for the study; the latter may not always be the decisionmaker himself, but he wants something done about the problem and commissions the study. The decisionmaker and his problem situation exist in an environment that affects them both, one that the decisionmaker can himself affect to some extent. Considerations arising as part of the problem situation or the environment place limits and constraints on the problem, the decisionmaker, and the problem-solving effort. These concepts and terms all need more detailed consideration.

The client, the decisionmaker, and the participants in the situation may perceive the problem situation in different ways. But the perception of a situation as problematic implies that there is a recognized need for change, and the systems analyst's task is to build a rich picture of who perceives what kind of change to be necessary and for what reasons. His own position should be one of disinterest. The analyst's response to client, decisionmaker, and participants alike, as he asks questions and explores their perceptions, should be neither "I agree with you" nor "I disagree," but rather a response in the sense of "I hear you." Questions that the analyst can usefully ask at this stage are of the following kinds (see also Jenkins, 1969; Pogson, 1972; Quade, 1982):

What is said to be the problem? Why is it a problem? How did it arise? What previous actions have led to it?

Who believes it to be a problem?

Why is it important to solve it?

Section 5.2. Formulating the Problem: The Concepts   157

If an analysis is made, what will be done with it? Who might act on the recommendations?

What would a solution look like? What sort of solution is at present regarded as acceptable? What kinds of changes would a solution imply?

Of what larger or deeper problem is the stated problem a part? What are the implications of tackling the problems related to the stated problem?

Does it seem likely that the return (in the problem-content system) will exceed the cost of the problem-solving effort? Where else may the analytic effort be applied?

A general set of questions concerning resource deployment can usefully follow the ones just posed (if it can be answered in detail, then the analyst has a reasonable initial knowledge of the structures and processes in the problem situation):

What resources are deployed in what operational processes under what planning procedures within what structure, in what environments and wider systems, and by whom; and how is this resource deployment monitored and controlled?

It has been found that the ideas of structure and process are very useful guides in obtaining a rich picture of the problem situation without imposing a spurious pattern upon it as technique-oriented approaches frequently do. (The queuing theory fanatic will always see the problem situation as a queuing problem!) Structure means the elements that do not change over a short time span such as, for example, the physical structure, the organizational structure, and the formal and informal reporting/communicating structure. Process means the elements that by their nature change continually (and/or continuously); in any organizational context these may be analyzed in terms of basic activities: planning to do something, doing it, monotoring how well it is done and its external effects, and taking action to correct deviations. More subtle, but an essential characteristic of any problem situation, is the relation between structure and process, the "climate" of the situation. Many problems are problems of mismatch between structure and process; it is worth pondering and repondering this relation as familiarity with the situation increases. In one study carried out in an engineering company that was organized functionally, prestige and power went with demonstrated technical competence within, for example, the electrical systems section or the procurement and purchasing department, but the overall organizational task was a project to create a new aircraft. The processes associated with this task did not match the functional structure, but middle-manager enthusiasm and commitment enabled unsuitable structures to survive. The problem posed concerned the need for improved information flow between the design department and other functions, but the real problem was the structural one, and the structure/process analysis revealed this clearly.

Building knowledge of the problem situation in this way enables the analyst to begin forming a view on a possible direction for his work, that is, a perspective on the work to be done within the problem-solving system. Is it to present alternatives (and their implications) among which a decisionmaker can choose, a "satisficing" solution feasible under various likely uncertainities, or is it to recommend a single specific solution arrived at by formal optimization procedures? In other words, the analyst will have decided on whether the problem is hard or soft, or whether it is to some extent both. This is crucial to the task of assembling an appropriate study team.

Exploring the problem situation in the way described will, of course, reveal much about both the client who initiates the study and the decisionmaker whose purposes it will serve. The analyst will learn about the problem perceptions of the client and decisionmaker, and about their expectations for the study. To focus on client and decisionmaker in this way is to focus on their objectives, and hence on any other objectives that may be present in the problem situation. It is useful to remember Kahn's statement (1960) that conflicting objectives are "an essential of good planning." Although the analyst will pay much attention to the client's and the decisionmaker's stated objectives, systems analysis should not assume that both parties actually know explicitly what their objectives are. The decision to undertake a systems analysis implies that objectives are to be debated, and examining the roles of client and decisionmaker by examining their objectives must include examining objectives counter to those most readily stated. Asking "whose objectives would these counter-objectives be?" initiates analysis of the political process through which the action to be taken will be decided. If the analysis concerns a matter of public policy within a climate of public debate, then skepticism concerning the decisionmaker's stated objectives is essential; the broader the policy issue under review, the more skeptical one should be. Concerning such high-level objectives, Hitch (1960, p.6) reminds us:

> Even in the best of circumstances ignorance and uncertainty about high-level objectives make reliance on official definitions a precarious procedure. We know little enough about our own personal objectives . . . National objectives can only be some combination or distillation of the objectives of people who comprise (or rule) the nation; and we should learn to be as skeptical and critical of the verbalizations and rationalizations that pass for national objectives as we have learned to be of apparent or claimed personal objectives.

This is no less true of objectives stated for problems of smaller organizations.

The scale and time-dependence of objectives are other important aspects to be examined. In a study carried out for a client that was a holding company, the decisionmakers were the managers of one of the constituent companies of the group. The issues concerned launching a new product that would take the company into a new market and a new kind of business. The decisionmakers had a number of specific local objectives related to the new product, linked to a relatively short time scale of one or two years. But the relation between the client and the decisionmaker in this study illustrated sharply that these objectives were themselves part of a larger objective tree, the higher levels of which concerned less concrete objectives (the new shape of the company's business) over a longer time (5 to 10 years). These more abstract and more distant objectives and purposes were very much a part of the problématique.

Clients and decisionmakers (and analysts!) can rarely define a hierarchy of objectives even at the end of a study; part of its purpose is to debate possible hierarchies and to elucidate and compare possibilities. If, on the other hand, the roles of client and decisionmaker, together with their relevant objectives, are clear and unequivocal, and resist challenge, then the study—by definition now hard—is more likely to involve, not debate and satisficing, but formal optimization.

5.3. The Problem Environment

The problem situation, which contains the study client and those who will make decisions in order to resolve the problems, is itself located in a number of environments, some of which are concrete, and some others of which are abstract; all are important in the analysis as a source of influences, possibilities, and constraints. The first point to note is that an environment is somehow "outside" the problem situation; that is to say, it is outside both the problem-content and the problem-solving systems. In other words, there must be boundaries between the systems that are the analyst's prime concern and the environments in which the systems are embedded. If we can define a system's boundaries (and there may be a number of different kinds), then we have said something important about the system's environments. Churchman (1971) suggests a method of doing this formally that I have found to be useful in a number of studies. He suggests that the decisionmaker role be defined by the precept that the decisionmaker has control over what is within the system. The boundary of the system encloses the set of things (physical and concrete) over which decisionmaking control can be exercised. An item outside the decisionmaker's control is by definition in the system's environment. In soft systems studies it is frequently illuminating to plot boundaries based on this definition and to compare the outcome with decisionmaking responsibilities in the real world. Problems in organizations often stem from a failure to match institutionalized system boundaries (the areas of responsibility of sections, departments, and so on) with actual managerial decisionmaking authority. Experience suggests that the existence of a role of "coordinator" is quite often an indicator of the existence of a mismatch of this kind.

Optner (1965), writing on business problem solving with the idea that business operations constitute a system, defines the environment as "a set of all objects, within some specific limit, that may conceivably have bearing upon the operation of the system." Since he allows that the "objects" may be abstract or concrete, this is a frightening definition for the systems analyst! Hall (1962, p. 149), who is more technologically oriented, but otherwise writes in the same vein, points out the importance of the environment in this way:

> Opportunities for new systems arise in the environment. Boundary conditions for new systems are determined by the environment. Facts for making all kinds of decisions come from the environment, as do all the resources needed for new developments.

He goes on to urge examining the physical and technical environment, the economic and business environment, and the social environment; to these, for most systems analyses, we may add the political and legislative environment, as well as the sets of attitudes, values, and standards of judgment—what Vickers (1965) terms the "appreciative" environment—that will profoundly affect what is possible and what is not.

Obviously, the systems analyst must pay great attention to the environment surrounding the problem situation; equally obviously, the full variety of all relevant environments cannot possibly be absorbed, and some means of reducing the potentially overwhelming inflow of information has to be found. This is a fundamental problem of the whole problem-formulation phase, and I shall return to it shortly. But at this stage we may note that the other major idea relevant to exploring the problem is here extremely useful: the idea of limits and constraints on the study. An initial scanning of environments may be done by regarding them as sources of constraints on the study that are "given," either because they are fundamental natural characteristics (such as physical limits imposed by geography), or because they are beyond any powers that the identified decisionmakers possess or are likely to possess in the future. Laws, for example, are not permanent and may be changed over a period of time. But in most studies the legislative environment is one that is given; knowing the limitations and restrictions it imposes may reduce the analyst's task, and help to define a solution.

Defining other limitations on the study is less straightforward when they derive from less explicit sources: convention, tradition, or common practice. Here the mood is one of impatience with such restrictions, and the analyst

> should seek to establish the boundaries of the issue under investigation where thought and analysis show them to be and not where off-the-cuff decision or convention, whether established by government jurisdiction, academic tradition, or industrial practice, would have them be [Quade, 1982, pp. 51–52].

What is most important of all is that the analyst should record at various times what he is accepting as limitations and constraints. Only if this information is clearly recorded will it be possible later on, as knowledge increases and perspectives change, to redefine limitations with clarity, or to lift constraints so that the implications of doing so can be explored coherently.

To summarize the ideas relevant to the problem-formulation stage of a systems analysis: In a perceived problem situation there is a client who causes a study to be carried out and there are decisionmakers. The problems perceived are hard or soft or, most often, a mixture of both. There are possible definitions of the relevant problem-content system, these depending upon decisionmakers' objectives, either explicitly stated or implicit in the situation. Such systems are affected by a number of environments that are a source of constraints on what can be achieved. The aim of problem formulation is to explore the study situation, making use of these ideas, so that a study outline can be prepared.

Now it is obvious that these concepts are related to each other, and that it is in fact not possible to examine any one of them in isolation from the others. This is the fundamental problem of the problem-formulation phase. The choice of decisionmaker determines which systems and which environments are relevant, and hence what constraints there are on the study. Decisionmakers' objectives are affected by various environments, but they also themselves affect these environments, and so on. The important consequence of these interactions is that it is essential that problem formulation be carried out, not in a straight-through, once-and-for-all way, but in a way that allows initial tentative findings and judgments to be modified continually as knowledge is gained.

5.4 Formulating the Problem: The Activities

It is not always easy to take seriously the activities involved in problem formulation. There is sometimes a feeling that, until models are being constructed, for example, or alternatives are being evaluated, the real work has not begun. But, in fact, which models to construct, which alternatives to compare, and whether the study outcome is to be a solution feasible under defined uncertainties, a formal optimization, or a presentation of alternative possibilities are all decided in the problem-formulation phase. In the kinds of situations in which systems analysis is appropriate, problems are far from obvious, and the way the problem is formulated determines the course of the remainder of the study. A philosopher of the process of inquiry, John Dewey (1938, p. 108), summarized the importance of the initial stages thus:

> It is a familiar and significant saying that a problem well put is half-solved. To find out *what* the problem and problems are which a problematic situation presents to be inquired into, is to be well along in inquiry. To mistake the problem involved is to cause subsequent inquiry to go astray . . . The way in which a problem is conceived decides what specific suggestions are entertained and which are dismissed; what data are selected and which rejected; it is the criterion for relevancy and irrelevancy of hypotheses and conceptual structures. [Emphasis in original.]

In order to decide "the way in which a problem is conceived" in "a problematic situation" it is necessary to decide which facts, out of the plethora available, are what Dewey calls "the facts of the case." The starting point must be the problem situation (rather than what is said to be the problem) and the first activity is to gain an understanding of the history of the situation. Using the kind of questions discussed above, the analyst seeks to understand how the problematic situation developed. What experiences led these particular role occupants, in this particular culture, embodying these particular values, to perceive a state of affairs as "a problem"?

Knowledge of how the situation evolved to its present form enables the analyst to begin the next activity: documenting the problem-content and problem-solving systems. The crucial question for the latter is: what are its resources? That for the former is: what is the nature of the study to be? and this may be answered by using the concepts discussed above. Answers to both questions enable problem-solving resources to be matched against problem-content requirements, and iteration enables a suitable balance to be achieved. The position at this point is somewhat analogous to that at which a scientist selects the most difficult problem that he has a reasonable chance of solving, given the intellectual and physical resources available to him (Medawar, 1967). Here the systems analyst's aim is to define the potentially most useful study that the problem-solving resources likely to be made available can carry out. Figure 5.1 shows how these activities interact, and includes, in the case of the problem-content system, iteration deriving from the basic ideas of client, decisionmakers, objectives, etc. (Appendix A includes a workbook, discussed below, that can help in the process of documenting the problem content.)

The sequence illustrated must be regarded as a single entity, in the sense that it is unlikely that any activity will be carried to completion at the first attempt. The problem-formulation stage may be taken as complete when iteration around the cycle of activities increases understanding to the point that a study outline or issue paper can be prepared. And even then it is, of course, possible at later stages of the study that new information, changing judgments, or new environmental forces may cause a return to problem formulation. If this happens, it is extremely valuable to find that the early work has been carefully documented. If it has, then it will be clear what changes are being made, which parts of the initial work stand, and what now needs to be done.

Experience with a large number of systems studies has suggested that the general shape of their initial stages was sufficiently similar to justify preparing a workbook to help in documenting problem-content and problem-solving systems. The context in which the workbook was developed (Checkland and Jenkins, 1974; Checkland, 1972, 1975) enabled its use to be studied experimentally. Initial difficulties pointed to the need for precise definitions of the main terms used in it; once this was done, it has been found helpful in both

```
                    ┌─→ Appreciate the history of the problem situation.
                    │                    │
                    │                    ▼
                    ├──── Document the problem-content and problem-solving systems.
                    │                    │
                    │         ┌──────────┴──────────┐
                    │         ▼                     ▼
                    │   ┌─────────────────┐   ┌─────────────────┐
                    │   │ Problem-Content │   │ Problem-Solving │
                    │   │     System      │   │     System      │
                    │   │  Client?        │   │ Likely resources│
                    │   │  Problem owners/│   │   human?        │
                    │   │  decision takers│   │   physical?     │
                    │   │  Their objectives│  │   intellectual? │
                    │   │  values?        │   │   financial?    │
                    │   │  Possible relev.│   │   time?         │
                    │   │  systems?       │   │ Likely constr.? │
                    │   │  Environmental  │   │                 │
                    │   │  constraints?   │   │                 │
                    │   └─────────┬───────┘   └────────┬────────┘
                    │             └────────┬───────────┘
                    │                      ▼
                    │         Check the match of the problem-content and
                    │                problem-solving systems.
                    │                      │
                    ├──── Modify the definitions of the problem-content and
                    │        problem-solving systems to achieve balance.
                    │                      │
                    ├──── Define and assemble the problem-solving team.
                    │                      │
                    ├──── Gather data relevant to the problem situation.
                    │                      │
                    │              Prepare issue papers.
                    │                      │
  ──────────────────┼──────────────────────┼──────────────────────
                    │                      │        Later stages of problem
                    │                      │             formulation
                    │                      ▼
                    │   ┌───────────────────────┐
                    │   │ Information from later│    ┌──┐
                    └───┤ stages may reopen     │    │  ├┐
                        │ the problem formulation│   │  ││
                        │                       │    └──┘│
                        │                       │     Issue papers
```

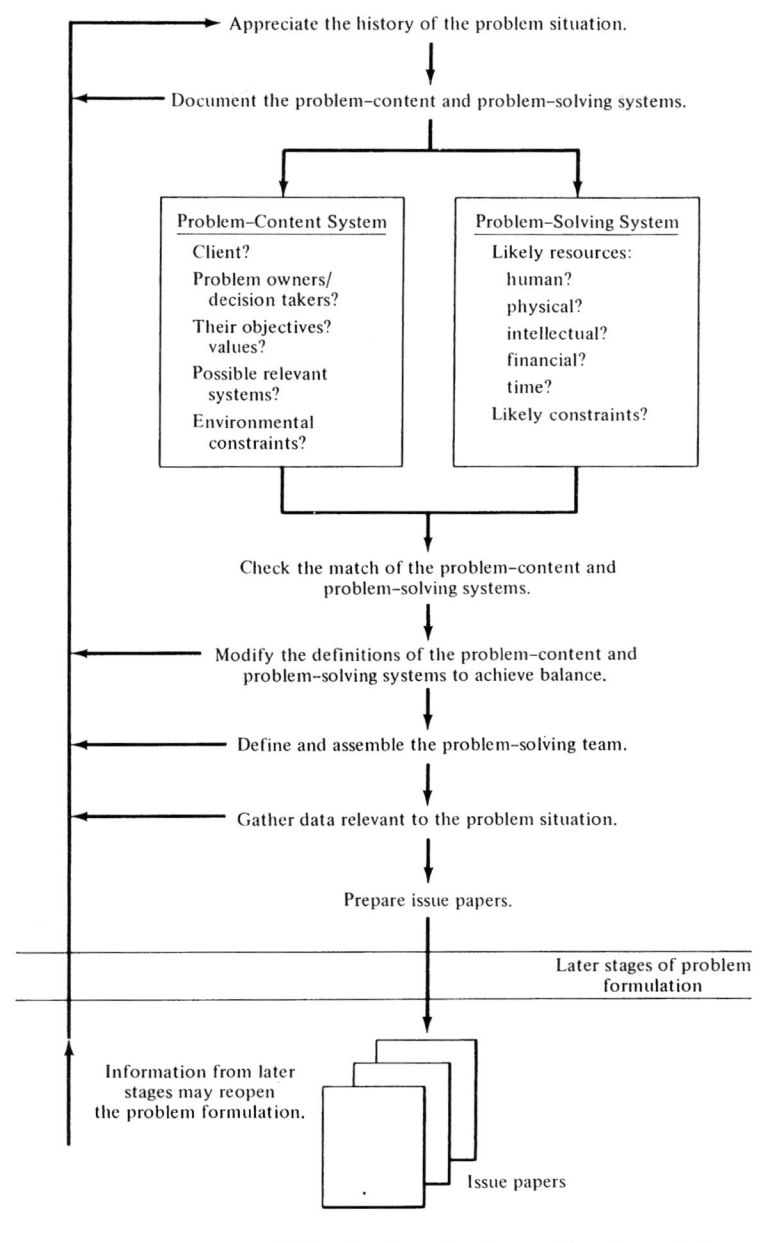

Figure 5.1. Concepts and activities involved in the problem-formulation stage of systems analysis.

large and small studies in industrial firms and in the public sector. The questions answered in the workbook are in Appendix A. Use of it in about 20 studies suggests that the most difficult question the systems analyst has to answer, and the one whose answer has the biggest effect on project outcome, is Who are the problem posers and decisionmakers?

Once documentation of problem-content and problem-solving systems has been completed and a balance achieved, so that the task defined is commensurate with the resources available, data collection can begin. The aim now is to explore the problem content further, so that papers can be produced that isolate the main issues, clarify the objectives of the study, and set out the major factors that will influence the final outcome. This must be done before the process starts, because there is always far too much data possibly relevant to the study; the analysts must therefore make prudent choices about what to gather and consider. It is here that the definition of the problem-content system begins to be useful: it provides an initial basis for data collection, it defines the starting points for gathering information (on the problem posers, decisionmakers, objectives, values, measures of performance, environmental constraints and so on), and gets the detailed work under way.

But when does the analyst stop? It is useful for the systems team to make a distinction between "data" (Latin "datum," what is given), and what we may call "capta" (Latin "captum," what the analysts decide to fetch from the problem area). When the team develops the feeling (and there can be no certain test that their feeling is appropriate) that they have moved from collecting data to defining and seeking out capta, then it is time to describe the problem area in some issue papers. Completing the study outline or issue papers may be taken as the formal end of the problem-formulation phase. They should set the scene for the study, indicate its scope, and define the kinds of alternatives that may be regarded as solving the problems perceived. These alternatives should not be the analysis itself, because they are based only on the most readily available data and capta. Quade (1982, p. 70) points out that, when the idea of such papers was developed, they were thought of as providing the person or group who had commissioned a study with the opportunity of calling a halt or going ahead:

> The original issue paper was supposed to be as complete an assessment of all that is currently known about a problem or issue as the readily available data would allow. The idea was to explore the problem at a depth sufficient to give the reader a good idea of its dimensions and the possible scope of the solution, so that it might be possible for management to conclude either to do nothing further or to commission a definitive study looking toward some sort of action recommendation.

Appendix B gives an outline content for issue papers.

It is difficult to say when such papers should be written, but experience is that in a well-conducted study the problem-formulation phase usually consumes 20–25 percent of the total effort.

5.5 Conclusion

A recent encyclopedia that aims to keep the educated man abreast of "modern thought" (Bullock and Stallybrass, 1977, p. 497) defines "problem solving" as

> that form of activity in which the organism is faced with a goal to be reached, a gap in the "route" to the goal and a set alternative means, none of which are immediately and obviously suitable.

Recent work on systems analysis has suggested that, the softer the problem, the more the emphasis must be placed on how concerned actors perceive problems; and on bringing out the underlying values and their conflicts, rather than on "engineering" a preferred alternative (Checkland, 1972, 1975, 1979, 1981; Vickers, 1965, 1970; Hammond, Klitz, and Cook, 1977). Checkland, for example, emphasizes the need to compare aspects of the problem situation with a number of systems models, each based on a "root definition" with one of a set of possible viewpoints. This process allows examination of what Vickers calls "appreciative systems" in which decisionmakers notice only certain aspects of reality and evaluate them according to particular standards of judgment; both the aspects noted and the standards of judgment change with time and experience, and from model to model. Hammond, Klitz, and Cook emphasize the need to examine, not only the "analytical models of external systems, that is, systems that exist outside of persons," but also models of the decisionmakers' "internal (cognitive) systems." But, despite these developments, and the uncertainty they introduce into our vision of what systems analysis might be in 10 to 15 years, it is certainly the case that most systems analysis is (and will continue to be) based upon the model of problem solving described so far in this handbook. It has been a useful model. It is also true that, no matter how systems analysis develops in the future, it will require an initial stage in which the area of concern is described and the issues to be faced are isolated. Such a stage will always be vital in any analysis, since it dictates subsequent work. It is not surprising that, in answering a questionnaire on systems analysis (Quade et al., 1976), more than 160 analysts and users of systems analysis rated "problem formulation and information gathering" as more important than the other stages of systems analysis.

Because early mistakes and false starts may be expensive in time and effort, the analyst needs a delicate touch in the early stages of problem formulation. He should be cautiously firm in making explicit use of the basic ideas that order the task, but he should be tentative in commitment. A commitment to a particular view of the problem content should emerge only slowly; the whole problem-formulation phase should be conducted in a spirit of inquiry. The analyst ought to expect to be surprised by what he learns.

In rating the problem hard or soft the analyst should err on the side of the latter, even though the specific techniques available to help during the main body of the study—modeling, simulation, optimization and the rest—are most useful in sharply defined situations in which, for example, a well-defined decisionmaker wants help in selecting among alternative ways of meeting a defined need. There has been much criticism of the insensitive use of hard systems analysis in public issues [see, for example, Hoos (1972, 1976) and Pollock (1972) for a rejoinder to Hoos's polemic] and it is certainly the case that taking a soft problem to be hard is more damaging to useful inquiry than the reverse. A soft analysis can always become harder if the study reveals this to be acceptable; but it is much more difficult to make a problem soft that was originally defined as hard.

Finally, the systems analyst engaged in problem formulation, although he is a would-be bringer of the light of reason to human decisionmaking, should not overestimate the part that overt rational thinking plays in most human situations. He must remember that a client setting up a systems analysis is making a political act—or at least it may be seen as such—and the political situation of which his study is a part should itself be studied. Whose political aims are served by the study? Who will be affected by the different possible kinds of recommendations? Who will be able to make the damaging claims that their views were not solicited? These are all questions the analyst should not ignore.

If the analyst's contribution to decisionmaking is ultimately less than he would wish, he may at least console himself with the thought that the very existence of his issue papers will have made more difficult the victory of the completely irrational. In a remarkable passage about the high-level decisionmaking prior to the Allied invasion of France in June 1944, Lord Zuckerman (1978) has recently described in his autobiography *From Apes to Warlords* the "nonsensical arguments" which went on, in those days before systems analysis existed, about the use of heavy bomber forces. The argument concerned whether or not they should aim to destroy the railway network ahead of Eisenhower's invasion force or should continue to bomb the industrial towns that sustained the enemy war effort, in particular, the towns concerned with aircraft production. Apparently no study ever considered more than one option; no attempt was made to compare rationally the likely costs and benefits of alternatives, and protagonists with an emotional commitment to one option simply sought to find facts to damage the others. Zuckerman writes (1978, pp. 236–237):

> After a thirty-year gap, I am utterly amazed by the nonsensical arguments about the plan [to destroy the railway network] to which one had to listen, and which are on record in contemporary documents and minutes of meetings. I had incorrectly assumed that planners were concerned to extract, as quickly as they could and for use in further planning, such facts as experimental enquiry and analysis of past operations could provide. This, however,

was clearly not general practice. Most of the people with whom I was now dealing seemed to prefer *a priori* belief to disciplined observation. . . . rational discussion . . . was at an end. All the opposing parties joined to defeat the apparent threat which the A[llied] E[xpeditionary] A[ir] F[orces] implied to the independence of the strategic air forces [who wished to continue bombing Germany]. It did not matter what considerations were advanced to upturn it.

We may be sure that, for any instance of judgmental decisionmaking, what is formulated as a problem in accordance with the guidelines described here will at the very least provide an opportunity through which experimental inquiry, analysis of past operations, disciplined observation, and rational discussion can bring the voice of reason into what might otherwise be an uncivilized wrangle.

Appendix A

A Workbook Outline to Aid Documenting the Problem-Content and Problem-Solving Systems

Definitions of Terms

Client: The person who wants to know or do something; he may commission the study. The implication is that he can cause something to happen as a result of the work. (He may also have the decisionmaker role.)

Decisionmaker: The role player in a human activity system who can alter (or at least try to alter) its content and activities and their arrangement and who makes resource allocations in it.

Problem poser: The person who has a feeling of unease about a situation, either a sense of mismatch between what is and what might be, or a vague feeling that things could be better, and who wants something done about it. The problem poser may not be able to define what he would regard as a "solution," and may not be able to articulate the feeling of unease in any precise way. (The analyst may assign to the role problem poser someone who does not himself recognize that he has posed the problem, and the problem poser may not be the decisionmaker. However, usually systems analyses are carried out for decisionmakers who are also problem posers.)

The Outline

1. *The study situation.* Take it to be one in which a client has commissioned the analysis; there is a problem-solving system (containing the analyst as

problem solver) whose efforts are brought to bear on a problem-content system (containing the roles of problem poser and decisionmaker, which may be coincident).
   1.1. The client.
   1.2. His aspirations.
2. *The problem-content system.*
   2.1. The occupants of the roles of problem poser and decisionmaker.
   2.2. The decisionmaker's and problem poser's versions of the nature of the problem.
   2.3. The decisionmaker's and problem poser's reasons for regarding the problem as a problem.
   2.4. The decisionmaker's and problem poser's expectations of the problem-solving system.
   2.5. The matters that the expectations listed in 2.4. suggest as highly valued by the decisionmaker and problem poser.
   2.6. Some possible names for the problem-content system.
   2.7. In describing the problem-content system initially, the likely relevant elements:
   nouns.
   verbs.
   2.8. Environmental constraints on the problem-content system.
3. *The problem-solving system.*
   3.1. The occupant(s) of the role of problem solver.
   3.2. The other persons (and roles) in the problem-solving system.
   3.3. The resources of the problem-solving system:
   people.
   physical resources.
   skills.
   finance.
   time.
   3.4. Likely or known environmental constraints on the problem-solving system.

Appendix B

A Format for Issue Papers

An issue paper is as complete an assessment of all that is currently known about the problem or issues as the readily available data will allow. The idea of an issue paper is to explore the problem in sufficient depth to give the reader a good idea both of its dimensions and the possible scope of a solution, so that a decisionmaker can decide either to do nothing further or to commission a study looking toward some sort of action recommendation.

A standard issue-paper format includes these main sections:

A. Source and background of the problem.
B. Reasons for attention.
C. Groups or institutions toward which corrective activity is directed.
D. Beneficiaries and losers.
E. Related programs and activities.
F. Goals and objectives.
G. Measures of effectiveness.
H. Framework for the analysis.
   1. Kinds of alternatives
   2. Possible methods.
   3. Critical assumptions.
I. Alternatives.
   1. Descriptions.
   2. Effectivenesses.
   3. Costs.
   4. Spillovers (side effects).
   5. Comments on ranking of alternatives.
   6. Other considerations.
J. Recommendations that may emerge.
K. Appendices (as needed).

This outline is adapted from Quade (1982, pp. 71–76).

References

Ackoff, R. L. (1974). *Redesigning the Future.* New York: Wiley.

Bullock, A., and O. Stallybrass, eds. (1977). *The Fontana Dictionary of Modern Thought.* London: Fontana/Collins. Also published as *The Harper Dictionary of Modern Thought,* New York: Harper and Row.

Checkland, P. B. (1972). Towards a system-based methodology for real-world problem solving. *Journal of Systems Engineering* 3(2), 87–116.

———(1975). The development of systems thinking by systems practice—a methodology from an action research programme. In *Progress in Cybernetics and Systems Research* (R. Trappl and F. de P. Hanika, eds.). Washington D.C.: Hemisphere Publications.

———(1979). The problem of problem formulation in the application of a systems approach. In *Education in Systems Science* (B. A. Bayraktar et al., eds.). London: Taylor and Francis.

———(1981). *Systems Thinking, Systems Practice.* Chichester, England: Wiley.

———and G. M. Jenkins (1974). Learning by doing: Systems education at Lancaster University. *Journal of Systems Engineering* 4(1), 40–51.

Churchman, C. W. (1968). *Challenge to Reason.* New York: McGraw-Hill.

_____(1971). *The Design of Inquiring Systems.* New York: Basic Books.

Dewey, John (1938). *Logic, the Theory of Inquiry.* New York: Holt.

Hall, A. D. (1962). *A Methodology for Systems Engineering.* Princeton, New Jersey: Van Nostrand.

Hammond, K. R., J. K. Klitz, and R. I. Cook (1977). *How Systems Analysis Can Provide More Effective Assistance to the Policy Maker,* RM-77-50. Laxenburg, Austria: International Institute for Applied Systems Analysis.

Hitch, C. J. (1960). *On the Choice of Objectives in Systems Studies,* P-1955. Santa Monica, California: The Rand Corporation.

Hoos, Ida R. (1972). *Systems Analysis in Public Policy: A Critique.* Berkeley, California: University of California Press.

_____(1976). Engineers as analysts of social systems: A critical enquiry. *Journal of Systems Engineering* 4(2), 81–88.

Jenkins, G. M. (1969). The systems approach. *Journal of Systems Engineering* 1(1), 3–49.

Kahn, Herman (1960). *On Thermonuclear War.* Princeton, New Jersey: Princeton University Press.

Koestler, A. (1969). In *Beyond Reductionism: New Perspectives in the Life Sciences.* (A. Koestler and J. R. Smithies, eds.). London: Hutchinson.

Medawar, P. B. (1967). *The Art of the Soluble.* London: Methuen.

Optner, S. L. (1965). *Systems Analysis for Business and Industrial Problem Solving.* Englewood Cliffs, New Jersey: Prentice-Hall.

Pogson, C. H. (1972). Defining the "right" problem: A production control problem. *Journal of Systems Engineering* 3(2), 137–143.

Pollock, S. M. (1972). Review of *Systems Analysis in Public Policy: A Critique,* by Ida Hoos. *Science* 178, 739–740.

Quade, E. S. (1982). *Analysis for Public Decisions,* 2nd ed. New York: North-Holland.

_____, K. Brown, R. Levien, G. Majone, and V. Rakhmankulov (1976). *The State of the Art Questionnaire on Applied Systems Analysis: A Report on the Responses,* RR-76-17. Laxenburg, Austria: IIASA.

Raiffa, Howard (1976). Creating an international research institute. In *IIASA Conference '76.* Laxenburg, Austria: International Institute for Applied Systems Analysis, Vol. 1.

Rapoport, A. (1970). Modern systems theory—an outlook for coping with change. In *General Systems Yearbook.* Society for General Systems Research, Vol. 15.

Vickers, G. (1965). *The Art of Judgment.* London: Chapman and Hall.

_____(1970). *Freedom in a Rocking Boat.* London: Allen Lane, Penguin.

Zuckerman, Solly (1978). *From Apes to Warlords.* London: Hamish Hamilton; New York: Harper and Row.

Chapter 6
Objectives, Constraints, and Alternatives

Edward S. Quade

To help a decisionmaker means to help him achieve his true objectives; to do so, it is crucial to discover what they are. To find feasible alternatives (i.e., ways to achieve the objectives that are not ruled out by the constraints imposed on possible actions by nature, circumstance, authority, or the decisionmakers themselves) is often a central task of systems analysis, and frequently the most appreciated one. This chapter, expanding the remarks in Chapter 4, discusses problems of clarification and measurement related to objectives, the roles of objectives and constraints in determining alternatives, and methods for discovering and improving alternatives, and for eliminating the inferior possibilities.

6.1. Objectives

Ideally, objectives (and constraints, since they play a role similar to that of objectives) should be identified very early in a systems analysis study. In practice, however, even for hard problems (as Checkland defined them in Section 5.2) this is seldom possible. A clear, well thought through, precisely spelled out, and analytically useful statement that correctly reflects what the decisionmakers really want to accomplish is rarely presented to the analyst at the time the study is commissioned. Nevertheless, some idea of what is wanted is available. Tentative objectives, specific enough to get the analysis started, can be selected; these should suggest possible ways to achieve what is wanted. The impacts, or consequences, of implementing these alternatives are then imagined or estimated, taking into consideration any constraints known to exist, and their projected implications used to reexamine the first formulation of objectives and introduce modifications. As the study progresses, the analysts, their sponsors, and others learn from this early work. The decisionmakers for whom the work is being done are also influenced by pressure from interested constituents, and from other decisionmakers who may see their domain adversely affected by what they anticipate may occur as a result of the study. Hence objectives and alternatives change and constraints are introduced or removed. This is one of the major reasons why systems analysis must be an iterative process.

To someone without systems analysis experience it may seem odd that we begin here with the assumption that the objectives will not be spelled out sufficiently to allow the analysis team to adopt them as given and proceed to their work. However, experience is almost universal on this point: decisionmakers seldom have carefully articulated objectives. This apparently troublesome fact—which leads to the iterative search for realistic and acceptable objectives as part of the systems analysis—may lead the wishful analyst into dreaming of the "perfect client" who is the exception, so that he can get quickly beyond the beginning statement of objectives to what he may think of as the real analysis. However, here again the voice of experience suggests that it may be better not to have such clearly defined objectives right at the beginning before at least some preliminary analysis has taken place, for the objectives stated at the beginning will probably not be as well thought through as they should be; as a result of using such early primitive objectives, the analyst will face the dilemma of tailoring his work to goals he suspects to be defective, or trying at the end to alter what he has done in order to squeeze in new perspectives. The experienced analyst does not rue the existence of hazy starting objectives, but is thankful for them, as they offer him the opportunity to help his clients consider their objectives carefully while the study is still in its formative stage.

The objectives of individuals or organizations are the principles that are supposed to motivate how they act. As Sugden and Williams (1978, p. 233) put it, "They are not pious incantations of ethical or ideological beliefs which unfortunately cannot be acted on because of 'political constraints'; they express intentions to act." The analyst needs information specific enough to identify a set of alternatives and to guide the choice among them. In particular, he would like enough specificity to be able to tell what sorts of alternatives to investigate and what types of consequences are likely to be significant.

Even when objectives appear to be well specified at the outset, they should not always be adopted uncritically by the analyst. Means are sometimes taken for ends: A decisionmaker may say that his objective is to find out where in his district to place a new comprehensive medical center, but his real objective may be broader, perhaps to improve all health services in his community; better ways to achieve the real objective may be to provide several neighborhood health centers or services through other mechanisms (hospital outpatient clinics or health maintenance organizations). Perhaps programs focusing on maternal and child health services or screening apparently well people to discover heart and cancer conditions should be considered. Unless the broader objective is investigated by the analyst, these latter alternatives will not appear and the decisionmaker may never realize how much more he could do with his resources.

Desired goals (or aspirations) can be stated easily, even in soft problems (as defined in Section 5.2); however, specifying objectives (or targets) one has a reasonable hope of attaining and assigning priorities to them may take considerable thought, and even research. It does not make sense for a person to make up his mind as to what he wants until he has a fair idea of what he can get and when. Thus, the investigation of objectives usually must extend beyond the problem-formulation phase of the work. An important way in which analysis helps in clarifying objectives is that it determines the undesirable as well as the desirable consequences of the alternatives that follow an assumption about objectives. The decisionmaker, when confronted with these consequences, can ask himself whether he is willing to accept what they imply. If not, he will have to modify his goals.

In the effort to clarify objectives and find ways to measure their attainment, it is helpful to discuss the issue under analysis with critical and skeptical outsiders who have no stake in the outcome. One seeks answers to questions such as "What is really at stake here?" Since attainment of the ultimate goal may be many years off, what practical intermediate goals should we strive for? Techniques such as "value clarification" and "value critique" may also be helpful (as described by Dunn, 1981).

For certain issues, the question of whose objectives are relevant must be considered. For public issues, is it some subset of today's citizens or of future generations? The decisionmaker is merely the person or organization charged with the responsibility for changing the system, and the analyst may have to find some discreet way to make this clear (Sugden and Williams, 1978, pp. 232–242). Moreover, different interest groups have different objectives.

High-level objectives tend to be ambiguous, one reason being that it is a political advantage to appeal to as many people as possible. In fact, it is often much easier in the political process to agree on an action or program than on a goal (unless the latter is indefinite), for people may have different motives for what they are willing to do. High-level objectives that express general good intentions are valid over a long time period and are the easiest for the decisionmaker to state (Hovey, 1968). A frequent problem is that such objectives are too general for direct use in analytical studies. A lower-level objective that is a means to achieve the higher-level objective may be required for analysis. To build a new health center is both a low-level objective and a means to improve health services, a higher-level objective. Clear definitions of low-level objectives are usually more easily provided and are technically easier to use for finding and ranking alternatives. However, misleading results may occur if the low-level objectives are not, under all circumstances, an appropriate means to achieve the higher-level objectives. The relation need not be direct; for example, to relocate fire stations to provide better fire service, the low-level objective of reducing the average travel time from fire stations to fires serves well as a substitute for the higher-level objective of providing better protection of lives and property (Section 3.3 and Walker, Chaiken, and Ignall, 1979). Travel time is, moreover, easily measurable and can thus serve as an estimate of the extent to which the alternatives attain the objective.

Alternatives designed with one objective in mind can differ considerably from those designed with another uppermost, even though both have the same higher-level goal. This is a difficulty that can arise when one attempts to make a relatively vague higher-level objective operational by using a more specific lower-level formulation. Wohlstetter (1964, p. 123) illustrates this point for the case of automobile traffic safety:

> The city fathers would like to reduce the number of violations of the law. They would also like to fine or put in the clink as many violators as they can. There are two well known alternative techniques for accomplishing these ends; one is the familiar ambush technique; the other is sometimes called the visible patrol technique. The first increases the probability of interception and arrest. The second discourages culpability. Now if our goal is to maximize the number or proportion of speeders punished, or the total of municipal revenue through fines, probably the best way to do the job is by ambush, however uneasy such a sneaky tactic makes us. If our goal, on the other hand, is a reduction in the total number of traffic accidents, say, or in the number of attempts to violate the law (even if on the whole such attempts at evasion as do take place are more likely to be successful, since the culprit is aware of the cop's presence), it may very well be that the most frequent, obvious presence of policemen capable of instantaneous retaliation against speeders would encourage caution, and so achieve such goals best.

It is interesting to review the cases discussed in Chapter 3 in the light of these remarks about objectives.

The basic objective of the Greater New York Blood Program is to have blood available when and where needed—always. The only admissible exception is that elective uses can possibly be be postponed when necessary, although the costs of such decisions are recognized as making them undesirable. Deriving from this basic objective—which was being met adequately when the systems analysis was undertaken—are two subordinate objectives: to reduce the amount of blood being outdated (and hence discarded) to the lowest level consistent with the basic objective, and to reduce the costs of maintaining the blood supply at the points of use as much as possible consistent with the basic objective. The direct simplicity of these objectives contributed a great deal to the crisp clarity of the analysis and its successful implementation, because these objectives were widely accepted.

The basic objective of the Wilmington Bureau of Fire is that of any fire department: to hold down as much as possible the human (death and injury)

Section 6.1. Objectives

and property losses from fire. However, owing to the lack of information in the firefighting community about the relations between this objective and firefighting deployments and activities, this bureau—and the systems analysts called in to help with its planning problem—accepted three objectives that were proxies for the basic objective: to keep travel times to individual locations down to an acceptably low level, to keep the average travel time in a region at an acceptable level, and to maintain reasonable workloads for fire companies. As in the case of the Greater New York Blood Program, before the systems analysis began the Wilmington firefighters were achieving their basic objective to a level that the community accepted without protest, so that one could argue pragmatically that the existing level met the basic objective. Their experience did not include the idea of searching systematically for ways to maintain the level of service while lowering costs to the city by redeployment or other means. Analysts from outside with a different background, however, took the objective of the analysis to be to achieve a redeployment pattern that maintained the level of achievement of the basic objective, while reducing the cost of the service or raising its standard, or both, as judged by the proxy objectives.

In the study of the Oosterschelde estuary, the basic objective was to protect it from future flooding caused by violent storms, but the level of protection to be provided, as well as the myriad other objectives (ranging from the concerns about microscopic organisms to those about humans) were not clear at the beginning of the work and thus were open for analysis. While the basic objective was widely agreed upon, the analysts could count on no such consensus for the others, and, for this reason, had to keep them all flexibly in view until the time for decision, in order to allow the many concerned parties to make their own judgments about them. (In fact, in many analyses in which conflicting social and political objectives are strong, this flexibility with respect to secondary objectives may have to be retained.)

In the IIASA study of the world's energy future for the next 50 years, since there was no world energy executive—or even a closely knit set of officials who could be thought of as an approximation—the analysts had to attribute objectives to the world that would seem reasonable to the many executives and analysts who might later want to use the study's findings as a contribution to their own thinking about their particular energy problems. In broad terms the basic objective assumed by the analysts was that the world would want to sustain its use of energy indefinitely at a level that would maintain the standard of living in developed parts of the world and allow the developing parts to improve their standard, while accepting an expected population growth. Supporting this basic objective were many other objectives, for example, making the world's energy future grow by a natural and fairly smooth evolution from the present world energy posture. While most of these supporting objectives were expected to be widely subscribed to, variant views were expected on some—an expectation that proved to be realistic. For example, some solar energy enthusiasts feel that the assumption of a sustained standard of living is inappropriate, that a smooth transition should be replaced by a sudden switch to solar energy, and that future world energy use should be assumed to undergo a significant per capita reduction.

In sum, it is important to consider and evolve a clear concept of the objectives. Agreement on a single objective can do much to simplify the work. However, our examples suggest that a consensus may not be achievable, particularly at the beginning of the analysis, when the consequences of various objectives may not be perceived realistically by all concerned. On the other hand, when there are myriad and conflicting objectives (as in the Oosterschelde example), analysis can illuminate them and their consequences so as to allow accommodation among potentially conflicting parties in the process of deciding on a course of action. All of these matters emphasize the importance of having a clear view of all relevant objectives, even if they cannot be organized into a coherent and congenial set.

In brief, finding the right objective is crucial, more important than finding the very best alternative. The wrong objective means the research is devoted to solving the wrong problem; to designate a slightly inferior alternative as best is not nearly so serious.

Measuring Effectiveness

To be considered an alternative, a course of action must be consistent with the decisionmaker's objectives, i.e., offer some hope of attaining the objectives, or at least of coming closer to them. For the purpose of quantitative analysis we would like a scale on which the effectivenesses of the various alternatives in attaining the objectives can be measured. The alternatives can then be compared and ranked in terms of effectiveness, that is, by their standings on the effectiveness scale.

Unfortunately, a satisfactory scale cannot always be easily found. The problem is that many objectives are difficult or impossible to quantify directly in any useful fashion. It is therefore necessary to use a surrogate or proxy, a substitute objective that can be measured and that approximates the extent to which the real objective is attained. The problem is to get a good approximation. Thus, to measure the quality of medical care in a community, the infant mortality rate is often used as a proxy, even though it merely measures one aspect of the quality of medical care; to measure fire-department performance, response time is often used (Walker, Chaiken, and Ignall, 1979, p. 81).

One technique for finding quantifiable ways to measure effectiveness is to try several successive modifications of tentative possibilities for stating the objective to see whether any substitutes or proxies are suggested. Sometimes it can be easier to examine several possible proxies to see whether, if they were attained, the desired end would also be achieved.

Section 6.1. Objectives

The mark of a good proxy is that its achievement closely reflects achieving the real objective. Unfortunately, there are a number of inadequate but common approaches in use.

One approach that is not only inadequate but conceptually wrong is to use input to measure output; for example, to compare the quality of primary school education in various districts in terms of expenditures per pupil. A second is to use workload measures or efficiency measures to compare quality of output, say, to compare the quality of primary education on the basis of teacher-pupil ratios.

Consider a single unambiguous objective, say, to improve garbage collection. To facilitate comparisons, it is useful to have a scale on which to measure the effectiveness of the various possibilities. But there is no obvious scale to measure better garbage collection, so we need a proxy—a substitute objective measured by, to give a few examples, the percentage of city blocks remaining without health hazards, the reduction in the number of fires involving uncollected solid waste, rodent bites, or valid citizen complaints. All of these unfortunately, treat only an aspect, not the full value, of better garbage collection. In practice, people often use even less satisfactory scales, for instance, an input measure (expenditure per household) or an efficiency measure (number of tons collected per man-hour) or a workload measure (tons of waste collected) that indicate nothing about the quality of the service.

When several attributes need to be considered, a combination is sometimes used in which the various attributes are assigned weights, resulting in an ordinal or cardinal utility function. The failing here is that the function is to a large extent the product of the analyst's judgment of the relative importance of the attributes and not that of the responsible decisionmakers. The decisionmakers, if they were willing to spend the time, could work out their own set of weights [with guidance from the analyst (Raiffa, 1968)] but even here the analyst's influence would be powerful. Hatry (1970, p. 774) comments:

> There is no doubt that the job of decisionmakers would be easier if a single effectiveness measure could appropriately be used. However, I contend that such procedures place the analyst in the position of making a considerable number of value judgments that rightfully should be made in the *political* decision-making process, and *not* by the analyst. Such value judgments are buried in the procedures used by the analysts and are seldom revealed to, or understood by, the decision makers.
>
> Such hocus pocus in the long run tends to discredit analysis and distract significantly from what should be its principal role: to present to decision makers alternative ways of achieving objectives, and to estimate and display all the major tradeoffs of cost and effectiveness that exist among these alternatives. [Emphasis in the original.]

The Oosterschelde analysis described in Section 3.4 shows, not only that it is not necessary to push disparate measures of effectiveness into a common measure, but also that displaying them with their relevant objectives can have important benefits for the decisionmakers.

In selecting a scheme to measure effectiveness, we are not only looking for a scale that is positively correlated with the objective under consideration but also for one for which the required data can be obtained.

Suppose, for example, an analyst evaluates an ongoing government program for training computer operators. If the objective of the program is the eventual increase in the gross domestic product (GDP), how can effectiveness be measured? One possibility is to calculate the increase in GDP caused by the increase in the income of the trainee that results from the training he receives; this requires that the income of the trainee be total compensation (i.e., including fringe benefits) and that adjustment be made for displacing any previous workers by the trainees.

But how do we actually get the needed information? By following the history of the trainees after they leave the program, it is possible to estimate their actual income, but how much of any change can be attributed to the training? One way to get the desired information would be to carry out a social experiment (Section 7.6) in which participants are assigned randomly either to the program or to a control group, and then follow the wage experience of both groups. But the experiment could well be much more costly than the training program alone. A practical substitute would be to use the wage experience of a group of people having similar backgrounds to the trainees for comparison purposes. It is imperfect, but conceptually correct; a measure based on it is likely to be superior to an output measure such as the percentage of trainees who get jobs as computer operators.

Multiple Objectives

A decisionmaker may have more than one objective. If so, they may conflict; he may wish to reduce expenses but increase staff or to increase highway safety on a motorway between two cities but to decrease the travel time. In any event, if there are two or more objectives, they compete (except possibly for pairs where one is the means to the other) in the sense that, for given resources, if the decisionmaker strives for maximum attainment of a particular one, he must accept less than maximum attainment of the others.

It is obvious that one cannot maximize benefits and minimize cost simultaneously or do something similar for any other pair of goals. But if the measures of attainment for these goals have a common unit, one can create a new goal to achieve the most advantageous combination. For instance, one can maximize benefits minus costs (as in cost–benefit analysis) provided both can be expressed in monetary units (Nagel and Neef, 1979).

If there are several decisionmakers, each with his own set of objectives, a number of different approaches can be used to expedite the process of reducing the number of objectives to some that can be used as a basis for analysis

Section 6.1. Objectives

(Eilon, 1972; Keeney and Raiffa, 1976). The following list gives some examples—each of these approaches requires discussion among the decisionmakers holding competing objectives and a certain amount of compromise and concession:

Objectives that are only means to achieve other objectives can be eliminated.

If all the objectives can be interpreted as means to achieve some higher-level objective, and a relevant way to measure its effectiveness or that of a good proxy corresponding to this objective can be found, then this higher-level objective may serve as the single objective.

A preference ordering of objectives can sometimes be set up and used to effect tradeoffs among them. A solution is first determined using the highest-ranking objective; then an effort is made to achieve as much of the second as possible without sacrificing too much of the first; and so on.

All objectives except the most important one can be converted into constraints, by agreement on a minimum level of attainment acceptable on each.

Tradeoffs among the objectives can be worked out and used to construct a composite index of worth, a value or utility function (decision analysis; see Raiffa, 1968).

No effort can be made to "optimize" with respect to any specific objective. Instead, all objectives can be converted into constraints and a solution determined under the agreement that any solution satisfying all constraints—called a *satisficing* solution—will be "good enough."

It is, of course, not always possible to reach the agreement necessary to implement any of these simplifications, although the use of special techniques to increase the value sensitivity of decisionmakers (Dror, 1975, p. 250) may make them more amenable to compromise. We will treat value sensitivity in Section 8.9 after discussing satisficing and the more common schemes for presenting results: cost-effectiveness and cost–benefit analysis, decision analysis, and the so-called "scorecards."

What we cannot do satisfactorily is construct a unique group objective from all the individual objectives that automatically weights all the separate ones. Arrow (1951) has proved, for example, that, under a few reasonable assumptions, there is no completely satisfactory general procedure for obtaining a group ranking from the rankings of the individual group members.

Some idea of the interplay among objectives and their measures can be gained from looking more closely at the blood availability and utilization example. According to the prevailing doctrine, the basic objective is, as we said earlier, to have blood available when and where needed. However, to this baldly idealistic objective—which could well entail very high costs—was added a qualification: that elective uses of blood be allowed to be postponed when supplies are short. Within the framework of a system meeting this goal, the analysts considered two additional objectives: to reduce the amount of blood being outdated (and hence discarded) and to reduce the costs of maintaining the blood supply at the points of use (the proxy measure for this objective being the average number of weekly deliveries to a hospital blood bank).

The basic objective could be achieved by maintaining very large supplies at the hospital blood banks at all times, but this policy would entail very large outdating rates; in fact, at the time of the study most areas in the United States maintained policies with this approach and had outdating rates of 0.20—a fifth of the blood donated was not put to its ultimate good use. On the other hand, very low outdating rates could be achieved merely by keeping minimal stocks at the hospital blood banks, but this would run the risk of seriously prejudicing the basic objective of availability where needed whenever needed. Another policy could perhaps be imagined as meeting the demands of the basic objective and the desire to reduce outdating to a minimum: keep all blood centrally and deliver expeditiously when needed. Very little speculation is needed to determine this policy's unacceptability; besides escalating delivery costs, there would be unacceptable time delays in the face of short-term health emergencies.

The study actually aimed at a compromise among all of these objectives, and achieved it by keeping the basic objective at its former high and acceptable level while reducing the outdating and shortage rates (these latter causing extra deliveries to be made from the center to the hospital blood banks). The results of implementing the policy suggested by the analysis were: outdating reduced from 20 percent to 4 percent, average weekly deliveries per hospital blood bank reduced from 7.8 to 4.2 (these figures were also an indication of the increased adequacy of the hospital blood bank's supply, especially since 1.4 of the 4.2 weekly deliveries were to cover shortages, the other 2.8 being routine prescheduled deliveries). Some experimentation with their models convinced the analysts that the 4 percent outdate rate was about the smallest that could be achieved in this balance among the three objectives; in other words, this outdate rate represented a cost of pursuing a balance, rather than just this one objective.

Similar discussions could be generated for the other examples in Chapter 3, but they would be too long for the space available here. Nor would they contribute essentially new insights. However, the diligent reader would find the sources from which we have drawn our brief accounts a rich mine of instructive issues of the sort indicated in the blood-bank discussion.

6.2. Constraints

The objectives suggest the alternatives; the constraints restrict them and reduce the number of possibilities that can be considered. Constraints are thus more likely to simplify than to complicate the work of the analyst.

Section 6.2. Constraints

Constraints often perform a function similar to that of objectives from an evaluation point of view. Simon (1964, p. 20) writes:

> It is doubtful whether decisions are generally directed towards a goal. It is easier and clearer to view decisions as being concerned with discovering courses of action that satisfy a whole set of constraints. It is this set, and not any one of its members, that is most accurately viewed as the goal of the action.
>
> If we select any of the constraints for special attention, it is (a) because of its relation to the motivations of the decisionmaker, or (b) because of its relation to the search process that is generating or designing particular courses of action. These constraints that motivate the decisionmaker and those that guide his search for actions are sometimes regarded as more "goal-like" than those that limit the actions he may consider, or those that are used to test whether a potential course of action he has designed is satisfactory. Whether we treat all the contraints symmetrically or refer to some asymmetrically, as goals, is largely a matter of linguistic or analytic convenience.

When a distinction between objectives and constraints is made, it is usually based on the idea of accepting the constraint as an absolute restriction, in contrast to an objective or goal that may be open ended. Majone (1978) suggests, and we concur, that when there are several objectives they can always be traded off at the margin if this leads to an improvement in the total utility. In other words, it is reasonable to sacrifice a particular objective if it thereby improves the situation as a whole. A constraint cannot be so exchanged, for its logical force resides wholly in its inviolability, but the analyst should look beyond the less rigid constraints set by the decisionmaker to see if the gain resulting from relaxing them would justify the sacrifice. Thus, the translations of a decisionmaker's desires into a problem formulation, including the definitions of limit values (constraints), must be very carefully done, for, once a constraint (or limit value) is established by or in concurrence with the decisionmaker, it will be held to during analysis (although, of course, it may be changed in a later analysis). Majone (1978, p. 20) remarks:

> The opportunity cost of a proposed policy constraint must be carefully considered before the constraint becomes firmly embedded in the analytic structure. As Hitch and McKean (1960, p. 196) write, "casually selected or arbitrary constraints can easily increase system cost or degrade system performance manifold, and lead to solutions that would be unacceptable to the person who set the constraints in the first place." They cite the example of a weapon-systems study, where a constraint on acceptable casualities led to solutions in which 100 million dollars was being spent, at the margin, to save a single life. Many more lives could have been saved with the same resources. Had the policymakers realized the opportunity cost of their safety requirements, they would probably have set them at a lower level. Or, like good utilitarians, they may have chosen to treat the risk factor as a subgoal, to be optimized compatibly with other system's requirements and the available resources.

The constraints may be so restrictive that no alternative will attain the objective. To demonstrate that something cannot be done, or can only be done if certain constraints are removed, may be just as important as to show that something can be done, for doing so can save a great deal of wasted effort.

Here again the blood availability example illustrates the points. We have so far treated the desirability of always having blood available when and where needed as an objective, because the existing system allowed modest shortfalls affecting elective procedures. However, if it had been considered and treated as an inviolable constraint—one that could easily be advocated by someone not familiar with the usual working of the health system—the analysis and its findings would have been violently transformed, as also would the results of implementing them.

On the other hand, a constraint that is not within the decisionmaking system may be intrinsically inviolable. For example, the IIASA energy study could not yield a use of fossil fuels over the next 50 years greater than the available supply. However, careful scrutiny of the technical possibilities yielded new views of this constraint, as new forms of fossil resources could be exploited as fuels when technology and economics become favorable (example: oil from oil shales) or the available supplies could be extended by combining them with more advanced technologies (example: using breeder reactors to fuel coal gasification).

The lesson is simple: objectives and constraints must not be treated as inviolable, but must be scrutinized from many points of view as the analysis proceeds and new possibilities emerge, and their roles should be subject to change. Also, as Checkland suggests in Section 5.3, it is important for the analyst to keep track throughout his work of the constraints under which he believes he is operating.

6.3. Alternatives

The search for alternatives is the activity that gives form and structure to systems analysis—and is probably the most creative aspect of the profession's work. No amount of modeling and evaluation will help attain a solution unless the analyst can discover, design, or invent one or more satisfactory alternatives, that is to say, actions or policies that offer hope of accomplishing what the decisionmaker wants. No amount of evaluation will uncover a best alternative available unless it appears among those investigated.

An obvious illustration is suggested by Sugden and Williams (1978, p. 231):

> Consider, for example, a cost–benefit analysis that compares the effects of undertaking a large programme of road-building in a city with the effects of taking no action and which finds that the former policy is to be preferred.

Section 6.3. Alternatives

This might then be used as an argument that the whole programme ought to be undertaken even though all that has been shown is that this is better than doing nothing at all. It might well be that undertaking only a part of the programme is preferable to either of the alternatives that has been studied.

To generate alternatives at the start of a study is clearly a creative act. Once we have one, it is easy to design many related alternatives that are more costly or less efficient or possibly even marginally better, but significant improvement is harder to achieve. One must make a deliberate effort to think of possibilities; a systematic search for alternatives should be aided by brainstorming and talking to a variety of people.

To design alternatives frequently requires becoming well acquainted with the relevant technologies and working closely with specialists who have detailed knowledge of the technical possibilities. For example, the flood-control engineers developed the options for protecting the Oosterschelde estuary that were considered by the Rand team of systems analysts. In the IIASA study of world energy supply and demand a great deal of effort was expended on detailed inquiries into the possible technical options that might be available for use with many forms of energy sources: coal, oil, solar, ocean thermal, water power, and so on. The characteristic properties of these technical options could then enter the systems analysis calculations in the forms of contributions to the total energy supply, costs, material requirements, demands on the available stock of capital, and so on.

This is not to say that the systems analyst should just consult a few technologists and then adopt some of their ideas as alternatives. Experience shows that an interplay between the original ideas and the issues in the analysis may suggest new and important options, with much improved properties in the light of the compromises and tradeoffs that the analysis reveals as required. For example, although the IIASA study of world energy supply and demand started with the presumption that it would be possible for the world to move in 50 years from a major dependence on exhaustible sources of energy to principal reliance on renewable sources, the analysis showed that, with the alternatives first proposed, this would be so difficult as to be virtually impossible in so short a period. New alternatives projecting a significant increase in the use of energy from exhaustible sources had to be considered (as Table 3.6 shows), although the proportion of the total supply from such sources could be expected to decrease somewhat (as Figure 3.10 shows). Furthermore, in designing these new alternatives, the analysts were forced to project a continuing high use of gas and easily transportable liquid fuels. With use of oil and gas from fossil sources having to decline for both supply and cost-of-production reasons, attention turned, as Figure 3.10 shows, to coal liquefaction, since the world has huge coal reserves.

In the usual autothermal process for converting coal into a liquid form, a large amount of energy is lost, and the resulting liquid contains only about half of the energy content of the coal that enters the process. Hence, the analysts turned to a new (allothermal) process yet to be developed. The IIASA analysis team observed (Energy Systems Program Group, 1981, p. 33):

> For the allothermal process the process heat and the required hydrogen are supplied exogenously, preferably by means of heat from a nuclear reactor . . . or in more futuristic schemes by means of hydrogen gas from a solar plant. The synfuels thus produced have a higher energy content than the original coal. While in both processes the combustion of coal releases carbon dioxide into the atmosphere, the allothermal process requires less coal (by a factor of 3 to 4) and accordingly releases a smaller amount of carbon dioxide than the autothermal method. . . .

The detailed calculations showed this hybrid option to have important advantages (when development and investment allow it to be introduced): extending the useful life of the coal reserves, allowing the shift from readily transportable gas and liquid fuels to take place over a longer period, and reducing the amount of carbon dioxide released into the atmosphere.

There are many forces that tend to restrict the range of alternatives likely to be examined. Some of the strongest are biases of various sorts due to the unconscious adherence to an organization's "party line" or cherished beliefs or even mere loyalty (Kahn and Mann, 1957). When a problem is first discovered in an organization there is a tendency to look for a solution that can be controlled within the organization. An administrator may initially bar analysts from considering certain kinds of alternatives for no better reason than that "we don't do things that way." Staff analysts are particularly vulnerable to biases of this sort.

It can also happen that the analyst, in talking with the decisionmaker or his staff, becomes aware that the decisionmaker (or his superior) doesn't like certain kinds of alternatives. He may sense that it is both useless and hazardous to even give the impression that he might advocate these alternatives as possible solutions. As a result, the development of such alternatives is likely to be neglected or forgotten, thus leading to inferior results.

Various alternatives can also be advocated by enthusiasts, each of whom honestly believes that his alternative is the royal road to the problem's solution. One could easily imagine, in the blood supply example, one enthusiast advocating that all blood be delivered to the hospital blood banks on a prescheduled basis, with another advocating with equal enthusiasm that all deliveries be made on demand. With the analysis in hand, we now know that the best compromise is a set schedule supplemented by a few demand deliveries when blood-bank supplies run short—in sum, a hybrid option with an average of 4.2 deliveries per hospital per week, two-thirds prescheduled and the other one-third on demand. Similarly, any citizen with even passing interest in the energy problem recalls that various enthusiasts advocate singular solutions. One of the most vocal groups feels that the world must soon adopt solar energy. On the other hand, perhaps the most important finding of the IIASA energy systems analysis is that—at least for the next 50 years—no one energy

Section 6.3. Alternatives

option can be relied on to solve the world's energy supply problem; rather, a large spectrum of such options, as Figure 3.10 suggests, must be combined appropriately, with the totality managed with a view to having a completely sustainable system within the next century. In sum, the enthusiastically sponsored unitary solar option cannot do the job within the next 50 years, according to the IIASA study.

Alternatives need not represent the same approach to obtaining the objective. Suppose, for instance, the objective were to reduce crime. There are at least two categories of alternatives that might help to attain this goal, social measures such as preventive education and antipoverty legislation, or police measures such as more severe punishment and more certain apprehension of criminals. In the investigation, police measures as a whole might be one alternative, or a specific police measure such as a 50 percent increase in the number of police cars might be another, or a combination of several police measures with social measures might be a further alternative.

The point is that much thought must be devoted to designing alternatives. They will be eliminated or modified to remove or add certain features as constraints are discovered and applied, or as their effectiveness is estimated. Preliminary evaluation can be used to screen out grossly inferior alternatives and those that are dominated by others. During the evaluation process the good features of the better alternatives may suggest ways for the analyst to design new and still better ones.

Once the analyst has a model or set of models enabling him to determine the significant consequences of a class of alternatives, he can improve some of the alternatives by investigating how the spectrum of consequences varies with changes in these alternatives, being careful, of course, to revise the model if the changes are so radical that the credibility of the original model is brought into question. He must, however, not carry this process too far, for, although the model results may show differences, they may really be insignificant considering how crude our models are likely to be. There are, of course, certain relatively narrow problems that permit a closed mathematical formulation or model where some type of algorithm, such as linear programming, permits the analyst to investigate all alternatives of a certain class and designate one as best. There are relatively few, if any, problems (other than purely tactical ones) where such a formulation is possible, however.

Certain properties of the alternatives, while they may not be specifically demanded by the objectives and criteria, as stated by the decisionmaker, nevertheless are important and likely to be considered later in his evaluation—and hence should be considered by the analyst in the design of the alternatives.

One of these, an almost indispensable feature of an acceptable alternative, is its insensitivity (robustness), measured by the degree to which attainment of the objectives will be sustained despite disturbances encountered in normal operation, such as varying loads, changing weather conditions, etc. In urban transportation, insensitivity could mean, for example, that the average travel time does not greatly increase even when the peak-load and street traffic are increased by 25% or more.

Another feature important for many applications is reliability, which is the probability that the system is operational at any given time, as opposed to being out of order. In some cases, it is important for the proposed system never to fail; in others, that it not fail for a time longer than some threshold value; and in still other cases, a failure is tolerable if it can be repaired quickly. Reliability brings us in turn to questions of maintenance and, consequently, logistics.

A system is vulnerable if damage or failure of an element causes considerable trouble in meeting the objectives (vulnerability does not mean, or does not necessarily mean, complete failure). In urban transportation, a bus system is vulnerable to snow storms. One would like an alternative with low vulnerability.

Flexibility is a property exhibited by an alternative designed to do a certain job that can also be used with reasonable success for a modified, or even an entirely different, purpose. It is important to have a flexible alternative when the objectives may change or when the uncertainties are very great. For example, for transferring fuel, rail transportation is more flexible than pipelines.

In addition, each alternative that survives the other feasibility tests must be examined with implementation in mind. Some alternatives will be easier to implement than others; those impossible to implement must be eliminated, and the cost of implementation associated with each of the others must be taken into account.

One alternative usually available to the decisionmakers is to do nothing, that is, to maintain current policies and practices. This alternative must at least be examined—and sometimes investigated in detail—for change does not always bring improvement.

Generating alternatives is above all a craft or art, an exercise of imagination, creativity, criticism, and experience. The diversity of alternative ways of attaining an objective, so often encountered in systems problems, calls for creativity, ingenuity, and a deep knowledge of the real-world situation, rather than for complete mastery of formal tools. Therefore, what we say below about generating alternatives can only be a loose guideline, a framework, which may help in some cases, but not in others.

Whenever a diversity of means exists to achieve the objectives, generating and selecting alternatives are best done in steps or stages. Initially, it is appropriate to consider a fairly large number of possibilities as alternatives; any scheme that has a chance of being feasible and of meeting the objectives should be investigated. At the beginning, it is good to encourage invention and unconventionally; foolish ideas may not appear so foolish when looked at more closely. It may often be advisable to reach beyond the less rigid constraints, to broaden the scope of the study outside the limits that were

Section 6.3. Alternatives

initially set by the client. See, for instance, Ackoff (1974) and Brill, Chang, and Hopkins (1982).

The many alternatives that are considered initially cannot be investigated in detail. It would be too costly and, above all, excessively time-consuming. Some kind of screening, based on expert judgment, evidence from past cases, or simple models, can often be used to select a few of the alternatives as more promising for the next stages of investigation. It may, for example, be possible to reject some alternatives by dominance; i.e., because another alternative exists that is better in at least one aspect and equally good in all the remaining significant aspects. See Walker and Veen (1981).

The stages that follow the initial scrutiny should include an increasing amount of quantitative assessment. At first, the assessment of the consequences of each alternative may still miss many details, but it should be adequate to permit rejecting a fair percentage of the original alternatives on the ground that the other cases are more promising. Care should be taken that measures of effectiveness are treated only as approximations; that is, what is really better is not necessarily demonstrated by a simple arithmetic comparison. Here an *a fortiori* approach may be useful. In such an analysis, two alternatives are compared by resolving a number of uncertainties in favor of the one that appears to be the weaker of the two, say, by estimating its cost at the low end of the range of possibilities or its reliability at the high end. If the apparently stronger alternative still appears stronger, the case for preferring it is strengthened.

The last stage of the selection procedure should investigate relatively few alternatives, but in considerable detail. These alternatives should be serious candidates for implementation. At this stage every effort should be made to assess each alternative as accurately as possible, and each one may have to be fine-tuned to yield the best results possible. At this stage, systems analysis sometimes overlaps with systems design or systems engineering, where—for example, for an industrial plant—the job is to determine all specifications for the consecutive design of the particular parts of the plant.

Fine tuning is an activity that may, in appropriate cases, make good use of mathematical models. The problems are usually well defined when fine tuning is appropriate and setting the details may be ideal for formal procedures for optimization, such as linear programming.

As can be seen, we favor a procedure of step-by-step rejection of alternatives rather than one of focusing on selecting the best alternative in a single operation. This procedure has some rationale; first, the alternatives that are shown to be infeasible can be rejected (regardless of what they promise in terms of benefits); next, the alternatives that can be shown to be markedly sensitive or vulnerable can be rejected, etc. It is, in many cases of judgment, easier to agree on rejection than to agree on positive selection. In addition, it is a good idea to see and think about several alternatives instead of just one. Indeed, some decisionmakers have expressed the view that the opportunity to view a number of well-developed options is the most positive contribution systems analysis can make.

In sum, it is important to begin the analysis with good alternatives, and end with better ones. The time and effort needed to develop them must be adequate to the task, and all of the relevant sources of technical expertise must be tapped in the process. On the one hand, the analysts should beware of the glib technologist who alleges that there are only two or three possibilities. On the other, he should be equally suspicious of alternatives developed entirely within the systems analysis team, for they will usually not contain representatives of all of the useful technologies. The client's organization, with its built-in expertise, may be the best source of ideas, but it has no way of separating the good ones from the bad until the analyst's models come along. It is a synthesis that is called for, led by the systems analysis team with its eye clearly on the problem in hand.

In summary, the continuing awareness of the need for newer and better alternatives throughout the analysis holds the key to outstandingly useful results.

References

Ackoff, R. L. (1974). *Redesigning the Future: A Systems Approach to Societal Problems.* New York: Wiley.

Arrow, K. J. (1951). *Social Choice and Individual Values.* New York: Wiley.

Brill, E. D., Jr., S. Chang, and L. D. Hopkins (1982). Modeling to generate alternatives: The HSJ approach and an illustration using a problem in land use planning. *Management Science* 28(3), 221–235.

Dror, Y. (1975). Some features of a meta-model for policy studies. *Policy Studies Journal,* 3(3), 247–255.

Dunn, W. N. (1981). *Public Policy Analysis: An Introduction.* Englewood Cliffs, New Jersey: Prentice-Hall.

Eilon, S. (1972). Goals and constraints in decisionmaking. *Operational Research Quarterly* 23(1), 3–15.

Energy Systems Program Group of IIASA, Wolf Haefele, Program Director (1981). *Energy in a Finite World: Volume 1. Paths to a Sustainable Future.* Cambridge, Massachusetts: Ballinger.

Hatry, H. P. (1970). Measuring the effectiveness of nondefense public programs. *Operations Research* 18(5), 772–784.

Hitch, C. H. and R. McKean (1960). *The Economics of Defense in the Nuclear Age.* Cambridge, Massachusetts: Harvard University Press.

Hovey, H. A. (1968). *The Planning–Programming Approach to Government Decisionmaking.* New York: Praeger.

Kahn, H., and I. Mann (1957). *Ten Common Pitfalls,* RM-1937. Santa Monica, California: The Rand Corporation.

Keeney, R. L., and H. Raiffa (1976). *Decisions with Multiple Objectives: Preference and Value Tradeoffs.* New York: Wiley.

References

Majone, G. (1978). *The ABC's of Constraint Analysis,* unpublished manuscript.

Nagel, S. S., and M. Neef (1979). *Policy Analysis: In Social Science Research.* Beverly Hills, California: Sage.

Raiffa, Howard (1968). *Decision Analysis: Introductory Lectures on Choices under Uncertainty.* Reading, Massachusetts: Addison-Wesley.

Simon, H. (1964). On the concept of organization goal. *Administrative Science Quarterly* 9(1), 1–22.

Sugden R., and A. Williams (1978). *The Principles of Practical Cost–Benefit Analysis.* Oxford, England: Oxford University Press.

Walker, W. E., J. M. Chaiken, and E. J. Ignall, eds. (1979). *Fire Department Deployment Analysis: A Public Policy Analysis Case Study.* New York: North-Holland.

Walker, W. E., and M. A. Veen (1981). *Policy Analysis of Water Management for the Netherlands: Vol. II. Screening of Technical and Managerial Tactics.* N-1500/2-NETH. Santa Monica, California: The Rand Corporation.

Wohlstetter, A. (1964). The analysis and design of conflict systems. In *Analysis for Military Decisions.* (E. S. Quade, ed.). Amsterdam: North-Holland, pp. 103–148.

Chapter 7
Predicting the Consequences: Models and Modeling

Edward S. Quade

> Any model is a caricature of reality. A caricature achieves its effectiveness by leaving out all but the essential; the model achieves its utility by ignoring irrelevant detail. There is always some level of detail that an effective model will not seek to predict, just as there are aspects of realism that no forceful caricature would attempt to depict. Selective focus on the essentials is the key to good modeling.
>
> C. S. Holling (1978, p. 96)

7.1. Introduction

Assume that a problem has been clearly defined, the objective specified, and a number of alternatives identified that seem worth further investigation. Before a decision is made, the decisionmaker ought to know, insofar as possible, what the consequences of his choice will be. To predict these consequences, one or more models are required, generally much more elaborate than the models employed earlier in the study to screen the alternatives or to define the limits of the inquiry. The purpose of this chapter is to show how models are developed, used, and refined to increase our confidence in what they tell us.

For the problems that systems analysis addresses, the information required for decision is usually obtained by means of carefully constructed, explicit models, represented quantitatively (i.e., by using numbers and mathematical relations) and expressed in part by a computer program. These models are frequently the synthesis of a host of other models, simpler in varying degrees, many of them mental, implicit in the minds of the model builders, others explicit, expressed by words, diagrams, mathematical equations, random numbers, physical forms, or in other ways. There are, of course, still other models everywhere throughout the analytic process: in problem formulation to define the scope of what is to be included; in applying dominance or other schemes to reduce the number of alternatives; in procedures to present the results; and indeed wherever a decision has to be made.

Because modeling plays such an important role in systems analysis, the two are sometimes assumed to be identical. Many studies do have one model—the one used to predict the consequences of a choice of alternatives—so dominant that the other models employed are seldom mentioned; the global-modeling community offers examples (Meadows, Richardson, and Bruckmann, 1982). Other models are, nevertheless, present and used through the process, although most of them may be mental and never made explicit. The model (or the group of models considered as a single model) used to predict the consequences of the alternatives is usually spoken of as "the model" when systems analysis is discussed. These dominant models are the subject of this chapter; we do not, for instance, discuss the models a decisionmaker may employ to make use of the information the analysis provides.

This chapter, building on Chapter 4, begins with an explanation of what models are and why they are needed in systems analysis. It then discusses the four broad modeling techniques most used in systems analysis. Next, to show how models are built and tested, it works through an example and expands the topic. It follows this with an explanation of the way these models are used to produce the necessary predictions. Finally, after a brief discussion of social experimentation, model documentation, and model cost, it closes with a statement of what one can expect to get from models and modeling.

7.2. The Need for Models

Everyday decisions by individuals and the predictions on which they depend are most often based on judgments derived from implicit models that exist only in the mind. Such a judgmental or mental model is composed of the assumptions and intuitions its holder has about the issue with which he is concerned. Most decisions, even some of considerable significance to others as well as to the decisionmaker himself, are based largely on implicit or mental models. When the analysis is done by someone other than the decisionmaker himself, however, the models the analyst uses tend to be made explicit before the decision is taken, as when an advisor lists the pros and cons of an action he is about to recommend and assigns weights. In technical situations, an originally implicit model is not only made explicit but usually supplemented by other explicit models such as diagrams, graphs, tables, and mathematical formulas. Formal studies of even relatively simple issues, in fact, demand that the models be as explicit as possible so that others can judge the assumptions, follow the reasoning, and check the outcome.

Systems analysis needs models to predict the consequences that would follow were an alternative to be chosen and implemented. However, these models should not be confused with the many scientific models that are the

Section 7.2. The Need for Models

mathematical expression of well-established and accepted theories and that produce very reliable predictions for well-understood phenomena. Systems analysis models are seldom fully developed theories (although they include elements of such theories), for they must often include much that is little more than conjecture; hence, their predictions must be used with caution. Like scientific models, they are explicit and subject to testing; however, the nature of the problem and the conditions of inquiry may make testing difficult.

Why are elaborate models required in systems analysis? Why not, for instance, try out each alternative on a full scale for a time sufficiently long to determine what would happen? There may be exceptions, but, in almost every case, this would be too expensive, or too dangerous, or otherwise impractical. Consider, for example, the construction required to test each alternative in the Oosterschelde example of Section 3.4. In the firefighting example (Section 3.3), it might be possible to try some arrangements of fire companies for short periods of time (or, more practically, alternative dispatching policies); but, if the alternative were not a good one, it could result in increases in life and property losses.

A small-scale experiment with a segment of the real world is sometimes a possible, even a desirable, way to predict what might happen (see Section 7.6), but even this would not avoid sophisticated mathematical models, for they would be needed to design the experiment and to analyze the data.

Many psychologists and philosophers believe that the human mind operates entirely through models. Mental models have many advantages. They can contain rich stores of information, they can handle incommensurable factors, and they can balance conflicting values (Meadows, Richardson, and Bruckmann, 1982), but they have biases and gaps that may be completely unknown to the holder and undiscoverable by anyone else. They cannot, moreover, handle problems that demand an extremely precise answer or require knowledge from too many disciplines.

Meadows and Robinson (1984, Ch. 1) list five reasons why promoters of the computer as a forecasting tool claim that mathematical models should be superior to the best mental models:

1. *Rigor.* The assumptions in computer models must be specified explicitly, completely, and precisely; no ambiguities are possible. Every variable must be defined, and assumptions must be mutually consistent. Computer modelers often mention that the discipline required to formulate a mathematical model is helpful in organizing and clarifying their own mental models, even before any computer analysis takes place.
2. *Comprehensiveness.* A computer model can manipulate more information than the human mind and can keep track of many more interrelationships at one time. It can combine observations from many mental models into a more comprehensive picture than could ever be contained in a single human head.

3. *Logic.* If programmed correctly, the computer can process even a very complicated set of assumptions to draw logical, error-free conclusions. The human mind is quite likely to make errors in logic, especially if the logical chain is complex. Different people may agree completely about a set of assumptions and still disagree about the conclusion to be drawn from them. A computer model should always reach the same conclusion from a single set of assumptions.
4. *Accessibility.* Because all the assumptions must be explicit, precise, and unambiguous in order to communicate them to the computer, critics can examine, assess, and alter computer models, whereas mental models are virtually unexaminable and uncriticizable.
5. *Flexibility.* Computer models can easily test a wide variety of different conditions and policies, providing a form of social experimentation that is much less costly and time-consuming than tests within the real social system.

Computer models have not had either the acceptance or the success that many of their advocates feel they should have. Even though a model of this type may be an appropriate tool for most problems to which systems analysis is applied, they are, as Meadows and Robinson go on to say, "more often made than used, more often criticized than praised." Judgment, by committees and individual experts, largely based on individual mental models, is still widely used for tasks that systems analysts feel would benefit from the use of more explicit models. Judgment by committee and individuals can be improved, however, through structured discussion, a form of modeling as yet little employed in systems analysis (Helmer, 1966, 1978, 1983; Holling, 1978; Checkland, 1981).

As said earlier and in Chapter 4, models have many roles in systems analysis. In this chapter we are interested in models as devices, processes, or procedures to predict, or to at least provide insight concerning, the consequences that result from the choice of an alternative.

7.3. Modeling Techniques

Models differ in many aspects—in degree of abstraction or complexity, in how time or chance events are handled, and in many other ways—and may be classified accordingly. Specht (1968) separates models into five categories: verbal, people, people and computers, computers, and analytical. Greenberger, Crenson, and Crissey (1976) distinguish four classes: schematic, physical, symbolic, and role playing. A simple road map used to give a motorist directions is a schematic model; a wooden airfoil in a wind tunnel is a physical model. The models used for predicting the consequences, the so-called systems analysis models, while they make use of mental, schematic, and sometimes (but rarely) physical modeling, depend for the most part on four basic modeling techniques: analytic, simulation, gaming, and judgmental. A given model may employ more than one of these techniques. The common man–machine

Section 7.3. Modeling Techniques   195

model, the people and computer model of Specht's classification, employs simulation, gaming, and judgmental models, for instance.

The modeling techniques most used for applied systems analysis are quantitative (for instance, represented by mathematical equations or a coded set of instructions for a computer). Often they are the only modeling techniques considered for "the model." These models resemble those used in the physical sciences, consisting of a set of logical relations from which one obtains the outcome by solving the equations in closed mathematical form or by statistical analysis. For a model to be strictly quantitative, it would have to represent the situation and the activity under investigation so faithfully that a decision could be based solely on the results obtained from the model. For some questions, such models may exist, but not when social and political factors are as prevalent as they are in the applications of systems analysis; in such cases, the model results must always be tempered with judgment, i.e., modified by the decisionmaker's and the analyst's mental models. Nevertheless, the adjective *quantitative* is applied to any model where most of the relations are represented analytically or on a computer. Quantitative models are of two types; analytic models and simulations, although not all analytic models and simulations are quantitative.

Many issues have major aspects that cannot be expressed satisfactorily by quantitative means. Frequently these are aspects that depend for understanding on the social sciences where, because of the nature of their subject matter, few models with the predictive quality comparable to the models found in the physical sciences, or even in economics, have been developed. Without such building blocks, the predictive models for systems analysis must depend on a more direct use of judgment and intuition and less on quantitative relations. To achieve this dependence, human participants, usually experts or especially qualified people, are brought into the model structure. Gaming and group judgment are two ways to bring human participants into systems analysis models.

The four modeling techniques will be discussed in turn, the latter two in greater detail than the former. For more information on analytic models and simulations see operations research textbooks, as well as Mood (1982) and Greenberger, Crenson, and Crissey (1976, Chapters 3 and 4) for good introductory treatments of this type of modeling. In addition, Moder and Elmaghraby (1978) and Drake, Keeney, and Morse (1972) cover more sophisticated methods and give numerous applications. Meadows and Robinson (1984) compare nine studies that make use of systems dynamic, econometric, input-output, and optimization models in various combinations and provide useful insights on the effectiveness of computer modeling.

Analytic Models

In an analytic model mathematical statements are used to represent the relations that hold between the variables of interest. The use of mathematics as a surrogate for reality has a long and successful tradition in physics and engineering and more recently in operations research. An analytic model is particularly desirable because the outcome for a full set of alternatives can often be predicted by a closed mathematical form (as by the square root law of the fire deployment example of Section 3.3) or graphically (as from Figure 3.1 for the blood-supply example). Problems of flows in networks, queueing, search, inventory control, and others can often be modeled analytically. Numerical analysis and a computer may be needed to aid in finding a solution, but it is a use of the computer different from that in simulation.

Most systems analysis models are descriptive (although this is the common adjective, informative would be better, as their outputs are decision-relevant information). That is, they predict the values of a set of consequences for a particular alternative under a specified set of conditions. Ranking the alternatives is done externally to the model. Sometimes, when the alternatives are similar and differ only in a set of parameter values, it is possible to design a "prescriptive" model that ranks the alternatives on a performance scale. The user then does not have to compare the alternatives to select the one he prefers; he merely has to agree on the scale. The model contains an optimization procedure (linear programming, for instance) that indicates the set of parameter values that yields the best value of the performance measure (say, the minimum monetary cost to set up a system). The selection is best, however, in an overall sense only to the extent that the one-dimensional scale on which the model measures performance incorporates and weighs properly all the factors that the decisionmaker has in mind when he seeks a best solution. Nevertheless, in spite of their defects, prescriptive models are the ones most sought after by analysts, possibly owing to academic goals (Majone and Quade, 1980).

Simulation

Although every model is a simulation, in operations research and systems analysis parlance the term simulation is used in a special sense: simulation is the process of representing item by item and step by step the essential features of whatever it is we are interested in and then predicting what is likely to happen by operating with the model case by case, i.e., by estimating the results of a proposed action from a series of pseudo-experiments (pseudo because they are performed on the model rather than in the real world). The series of experiments is needed to take account of the effects of chance on the system (simulation, in systems analysis, is seldom used in a deterministic situation, i.e., one where the random elements in the system can be assumed negligible), for each individual experiment with the model may produce a different outcome. After a large number of experiments, what is likely to happen can then be determined by statistical analysis of the set of outcomes.

More often than not, the simulation is a computer simulation in which the representation is carried out numerically on a digital computer, using computer-generated random numbers, frequently without employing any formal analytic techniques. A great advantage of this type of simulation is that a digital computer, using random numbers, can represent with precision processes for which satisfactory analytic approximations do not exist. For example, the intricate process of traffic flow can be expressed in terms of simple events (such as a car turning left at an intersection or a vehicle parking) and simple rules (such as when attempting to turn left the car waits until oncoming traffic has gone by, or a vehicle attempting to park forces the following cars to stop). As is typical of many real systems, traffic flow is subject to chance elements; thus, by selecting random numbers from the appropriate distributions, the computer determines, say, whether a given car turns left and for how many oncoming cars it has to wait. The computation is carried out at high speed with relations that indicate the manner in which real activities might take place in real time. A large measure of realism can thus be attained. In fact, the analyst has to guard against attempting to provide a one-to-one representation of the real-world process rather than abstracting just the features essential to his problem, since the computer time (and cost) to run a simulation increases with its complexity.

Simulation with a high-speed digital computer is an extremely powerful technique. A system that is not well enough understood for mathematical relations between variables to be set up may often be modeled as a simulation and the relations discovered. The costs of building and using a large simulation model or of an operational game can be significant. An idea of what these costs might be is given by Shubik and Brewer (1972). Nevertheless, while analytic models are cheaper to use in both time and money, simulation is often chosen because it is easier to set up and not costly at the model building stage. Nevertheless, Bowen (1978a, p. 4) remarks: "In principle, . . . a simulation is the least desirable of models. It has low insight, since it does not provide explanation of the observed outcomes, and it may involve an undesirably long, confusing, and expensive analysis phase. Nevertheless, it may be a correct choice as a model, if only because no other choice is open."

Gaming

Gaming or operational gaming (recently called interactive simulation by some who feel gaming is not a suitable term for a serious research effort) is a form of simulation modeling in which analysts, expert consultants, and sometimes decisionmakers simulate the behavior of major elements in the model. A human "player" may, for instance, simulate the actions of a plant manager or of a political party or the changes that take place in a sector of the economy. The players may be assisted by computer simulations and analytic models or even play against such models.

Gaming originated with the military. Military staffs found that map exercises in which opposing teams acted out the moves that might be made by opposing armies were useful for examining the feasibility of war plans and the adequacy of logistics. Since the activities of the participants in such an encounter bore considerable resemblance to playing a game, the activity came to be called gaming. Gaming is now used also to study the usefulness of future weapons and potential conflict between nations. In business its use is widespread, particularly for training. Although gaming is little used to study public problems, its use is increasing (for an example, see Thomas, 1982), and it can be argued that some form of gaming is needed if human judgment is to be introduced into models to investigate such problems (Bowen, 1978b).

To illustrate, a game to investigate policy options to counter organized crime might be set up as follows (Quade, 1975, p. 10). Three teams would be used:

1. A player team, Blue, to simulate in some sense a National Council on Organized Crime plus local authorities;
2. A player team, Red, simulating the activities of organized crime in city X;
3. A control or umpire team, Green, to structure the game, provide a startup situation, rule on moves, etc.

The game would start from an initial situation (prepared by Green) with a move by Red, e.g., various actions involving gambling, loansharking, dishonest businesses, and the like. This would be followed by Blue's move, involving mainly actions by the local authorities. The results would then be evaluated by the control team, taking into account both the local moves and the legislative and operational components of an overall strategy to combat organized crime previously formulated by Blue in its role as a National Council: the activity of preparing this latter is probably the most important aspect of the game.

After the results are communicated (in part) to the player teams, another move follows. The control team determines the number of moves and the timing, updates the scenario, and provides information about such factors as the state of the economy and the political situation. Conclusions are drawn at the end based on the experience of all concerned.

Gaming can be used to tackle many problems for which no satisfactory quantitative model can be constructed. The players can use their intuition and judgment to take into account such hard-to-measure factors as courage, cooperation, commitment, and morale. A realistic environment and intelligent opponent can force the players in a two-sided game to consider aspects of the issue that might be overlooked were they working in isolation without teammates and without an intelligent opposition searching for flaws in every move. Gaming works well to educate and to improve communication among players of different disciplines. Its predictive quality, however, is questionable, for it so clearly depends on the intuitive insights provided by the participants (Quade, 1982, pp. 193–203). For additional discussion, see Helmer (1978, 1983).

Difficulties sometimes arise with analytic models and computer simulations when the system being modeled contains one or more decisionmakers whose decisions have an important influence on the model outcome. If these decisionmakers follow some simple rules—for example, if they maximize their net benefits—then it may be possible to describe their behavior by mathmatical models. Demand functions, which express how much of a commodity a consumer will buy at various prices, are one version of such models. The decisionmaker, however, may be something like a legislative body, a political party, a protest group, a particular individual, or even inanimate, say a sector of the economy that in our present state of knowledge we do not know how to model satisfactorily. Another approach is then needed.

One such approach is to insert individual "players" into the model to represent these internal decisionmakers. These players are then supposed to act as their real-life counterparts would or, in some circumstances, to optimize with an assigned goal in mind (Helmer, 1966). In other words, if we know of the existence, position, and action possibilities of these decisionmakers whose intervention may affect the choice of alternatives, we may try to imitate their behavior by using appropriately chosen actors. We hope that these actors will behave, in the model, in a way that corresponds to what the actual decisionmakers would do, or should do, in real-world situations, with all the ambiguity and uncertainty there present. Incidently, this is a reason for the growing importance for systems analysis of the psychological and sociological theory of value and choice. We are unable to model—and thus predict—the consequences of a course of action unless we understand the laws of behavior of the group that will be affected by it.

If all the dependencies, except for human decisionmaking, are programmed into a computer, the whole model becomes an interactive model, or man–machine model, where human decisions interact with input and output data from the computer program. Models of this type are frequently called "role-playing" models and are usually classed as a form of gaming.

Judgmental Models

In addition to the judgment and intuition of individuals applied through their implicit mental models, the multidisciplinary nature of applied systems analysis usually makes reliance on the judgment of several people indispensable. One way is through gaming; a second is through a committee. A committee or panel exercising its judgment as a group is a firmly established and much used substitute for explicit modeling to provide advice or predictions. It is one, however, that is open to a number of objections, based on the well-known deficiencies of committee deliberations that affect the quality of the end product (Helmer, 1983, 1978, 1966). There are, in addition to gaming, a number of ways to structure group discussion that will improve the focus of its judgment. These devices include scenario writing, Delphi, cross-impact analysis, and various team and workshop approaches. They are models, or at least surrogates for models, that play the same role in systems analysis as simulation, mathematical modeling, or gaming. The team-workshop approaches, such as Lasswell's decision seminar (Brewer, 1972; Brewer and Shubik, 1979), the one used by Holling and his colleagues (1978) to investigate environmental management problems, and the scheme used by Checkland (1981) for business problems, employ many of the other modeling techniques, such as simulation and cross-impact analysis, during their sessions. Except for a remark about individual judgment, the discussion will be confined to Delphi and scenario writing.

The judgment of an individual is sometimes used as a direct link in an otherwise analytic model to model processes that would otherwise be difficult or costly to handle. For instance, there are models for finding efficient vehicle routes and schedules through a network of city streets in which the selection of routes by a traffic expert, based on his experience and justified by heuristic arguments, is combined with the formal mathematical techniques of graph theory to avoid the computational difficulties that would be required were graph theory to be used alone. In IIASA's Energy Program (see Section 3.5), individual judgmental models were used to link together the various (sub)models where each model evaluated only a particular aspect of the problem (Energy Systems Program Group, 1981, Vol. 2, p. 28).

Delphi. Delphi is an iterative procedure for eliciting and refining the opinions of a group of people by means of a series of individual interrogations. Originally the interrogation was by written questionnaire, but more recently on-line computer consoles are used to speed up the process. Ideally for systems analysis purposes, the group should consist of subject-matter experts and especially knowledgeable individuals, possibly including some of the responsible decisionmakers. The idea is to improve on the committee process for arriving at a prediction or recommendation by subjecting the views of the individual participants to each other's criticism in ways that avoid the psychological drawbacks associated with face-to-face confrontation. To this end, anonymity, to the extent that the responses to a question when supplied to the participants are not attributed to the responders, is usually preserved during the exercise and sometimes even when it is over.

Discussion is replaced by exchanging information under the control of a steering group. In each round of questions after the first, information about the outcome of the previous round is fed back to the participants (without letting them know, however, which opinion was contributed by which particular participant). As Helmer (1978, pp. 31–32), one of the developers of the technique, describes it:

> Some of the questions directed to the participating experts may, for instance, inquire into the reasons for previously expressed opinions; and a collection of such reasons may then be presented to each respondent in the group,

Section 7.3. Modeling Techniques

together with an invitation to reconsider and possibly revise his earlier estimate or, conversely, to state counterarguments explaining why the reasons presented are found unconvincing. This inquiry into the reasons for stated opinions and the subsequent feedback of the reasons adduced by others constitutes the elements of what may be thought of as an anonymous debate which serves to stimulate the experts into considering pertinent factors they might through inadvertence have overlooked, and to give due weight to considerations they may at first have been inclined to dismiss as unimportant. As the communication channel is controlled, noise, material judged irrelevant or redundant, can be reduced.

Four rounds are usually adequate: a second giving reasons for deviations from the first-round median; followed by a third with new estimates in the light of the reasons for deviation on the second with counterarguments; followed by a fourth estimate in the light of the counterarguments. The median of the fourth round is then used to substitute for a consensus. (If the result sought is not expressed numerically, it can usually be rephrased to permit quantitative valuation.)

Although the group opinion tends to converge with iteration (as measured, for example, by the interquartile range), the normal outcome is a spread of opinion. Using the median to represent the group response reduces pressure for conformity and ensures that the opinion of every member plays some role in determining the final outcome.

Delphi can be employed whenever expert judgment is required. For this reason, it is often used in conjunction with gaming. Its purpose is to estimate the answers to questions for which there is no "hard" model way to find the answer. There is some experimental evidence that Delphi results are usually more accurate than those obtained from a committee, particularly for numerical estimates such as forecasts as to when an event will happen or the future value of some index; the evidence, however, is not adequate enough to convince all analysts. Thus Delphi is not a substitute for an analytic model or simulation unless one feels so little confidence in the validity of the analytic models he can construct that he would prefer to depend on committee judgment instead (see also Linstone and Turoff, 1975).

Scenario writing. Before alternative actions can be designed, compared, or evaluated, the conditions under which they are to take place must be known or forecast. In systems analysis, a *scenario* is the set of conditions and characteristics that define the situation or environment under which a system or policy is assumed to perform. It is a description of the essential features (in the sense that they affect the actions under investigation) of the hypothetical context or contingency in which the action is to take place. *Scenario writing*, done properly, should include the preparation of a logical sequence of hypothetical (but credible) events that leads from the present to the scenario.

As a form of model building, scenario writing is clearly an art. There is not much that can be formalized or codified about how to do it well. Olaf Helmer (1966, p. 10) describes it as follows:

> Scenario writing involves a constructive use of the imagination. It aims at describing some aspects of the future, but, instead of building up a picture of unrestrained fiction or even of constructing a utopian invention that the author considers highly desirable, an operations-analytical scenario starts with the present state of the world and shows how, step by step, a future state might evolve in a plausible fashion out of the present one. Thus, though the purpose of such a scenario is not to predict the future, it nevertheless sets out to demonstrate the possibility of a certain future state of affairs by exhibiting a reasonable chain of events that might lead to it.

A scenario can be generated from a simulation or through the sequence of plays in an operational game, but it is most commonly developed from the mental models of one or several individuals. Scenario writing is not only the most frequently used means of exploring the future contingencies in which alternatives are to be compared, but it is also a useful device for beginning the construction of a more analytic model. For further information, see Brown (1968), DeWeerd (1973), Schwarz et al. (1982), and Section 9.5.

The central purpose of the IIASA energy study described in Section 3.5 was to look at the energy supply and demand balance for the next 50 years of a world that is notably heterogeneous, at least as we view it today. Not the least of the highly variable factors is the present per capita energy consumption, which in one major world region (North America) is over 40 times what it is in another (south and southeast Asia and sub-Sahara Africa excluding South Africa), thus implying the need for much more economic growth in the latter region than in the former. The approach the energy analysis team took was to write scenarios, from this point of view (Energy Systems Program Group, 1981, Vol. 1, pp. 19, 132):

> In writing scenarios, we were in no sense attempting to make predictions. Rather, we viewed scenario writing as a way to organize our thinking about available information; specifically we insisted rigorously on two criteria—internal consistency and global comprehensiveness . . .
>
> The purpose of the scenarios is to detail realistically the engineering and economic consequences that might follow from two sets of reasonable assumptions [embodied in the high and low scenarios]. The results should be interpreted carefully. The numbers are meant to provide insights and to help in meeting the intellectual challenge of grasping the dominant characteristics, trends, possibilities, and constraints on global and regional energy considerations. They are not predictions, and should serve only as guidelines for determining what is feasible over the coming five decades, assuming there are no social and political constraints.

Table 3.6 and Figure 3.10 give some of the central results—which we have commented on earlier—emerging from the analyses based on the energy scenarios.

Section 7.4. Model Building   203

7.4 Model Building

Even in well established scientific fields model building is not a cut-and-dried process but a highly creative activity.

Developing a Simple Model

Before listing some general precepts, consider, as an illustration of model building, the development of the square root law used in the fire department deployment example of Section 3.3. In its simplest form, this model is expressed by the equation.

$$E(D_1) = k_1\sqrt{A/N},$$

where $E(D_1)$ is the expected distance between points in the region at which fires occur and the closest available engine company, k_1 is a constant, A is the area of the region, and N is the number of firehouses that have engines available to respond.

The analysts, Kolesar and Blum (1973), had a feeling that there might be a relation between average travel distance in a region and the area of the region. With this in mind, they set out to investigate the possibility for a square city whose streets form a rectangular grid with a single firehouse located at the center (Figure 7.1).Within this city, fires were assumed to occur at random, with equal probability and severity everywhere.

The derivation of the model in this case, as described in Walker, Chaiken, and Ignall (1979, pp. 181–182), is as follows:

> We would like to determine the expected response distance for this city's fire company. We begin by answering the question. "What is the chance that the fire company will have to travel less that s miles?" for any distance s that lies between O and $\sqrt{A}/2$. To answer the question, consider a square that is $s\sqrt{2}$ on a side, which is centered inside the original one and is oriented the same way. Every point inside this square is no further than s from the firehouse, while every point outside it is further than s from the firehouse. [Because the fire company in traveling must follow the streets, which are parallel to the axes; all points on the boundary are thus the same distance from the firehouse.] The chance that the company will have to travel less than s miles is, then, the probability that an alarm occurs within the smaller square. This probability is the same as the ratio of the area of the small square to the area of the city. That is,
>
> $$P(\text{response distance} \leq s) = (s\sqrt{2})^2/A.$$
>
> The probability density of response distance, $f(s)$, can then be obtained by differentiation: $f(s) = 4s/A$. So the expected response distance is given by
>
> $$E(D_1) = \int_0^{\sqrt{A/2}} sf(s)\, ds = \int_0^{\sqrt{A/2}} (4s^2/A)\, ds \cdots = (\sqrt{2}/3)\sqrt{A}.$$

204   Chapter 7. Predicting the Consequences

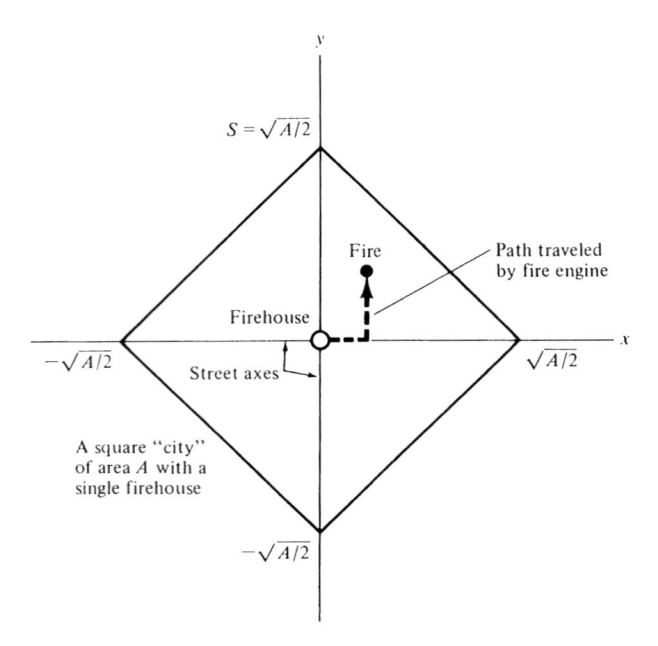

Figure 7.1. An idealized city with one firehouse. (*From Walker, Chaiken, and Ignall, 1979.*)

Hence, in the case of a single company ($N = 1$) in a square city, the square-root law holds with $k_1 = \sqrt{2}/3 = 0.4714$.

The model was then extended; first to a square city made up of smaller square cities, then through stages to more general configurations. In order to simplify the mathematical analysis required for these extensions, the analysts made a number of assumptions:

Alarms are distributed randomly but with uniform probability density throughout the region of interest

Firehouses are spread either in a regular pattern or randomly throughout the region of interest

Boundary effects are insignificant

Units are always available to respond

Fire companies travel either on a straight line between two points or on a dense rectangular grid of streets.

In the real world, of course, none of these assumptions is strictly true. Complications that are not consistent with this simple model abound: a city is of finite size and irregular shape: the distribution of units is not homogenous: several companies (in varying numbers) are dispatched to each alarm: in the event of a very serious fire, companies from other regions may be

Section 7.4. Model Building   205

>relocated into the depleted area: and responding units must follow actual street patterns that are often irregular, observe one-way streets, and route themselves around obstacles such as parks and rivers. [Walker, Chaiken, and Ignall, 1979, p. 185.]

Nothwithstanding such complications, the square-root model provides estimates useful for the purpose for which the model was intended—to estimate the average travel distance in a reasonably large region over an extended period of time. Before this statement could be made with confidence, however, the model had to be extensively tested. The mathematical derivations lent an air of plausibility to it, but, as these were based on simplifying assumptions that were not true in the real world, checks were needed. The testing involved the use of alternative models, historical data (see Figure 3.5), and simulation (Kolesar and Blum, 1973).

General Remarks

In systems analysis, a model builder is likely to find himself working in an area where the relations between the variables important to his problem are very imprecisely known and the data for improving them, while often abundant, were not collected for this purpose, and therefore must first be turned into useful information. His first step is to select certain elements as being relevant (and to set aside for the present all others) and to make the relations between them explicit. To do so, he uses established models from the disciplines involved, where such models are known, and conjectures the other relations using judgmental models based on his own intuition and that of experts he consults. The choice of techniques should follow from the nature of the problem, not the other way around, for, if the choice of analytic approach or modeling style comes first, the problem may have to be altered or even redefined to suit it.

At every stage, the process is full of pitfalls (Majone and Quade, 1980). For instance, during data analysis:

>This transformation of data into information involves three basic judgments, which all present the risk of serious pitfalls. The first is that the advantages achieved through data reduction compensate for the probable loss of information; generally speaking, the existence of "sufficient statistics," i.e., of summaries of the data which contain exactly the same amount of information as the original sample, is the exception rather than the rule. The second is a judgment of the goodness of fit of the model to the original data. The third is that this particular model, among the infinitely many possible ones, is the significant one for the problem under examination. All the operations and judgments involved in data reduction, transformation, and testing are, of course, craft operations. [Majone 1980, p. 14.]

To build a model means that most aspects of the real world must be aggregated or simplified.

Simplifications are of many types. One is to omit factors because they are judged to be irrelevant to the outcome. The analyst does not, however, omit factors because data or theory do not exist; one simply models them as best he can (see Forrester, as quoted in Section 3.4). Sometimes factors are omitted because the analyst finds them too difficult to quantify. If that is the case, however, they must be handled in some other way; preferably by changing the model to a type that will accommodate factors that are unquantified. Other simplifications are to assume that variables are constants and that complicated relations are linear. (There is always a preference for linear models because well known techniques exist for solving many such models.) Another is to assume that the average value of a function of a variable is equal to the function of the average value of that variable. All such simplifications must be used with great caution, particularly the last one.

Aggregation, such as treating areas as points or all members of a class as being of one "average" type, or replacing stochastic processes by deterministic rules, are common simplifications.

Simplifications are introduced for analytical or computational convenience (for instance, the assumptions used in deriving the square-root model of the preceding section) or sometimes to avoid the cost of gathering the data that would be required were the more realistic assumptions to be used. It is, of course, the purpose of the analysis that tells us what to include and what to leave out. Detail that later turns out to be unneeded may be included at the start, for it may take investigation by the analyst to find out what can be omitted or aggregated. Compromises are always necessary; sometimes a detail that the sponsor thinks should be important is included, at least in early models, merely to retain his confidence.

It should be clearly stated what has been assumed in the way of simplification and why, and, insofar as possible, the sort of uncertainty or bias that the assumption is likely to introduce in the model output. It should also be made clear how the aggregations and simplifications restrict the types of questions that can and cannot be addressed.

Improving a Model

The ad hoc and tentative model that represents the analyst's first cut is improved as new information and insight become available. To do this, the analyst works with his model, trying it out for cases in which the results he would like it to produce are known or can be conjectured from other models. He heeds the judgment of people experienced in the subject matter who feel they can recognize when the model results "seem reasonable." He checks his model against historical data. If it can be made to fit, this does not prove the revised model to be true, for by manipulating a few parameters this can usually be achieved (Bush and Mosteller, 1966, p. 335). But, if the data are

Section 7.4. Model Building

extensive and the adjustments slight, it tends to increase his confidence in the model.

Verification. A computer model is said to be *verified* if the program does what the model builder intended it to do. This requires that everything has been properly programmed. Typically, an attempt is made to verify such a model by setting some of the data input to extreme values, say zero, or by holding some of the input variables constant to determine whether the output changes in anticipated ways as the other inputs change. Using such trivial or degenerate cases, however, is not an adequate check. It is better to check the output against results provided by previously verified models or by testing with sample data that correspond to known output. As models become more elaborate, verification can become extremely difficult (Meadows and Robinson, 1984).

Validation. Validation is the process of determining that the outputs of a model conform to reality. No model can be validated in an absolute sense. As Holling (1978, p.95) and his coworkers express it:

> In fact, it is the central tenet of modern scientific method that hypotheses, including models, can never be proved right; they can only be proved wrong (Popper, 1959). This is why the frequent claims of—and demands for—"valid" models in ecological management, impact assessment, and policy design are so unsound. Provisional acceptance of any model implies not certainty, but rather a sufficient *degree of belief* to justify further action. In practice, the problem is one of model invalidation—of setting the model at risk so as to suggest the limits of its credibility. [Emphasis in the original.]

Some recent writers hold absolute invalidation impossible also (Toulmin, 1974, p. 605; Majone, 1980). Nevertheless, one has no confidence in a model that appears invalid; for a good description of how invalidation is attempted, see Holling (1978).

The more difficult it is to invalidate a model, the more confidence we have in it. To increase our confidence in a model to the stage at which we are willing for it to be used as a laboratory world to predict the consequences of alternative policies, we subject it to a range of tests and comparisons designed to reveal where it fails. For instance, one test is to compare the results to those of a more detailed model in which one already has great confidence. In such a case, a simulation model has been used to test an analytic model of the same process (as described in Ignall, Kolesar, and Walker, 1978). When such tests of the model have been completed, the model will not have been proved valid and not all the uncertainties will have been eliminated; the user will, however, have an understanding of the extent and limits of the model's predictive capabilities.

Often there is empirical evidence that can be used to calibrate the model until it will predict results that are consonant with other existing data. Curve fitting is an example of such calibration. This calibration does not, however, ensure that the model is a good predictor of the future, although it contributes to our confidence.

7.5. Predicting the Consequences

The consequences that result from implementation depend both on the nature of the alternative and on the context or environment in which it is implemented. The common practice in systems analysis is, first, to generate by scenario writing, by qualitative forecasting methods, or by some other means one or more possible future contexts and then, for each such context of interest, or for a representative set of such contexts, to determine the consequences that follow from selecting and implementing each alternative.

By the context—also called the environment, state of the world, state of nature, or scenario—we mean the aspects of the world existing at the time the alternative is implemented that influence what its consequences will be. Thus, in the Oosterschelde example of Section 3.4, to predict the impacts of the three alternatives, for instance, the change in attendance at the sea beaches, a context had to be forecasted (called a scenario there) that specified the growth of population, the recreational investment policy, the state of the economy, and so on, at the time the alternative under consideration was to be implemented.

Establishing the Context

The implementation of alternatives takes place in the future. Hence prediction is necessary to specify each possible context. More often than not, prediction is by mental model and amounts to no more than a judgment that the future will be much like the present. Occasionally, only a few factors are significant and various mathematical forecasting models can be used to define the context.

In forecasting we make the essential assumption that the future is largely determined by the past, on which data can be made available. This assumption implies a number of important questions related to the data needed for a reliable forecast:

> How far into the past should the record reach?
>
> How broad should the observations be, i.e., how many related phenomena must be observed to forecast one selected phenomenon?
>
> To what extent can we trade the length of record for number of observations, or weigh scanty new data against abundant old data?
>
> How far ahead can we infer from the data available?
>
> One should not overestimate the power and possibilities of forecasting

Section 7.5. Predicting the Consequences

techniques based on statistical data and formal models. For one thing, the data may not be rich enough to provide the necessary length and breadth of the record. Secondly, the phenomena in the past were observed (measured) with errors. Thirdly, there are phenomena to be forecast in some systems analyses that relate to phenomena in the past that are either not measurable or missing from the statistics. There are also cases where extrapolating the future from the past may be completely inappropriate. For example, in making long-term forecasts of changes in technology due to inventions or forecasts of changes in societal and political attitudes, judgment may do as well (or as poorly) as any computer model we have today.

There certainly are many other cases where expert-based, judgmental forecasting may be appropriate, because human experience and intuition may, implicitly and even unconsciously, make use of correlations and associations that cannot readily be formalized. The most frequent use of Delphi has been for forecasting and parameter estimation.

Whatever the forecasting techniques, the ability to determine the future in terms of reasonable probabilistic confidence is limited. There are many cases in analysis where the future that we must consider is more distant than any explicit theory-based forecast of the external conditions can reach with confidence (as in the energy study described in Section 3.5). In these cases, the analyst tends to predict the future environment by scenarios, i.e., hypothesized chains of events. He is still able to say: if the external events follow scenario No. 1, the results of the action will be . . ., but he cannot say much about the probabilities.

For questions where there is a considerable interval of time between the decision and full implementation, say the time between the decision to design a new supersonic transport and the time it is put into commercial operation, predicting the future can be so uncertain that it becomes desirable to compare alternatives in many different contexts or contingencies (also sometimes called alternative futures) that might come about. A common method for preparing these contingencies is by scenario writing. Those that are selected for use in comparing the alternatives are chosen as representative of the full set of possibilities. How this should be done is not at all clear. Among those selected would be the one considered to be the most likely; others would be selected because, although less likely, they might have high impact, or because the analyst feels they might affect the ordering of the alternatives. In military analyses, for instance, a "pessimistic" contingency, one in which the enemy is assumed to be best prepared to counter the alternatives, would certainly be included as well as an "optimistic" contingency, say one in which it was assumed that enemy intelligence had not anticipated certain of the alternatives under investigation. Calculation of the consequences for several contingencies may then give an idea of the range of uncertainty to be expected. The energy study summarized in Section 3.5 centered most of its attention on two scenarios looking 50 years into the future: a high scenario and a low scenario, the former assuming a higher economic growth throughout the world and the latter assuming a lower worldwide economic growth (and Table 3.6 and Figure 3.10 give results that emerged from these two scenarios). However, to explore the appropriate sensitivities, the analysis team also looked at three other scenarios: one involved a nuclear moratorium, one involved a significantly enhanced nuclear energy capability worldwide, and the third assumed that the 2030 energy demand and use would be only about double what it is today (or a third less than that in the low scenario, a result that keeps the world's per capita energy consumption constant over the next 50 years). Important insights emerged from all three cases.

A few summary remarks are appropriate here. First, as the probabilities of the scenarios are not known, nothing can be said about the expected outcome of the action.

It is important to consider several scenarios, and to choose them in a systematic way. One of these should be the scenario that seems most likely to come about, but comparisons based on others may present special insights. Thus, for example, we also want to consider, among others, scenarios that are structured so as to present circumstances unfavorable to achieving the objective, but which we feel are still reasonable possibilities.

An alternative that is very sensitive to small changes in the scenario assumptions should probably be rejected, or redesigned with the purpose of decreasing the sensitivity, even though it may rank high for certain favorable circumstances.

Scenarios that represent positions being widely or influentially held, even if they are at extremes, may be important to be explored. For example, the three energy study scenarios just cited clearly respond to the interests of the communities wishing to (1) ban nuclear energy altogether, (2) place principal reliance on it in the world's energy future, and (3) reduce greatly the world's consumption of energy, respectively. The findings also shed important light on the potential consequences of these extreme positions.

Establishing the Consequences

Given a context, a model or set of models is then used to predict the consequences of each alternative. This same model set may also serve for the other contexts and all alternatives unless the alternatives are radically different. If they are, another model or set of models may have to be constructed. For example, unless the alternatives are of essentially the same type, differing only in parameter values, they may generate consequences of different types and hence may require different models. Thus, in a benefit–cost comparison to determine whether public money should be spent for flood control, a new hospital, or an urban park different models would be required to determine the benefits of each alternative.

One of the major difficulties in systems analysis is that the ranking of the alternatives may not be the same in all contingencies. Further models, those of decision theory, are sometimes used in such cases (Schlaifer, 1969); one argues that certain of the contingencies are more likely to occur than others and hence probabilities can be assigned to them subjectively. An approach that would be appropriate were the probabilities known can then be used (White and Bowen, 1975).

In spite of the many difficulties with large computer models (these difficulties are well treated in Meadows and Robinson, 1984), many analysts try to design an elaborate computer model that will predict the full spectrum of impacts. A better approach, in the view of many analysts, is to use a collection of smaller-scale models that can be linked together (Goeller, 1973, and as quoted at the end of this chapter; Paxson, 1971; Raiffa, 1982) by means of various logical connections (which are in themselves models). These smaller models can be set up on-line on a large computer and, during presentations by telephone connection through a portable terminal, they can be used to answer questions from the decisionmaker regarding changes in the impacts that follow from changes in the contingencies and other assumptions.

Sensitivity Analysis

To analyze a model's sensitivity, the analyst changes some assumption, parameter value, or structural specification within the limits of uncertainty and then determines the new outcome to discover the extent to which it differs from that of the standard, or base-line, case. In fact, this process is usually repeated for several new values—often high and low estimates—that represent reasonable variations of the item of interest. If the changes in the outcomes are sufficient to suggest modifying the decision or policy that was preferred on the basis of the base-line results, then the model is said to be sensitive to the factor involved. "Within the limits of uncertainty" is, of course, a subjective judgment; other authors say "realistic" changes (Holling, 1978). Models that are not sensitive are more credible in the sense that their outcomes do not depend so critically on questionable assumptions. The analyst may, however, need to consider whether or not a lack of sensitivity is due to an inadequate model.

When the assumptions about the context, environment, or scenario are changed, rather than those related to the systems model, and the resulting changes in the results examined, the process is sometimes called a "contingency" analysis.

In the usual form of sensitivity testing, just one parameter is varied at a time. This is seldom good enough (Holling, 1978, p. 103); it is almost always necessary to test for interactive variation by changing more than one factor at once. However, this approach can easily generate so many cases that running them all becomes prohibitively time-consuming. Another way to test for sensitivity to a number of parameters simultaneously is to use a Monte

Carlo sampling process (Emerson, 1969). This can be done by selecting values of the uncertain parameters randomly from their frequency distributions for each one of a series of trials. The model result is then determined for each set of parameters. If this is done enough times, we can get an idea of what is required in the way of parameter changes to alter the outcome.

Sensitivity analysis must of necessity be undertaken in close communication with the decisionmaker, since it takes his judgment to decide when a modification in his decision is called for. The analyst needs his guidance also in deciding where to check for sensitivity.

What sensitivity testing does is help to make explicit the types and degrees of uncertainty that exist in the model outcome and to identify the dominant and controlling parameters. There is a misconception about sensitivity analysis (Bowen, 1978a) that sometimes occurs; namely, that it can compensate for the simplification that occurs in a model when expected values replace stochastic processes. Sensitivity testing, however, questions assumed values, whereas a stochastic formulation allows a value to vary from event to event in some assumed manner.

Sensitivity testing is a powerful way to tackle uncertainty but, if the model is elaborate, it can cost a lot in computer time. The claim made earlier in Section 7.2 that computer models can be easily tested is true in theory but, in practice, the expense and the time required tend to rule out extensive testing (Meadows and Robinson, 1984).

7.6. Social Experimentation

One way to determine the consequences of a proposed program may be to perform an experiment, to actually implement a number of alternatives for doing what one proposes to do under controlled conditions and observe the consequences that follow. A social experiment compares people who receive a certain treatment (the experimental program) with similar people who receive some other treatment, or none at all. Great care must be taken to ensure that the groups are indeed similar. Social experiments have been used to determine the degree to which families might change their hours of work as support levels and tax rates vary, and to measure how the use of medical care varies with insurance coverage; Section 1.2 describes a housing-maintenance experiment. When an experiment can be used and is properly designed and executed, the consequences can be inferred with greater confidence than from any other method.

Unfortunately, there are drawbacks to the social-experimentation method. It is often a completely impractical approach (for example, in the flood-control example of Section 3.4), or it cannot be properly controlled (Nagel and Neef, 1979, pp. 180ff, give some examples), or it may be too expensive. There are also ethical questions regarding equity and interfering with lives while running the risk of negative consequences, while still having enough variation in the experiment to learn something. See also Section 9.5. For a discussion of when to conduct a social experiment, how to manage one, and some practical advice, see Archibald and Newhouse (1980).

7.7. What Do Models Give Us?

In many clearly defined situations, particularly where repetitive operations are involved, models can be designed to give predictions in which the analyst can place great confidence. The statistical models used in the blood-supply study of Section 3.2 and the deployment models used in the Wilmington fire study of Section 3.3 are examples. In contrast, the safety models for the Oosterschelde study yield predictions that are far less firm; there the analysts had nothing but fragmentary data from which to estimate at what water level a dike would fail or how much damage would result from a particular set of dike failures. On account of such uncertain elements, the models used were challengeable, but until the basic data are improved, so are any other models that might be used. Because a model, by its nature, is a simplification, it distorts what is modeled; hence, the results it generates must be viewed with appropriate circumspection.

The predictive models for the sociotechnical problems of systems analysis are not like the scientific models of, say, mathematical physics or the life sciences. They have not yet been shown to be the appropriate models for identifiable classes of real situations. They must be freshly devised—or at least modified—for each particular application. They cannot always be expected to give good results when the contingencies with which they are associated are changeable (Boothroyd, 1978). The world is just too complex, unpredictable, and disordered for models of large-scale problems with social impacts to do much more than provide useful insights. As Hitch (1957, p. 718) said of systems analysis 25 years ago (he called it operations research):

> Operations research is the art of sub-optimizing, i.e., of solving some lower-level problems[;] . . . difficulties increase and our special competence diminishes by an order of magnitude with every level of decision making we attempt to ascend. The sort of simple explicit model which operations researchers are so proficient in using can certainly reflect most of the significant factors influencing traffic control on the George Washington Bridge, but the proportion of the relevant reality which we can represent by any such model or models in studying, say, a major foreign-policy decision, appears to be almost trivial.

Our computer capabilities have increased at least a hundred fold since then and we can do better, but not a great deal better; we are not calculation-limited, we are understanding-limited.

Models for economic management, impact assessment, social policy design, and for many other issues to which systems analysis is applied have turned out to give predictions in which our confidence is low. Yet these are important concerns that must be investigated and the policymaker's choice is limited; either he must base his predictions and actions on judgment alone, or use information from the explicit models developed by analysts.

What then do we get from our models if their predictions are so tentative? At the very least we get insight into the consequences of our alternatives, information that may enable us to get a feel from the model about the significant factors that will guide us toward better alternatives. Indeed, the process of building the model may often be more valuable than the results we get from the model itself. "Experts create models, but models also create experts" (Greenberger, Crenson, and Crissey, 1976). Almost everyone agrees that the people involved in modeling learn a great deal about the problem. This is one of the reasons why many modelers so often push for gaming, for it offers a chance to involve the actual policymakers.

We should not look on systems analysis models as mere "black boxes" that produce predictions when properly stimulated. So narrow a view ignores an important process: in using and building models, analysts learn about the problem. An explicit model of any kind introduces structure and terminology to a problem, and provides a means for breaking a complicated decision into smaller tasks that can be handled one at a time. It also serves as an effective means of communication, enabling the participants in a study to make their judgments within a defined context and in proper relation to the judgments of others. Moreover, through feedback—for example, the results of computation in a mathematical model or the criticism of an expert's judgment—the model can help the analysts and the experts on whom they depend to revise their earlier judgments and arrive at a clearer understanding of their subject matter and of the problem, thus starting another cycle of analysis from an improved background.

These characteristics of a model—separating tasks and providing a systematic, efficient, and explicit way to focus judgment and intuition—are crucial, for they provide a way of conjecturing what the major consequences may be when adequate quantitative methods are not available.

In connection with the San Diego Clean Air Project (Goeller et al., 1973), Bruce Goeller developed a number of modeling premises that should be considered by every analyst:[1]

> The first, and most basic, premise holds that it is impossible for a comprehensive model to realistically internalize the policymaking process, that is, to individually weigh and trade off the numerous factors involved in making a policy decision and to select the preferred alternatives. Past attempts to do so were not considered credible to either the researcher or the policymaker.
>
> To overcome this deficiency, the policy analyst is viewed as a person who

---

[1] The text presented here was revised by Goeller from an early version of (Goeller, 1984); a slightly different version appears in House and McLeod (1977).

Section 7.7. What Do Models Give Us?   215

constructs and maintains a toolkit of models and analytical techniques that can be brought to bear on specific policy issues; the specific mix of these tools is variable and determined by the specific problem.

The interaction between analysts and policymakers is viewed as an iterative one; in response to questions and concerns of the policymaker, the analysts will modify the menu of alternatives or enrich the menu of impacts by which they are compared.

The second premise is that the methodological approach of policy analysis models should often differ from that of implementation planning models because their purposes differ. *Policy analysis,* in our view, is primarily concerned with deciding *what* to do; that is, what are preferred. *Implementation planning* is concerned with deciding *how* to do something; that is, what actions by what institutions will bring a particular preferred policy into being. Since they must evaluate many possible policies in terms of many possible impacts, policy analysis models should strive for flexibility, inexpensive operation (both in terms of computer and human costs), and relatively fast response; moreover, they should allow policies to be described at a relatively gross and conceptual level. Implementation planning models, in contrast, can, and generally do, operate at a considerably more detailed and concrete level, since they will be used to evaluate only a few alternatives.

As an example of the distinction between implementation planning and policy analysis, suppose the decision problem is how to improve a regional bus system. During implementation planning, one is concerned with such questions as whether the buses should run on First and Third Streets rather than Second and Fourth Streets. During policy analysis, in contrast, one is concerned with such questions as whether the route-spacing should be two blocks rather than four or six blocks—or whether the fare should be reduced instead—and how many people will ride on the buses.

The third premise is that a policy model's primary purpose is to improve decision making rather than to improve forecasting per se. For example, a relatively crude model that can clearly demonstrate that alternative *A* performs better than alternative *B* under both favorable and unfavorable assumptions will probably lead to a better decision than a complex model that can perform only a highly detailed expected value extrapolation. Policy models generally need the capability easily to perform various kinds of sensitivity analyses, not only on the policies themselves, but on the basic technical and scenario assumptions as well.

The fourth premise is that our toolkit approach to a comprehensive model (where a set of partial models that may be used in different combinations) is better suited to many kinds of policy problems than the *monolithic* model approach. With the toolkit approach, the component models, which relate to different parts of the problem, may be used separately to analyze a particular part of the problem in many different ways, with a minimum of data inertia or housekeeping problems, thereby increasing the analyst's understanding of that part of the problem and his ability to design effective policies for it. When the component models are used in combination, the output data set from one model is generally part of the input data set of a subsequent model. Although the analyst could submit a combination of models as one computer run, he often gains advantages from making separate serial runs. This enables him to see various intermediate results, to check the output data from one model for reasonableness and, if necessary, to modify them before they are input to the next step. He can adaptively intervene in the interaction process between the models to reflect the effect of factors that the models do not explicitly treat or to heuristically increase the efficiency of search or convergence (Paxson, 1971).

The fifth premise is that the design of a comprehensive policy model should be decision-maker-oriented from the start. Initially, the model should be considered as a black box (toolkit!) and the question should be what knobs, representing policy variables (and the scenario), and what dials, representing impacts, should be put on the front of the box to make it useful to the decision makers. Only after this exercise should attention be given to designing the algorithmic contents of the box.

The sixth premise is that there might be synergistic complementarities from developing comprehensive policy models, using the toolkit approach in a region that already has a fairly well-developed system of planning models. First, and most obvious, the planning models could be used as part of the detailed implementation planning process after the preferred policy is chosen. Second, they could be used as a pump-primer for the policy analysis methodology: By generating detailed forecasts of numerous regional characteristics (population and land use by small areas, etc.) in machine-readable form, planning models provide a voluminous but internally consistent and systematic data base that may be aggregated, incorporated, and used in various ways by the policy models. This approach can be particularly effective for studying the near-term effects of near-term policies, since it is common to treat land use and other slowly varying regional quantities as exogenous in such studies. In this context, we use the planning methodology to provide a detailed forecast of the region in the near term assuming that the "do nothing" or "existing trends" policies prevail, and then use the policy model to predict the impacts of changes in policy. We call this a perturbation approach.

The final premise is that the practicality and usefulness of a particular policy model for other (related) policy problems is strongly determined by the concreteness of the original policy problem for which it was developed. [Italics in the original.]

Goeller's comments, although they refer to particular policy studies, represent a summary of many of the points we have tried to impart in this chapter.

References

Archibald, R. W. and J. P. Newhouse (1980). *Social Experimentation: Some Whys and How.* R-2479-HEW. Santa Monica, California: The Rand Corporation.

Boothroyd, H. (1978). *Articulate Intervention.* London: Taylor and Francis.

Bowen, K. C. (1978a). Analysis of models, unpublished paper. Laxenburg, Austria, International Institute for Applied Systems Analysis.

References

———(1978b). *Research Games.* London: Taylor and Francis.

Brewer, G. D. (1972). Dealing with complex social problems: The potential of the decision seminar, P-4894, August 1972. Santa Monica, California: The Rand Corporation.

———and M. Shubik (1979). *The War Game.* Cambridge, Massachusetts: Harvard University Press.

Brown, Seyom (1968). Scenarios in systems analysis. In *Systems Analysis and Policy Planning: Applications in Defense* (E. S. Quade and W. I. Boucher, eds.). New York: Elsevier.

Bush, R. P., and F. Mosteller (1966). A comparison of eight models. In *Readings in Mathematical Social Sciences* (P. Lazarsfeld and N. W. Henry, eds.). Chicago: Science Research Associates.

Checkland, Peter (1981). *Systems Thinking, Systems Practice.* Chichester, England: Wiley.

DeWeerd, H. A. (1973). *A Conceptual Approach to Scenario Construction,* P-5084. Santa Monica, California: The Rand Corporation.

Drake, A. W., R. L. Keeney, and P. M. Morse, eds. (1972). *Analysis of Public Systems.* Cambridge, Massachusetts: MIT Press.

Emerson, D. E. (1969). *UNCLE—A New Force Exchange Model for Analyzing Strategic Uncertainty,* R-480, November 1969. Santa Monica, California: The Rand Corporation.

Energy Systems Program Group of IIASA, Wolf Haefele, Program Leader (1981). *Engergy in a Finite World: Volume 1. Paths to a Sustainable World; Volume 2. A Global Systems Analysis.* Cambridge, Massachusetts: Ballinger.

Goeller, B. F., et al. (1973). *San Diego Clean Air Project: Summary Report,* R-1362-SD, December (1973). Santa Monica, California: The Rand Corporation.

———(1984). *Guidelines for Constructing Policy Analysis Models,* P-6975. Santa Monica, California: The Rand Corporation.

Greenberger, M., M. Crenson, and B. Crissey (1976). *Models in the Policy Process.* New York: Russell Sage Foundation.

Helmer, Olaf (1966). *Social Technology.* New York: Basic Books.

———(1978). Role-playing and other judgmental techniques. Unpublished paper. Laxenburg, Austria: IIASA.

———(1983). *Looking Forward: A Guide to Futures Research.* Beverly Hills, California: Sage.

Hitch, C. J. (1957). Operations research and national planning—a dissent. *Operations Research* 5, 718–723.

Holling, C. S., ed. (1978). *Adaptive Environmental Assessment and Management.* Chichester, England: Wiley.

House, P. W., and John McLeod (1977). *Large Scale Models for Policy Evaluations.* New York: Wiley Interscience.

Ignall, E. J., P. Kolesar, and W. E. Walker (1978). Using simulation to develop and validate analytic models: some case studies. *Operations Research* 26, 237–253.

Kolesar, P., and E. Blum (1973). Square root laws for fire engine response distances. *Management Science* 19, 1368–1378.

Linstone, H. A., and M. Turoff, eds. (1975). *The Delphi Method: Techniques and Applications.* Reading, Massachusetts: Addison-Wesley.

Majone, G. (1980). *The Craft of Applied Systems Analysis,* WP-80-73, April 1980. Laxenburg, Austria: International Institute for Applied Systems Analysis.

———and E. S. Quade (1980). *Pitfalls of Analysis.* Chichester, England: Wiley.

Meadows, D., J. Richardson, and G. Bruckmann (1982). *Groping in the Dark,* Chichester, England: Wiley.

———and J. M. Robinson (1984). *The Electronic Oracle: Computer Models and Social Decisions.* Chichester, England: Wiley.

Moder, J. J., and S. E. Elmaghraby, eds. (1978). *Handbook of Operations Research: Models and Applications.* New York: Van Nostrand Reinhold.

Mood, A. M. (1982). *Introduction to Policy Analysis.* New York: North-Holland.

Nagel, S. S., and M. Neef (1979). *Policy Analysis in Social Science Research.* Beverly Hills, California: Sage.

Paxson, E. W. (1971). XRAY Game. In *Cost Considerations in Systems Analysis* (G. H. Fischer, ed.). New York: Elsevier.

Popper, K. R. (1959). *The Logic of Scientific Discovery.* New York: Basic Books.

Quade, E. S. (1975). Models and their use. In *Criminal Justice Models: An Overview* R-1859-DOJ (J. Chaiken et al.). Santa Monica, California: The Rand Corporation.

———(1982). *Analysis for Public Decisions,* 2nd ed. New York: North-Holland.

Raiffa, Howard (1982). *Policy Analysis: A Checklist of Concerns,* PP-82-2. Laxenburg, Austria: International Institute for Applied Systems Analysis.

Schlaifer, Robert (1969). *Analysis of Decisions Under Uncertainty.* New York: McGraw-Hill.

Schwarz, B., U. Svedin, and B. Wittrock (1982). *Methods in Futures Studies: Problems and Applications.* Boulder, Colorado: Westview Press.

Shubik, M., and Brewer, G. D. (1972). *Models, Simulations, and Games—A Survey,* R-1060-ARPA/RC. Santa Monica, California: The Rand Corporation.

Specht, R. D. (1968). The nature of models. In *Systems Analysis and Policy Planning: Applications in Defense* (E. S. Quade and W. I. Boucher, eds.). New York: Elsevier.

Thomas, M. A. (1982). *An Energy Crisis Management Simulation for the State of California,* R-2899-CEC. Santa Monica, California: The Rand Corporation.

Toulmin, S. (1974). The structure of scientific theories. In *The Structure of Scientific Theories,* (F. Suppe, ed.). Urbana, Illinois: University of Illinois Press.

Walker, W. E., J. M. Chaiken, and E. J. Ignall, eds. (1979). *Fire Department Deployment Analysis.* New York: North-Holland.

White, D. J., and K. C. Bowen, eds. (1975). *The Role and Effectiveness of Theories of Decision in Practice.* London: Hodder and Stoughton.

Chapter 8
Guidance For Decision

Brita Schwarz, Kenneth C. Bowen,
István Kiss, and Edward S. Quade

8.1. Introduction

This chapter deals with the guidance a systems study can provide, guidance that varies considerably with the kind of problem being studied, the purpose of the work, and the decisionmaking structure. Some systems studies, such as the IIASA global energy study (as summarized in Section 3.5), may be designed merely to provide improved insights into a problem area and into the effects on its relevant system of various contingencies and technological, social, and economic developments, as well as the actions of various categories of decisionmakers. Such work can serve as a background for other studies that focus more directly on the problem of identifying specific alternatives for narrower and more sharply defined contexts [for an example that relates the findings of the IIASA global energy study to the European Communities, see Sassin et al. (1983)]. However, this chapter limits most of its discussion to studies that include the explicit evaluation of decision alternatives.

The guidance an analysis can provide those responsible for selecting an action, based on the information the study has produced about the advantages and disadvantages of the various alternatives, may sometimes be quite uncomplicated, and may consist of recommending one of the alternatives. More often, however, when there are competing objectives, multiple decisionmakers, or great uncertainty about future conditions, it becomes a complex process in which conflicts tend to be resolved by bargaining, and political pressures may overpower research findings. The way the results are presented and the information and evidence presented with them can both facilitate and improve the choice.

An analyst can almost never, based on his analysis alone, tell the decisionmaker with confidence: "This alternative should be selected." A mathematical model may designate an optimum action, but it is an optimum only in the domain of the model, for even the most perfect of models corresponds only imperfectly to the real world. Optimization is a technical concept, inapplicable in situations where differing values, uncertainty, ambiguity, multidimensionality, and qualitative judgment are present and possibly dominant. Even with perfect information, the most that can be done is to find the alternative that best satisfies a certain criterion under a given set of assumptions. This is far from full optimization, which would require considering simultaneously the complete set of consequences for every choice of alternative, taking into account the full range of future events and their associated probabilities.

For multiple decisionmakers, there can, in fact, be no optimality; any such concept depends on a particular decisionmaker's values, purposes, abilities, and needs. Consequently, as Boothroyd (1978, p. 73) puts it, ". . . would-be-scientific intervention is at best a way of getting things righter, not of getting them right." Earlier, citing other reasons, Hitch (1960b, p. 444) had laid the ghost of optimization to rest in his retiring address as President of the Operations Research Society of America: ". . . Most of our relations are so unpredictable that we do well to get the right sign and order of magnitude of first differentials. In most of our attempted optimizations we are kidding our customers or ourselves or both. If we can show our customer how to make a better decision than he would otherwise have made, we are doing well, and all that can reasonably be expected of us."

Thus, in systems analysis, whenever the terms optimum, optimal, and optimization are found, they must be interpreted with great caution, for they refer to something that is, at best, a suboptimization.

The goal of the analyst is, nevertheless to do more than to produce, by cost–benefit or other criteria selected by the decisionmaker, a correct ranking of the limited set of alternatives with which he is presented, or that he designs, so that a "best" one can be selected from among them. To do this much he must, of necessity, learn a great deal about the subject of inquiry; but, in designing possible alternatives, he may remain far from having the expertise of the client and his staff. Thus, to do better he must instead, as Goeller (1972, 1977, and Section 3.4) and Holling and his colleagues (1978) suggest (see Section 8.8), seek a presentation that will enable the decisionmaker and his staff to understand the strengths and weaknesses of—and the tradeoffs among—the various alternatives, so that their expertise can be applied to generate new and better possibilities before a decision is taken.

8.2. Criteria

A criterion is a rule or standard by which the analyst can rank alternatives for the decisionmaker. As an example, suppose a decisionmaker's objective were to provide electric power for his constituents by building a dam on a certain stretch of river. Assume he has a budget of 200 million dollars available for the project. If acceptable to the decisionmaker, a criterion for ranking the various dams that might be built in different designs and locations along the river could be to rank the ones that can be constructed for the available budget in decreasing order of power output. (Although the purpose of a criterion is distinct from that of an objective, the decisionmaker could have stated his objective in exactly the words of the criterion, namely, to build the dam with the greatest power output that can be constructed within the available budget. Because statements of objectives are frequently made in this way, the terms criteria and objectives are sometimes confused.)

To maximize a benefit such as power output from a project subject to a cost constraint (as above) or its equivalent, to minimize the cost subject to a benefit constraint, is a commonly used criterion. It works well when the significant costs are monetary and there is a single dominant benefit and desirable consequence. It is also used when the benefits are difficult to measure in monetary terms, say for something like crime reduction. This criterion is called cost-effectiveness.

For public decisions, for example, the choice of an airport location, a common criterion is that used in cost–benefit analysis, that is, one chooses the location for which the net benefits exceed the net costs by the largest amount. A benefit may be interpreted as something that brings about a Pareto improvement—a change that makes at least one member of the community better off and none worse off. A cost does the opposite. The measurement problems associated with cost–benefit analysis are enormous and are discussed later in Section 8.5; for an explanation of the underlying principles, see Sugden and Williams (1978).

Many other schemes have been used to combine various indicators into a single index, particularly when the impacts or consequences are ones whose measurements indicate the worths of the alternatives. One type of index much used in the past is a quotient with the product of the measurements of impacts for which an increase is desirable in the numerator and with the products of the measurements of impacts for which a decrease is desirable in the denominator. Thus, to compare alternative aircraft designs, if the significant indicators are the speed V, reliability R, cost C, payload P, and fuel consumption F, the index might be VRP/CF. To take account of the differing importance of the factors, exponents might be used. However, this is not a recommended approach, one reason being that it is a ratio (Hitch and McKean, 1960).

A far better form of index, if a single index of worth is to be used, is one developed by utility analysis. This form of analysis permits the decisionmaker (or a group of decisionmakers) to determine both the "utility" or "satisfaction" that is associated with different values of the set of consequences and the tradeoffs among them. The theory offers a way, through formal questioning, for an analyst to help the decisionmaker to develop an index (Raiffa, 1968; Keeney and Raiffa, 1976). It is the best of the single-index approaches developed so far.

Criteria are tied to objectives; the criterion the analyst would like to use is the one that ranks the alternatives in order of consistency with the decisionmaker's objectives. The decisionmaker may, and probably does, have objectives that he does not reveal to the analyst, possibly because he does not realize he has them until he is forced to make his decision. Hence, for this reason and because the analysis itself is always imperfect in one way or another, the analyst should regard his rankings as guidance rather than a rule for choice. He may want to present rankings according to several criteria; to say to his client "If you regard X of overriding importance, then C is indicated; but if, as many people do, you regard Y of essentially equal importance, then B may be your choice."

8.3. Satisficing

Since true optimization is impossible, satisficing, or replacing objectives by constraints, moves closer to the world as it actually is. The reasons, as summarized by Simon (1969, pp. 64–65), who supplied the name, are these:

> In the real world we usually do not have a choice between satisfactory and optimal solutions, for we only rarely have a method of finding the optimum, . . . We cannot, within practicable computational limits, generate all the admissible alternatives and compare their relative merits. Nor can we recognize the best alternative, even if we are fortunate enough to generate it early, until we have seen all of them. We satisfice by looking for alternatives in such a way that we can generally find an acceptable one after only moderate search.

To satisfice, lower bounds are set for the various goals that, if attained, are "good enough." An alternative is sought that will at least exceed these bounds. A unique solution is not sought and conflicts between goals do not have to be resolved. The satisficer does have to worry that the performance standards are not set too high, for then it may be impossible to satisfy the constraints. An alternative is usually considered to be good enough if it promises to do better than has been done previously.

Satisficing is, in fact, far more common than the relatively infrequent use of the term in the literature of systems analysis would indicate. The applied systems analyst normally works under sharp time restrictions. He may have barely enough time to produce a solution that is "good enough" for the momentary situation, i.e., better than what is currently being done, and this may be all that the decisionmaker really needs at the moment.

Once a satisficing alternative has been found, the analysis should not necessarily stop (although it may if the decisionmaker is completely satisfied), for there may be—and very likely are—more and better alternatives to be found by further analysis; for example, the analyst could seek to "optimize" on the basis of the variables that the satisficing solution leaves free. Looked

Section 8.4. Suboptimization

at in this way, satisficing is primarily a scheme for screening out and eliminating undesirable alternatives.

8.4. Suboptimization

The choice of criteria and objectives is made more difficult than otherwise when a decisionmaker undertakes to contribute to the solution of a broad problem by finding a better way to handle the one aspect within his span of control. Authority is everywhere divided; all decisions cannot be made at the highest level, even when the authority to do so exists. Thus, many problems are sub-problems, parts of problems that for an "optimum" solution should be considered in the "big picture," but the decisionmaker does not have the time or the authority to do more than to see to the improvement of his sector. Analysts, like decisionmakers, for these reasons as well as being forced by the difficulties of solving their problems, must frequently devote their attention to actions that pertain to only part of the problem. In the language of systems analysis, they "suboptimize."

These attempts are suboptimizations because it is almost always possible to do better if all of the factors that could influence a solution could be considered simultaneously and the decisionmaker were able to make his selection from a larger net of alternatives.

There are reasons to reject suboptimization, but as Hitch (1960a, pp. 1–2) comments:

> It might appear then that it would make sense to *begin* with some broad "given" or accepted objectives; to derive from them appropriate local or sub-objectives for the systems problem in hand; and then to design the analysis to maximize, in some sense, the proximate objectives. . . .
>
> Not only is this a plausible approach; it is in some special cases an acceptable one; it is usually (not always) better than making no systems study at all; and it is frequently, given limitations on available time or manpower, the only feasible approach. I think I was the first to use the term "sub-optimization" to describe this style of operations research (in 1952), and I am no implacable or dogmatic foe of its use. Some of the most rewarding systems studies have in fact been low level sub-optimizations. [Italics in the original.]

But as Hitch goes on to say, a suboptimization may not be satisfactory unless the criteria for the lower-level problem are consistent with those for the higher-level problem. Thus, to avoid inconsistencies, the analyst must give careful thought to the criteria and objectives for the full problem before deciding on the ones that should be used in the subproblem. An illustration may help (Quade, 1982, pp. 211–212):

> For example, in the design of a car-parking operation for an amusement park, one size of lot and pricing system might be derived from a suboptimization in which the criterion is that of maximizing net revenues from parking

and another size lot and pricing policy from an analysis that sought to maximize net revenues from the amusement park as a whole. Lack of parking for a few people, who then go elsewhere, might lead to considerable saving in land costs for parking and in salary for attendants, and thus in revenues for the lot, but the loss in goodwill, and thus in revenues for the park as a whole, might be serious.

A policy more consistent with the higher-level objective, and thus a better policy for the lot, might simply be to provide parking for all customers—or even to provide it free. We cannot know *a priori*, however, that income from a parking lot should be small relative to the income for the facility it serves. Whenever there is little opportunity for visiting the facility except by private car, a significant general admission might be more acceptable if disguised as a parking fee.

The advantage of suboptimization is that more detail can be taken into account in the narrower analysis. Models, because they involve fewer factors may, within their limitations, yield more accurate predictions. But the need for consistency between criteria for the full problem and those of the subproblem poses difficulties in selection.

8.5. Cost–Benefit Analysis and the Cost–Benefit Criterion

Decisionmaking is often described as a weighing of benefits against costs if the benefits and costs are interpreted in the broad sense of referring to *all* kinds of advantages and disadvantages of different decision alternatives. Sometimes risk is considered as a cost, sometimes as a separate dimension but rarely as a benefit. However, it is clearly a cost whenever we are willing to pay to avoid or hedge against it. Comparisons of various alternatives in terms of benefit–cost–risk can therefore be considered a general framework of analysis (Dror, 1975). Nevertheless, when the term cost–benefit analysis is used, it usually refers to a specific type of analysis, well known to economists, and having its origin in welfare economics.

In economic cost–benefit analysis, the analyst identifies the different types of consequences of each alternative, usually a governmental project (e.g., the location of an airport or a power station). The consequences are estimated quantitatively and the quantities converted to monetary units (while this conversion can almost always be done in one way or another, we do not believe that it can be done satisfactorily). Monetary benefits and costs are then summed separately with proper attention to probability and time of occurrence. The cost–benefit criterion means a ranking of the alternatives in decreasing order of the excess of benefits over costs. It should be borne in mind that not all costs and benefits, even though expressed in the same monetary units, can necessarily be added in a straightforward way without additional scaling: costs, like benefits, have to be treated initially as multidimensional variables. And, in addition, a given sum of money is not necessarily valued the same by different people or groups.

Section 8.5. Cost–Benefit Analysis and the Cost–Benefit Criterion

A cost–benefit approach has several attractive characteristics. The cost–benefit criterion seems relevant for decisionmaking and defines an unequivocal method for ranking alternatives. Also, theoretically, it can be used to guide choice between such diverse alternatives as allocating funds between a water project (with irrigation, electric power, flood control, and recreation as goals) and a health program (with reduced mortality, morbidity, and cost to the state as goals). If the projects are roughly of the same scale, one prefers the project with the greater excess of benefits over costs; if the projected benefits are less than the costs, then the project should not be undertaken.

In contemporary applications, analysts seek to identify all consequences associated with implementing each alternative for all future time, and then to determine their benefits and costs, together with the probabilities associated with their occurrence. The expected loss or gain for each cost or benefit is calculated by multiplying each amount by the probability of occurrence. A discount rate is then assumed, and the time streams of costs and benefits are discounted and summed to obtain their present values. The alternatives are ranked by the totality of benefits minus the totality of costs, or by the "internal rate of return," the rate of discount that reduces present worth to zero (Fisher, 1971). The translation of consequences of implementation into monetary terms includes estimates by the analyst of the prices that would have been attached to various goods and services if a perfectly competitive market had existed. In principle, cost–benefit analysis can thus associate with each possible choice all the inputs and outputs, all the positive and negative effects, including spillovers, with their probabilities and times of occurrence, condensing everything into a single number. For detailed discussion, see Mishan (1971) or Sugden and Williams (1978); Dunn (1981) gives a short treatment from a social science point of view.

In practice, to quantify all types of effects and translate them into monetary terms is very difficult, and any method used will be open to question. For instance, pollution effects can often not be considered as quite equivalent to some sum of money. Different decisionmakers may also have different time preferences, and these may not be conveniently expressed through the discount rate. Further, a general assumption behind the cost–benefit approach is that undesirable distributional effects can be corrected by transfer payments; costs and benefits, however, often accrue to different categories of people and satisfactory compensation to those who lose can often not be found.

As a consequence of the complications mentioned above there are numerous objections to using a cost–benefit approach. One is that it is easily subject to abuse, since so many critical assumptions tend to be buried in the computation. The choice of a discount rate is particularly tricky. For instance, to promote a project with high installation costs but with the benefits deferred in time, advocates would argue for a low discount rate (2 percent has been used for some water projects where the benefits were marginal and a long time in the future). Perhaps the most fundamental objection to the cost–

benefit criterion is that it requires the analyst to make judgments (for instance in connection with distributional effects) which in fact are value judgments of the sort that should be left to the responsible decisionmaking body.

An apparent advantage of the cost–benefit criterion is that it permits comparisons of very different policies and projects. Experience in applications, however, indicates that it is more likely to be used successfully when the decision alternatives are rather similar, i.e., with consequences similar in type and involving the same scale of effort.

Traditional cost–benefit analysis had no association with "systems thinking;" the concepts, so important to systems analysis, of iteration and feedback to improve the predictions of consequences and to screen and refine the set of alternatives have been until relatively recently foreign to the practice of cost–benefit analysis. The literature of cost–benefit analysis rarely mentions iteration. However, this literature has devoted some attention to identifying the alternatives and predicting the outcomes that might affect their adoption, emphasizing valuing them in commensurate units so that they can be ranked. Feasibility investigations have only recently been extended to implementation problems. For this latter purpose, Luft (1976) suggests additional cost–benefit analyses, a form of iteration.

To give an illustration of the possibilities and limitations of cost–benefit analysis, we will use a hypothetical application. Assume that an additional airport is considered to be required in a city area because of increasing air traffic. As the existing one cannot be extended, the problem is to find a suitable location for a second airport. To simplify, we assume further that there are several suitable and uninhabited land areas and that air traffic does not cause any negative side effects; i.e., there are no noise or air pollution problems. To calculate the costs and benefits of the different locations, the analyst has to estimate the impact on future air and surface travel, the monetary worth of savings in travel time, etc. These estimates may involve considerable uncertainties, but rough approximations are likely to be obtainable. Because of the uncertainties, it may not be possible to arrive at a definite ranking order. Nevertheless, very bad alternatives can probably be screened out and the analysis can help the decisionmakers to focus their further attention on a subset of the original alternatives, one that is likely to contain only reasonably good alternatives.

To make our hypothetical airport example somewhat more realistic, let us now assume that the alternative airport locations will, to a varying extent, bring noise disturbances into residential areas and also require that some residents, factories, etc., be displaced. This means that there will be a group of people who probably cannot be compensated in a way they find quite satisfactory. Surely this information is important to the decisionmakers and should be brought to their attention; the cost–benefit criterion alone, in this case, is not the most suitable basis for ranking the alternatives and needs to

Section 8.6. Cost-Effectiveness Analysis   227

be supplemented in some way, say by a "scorecard" presentation, as discussed in Section 8.8.

The term cost–benefit analysis is also used to describe studies whose results are not quite as condensed as a strict cost–benefit criterion requires. In such cost–benefit analysis, it is usually recommended that benefits and costs that cannot be expressed in monetary units in a satisfactory way be displayed separately. When there are such effects, more complex information has thus to be communicated from the analyst to the decisionmakers. For the analyst to choose when and how to do this, the information exchange between the analyst and the decisionmakers is of considerable importance. The analyst needs information about the decisionmaking situation and about what the decisionmakers consider important, and he has to structure the communication of his results in a way to fit the prevailing decision situation and in the language of the decisionmaker.

In evaluating risky projects with highly adverse but rare consequences and negligible monetary costs, a risk–benefit rather than a cost–benefit analysis is frequently used (Jennergren and Keeney, 1979; Fischhoff, 1977). The fundamental idea is to appraise whether or not the benefits outweigh the risks. It has been used, for example, in deciding whether various food additives and drugs should be barred from public consumption.

8.6. Cost-Effectiveness Analysis

If we now turn back to our simplified airport example, it may happen that the study is being carried out when the decision to build a second airport has already been taken. Perhaps several feasible and quite attractive alternative locations have been found, and general estimates or judgments have indicated that the benefits of a second airport will exceed the costs. In this case it may be an unnecessary complication to try to estimate the benefits in monetary terms, for some other measure of effectiveness (e.g., some kind of air-travel capacity measure) may be of more interest. More generally, a project is usually undertaken to achieve some objective; the measure of effectiveness should indicate the extent to which the objective is achieved.

This leads us to a type of criterion of choice that can be termed cost-effectiveness. In this, alternatives are ranked either in terms of decreasing effectiveness for equal cost, or in terms of increasing cost for equal effectiveness. Sometimes the maximum of the ratio of effectiveness to cost is used to indicate the preferred choice, but this is open to all the objections that apply to the use of ratios for criteria (Hitch and McKean, 1960) and requires additional information to fix the scale of the effort, as seen in Figure 8.1. Here, typical cost-effectiveness behavior for two projects is shown by the two curves. Although project 1 clearly has a higher ratio of effectiveness to cost (at K_1, where the tangent from the origin touches the curve) than any point

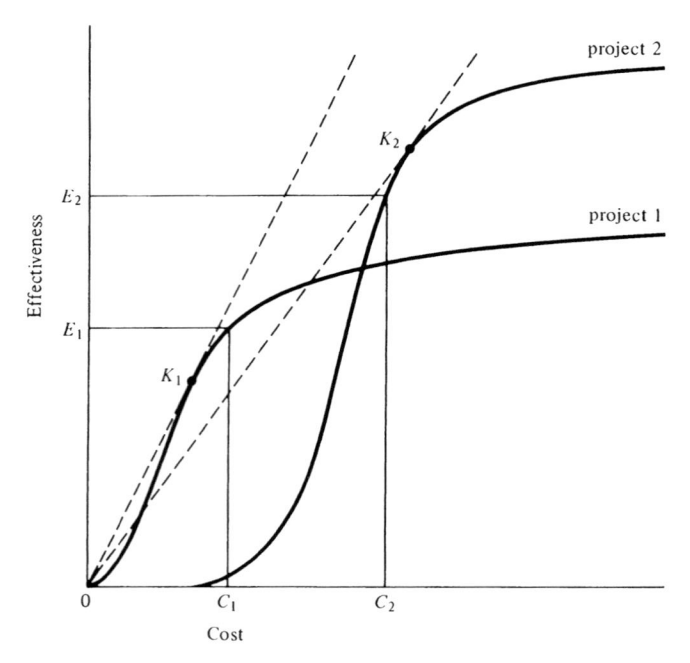

Figure 8.1. Typical cost-effectivess curves for two projects. The dotted lines are lines of the maximum cost-effectiveness ratio for each project.

on the curve for project 2, whether project 1 is preferred to project 2 depends on the scale of the effort. If, for instance, the effectiveness must be at least E_2, then project 2 must be preferred (Attaway, 1968). If, however, the cost cannot exceed C_1, 1 is preferred, for at this cost project 1 is more effective.

Cost-effectiveness is probably the most commonly used criterion for ranking alternatives. The reason is clear; it provides a comparison in terms of two factors of crucial importance to every decisionmaker—how much he will need to spend, and to what extent the action he takes will get him what he wants. It may be a sufficient basis for choice only in those rare instances when "other considerations" are not significant (and thus at a relatively low level of suboptimization), but the information it provides is always helpful.

The cost-effectiveness criterion is open to a number of objections. One is that cost as used in cost-effectiveness reflects only the costs that are inputs—the money, resources, time, and manpower required to implement and maintain an alternative. The penalties or losses that may accompany an implemented alternative—it may, for instance, interfere with something else that is wanted or bring undesirable consequences to other people—are costs that are not taken into account.

Ordinarily, effectiveness does not measure value, but is merely a proxy for some aspect of it. A different choice of how we measure effectiveness can lead to a different preference among alternatives. For example, if the objective is to increase traffic safety and we choose as our measure of effectiveness the decrease in fatalities, we may then give high priority to reducing accidents where two cars collide at high speed, for these are very serious. But if our measure is the decrease in the economic cost of accidents, then priority may go to the avoidance of low-speed collisions in rush-hour traffic, for these are very numerous.

Another defect is that the people who must pay the costs of a decision and those who stand to gain may not be the same. Unless the alternatives are so similar that this aspect can be neglected, a decision based on a cost-effectiveness criterion may mean trouble for the decisionmaker. Again, there is a likely clash of values.

Finally, even if cost and effectiveness were fully and properly determined, the decisionmaker would still be faced with the problem of what to choose. He needs some way to set the scale of effort—either the cost he must not exceed or the effectiveness level he needs to achieve. Sometimes this can be provided by setting the maximum cost so that it corresponds to the "knee" of the cost-effectiveness curve (Figure 8.1), since very little additional effectiveness is gained by further investment.

It is clear that the cost-effectiveness criterion we have discussed here is inadequate for decisionmaking problems for which multiple objectives, spillover effects, or the distributional aspects are important characteristics. Other approaches, as discussed below, must be used.

8.7. Decision Analysis

Cost–benefit analysis can be considered as a means of reconciling competing objectives through converting the various consequences into monetary units. This process, in effect, sets up a system for assigning weights to the various consequences. The analysis is then done for a less specialized objective—to find the course of action, no matter what particular set of objectives brought it into existence, that brings the greatest excess of benefits over costs.

Numerous other schemes for using a weighted combination of the consequences to provide a preference ranking of the alternatives have been tried. Many of these work satisfactorily when the decisions involved are of a repetitive type. Under the name of decision analysis a considerable body of knowledge has been developed which, in principle, is applicable both to one-time decisions and repetitive decisions.

In the decision analysis approach, the analyst models the value system or preference structure of the decisionmakers so as to be able to predict with the model what the decisions would be, were the decisionmakers to be presented with the full set of alternatives and their consequences. To do this, the analyst constructs a function of the consequences associated with the alternatives that represents the decisionmaker's value or utility rating for each alternative. For a simple example, see Mood (1982, pp. 13ff). Here the inputs to the function are measures (on appropriate scales) of the consequences, properties, aspects, or anything else associated with an alternative that the decisionmaker would take into account in estimating the value of the alternative. For a more detailed description of the paradigms of decision analysis, see Chapter 1 in Keeney and Raiffa (1976). Thus, if competing designs for communication satellites were being ranked, one variable might be the initial investment cost, a second the expected mean time to failure, a third the number of available communication channels, and so on.

Any aggregate approach of this type, like the cost–benefit approach, has two serious disadvantages. One is that a great deal of information is lost by aggregation; the fact that alternative A has environmental problems whereas alternative B has political implementation problems is suppressed. The second is that any single measure of value depends on the relative weights assigned by the analyst and the assumptions he used to get them into commensurable units.

To produce anything resembling a valid value function is clearly difficult, and perhaps impossible in many situations. There are problems both with getting the preference information from the decisionmakers, which can require a substantial effort on their part, and with putting it together in a usable expression. For examination of the basic assumptions behind decision analysis and the consequential problems in applications, see Tribe (1972) and White and Bowen (1975).

Many analysts believe that, while such value functions are clearly useful for screening the alternatives, the final designation of a preferred alternative must be made by other means. Particularly when the decision concerns the public sector, and the preferences depend on basic values, the decision thus being essentially political, more disaggregated information needs to be communicated to the decisionmakers. Nevertheless, the analyst may, while developing and using value functions for his own initial inquiry, find that his understanding of the complexity of the problem (and consequently the quality of the advice that he finally offers) has been enhanced.

8.8. Dealing with the Criterion Problem

A hypothetical decisionmaker might say: "If someone is to help me decide whether something I think I would like to have is worth what I would have to give up to get it, the most informative way for him to do so is to present me with a full and honest description of what I would be getting, and getting into, including all negative aspects and side effects. I would judge this preferable to being told that, because of previous decisions or statements, if I am to be consistent, I should do so and so." Many decisionmakers, ranging from individuals to the body politic, have this same sort of feeling.

Section 8.8. Dealing with the Criterion Problem

The obvious way of presenting the information asked for is by means of a two-dimensional array or matrix. Until recently, Bruce Goeller has been almost alone in advocating the use of such an array as the replacement for ranking the alternatives by cost–benefit or other criteria in presenting the results of a systems study to policymakers. On a scorecard, as Goeller (1972) calls such an array, the consequences (impacts is the term Goeller uses) that ensue from a possible decision to select each of the alternatives—the costs, benefits, spillovers, risks, segments of society affected, and in fact, anything about an alternative that the analyst thinks the decisionmaker might want to consider in his decision (including its characteristics and origins if they seem pertinent) are displayed (in terms of the natural units commonly used to characterize them) in a matrix, or tabular array. In such an array, the entries in each column represent the consequences associated with a particular alternative and the entries in each row show how a particular consequence or other characteristic varies from alternative to alternative. [For examples see the displays in Section 3.4 and Goeller et al. (1977).] Goeller's improvement over the usual such presentation lies in the careful selection of units for characterizing the consequences, in grouping similar ones into categories, and in using underlining, shading, or colors to show a crude ranking of alternatives for each consequence. The aim is to provide the decisionmaker with an effective "gestalt" of the relative advantages and disadvantages of particular alternatives.

Consider noise impacts as an example. These have usually been reported in terms of land area exposed to a noise level above some specified threshold. But the decisionmaker is more interested in how many people noise affects and how it affects them. A scorecard can report the number of people exposed to various noise levels on a noise-annoyance scale.

To illustrate the detail with which the results can be presented, consider the group of "community impacts" reported in a transportation study (Goeller, 1972): changes in the activity patterns, tax base, and environment that would occur to the communities in the region as the result of building and operating alternative transportation systems. Specific impacts displayed in that study include the number of households annoyed by excessive noise, the amount of air pollution, the savings in petroleum consumption, the households displaced by system construction, the amount of land taken, the resulting revenue losses to the community, and even such an intangible as the loss of a community landmark (which very likely can not be satisfactorily quantified in any fashion, let alone in the monetary terms necessary for a cost–benefit comparison).

For oral presentation, color, in the form of transparent colored rectangles placed over the numerical values, can be used to give a quick indication of each alternative's ranking on a particular impact. Goeller used green to show the best value and red to show the worst, with two colors for intermediate values, blue for next best and orange for the next to worst. The numerical values themselves were visible through the colors. Sensitivities to changes in parameters or to different forecasts for the environment were shown by further transparent overlays and the use of multi-colored rectangles.

The scorecard is such a simple and obvious device that no argument for its use is needed. It is extremely flexible. A decisionmaker can see where an alternative he favors is deficient; he can ask what modifications would eliminate the unfavorable outcomes from an otherwise promising alternative and whether this action might turn some presently acceptable result into an unacceptable one. Goeller uses scorecards in conjunction with a toolkit of many relatively small models programmed for a computer and available on-line, so that the answers to many such questions can be supplied immediately. In addition, the decisionmaker can call for further analysis to show how changes in the assumptions originally made by the analyst will affect the results. Since he assigns his own weights to the different impacts, the scorecard can help him understand the tradeoffs implied by the decision he is to make. If he chooses A over B he may be trading off substantial increases in noise and future costs for savings in air pollution and initial investment costs. Such tradeoffs are implicit in every decision, but the decisionmaker who views an aggregate index may not see them, for they have been obscured by the process that combined the different impacts into a single measure, even though he played a part in developing this process and agreed to use it. The scorecard confronts the decisionmaker explicitly with the tradeoffs he must make. To decide, he must weight them subjectively, bringing to bear not only factual knowledge but his feeling for societal values.

A scorecard presentation can also be understood, and used, by the public. Different groups can, in the same way as the ultimate decisionmakers, ask "what if" questions, apply their own preferences, and confront the decisionmakers with their views based on much more information than if they had merely an index to go on. Given the logical structure that the scorecard presents, they might also be guided to propose new alternatives and to consider additional consequences.

The advantages of the scorecard over an aggregated index for providing guidance to decisionmakers may be summarized as follows:

The scorecard

> seeks convergence to a decision—not agreement on value judgments from the decisionmaker or decisionmakers;
>
> is understandable and usable by decisionmakers and other groups involved, including the public at large;
>
> enables impacts and alternatives to be evaluated, and improved alternatives to be developed, with minimal interposition of the analysts' biases and values;
>
> allows direct consideration of qualitative as well as quantitative impacts;
>
> retains multidimensionality, showing tradeoffs explicitly;
>
>> uses natural physical—and thus understandable—units.

Section 8.8. Dealing with the Criterion Problem

A disadvantage, for there is one, is that the scorecard may present too much information for a decisionmaker to absorb. But this can be handled by careful selection of what to present, holding other information for later presentation when requested, bearing in mind that this process must be kept as free from the analyst's values as possible.

In their adaptive approach to environmental management, Holling and his colleagues rejected cost–benefit and similar criteria in favor of a scorecard approach, noting that " . . . the process of policy comparison through direct reference to the individual indicators is the least ambiguous evaluation technique available. What it lacks in refinement is more than compensated for by the clear communication of relevant information" (Holling, 1978, p. 110).

For example, in their study of the interactions of a forest system with a pest called the budworm, the analysts considered 17 consequences (that they called "indicators", because they indicated the effects of the various forest-management policies) grouped into three categories, as shown in Table 8.1. "Extensive experimentation with the system model and interviews with relevant decisionmakers identified five of the indicators listed . . . as primary;" they were (1) the forest volume, measured in cubic meters per hectare, (2) the harvest cost, measured in dollars per cubic meter, (3) unemployment,

Table 8.1. Examples of Indicators of Known Interest Taken from the Forest-Pest (Budworm) Case Study

Socioeconomic Indicators
  Profits to the logging industry
  Profits as a proportion of total sales
  Cost per unit volume of harvested wood
  Cost of insecticide spraying
  Unemployment rate reflected by the proportion of mill capacity utilized

Resource Indicators
  Volume of wood in trees older than 20 years
  Volume of wood in trees older than 50 years
  Volume of wood harvested
  Proportion of total volume harvested
  Volume of wood killed by budworm
  Mill capacity
  Total forest volume

Environmental Indicators
  Visible damage due to budword defoliation
  Damage due to logging operations
  Age class diversity of the forest
  Number of high quality recreational areas
  Insecticide impact in terms of fraction of province sprayed

Source: Holling (1978, p. 109).

measured as a proportion of those normally employed in the forest-products industry, (4) recreational quality, measured by an index lying between zero and one, and (5) insecticide applications, measured by a proportion of a standard effort. However, we are interested, not only in values of these indicators, but also their history; therefore, the scorecard technique for this case requires displays of graphs of the indicator values over time, as shown in Figures 8.2–8.5. Holling (1978, pp. 110–112) summarizes the background of these figures as follows:

> ... The values assumed by these indicators in a simulation of the management policy historically used in New Brunswick are given in Figure [8.2]. In an attempt to improve this policy, new spray and harvest rules were developed and then tested on the simulation . . . . The results, presented in Figure [8.3], show improvement in some indicators, notably total forest volume, profits to the logging industry, and recreation, but a somewhat worse situation with regard to employment and insecticide spraying . . . .
>
> A modification of the alternative policy was next designed, explicitly tailored to decrease spraying by cutting down trees threatened by budworm. The results in Figure [8.4] show that spraying is indeed reduced, but at a cost of even more irregular employment due to the sporadic antibudworm harvest. The "good" forest volume, harvest cost, and recreational performance have been reasonably maintained, however. Since any preventive harvest scheme seemed likely to incur this disadvantage, we searched elsewhere and attempted to reduce spraying by adding a hypothetical but realistic budworm virus to the model. As shown in Figure [8.5], this succeeded in reducing spraying substantially without radically increasing unemployment. Forest volume was better than with any other policy, and recreation was superior to any but the antibudworm harvesting policy.

8.9. Value Analysis and Political Feasibility

Values and beliefs held by individuals and organizations affect analysis at all stages, from problem formulation to decision and implementation. Analysts must be particularly careful not to affect the analysis by unconsciously introducing their own values. Differences in values can lead decisionmakers to advocate different actions on the basis of the same study, and, after a choice is made, can lead the implementing bureaucracy to take actions the decisionmaker did not intend.

In ranking the alternatives in preparation for a decision, or in helping the decisionmaker in ranking the alternatives, the analyst needs to discover a great deal about the decisionmaker's values. This is not easily done; "we can always ask people about their values, but in the end, we can only infer what values they appear to hold by analyzing their behavior, including their statements, in a number of situations" (Bowen, 1979, p. 503). Other approaches are possible. Bowen (1979) suggests that such topics as the following merit

Section 8.9. Value Analysis and Political Feasibility

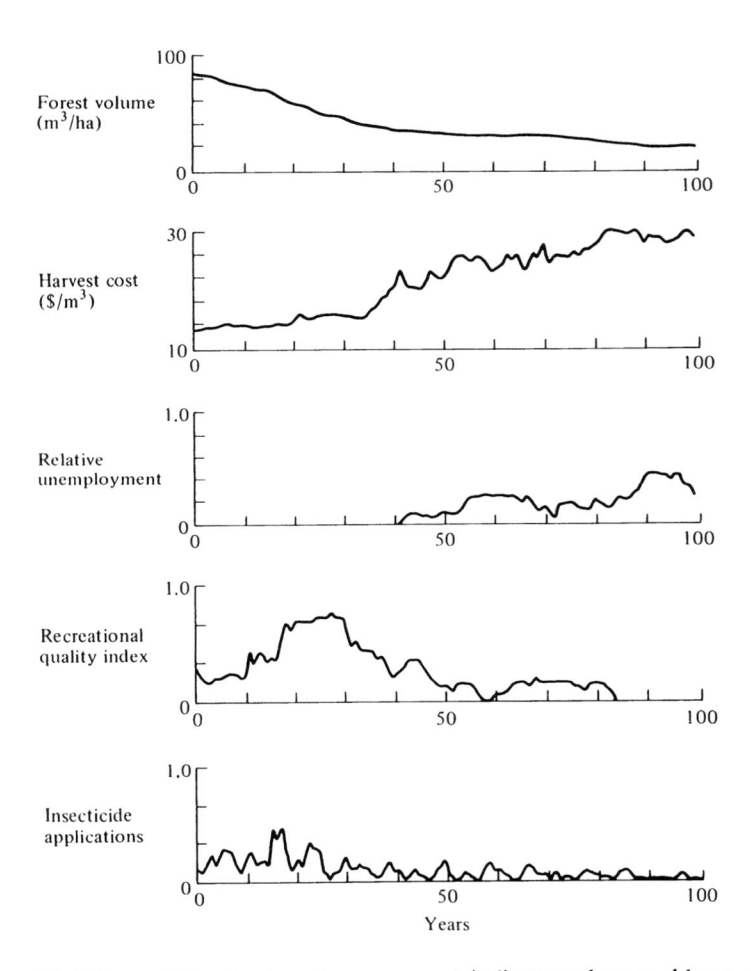

Figure 8.2. Values of the five forest-management indicators that would ensue from pursuing the historical management policy. (*From Holling, 1978*).

more attention than they have been given: analysis of options, hypergame theory, structural mapping, personal construct theory, fuzzy sets, and a number of ideas stemming from conflict research and research gaming. He also (Bowen, 1981) urges attention to social judgment theory as developed by K. R. Hammond and his colleagues (1975, 1977).

It is sometimes argued that decision problems that are "political" or value sensitive cannot be subjected to analysis. This may be true if ranking only according to cost–benefit or cost–effectiveness criteria is considered. However, many analysts are of the opinion that values can be properly taken into account for instance, when objectives, objective functions, constraints and

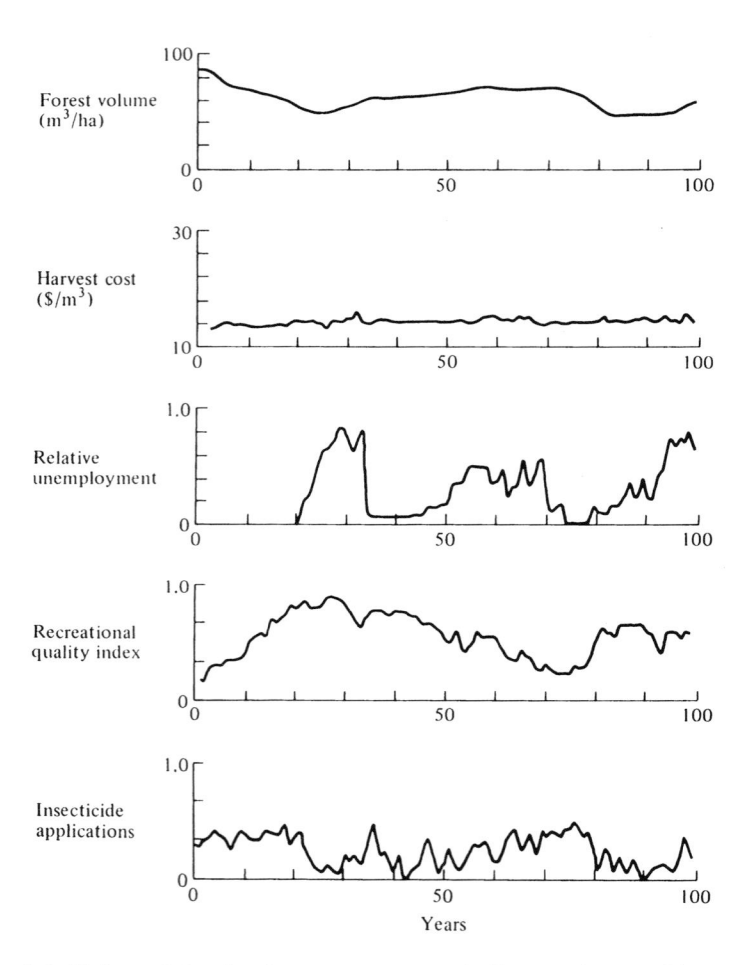

Figure 8.3. Values of the five forest-management indicators that would ensue from proposed new management rules involving new spray and harvesting policies. (*From Holling, 1978*).

alternatives are defined, or by an explicit display of various effects, for instance by a scorecard presentation, which enables decisionmakers to do the final ranking on the basis of their value preferences.

A frequent view is that values and facts are clearly distinguishable and that analysts (or experts, scientists, etc.) should contribute only facts to the decisionmaking process. But a clearcut value-fact dichotomy is not generally accepted, and estimates of future consequences of what we today regard as facts are not necessarily value-neutral. An example of a possible approach to value-sensitive issues is given in the IIASA energy study, which outlines a

Section 8.9. Value Analysis and Political Feasibility

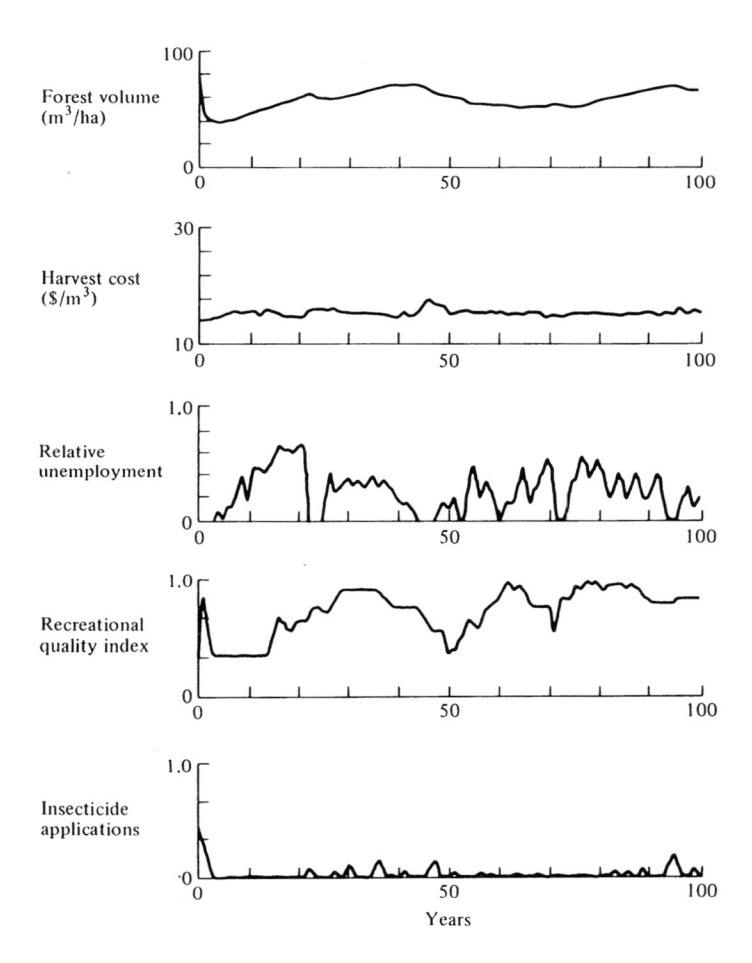

Figure 8.4. Values of the five forest-management indicators that would ensue from the proposed new management rules modified by cutting down trees threatened by budworm. (*From Holling, 1978*).

number of different scenarios for the global energy system. As mentioned in Section 7.5, three of the scenarios respond to the interests of the communities wishing to (1) ban nuclear energy altogether, (2) place principal reliance on it for the world's energy future, (3) reduce greatly the world's consumption of energy. The design of different decision alternatives for different sets of values and preferences, and efforts to illuminate their effects on future options can be important in analyzing value-sensitive issues (Soderbaum, 1982).

There are also arguments for a direct involvement of analysts in political feasibility and value analysis. This includes improving the value sensitivity

238   Chapter 8. Guidance For Decision

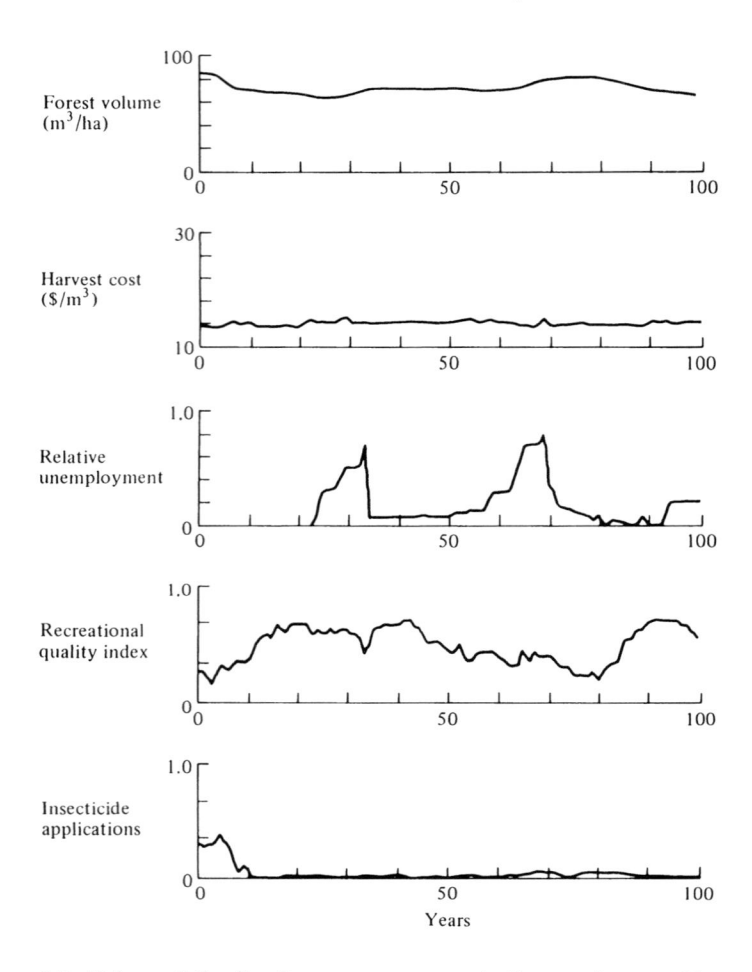

Figure 8.5. Values of the five forest-management indicators that would ensue from the proposed new management rules modified by introducing an antibudworm virus. (*From Holling, 1978*).

and the value judgment of "legitimate value judges" without usurping that function. To quote Dror (1975 pp. 250–251):

> ... this is achieved through methodologies designed to structure the judgment field and to explicate value dimensions in a way that permits more conscious, comprehensive and explicit judgment by the legitimate value judges. These processes help them to make more "responsible" value judgments on the basis of clarification of the fullest meanings of the involved values. Primary methods of value analysis include testing of value sensitivity, examination of value consistency, checking the completeness of the value set, explication

of tacit value dimensions (e.g., time preferences and lottery preferences), value mapping, consideration of value futures, design of value and goal taxonomies, and more.

The feasibility of implementation is an important aspect when decision alternatives are compared. Depending on the decisionmaking process, some alternatives may be almost impossible to implement if there are active groups who object to them. The analysis of such aspects is sometimes called "political feasibility" testing (Dror, 1968). It involves investigating the probability that a proposed action will be acceptable to various secondary decisionmakers—the special interest groups, the public, and the bureaucracy who must translate it into action. It is clearly important to identify these secondary decisionmakers and their influence at an early stage. If the probability of acceptance is too low (but the policy is very attractive for other reasons), compromises can be made to increase acceptability. Analysis can help find the preferable compromises—those that increase acceptability without a proportionate loss in attaining policy goals.

Cost–benefit and similar analyses designed to produce an economically efficient solution may encounter political opposition. For an alternative to be politically feasible, it may not only have to approximate the largest total benefit available to the affected parties as a whole, but, in addition, allocate the aggregate benefits and costs in a way that reflects the political strengths of the various interest groups or accords with the political majority's ideologies. Thus, the alternative selected must be acceptable to the most influential groups and not too strongly opposed by the others. When a group is asked to accept an alternative in a situation where a competing alternative would bring them greater benefit, then, if the losses can be estimated, the chosen alternative frequently can be made acceptable (and thus politically feasible), by arranging a compensation to the objecting group, say, by tax exemptions or deductions designed to benefit them specifically (Olson, 1971; Starling, 1979).

For further discussion of value problems, see Dunn (1981) and Rein (1976).

8.10. Uncertainties

In previous sections we have mentioned the existence of uncertainties, but have not sufficiently emphasized their dominant role and pervasiveness in systems analysis and decisionmaking. To evaluate decision alternatives we must estimate the future consequences of various courses of action, and the future is always uncertain. The effects of some uncertainties—say those in economic, technical, and operational parameters that can be identified, measured, or at least estimated, and treated statistically—can often be taken account of in the analysis proper by actual calculation of the probabilities, or by Monte Carlo methods, or, less precisely, by using means or expected values. Sensitivity testing and *a fortiori* analysis can also be done and presented to the decisionmaker. Other uncertainties, about future environments and contingencies, and about certain activities that depend on the actions of people (now as well as in the future), are more intractable.

The decisionmaker is always confronted with a certain amount of uncertainty when presented with the results of a systems analysis. When the issue has long-term implications, or involves a rapidly changing situation or one being manipulated by other decisionmakers, a number of different forecasts of the state of the world or scenarios may have to be considered. In this case, the results of the analysis as carried out for each contingency or forecast may not indicate the same order of preference among the alternatives. What then can the analyst suggest to the decisionmaker if, under one contingency with high probability of occurrence, alternative A is clearly superior, but, under another contingency of low probability but with catastrophic implications, alternative B is better?

Faced with such uncertainty the decisionmaker can, depending on the circumstances, take one or more of the following actions (Madansky, 1968):

Delay: Defer his action until better information is available. Delay, of course, is not always an option and, when it is, may be costly, particularly when competition or conflict is involved.

Buy information: Attempt to alleviate uncertainty by supporting further research and data collection. (This also involves delay and cost and may or may not improve the situation.)

Hedge: Adopt duplicate alternatives or modify an alternative to introduce greater flexibility—at a higher cost, of course.

Compromise: Select an alternative that, while it may not be best for the contingency judged to be most likely, does not rank too low on the less likely ones.

Be conservative: Choose the alternative that gives the best result if the environment is maximally unkind. This is the "maximin" approach, in which one resolves uncertainties by making the blanket assumption that the worst will happen.

Use decision theory: Argue that the probabilities of the various states of nature are not completely unknown and beyond human judgment, assign probabilities to them subjectively, and then use an approach that would be appropriate for the case in which the probabilities are known [precisely or in intervals, see Hederstierna (1981)].

The military in the United States (which may have had as long an experience with systems analysis under conditions of great uncertainty as any other institution) had at one time something like the following philosophy. Any attempt to determine a unique best solution to a problem involving a large number of uncertain factors, some of which may be under the influence of other decisionmakers, is doomed to failure. The aim instead should be to search out or design alternatives that perform well or even close to the best for what appears to be the most likely set of contingencies, and from such alternatives, whenever it can be done, select the one that gives some sort of reasonably satisfactory performance under the more unlikely and even most pessimistic circumstances.

8.11. Risk Evaluation

Side effects, or negative consequences that are not direct costs to be borne by the decisionmaker, but which may inhibit his actions in some way, may need special attention both when designing and when comparing the alternatives. Side effects are sometimes treated by imposing constraints. However, the elimination, or the reduction in the probability, of the occurrence of serious negative side effects must often be made an objective.

The term risk is often used in connection with uncertain negative side effects. More specifically, risk is often associated with highly negative consequences, which rarely occur. The exact meaning of risk varies somewhat. Sometimes it means the probability of a negative consequence. In other cases it may mean the negative consequences themselves. In yet other cases, it may refer to the statistical expectation of the negative consequences. Most commonly, however, risk refers to the entire spectrum of negative consequences with their associated probabilities [see Jennergren and Keeney (1979) for a fuller explanation].

Risk assessment is often thought of as consisting of two parts: risk estimation and risk evaluation. In risk estimation, one is concerned with identifying the various serious negative consequences of a project or activity, and assigning probabilities (or rates of occurrence) to those consequences. In risk evaluation, one appraises the acceptability of the risk to society.

A risk evaluation is a value judgment that sometimes includes comparisons with other risks that exist in society. This does not mean that such comparisons necessarily lead to definite conclusions. The acceptability of a risk depends on whether it is considered as a voluntary or an involuntary one, and also on the magnitude of the associated benefits. Also, the character of the risk is of importance. When two projects with the same benefits have risks with the same expected value people are not necessarily indifferent to them. If the worst that can happen is less serious in project A than in project B, many people will prefer A. Consequently, risk evaluation may depend on value preferences, in which case the analyst must leave the final evaluation to "the legitimate value judges."

8.12. Decision Processes, Planning, and Policies

We have thus far assumed that the guidance to be given to the decisionmakers concerns the choice among a number of alternatives that have been investigated in the analysis. Actually, the decisionmakers may make other types of decisions. If the alternatives studied have been different designs of a public project, the first decision to be taken may not be a decision in favor of one of the alternatives but may, for instance, be a decision:

- to study some of the designs in more detail, perhaps with new constraints;
- to accept a part of a design and keep the option open to choose later on among several alternatives;
- to include one design, perhaps vaguely described, in a plan that is to be reconsidered or reviewed later on (certain options are thus left open regarding the final version of the project);
- to make further studies.

The decision processes that follow a systems analysis may take many different forms, and the form to be chosen may be difficult to predict. However, some information about the likely decisionmaking process is usually available to the analysts, and this type of information can be important to take into account both in the design and the evaluation phases of a study. Much attention has also been devoted to decision processes (Allison, 1971, p. 10; Simon, 1957; Keen, 1977; Cyert and March, 1963; Lindblom, 1959; Inbar, 1979; Kicker, 1980; and George, 1980). Results from such descriptive–explanatory research is, of course, of considerable importance to the systems analyst.

It should be emphasized that a systems study frequently does not involve a ranking followed by choice from among a number of alternatives. Often, when the start of the study is a vaguely defined problem area, the work may include an analysis of the historic development of the problem issues and the effects of earlier policies, and only address issues concerning future development in a very general way. In such cases, the output consists of no more than some tentatively defined decision alternatives or, as in the IIASA energy study, some guidelines for developing future alternatives. In the United States, many systems studies are carried out in the form of "program evaluations." Here the study starts after the decision to launch a new program has been implemented and the program has been under way for some time. The problem defined at the outset may be "Has it worked as expected?" The result of the study is usually that it has not, but, more importantly, the study may suggest where to look for possible improvements (Hatry, 1980). One should not expect the need for analysis to stop with implementation. Policy decisions even supported by the best of analysis seldom result in a program needing only enforcement for implementation. Models are imperfect and circumstances change. As part of the analytic effort, it should be determined as soon as possible whether the results are as anticipated, and if not, how to correct the problems discovered. These monitoring and evaluating functions could, and perhaps should, be undertaken by someone other than the original analyst or policymaker (Walker, 1978).

8.13. Guidance from the Analyst

The effectiveness of the various schemes for presenting the results of analysis, and for carrying out the analysis itself, depends to an extent on the decisionmaking situation. It is best when this situation approximates the rational actor model. However, a knowledge of which other model—the process-oriented view (Simon, 1945), the organization-process view (Cyert and March, 1963; Allison, 1971), the political paradigm (Lindblom, 1959; Allison, 1971), or the apprehensive man (Keen, 1977)—best approximates the decisionmaking situation is useful to the analyst, not so much in finding a "best" solution, but in finding a way to get that "best" solution adopted and implemented by the relevant decisionmakers and organizations other than his client. Adoption of the results of systems analysis is, in fact, usually easier to achieve than successful implementation. At the decision stage, participants may not feel it necessary to resolve all uncertainties, for it is believed that they can be taken care of during implementation. All that is needed may be enough support to tip the decisionmaking body in favor of the proposal. This support can be verbal and soft; implementation, however, demands that the organizations involved contribute real resources and here is where the crunch may come. But, as Majone (1980) argues, technologically sound information and factual arguments are not always enough to win acceptance. A well written report, a carefully prepared visual presentation (briefing), and persuasive and continuing communication may be needed to change the current attitudes.

The type of guidance for decision that the analyst can give as a result of a systems analysis may, in rare cases, take the form of clearly specified recommendations, for example, in favor of a given decision alternative. Whether this is a satisfactory action depends on many issues, for example:

Have the criteria for the recommendations been thoroughly explored and agreed upon?

Are these criteria expressible in a quantifiable manner?

Has this quantification been based on value judgments with which the decisionmaker is in full agreement?

Are the models used satisfactory to the analyst and are their implications understood by the decisionmaker?

Are the situations tested by the models, and the alternative options explored in these situations, reasonably complete and unquestioned?

Are there agreed ways of weighing multiple criteria and multiple objectives?

Apprehension is sometimes said to dominate analysis (Keen, 1977). Decisionmakers may sometimes learn through apprehension rather than comprehension and rely on experience rather than on understanding and analytic methods.

It is often possible for decisionmakers to agree on the action to be taken, even though they disagree on objectives. A policymaker may concur in the decision to accept a study recommendation for reasons far different from those the analyst had in mind. He may do so, for instance, because he may forestall stronger action or because he may see how to divert to other purposes the money that will be appropriated to implement the recommendation.

It is not surprising then that, in general, it is safer and more satisfactory merely to provide pros and cons of the better options in many situations. In dialogue with the decisionmakers, there is a wide-ranging exploration and attempt to make less vague both the nature of the problem itself and the values that the various possible options for decision have for the decisionmaker. Most systems analysts have ways of doing this, although there seems to be no general methodology: there are different approaches depending on the values held by analysts and decisionmakers and the way in which they interact.

The aim of systems analysis, while it is to improve decisionmaking, is also to make the decisionmaker more satisfied that the basis for his decision is adequate and informed. The work done must provide new insights into the problem area under discussion, and it must be structured and presented in a way that facilitates the use of the information it contains. The analysis must be seen to be relevant and its communication must be readily understood. The mode of communication, continuous or at intervals, orally or in writing, diagrammatic or in words, technical or nontechnical, mathematical or nonmathematical, will vary with circumstances, but there must be good communication and it must be in terms familiar to the decisionmaker (Walker, 1978, and Chapter 10). Special communication aids include interactive computer modeling, scenario writing, games and game-theoretic processes, films, and even forms of counseling.

The important issue is how decisionmakers interpret the data put before them, because only some of these data will be seen by them as information relevant to their decisions [for some of the pitfalls, see Lynn (1980)]. Their previous experience, their general world view, their reaction to variables and constraints that the analyst has or has not been able to take fully into account, and particularly their attitude toward analysis and their prior beliefs, will all affect how they use what they are offered. Analysts should strive always to understand the total environment of decisionmaking so as to provide the maximum of information and the minimum of redundant data, although initial redundancies have a habit of being useful if the decisionmaker chooses to delay his decision in one way or another.

The fact, mentioned above, that no general methodology exists for the final stage of analysis and decision, leaves one important thing still to be said. Any analyst who can make explicit, for a stated systems analysis, how the communication process used was conceived and what its successes and failures were, will have added something of value to the literature on the subject. The trouble is that, because the process depends so much on personal values and understanding of values, it is difficult to write anything down in a way that can be used directly by others. In particular, it is difficult to define success or failure: on the one hand, although the results of an analysis may be accepted in a fairly short time, implementation may involve major resources, many people, and risks to key executives; on the other, apparently unaccepted findings may move into reality five to ten years later. Nevertheless, analysts with successful communication experiences should report them (thus adding both breadth and depth to the material summarized in Chapter 10). It is worth trying.[1]

References

Allison, Graham T. (1971). *Essence of Decision.* Boston: Little, Brown.

Attaway, L. D. (1968). Criteria and the measurement of effectiveness. In *Systems Analysis and Policy Planning* (E. S. Quade and W. I. Boucher, eds.). New York: Elsevier.

Boothroyd, Hylton (1978). *Articulate Intervention.* London: Taylor and Francis.

Bowen, K. C. (1979). Personal and organizational value systems: How should we treat these in OR studies? *Omega 7,* 503–512

____(1981). Decision-making models or decision-makers' models? *IMA Bulletin* 17, 110–112.

Checkland, Peter (1981). *Systems Thinking, Systems Practice.* Chichester, England: Wiley.

Cyert, R. M., and J. G. March (1963). *A Behavioral Theory of the Firm.* Englewood Cliffs, New Jersey: Prentice-Hall.

Dror, Y. (1968). *Public Policymaking Reexamined.* Scranton, Pennsylvania: Chandler.

____(1975). Some features of a meta-model for policy studies, *Policy Studies Journal* 3(3), 247–255.

Dunn, W. N. (1981). *Public Policy Analysis: An Introduction.* Englewood Cliffs, New Jersey: Prentice-Hall.

Eden, Colin, Sue Jones, and David Sims (1983). *Messing About in Problems: An Informal Structured Approach to Their Identification and Management.* Oxford, England: Pergamon.

Fischhoff, B. (1977). Cost–benefit analysis and the art of motorcycle maintenance. *Policy Sciences* 8, 177–202.

Fisher, G. H., ed. (1971). *Cost Considerations in Systems Analysis.* New York: Elsevier.

George, A. L. (1980). *Presidential Decisionmaking in Foreign Policy: The Effective Use of Information and Advice.* Boulder Colorado: Westview Press.

Goeller, B. F. (1972). The STAR study: impacts of alternative intercity transportation

---

[1] A few such reports are, in fact, beginning to emerge; for example, Checkland (1981) and Eden, Jones, and Sims (1983) report effective forms of experience in client-analyst communication based on extensive practical experience.

systems on the California corridor. In *Policy Analysis and the Problems of the 1970's.* Kamakura, Japan: Nomura Research Institute.

_____ A. F. Abrahamse, J. H. Bigelow, J. G. Bolten, D. M. de Ferranti, J. C. DeHaven, T. F. Kirkwood, and R. L. Petruschell (1977). *Protecting an Estuary from Floods— A Policy Analysis of the Oosterschelde. Vol. I: Summary Report,* R-2121/1-NETH. Santa Monica, California: The Rand Corporation.

Hammond, K. R., et al. (1975). Social judgment theory. In *Human Judgment and Decision Processes.* (M. F. Kaplan and S. Schwartz, eds.). New York: Academic.

_____(1977). Social judgment theory: Applications in policy formulation. In *Human Judgment and Decision Processes in Applied Settings* (M. F. Kaplan and S. Schwartz, eds). New York: Academic.

Hatry, Harry P. (1980). Pitfalls of evaluation. In *Pitfalls of Analysis.* (G. Majone and E. S. Quade, eds.). Chichester, England: Wiley.

Hederstierna, A. (1981). *Decision under Uncertainty: The Usefulness of an Indifference Method for Analysis of Dominance.* Stockholm, Sweden: Stockholm School of Economics.

Hitch, C. J. (1960a). *On the Choice of Objectives in Systems Studies,* P-1955. Santa Monica, California: The Rand Corporation, March 1960.

_____(1960b). Uncertainties in operations research. *Operations Research* 8, 437–445.

_____ and R. McKean (1960). *The Economics of Defense in the Nuclear Age.* Cambridge, Massachusetts: Harvard University Press.

Holling, C. S., ed. (1978). *Adaptive Environmental Assessment and Management,* Chichester, England: Wiley.

Inbar, M. (1979). *Routine Decision Making: The Future of Bureaucracy.* Beverly Hills, California: Sage.

Jennergren, L. P., and R. L. Keeney (1979). Risk assessment. Laxenburg, Austria: International Institute for Applied Systems Analysis. Unpublished draft.

Keen, P. G. W. (1977). The evolving concept of optimality. In *Multi-Criteria Decisionmaking.* (M. K. Starr and M. Zeleny, eds.). TIMS Studies in Management Science, Vol. 6., 31–57. Amsterdam: North–Holland.

Keeney, R. L. and H. Raiffa (1976). *Decisions with Multiple Objectives: Preference and Value Tradeoffs.* New York: Wiley.

Kicker, W. J. M. (1980). *Organization of Decision-Making.* Amsterdam: North-Holland.

Lindblom, C. W. (1959). The science of muddling through. *Public Administration Review* 19(2), 79–88.

Luft, H. S. (1976). Benefit–cost analysis and public policy implementation: From normative to positive analysis. *Public Policy* 24(4), 437–462.

Lynn, L. E., Jr. (1980). The user's perspective. In *Pitfalls of Analysis* (G. Majone and E. S. Quade, eds.). Chichester, England: Wiley.

Madansky, A. (1968). Uncertainty. In *Systems Analysis and Policy Planning: Applications in Defense* (E. S. Quade and W. Boucher, eds.). New York: Elsevier.

Majone, G. (1980). An anatomy of pitfalls. In *Pitfalls of Analysis* (G. Majone and E. S. Quade, eds.). Chichester, England: Wiley.

Mishan, E. J. (1971). *Cost-Benefit Analysis.* New York: Praeger.

Mood, A. M. (1982). *Introduction to Policy Analysis.* New York: North-Holland.

Olson, M. L. (1971). *The Logic of Collective Actions.* Cambridge, Massachusetts: Harvard University Press.

Quade, E. S. (1982). *Analysis for Public Decisions,* 2nd Ed. New York: North-Holland.

Raiffa, Howard (1968). *Decision Analysis.* Reading, Massachusetts: Addison-Wesley.

Rein, M. (1976). *Social Science and Public Policy.* New York: Penguin.

Sassin, W., A. Hoelzl, H.-H. Rogner, and L. Schrattenholzer (1983). *Fueling Europe in the Future—The Long-Term Energy Problem in the EC Countries: Alternative R&D Strategies,* RR-83-9/EUR 8421-EN. Laxenburg, Austria: International Institute for Applied Systems Analysis.

Simon, H. A. (1945). *Administrative Behavior,* New York: Macmillan.

_____(1957). A behavioral model of rational choice, In *Models of Man* (H. A. Simon). New York: Wiley, pp 241–260.

_____(1969). *The Sciences of the Artificial.* Cambridge, Massachusetts: MIT Press.

Soderbaum, P. (1982). Positional analysis and public decision making. *Journal of Economic Issues* 16, 391–400.

Starling, G. (1979). *The Politics of Economics and Public Policy.* Homewood, Illinois: Dorsey.

Sugden, R., and A. Williams (1978). *The Principles of Practical Cost–Benefit Analysis.* Oxford, England: Oxford University Press.

Tribe, L. H. (1972). Policy sciences: analysis or teleology? *Philosophy of Public Affairs* 12, 6–110.

Walker, Warren E. (1978). *Public Policy Analysis: A Partnership Between Analysts and Policymakers,* P-6074. Santa Monica, California: The Rand Corporation.

White, D. J., and K. C. Bowen, eds. (1975). *The Role and Effectiveness of Theories of Decision in Practice.* London: Hodder and Stoughton.

Chapter 9
Implementation

Rolfe Tomlinson, Edward S. Quade,
and Hugh J. Miser

> If to do were as easy as to know what were good to do, chapels had been churches, and poor men's cottages princes' palaces.
>
> William Shakespeare,
> *The Merchant of Venice,* Act I, scene ii

> The most important . . . results . . . come in the form of a vision felt by researchers as an outcome of deep, concentrated analysis . . . . The process of transferring this vision is difficult, lengthy, and delicate. There is no assurance that it will grow simpler as our vision comes closer to perfection.
>
> Jermen M. Gvishiani (1981, p. 17)

The agreement of the 16th-century English playwright and the 20th-century Russian academician that to bring vision to reality is difficult is widely shared, and nowhere more than in the contexts where systems analysis can help construct the vision of what is desired. But systems analysis is not intended just to aid in formulating what is desirable, its goal is also to help bring about change for the better, to see that what is done is what was decided—and what will bring the vision to reality.

However, change requires more than just words expressing a vision and the decision or policy mandate to bring it about; it requires the expenditure of energy, time, and resources. This change is implementation: the process of rearranging patterns of conduct so as to honor the prescriptions set forth in a decision.

When a systems analysis is commissioned, it is usually because the sponsor would like to discover a course of action that will do something he wants done at an acceptable cost, a course of action that he can adopt and can convince others with whom he shares authority to adopt. Moreover, he hopes the action, if chosen, can be successfully implemented, that is, that it not be so modified by the organization that carries it out (or by rival agencies), or constrained by the courts, or repudiated by the public, or resisted by those who must change their patterns of behavior, or otherwise frustrated, that it does not accomplish what was intended (or worse, produce results less desirable than those of existing policies).

Unfortunately, research on the implementation process has not yet yielded an established body of professional doctrine on which to base a strategy of implementation (Schultz and Slevin, 1982). Rather, it is important now not to pursue the perhaps vain hope of a universally effective strategy, but rather to be sensitive to the strategy problem and to respond appropriately to it (Hildebrandt, 1977).

On the other hand, the scattered literature does offer valuable insights, information, and advice that are useful as a background for devising an approach to implementation. Against such a background, the systems analyst must adapt his approach to implementation—as he always has—to the peculiar circumstances in which he works, selecting from the experiences of others what seems most appropriate to his own setting. For example, Hammond (1979) offers an imaginative and useful framework for management-science implementation in business firms that can easily be extended to other systems-analysis contexts; woven throughout Part 2 of Checkland (1981) there are useful insights that, although also derived from experience with business firms, can be extended to apply to how a systems analyst should relate to a client in other settings.

Thus, the purpose of this chapter is to offer what we judge to be key points from the best available knowledge and advice, based on the literature and our own professional experience. In a given case, a system analyst will undoubtedly have to consider not only the points in this chapter, but also some gleaned from the literature to which this chapter is a guide, as well as others arising from the situation in which he is working.

9.1. Background

The term implementation can have several meanings. Bardach (1980, p. 139) identifies four:

> *Adoption* of a policy recommendation by an authorized individual or institution, as in "The client has endorsed our analysis of airport landing fees and will soon promulgate regulations to implement it." This is typically an operations researcher's or planner's usage (. . . ; Huysmans, 1970; . . .).
>
> The *empirical details* that reflect, or represent, the application of a policy principle, as in "Effluent taxes are fine in principle, but when it comes to implementing them we see that they are often set too low." (It should be noted that "implementation" in this sense is bound to be somewhat imperfect, for the same logical reason that there is always a slippage between a theoretical construct and the operations that are used to measure it empirically.)
>
> The *operating routines* of an organization, or a network of organizations,

Section 9.1. Background

that have been brought into being or have been modified by some policy mandate, as in "Over the years we have found it necessary to shift our implementation methods away from a reliance on regular audits to voluntary compliance and self-reporting."

The *process* of rearranging patterns of social conduct so as to honor the prescriptions set forth in some policy mandate, as in "We are implementing the new workmen's compensation law just as fast as we can."

For this handbook, implementation is the process suggested by the fourth paragraph. It starts after the decision to adopt a specific course of action is made and continues until this course is well established and integrated into the activities of the system that had been subjected to study; it is successful provided the goals defined by the decision are achieved and the financial costs and the delay in reaching these goals are held to a reasonable level. The systems analyst's task is to assist with this process as needed, this being the eighth task of the nine listed in Section 1.4 as making up the full systems analysis process.

Implementation can, of course, have other meanings in other contexts. Recently, in some operations research and management science circles it has been used to describe the entire process described in this handbook (for example, see Hildebrandt, 1979); while this practice has considerable merit, since it serves to emphasize the essential unity of the entire process, it is not convenient for this handbook. Here the word implementation will be used in the more limited sense described above.

The importance of giving thought to implementation has long been recognized, along with the analyst's responsibility to do so. Witness Aesop's fable *The Mice in Council:*[1]

> A certain Cat that lived in a large countryhouse was so vigilant and active, that the Mice, finding their numbers grievously thinned, held a council, with closed doors, to consider what they had best do. Many plans had been started and dismissed, when a young Mouse, rising and catching the eye of the president, said that he had a proposal to make, that he was sure must meet the approval of all. "If," said he, "the Cat wore around her neck a bell, every step she took would make it tinkle; then, ever forewarned for her approach, we should have time to reach our holes. By this simple means we should live in safety, and defy her power." The speaker resumed his seat with a complacent air, and a murmur of applause arose from the audience. An old grey Mouse, with a merry twinkle in his eye, now got up, and said that the plan of the last speaker was an admirable one; but he feared it had one drawback. He had not told them who should put the bell around the Cat's neck.

One reason that, until fairly recently, analysts did not make implementation

---

[1] As quoted by the U. S. Senate Subcommittee on National Security and International Operations (U. S. Senate, 1968, p. 1).

of their proposed solutions a subject of investigation during their studies was the contexts in which they worked. Early operations research analysts worked for the military and were themselves essentially embedded within the implementing organization, usually vetting their ideas on the staff before they reached the commanders. Early systems analysts worked with large military and industrial organizations, both of which have strong lines of authority that can usually ensure that decisions made at the top will be carried out by the organization below, although not always efficiently and without modification. In fact, to get decisionmakers to accept results derived by analytic methods was more the problem at first, so that the early operations research analysts often equated implementation with the adoption and use of the results of their work by decisionmakers. In other words, if the analysis findings influenced a decision in some way, they were said to have been implemented (Schultz and Slevin, 1975, p. 6).

Later, when systems and policy analysts began to work on the social issues associated with housing, health, education, welfare, and other public affairs, implementation was found to be a much more serious problem. Indeed, so much so, that for social application systems analysis came to be regarded by some as a worthless approach that produced solutions only on paper (Hoos, 1972).

Analysts then turned their attention to implementation, the so-called "missing link" in analysis. K. A. Archibald (1970, pp. 81–82), one of the earlier analysts to mention implementation in the sense used in this chapter, stressed that it did not follow automatically and offered suggestions for handling it:

> . . . even if the policy alternative recommended by the analyst is accepted by top decisionmakers, the program that comes out of the organization may have little resemblance to the alternative originally envisaged by the analyst and the top decisionmakers. I am not merely saying that an alternative when implemented may not produce the consequences expected. Rather I am saying that the policy alternative actually executed is quite likely to have undergone radical revisions at the hands of operating levels. And since a policy is no better than its implementation, this suggests that analysts need to pay attention to the feasibility of a policy alternative at operating levels as well as to its acceptability at the top decisionmaking level.

Indeed, it may be argued that in many organizations decisions are really made from the bottom up. The policymakers may suggest, but it is the lower echelons who really decide.

Most early discussions of implementation were retrospective and contained more descriptive than prescriptive material. [For instance, Pressman and Wildavsky (1973); other material may be found in Bardach (1977, 1980), Williams and Elmore (1976), Rabinovitz et al. (1976), Berman (1976), Van Meter and Van Horn (1974), Hargrove (1975), Mintzberg (1979), and Hildebrandt (1980).] The last four references contain major reviews of the literature. Wolf (1979) ties the reasons for the implementation shortfalls in public policies to the predictable inadequacies of nonmarket organizations such as government itself.

The major responsibility for managing the implementation process lies with the decisionmaker, but, as it is the analyst's proposal and design that is being implemented, he must share responsibility for any failure of implementation. This means the analyst must give explicit attention to how particular policy alternatives are to be implemented, not only as his work draws to a close, but also throughout the study from problem formulation and alternative generation through to the final selection of a preferred course of action.

In the early 1970s Meltsner made a conscientious survey of policy analysis in the U.S. federal government and observed a disappointing lack of activity aimed at following up the findings of analysis. In his conclusions he emphasized the importance for the analyst of paying attention to the process of implementation (Meltsner, 1976, p. 269):

> Despite some ... limitations, there are some things that can be done. First, analysts should be encouraged to consider implementation concerns ... when defining the problem and presenting their recommendations. It is not enough to determine the policy, that is, what to do; analysts should also get into the business of how to do it. ... Second, clients could hold their analysts responsible for what happens in the field or at least judge them by results in practice and not merely by what is on paper. ... Third, where possible the analysts should get feedback, negative and positive, on the quality of their estimates.

9.2. Implementation Concerns Early in a Systems Study

There is a story that exists in different forms in many countries about a man from the big city who stayed for a few weeks in a small village. He did not like the life; he thought the villagers fools, and said so. Near the end of his stay he decided he ought to visit a friend who lived nearby and he asked a villager how to get there. "Oh, you want to go there," said the man, seeing his chance to get his own back. "Well, no one but a fool would start from here."

Similarly, consider the systems analyst, who, having completed his investigation with suitable technical sophistication, wonders how to ensure that his findings are implemented. "If you want your results implemented," he might well be told, "no one but a fool would start thinking about it now."

To begin, the conditions present where the problem exists will affect how a proposed solution will be implemented—and therefore what sorts of proposals may be feasible.

Giauque and Woolsey (1981, pp. 30–31) make this point with the tale of the well educated young analysts who were

> hired to increase the productivity of a third-world steel mill. A major problem lay in the scheduling of three electric arc furnaces. The time required to

process a charge depended upon the amount of power fed to the furnace, thus power scheduling was a critical decision variable. Furnace operators, who were on an incentive plan, had to work within a power capacity for each furnace, a total capacity for the plant, and had to schedule such resources as charging and pouring cranes so as not to interfere with one another.

The [analysts]. . . studied the problem, gathered operating and capacity data, and developed a complex model to handle furnace scheduling. A computer system, complete with video displays for each furnace operator, was procured, and massive amounts of time and money were expended in developing and debugging the code, report writers, system interfaces, and so forth. Total cost was approximately 2.5 million US dollars. All concerned settled back, confidently expecting major increases in productivity.

Unfortunately, productivity didn't change *at all.* The system designers had overlooked one minor detail; of the 24 people who operated the furnaces over three shifts, *only five could read!* The study team had never bothered to go to the furnaces, and had never studied the *actual* operations, much less learned how to *do* them.

What was wrong? The [analysts] . . . were undeniably bright; technically, the system was fine. What was lacking was a sense of perspective, a knowledge of reality, an understanding of the business, and an understanding of the cultural infrastructure. The furnace production was substantially increased . . . by junking the 2.5 million US dollar computer system and substituting a scheduling method based on colored blocks in a plastic frame. Cost . . . was less than 200 US dollars for the deluxe model. [Italics in the original.]

An initial familiarity with the setting—renewed at times throughout the analysis—is an essential basis, not only for choosing alternatives for analysis, but also for implementing the one that is found to be preferred. This familiarity also is an essential ingredient in a successful implementation plan, one carefully drawn and specifying actors, responsibilities, relations, activities, schedules, and desired outcomes.

To do his analysis competently, the systems analyst must have the real setting reflected adequately in his analysis from its inception. How decisions are actually taken in organizations—and, in particular, in the one involved in his study—also argues for early consideration of implementation matters.

Some descriptions of analytic work make it appear that the problem under consideration, and the decisions that must be taken with regard to it, exist in isolation. This is not the case. A single problem facing a decisionmaker is only a small part of a time-space continuum of problems that he has to deal with, and his problems are part of a still larger continuum of problems faced by his organization. The decisions taken with regard to his problem create new problems and affect others; similarly the decisions taken with regard to these other problems affect his. Furthermore, managers rarely take decisions at a given time in a dispassionate manner, using only the information provided at this time, without reference to other information acquired in the past, even though this other information may be hearsay, and discredited by what is available at the time of decision.

In any organization there is a gradual development of opinion as to how a decision should be structured. Even where this is not so, it is generally true that the final form of the information fed to the decisionmaker will have been influenced by arbitrary decisions taken earlier, often by people outside the apparent power structure relating to this decision. Other administrators and the rank and file all have their influence. Thus, even a one-time decision to deal with a unique situation appears on analysis to be the end point of a systems process.

Moreover, it soon appears that the systems analyst is himself part of this process. Indeed, from the start of the investigation—by the questions he asks, the information he collects, and the dialogue in which he engages—he becomes part of the decisionmaking system by virtue of his very existence. To be effective, he must design his actions to be in tune with the behavior of the system, involving, or at least informing, others of what he is doing. If he merely makes his input at the time of decision, he may affect the response of the system, but only in minor ways. The consequence is likely to be a perturbation in systems performance rather than the major improvement sought.

Whether he likes it or not, the systems analyst is part of the decisionmaking process. The interactions implied by this statement, however, work in both directions. Not only does the analyst affect this process from the beginning of his investigation, but the system also has its effect on his investigation (Churchman, 1978). It is as much a learning process for the systems analyst as for the system; in this way, and only in this way, is he able to tune his proposals to the needs of the system. Good systems analysis is adaptive as well as innovative.

In sum, for the systems analyst to do an effective analysis and to play his appropriate role in the decisionmaking process, he must concern himself with implementation issues early in his work, and throughout the entire analysis.

9.3. The Role of the Systems Analyst in Implementation

Nothing we have said about the analyst's concern for implementation is intended to say that the decisionmaker and his staff are relieved in any way of their traditional responsibilities and authorities for operating their organization. Although the systems analyst should consider possible implementation issues in his work and assist in preparing for it, during the implementation process he does not deal with the details that are the traditional staff responsibilities (see, for example, Anthony, 1965). Rather, he is on call for advice and consultation, and perhaps such additional work as may be needed to understand the implications of changed conditions since the basic study was completed.

The blood-distribution analysis described in Section 3.2 illustrates how the role of the analyst continues and changes as the study proceeds and moves into implementation.

At the beginning of the work the systems analyst familiarized himself thoroughly with the operations of the Greater New York Blood Program, and maintained this close contact throughout the study, a process made simple and direct by the fact that a member of the GNYBP worked as a principal member of the analysis team. This assured all concerned that the alternatives considered were in fact implementable. Indeed, implementability played a significant role in how these alternatives were fashioned.

Although this analysis of blood availability and utilization was sponsored by the GNYBP, which serves the needs of 262 hospitals and 18 million people, implementation began in the Long Island Blood Services area, which contains 34 hospitals and serves two million people. However, an initial pilot implementation began by involving a regional blood center (RBC) and only four hospital blood banks (HBBs). As Section 3.2 points out: "They were provided support to correct rapidly the start-up problems that occurred. Once these HBBs were working to the satisfaction of their supervisors, they described the system to the supervisors of the other HBBs at seminars where the operations research staff, wherever possible, played the passive role of providing information when requested to do so. Responding to this approach, all but four very small HBBs in Long Island voluntarily joined the program over a two-year period, and none have dropped out."

It is important to note in this account that the analysts quickly faded into the background (but remained present to help), while the supervisors who were using the system successfully sold it to others.

It is also important to note that the computer modules supporting the new blood-distribution system are run independently, and each allows the relevant officials to use their outputs as the basis for making the judgments for which they are responsible:

The policy selection module "presents the decisionmaker with alternative targets (shortage rate, outdate rate, scheduling factor) that can be obtained for different levels of blood supply in the region."

The distribution-schedule module provides "a detailed schedule of the shipments of rotation and retention blood for each blood type that each HBB will receive on each delivery day. These schedules are communicated to the HBBs for comment and feedback. Once this phase is completed, the . . . operation can begin."

The control procedure allows the RBC manager to keep his operation based on up-to-date estimates of the basic parameters of his region's operations.

Further, these modules are designed to make them as transferable as possible to other regions—one of the goals of the analysis, and one that is being

Section 9.3. The Role of the Systems Analyst in Implementation

achieved, not only in the Greater New York Area, but also elsewhere in the United States and Europe.

Similarly, the analysts doing the fire-protection analysis for Wilmington, Delaware, worked very closely with the relevant fire and city officials, so that these officials were able to manage the implementation almost independently; what the analysts did was to develop models that these officials could manipulate and that allowed them to exercise the judgments appropriate to their responsibilities. A mix of these judgments and supporting analytic results allowed the analysis team to derive and recommend a new deployment that preserved the former fire-protection coverage while achieving some economies. Then, the city officials took over the implementation, in this case largely a process of negotiation and step-by-step decision.

However, in both this and the blood-supply analysis, the analysts left behind a set of tools and personnel trained to use them, so that new problems and important changes could be analyzed without the analysis team's return.

A program for implementation depends, of course, both on the type of problem being investigated and the administrative and operational setting from which it arises. Preparing to implement a decision by the managers of an industrial organization to install a computer program to expedite its operations can be vastly different from preparing to implement a social program established by a legislature and having the force of law. Yet in the long run the successful implementation of either decision may depend on the flexibility and robustness of the associated program for implementation in coping with varying circumstances that cannot be predicted in advance and its ability to withstand human error and deliberate misuse.

To explore the role of the analyst further, we now turn to two additional examples. Both are somewhat narrower than the usual large-scale systems analysis, but are chosen to illustrate the points in modest space.

An Example: Improved Methods of Calculation

Consider developing a set of computer programs to assist in designing transport systems in coal mines conveying material from the coal face to the pit bottom. A typical colliery contains a number of productive faces from which the coal is transported to the shaft by means of conveyor belts. At each junction in the underground roadway system the coal is transferred from one conveyor to another and, since it is a converging system, a trunk belt may receive coal from a number of faces. The flow of coal from each face is variable, the peak output being several times the average output and there are a number of occasions during the shift when there is no coal forthcoming from the face at all. It is essential that no part of the system be overloaded, for this causes a belt stoppage, which is transferred backwards to the face itself, with the consequence that production is lost. Moreover, if a loaded belt stops, it may be difficult, if not impossible, to restart it in the loaded condition. It is, therefore, essential to uncouple the various parts of the system, and so bunkers are introduced.

The extractive nature of coal mining means that faces at a colliery are always advancing. Moreover, their average life is about one to two years, so that, in effect, the entire conveying system has to be redesigned at relatively frequent intervals. The problem is to decide on belt capacities, bunker sizes, and the control rules for deciding when to load and unload the bunkers.

From a modeling point of view, this is clearly a simulation problem. However, because the problem is common to many collieries and, indeed, reoccurs from time to time at the same colliery, it was desirable to develop a general method of calculation to be used by planning engineers and work-study staff in any situation. For the analysis team in the organization concerned, it was, moreover, the first exercise to be undertaken with a view to developing a general computer program of this kind. It was essential, therefore, that from the outset the system be accepted as effective, easy to use, and foolproof. A serious mistake in the early stages of its introduction could easily mean the failure of the whole project.

The first stage of the analysis was, therefore, to tackle the local design problem at two collieries. This meant developing computer programs for the local situation while observing the difficulties occurring in the process. The results of the work and how the method might be extended were also discussed in detail with the people concerned. These preparatory studies had two important consequences. In the first place, they made it possible to identify the major technical problems that would be involved in preparing a universal simulation program. Secondly, the management teams concerned were enthusiastic about the way they had themselves been able to use the techniques, and were thus able to talk to their professional colleagues about their potential use in a way that the systems analysts never could have. On the basis of the discussions held after this first study, the analysts resolved to go ahead and devise a more general program to be used at any colliery.

This work, however, led to a new difficulty. When working at a single colliery, the main contacts were the colliery planners, who provided the data on which the simulation was based, and who then used the completed computer program. When it came to developing a more general program, the managers responsible for the work were no longer those who would be using it personally. Nevertheless, it was essential that responsibility for developing the program and implementing it lie with the management. Accordingly, a joint committee was established consisting of three main elements: The chairman of the committee was a management representative and he had engineers on the committee whose joint task was to observe progress and advise on practical problems when they arose. The second element consisted of the systems team members, who advised on the methods to be used and undertook to develop the main part of the program. Finally, the team included staff from the computer service, who were to ensure that the proposals made were

Section 9.3. The Role of the Systems Analyst in Implementation

compatible with the available computer system and that the whole was effectively systematized, so that the programs, once developed, would run quickly and economically using relatively inexperienced staff. This committee followed progress and arranged trials of the program.

Once a program had been developed, it was necessary to test it for basic errors and then pass it to the management staff for training. The analysts developed a series of courses, and, over a period of 12 months, some 100 planning and work-study engineers were trained in its use. These courses also included some of the operations research personnel who would have to advise on the program's use and ensure its effective application in nonstandard situations. The important thing to remember with all simulation programs is that the mechanics of using them are often easy to explain, but it is not at all easy to describe how to use them efficiently. In inexperienced hands, simulation can prove to be an expensive way of undertaking calculations that are unnecessary.

Each person attending a course was able to run one simulation while there. However, it was usually found that some assistance was required back at the colliery from whence he came before he was completely at home with the technique. Therefore, the presence of local operations research personnel who could advise him was invaluable. After about a year the technique had been used at over 100 collieries, mostly without the need for professional advice. The programs, which have, of course, been continually improved and modified, have remained in use for many years.

The importance of this procedure is best illustrated by the fact that, when a major program improvement was developed three or four years later without such a careful process of introduction, all the first management users experienced major difficulties in using it. The rumor quickly spread that the program was unreliable and management staff refused to try it out. A lengthy trial under unusually rigid conditions was necessary before confidence began to be restored.

What, then, are the main lessons to be learned from this example?

- It is essential to have strong management support if a system like this is to be widely accepted.
- There must be joint responsibility for development and testing.
- Particular care must be paid to train the staff to use the new method of calculation.
- There must be an adequate back-up service while management staff are getting used to the technique, and, indeed, to educate new management staff.

An Example: An Organizational Computer System

This second kind of computer system is different from the one considered in the previous section in that, once installed, it will be mandatory; that is, it will be part of the routine operation of the organization, and the people concerned with its operation will have no discretion as to whether they use it or not. This is equally true whether the new system replaces work previously undertaken in some other way, or whether it provides some new service. It might be thought that the implementation problems of such a system are relatively easy, being confined to formal approval by the appropriate controller and the technical problems associated with the developing and debugging a computerized system. The reality is far more complex. For a system to operate successfully, the correct data must be fed into it, and the outputs must be both usable and used. All these call for control. As systems become larger, it also becomes more difficult for the people within them to have any understanding of the consequences of their actions, and the need for control increases.

Even the best control system, however, does not ensure the organizational system's effectiveness and use, unless the system is properly matched both to the organization as a whole and to the individuals who must use it; indeed, these persons must both understand and accept it. Thus, for an organizational system, matching and control are the essence of successful implementation.

Consider the problem of implementing a centralized computer system for provisioning (ordering, stocking, and distributing) spare parts and equipment for a large, dispersed engineering organization.

While this is too large a subject to be covered fully here, two points of organizational behavior need to be emphasized:

> There is an innate resistance on the part of many people to undertaking work that appears to them to happen without some system and against the perceived interests of their immediate group (or even that of the organization as a whole).

> Once a working procedure has been established, it develops an internal stability of its own. Attempts to make small changes often fail because there is a natural tendency to revert to old and previous practices that are understandable and feel comfortable.

The extent to which these factors can be controlled is discussed later, but control can never overcome the problems that arise from bad design or poor installation. There is only one way to overcome the dangers and distortions arising in most man/computer systems: to apply the principle of "inversion," which states that a proposed organizational design should be examined from the inside out, that is, the designer must explore the consequences of his design for the people in the system and analyze how they will react to the new pressures. Unless this is done, the new system will not be matched to the organization, and inefficiency and malfunction will result.

To this end, we shall look at the characteristics of some of the most important human elements in the system:

Section 9.3. The Role of the Systems Analyst in Implementation

1. the operators—who are involved with the detailed day-to-day operations of the stores;
2. the manager—who deals with complaints and takes responsibility for the smooth running of the system;
3. the maintainers—analysts who keep the system operational;
4. the controller—the executive who has overall responsibility for the system's performance as an element in the larger enterprise.

The operators. Human operators are not mere ciphers to be considered equivalent to the electronic units in the computer. By the standards of computer elements, they may be judged inferior in performance; but they possess specific positive characteristics far outweighing so casual an assessment, yet too often ignored both in systems design and implementation. More than one badly designed system has been saved from collapse because its operators had a better understanding of its performance than the designer. Unfortunately, as the system becomes larger and more computerized, the more difficult it is for operators to have this saving sense of what is happening.

People have at least four characteristics important for this context:

An extraordinary, even though fallible, memory;

An ability to relate cause to effect;

Flexibility;

A sense of purpose.

Not all operators have all these characteristics highly developed—perhaps only a minority do—but a system that does not make good use of them will almost certainly run into serious trouble, particularly during implementation, for it is then that these skills are most valuable. Indeed, if the system's designer is lucky, he will find that the operators to some degree redesign the system for him. He may find that he can never get a complicated system up to full operating efficiency without their help.

These human characteristics are also important in routine operation to cope with the inevitable mishaps that cannot be dealt with at the computer level. Thus, if the wrong part number is given in a requisition, the storekeeper very often remembers the right one. If the item has been misplaced in the store, he may guess where to look for it; if it still cannot be found, he may be able to identify another item that is like the one required. Efficient design demands that these human characteristics be used.

Implementing a system that denies the operator the opportunity to be human is likely to run into difficulties, for it reduces him not only to a cipher, but to a hostile and uncooperative element of the system.

Another important value of the human operator is his tendency to take short cuts. If it appears to him that effort, time, or money can be saved, he is likely to try to save it, and without consultation, unless there is some countervailing reason. Thus, if items are in short supply in his shop, he may do some private rationing to ensure that supplies last until the next delivery.

More importantly, he can report on any sudden changes of conditions, and thus bring corrective procedures into action faster than can the computer control system. On the other hand, if he has to perform a detailed calculation, but beforehand thinks he knows the answer from experience, he will give his answer. If he has to record information in difficult or dirty conditions, he is very likely to try to remember the information and record it later. He gives less attention to information believed to be irrelevant than to facts whose value is apparent.

The advantages of having human operators can be exploited if the system is matched properly to their actual characteristics. Thus, because an operation can be done best in different ways by different people in different places, there is an important place for flexibility in system design. Failure to appreciate the needs for flexibility and matching has led to serious system failures when transferring a general computer system from one context to another, from one country to another, or one administrative unit to another; the principle also sometimes holds when one person replaces another. Matching needs to be examined in detail when the implementation stage is being considered, and to be reviewed continually throughout the life of a system. It is as much a problem of implementation as design.

One must not, of course, assume that the operators are unalterable in their abilities or their understandings: they too are capable of adapting, but they need training and teaching (the former for acquiring specific skills, the latter for developing understanding). How to proceed requires careful analysis. If a mismatch exists it must be identified, and then analyzed. Often the best people to undertake this analysis are the operators themselves. They do not need to know the details of the whole system, which they could hardly be expected to understand, but they do not need to know the consequences of their possible actions on the system as well as to be able to comment on the consequences for themselves.

Finally, there remains the question of control. Whether from direct disobedience, unconscious drift, or changing conditions, operator performance will, from time to time, become unsatisfactory, and a control system must exist to ensure that it continues to meet the objectives of the system. How can such control be instituted? What indices can be used to ensure that departures from the desired performance are detected? While the answers to such questions must be specific to a given system, they are seldom obvious. Thus, a provisioning service must minimize costs subject to a given level of service. The costs can be measured in part, but the level of service is much more difficult to identify. Similarly, one can check that all necessary forms have been filled in, but not that they have been filled in correctly. Checks on stock levels are expensive to carry out, and are undertaken infrequently, and mistakes that may have occurred can rarely be traced to their origins.

The problem of control is one of management as much as systems design (Anthony, 1965), but it is essential that such indices as the system produces be well understood and related to the real control problem, not simply to the computer's functioning.

The managers. In this context a manager is one who is responsible to a group of customers for a service or function, for which the computer system is intended to provide the routine operating element. As a result, his work has a highly discretionary element. For example, one of the issues on which he must rule is whether or not to make a special order for items in short supply. An analytically designed provisioning system, of course, has reordering routines applicable when there is an established pattern of use. However, what happens with spare-parts ordering when a machine has only been in use for a short time, or when the operating divisions place a large new order for some well-established piece of equipment? In order to be able to cope with such situations, the manager must have an awareness of such special actions as may be necessary when the standard routines no longer apply. It is, of course, conceivable in theory for the system to be able to cope with all occurrences, but in practice it may not be worth while programming rare possibilities into it. In any case, trouble shooting when serious deviations occur provides managers with their most difficult and interesting tasks.

When an emergency occurs, the manager must be able to act with some knowledge of what the consequences may be. Suppose, for instance, that a supplier has production problems that greatly increase the lead times on orders. What will the effect of this be on the company's stocks? What will be the consequence of remedial actions? It is unlikely for the manager to know how to handle every eventuality himself, so he must be able to get this knowledge promptly. Thus, he must have quick and easy access to people who know and who can undertake the appropriate analyses. These people are called the "maintainers."

It is also important to realize that all systems have to cope occasionally with unexpected events, and that robustness and flexibility are part of an optimal solution. A system that can cope with a variety of inputs is better than one that is highly efficient for a single kind of input. Again, these may be thought to be questions of design, but they are critical when it comes to implementation. The manager knows only too well the problems with which he must cope. If he feels the system does not help, implementation will be slow. He may not be able to explain why, but his reluctance may be justified.

Managers have powers of discretion, which are, of course, part of the overall system, and thus subject to checks and controls. Because of these powers of discretion, however, the controls need to be primarily through indices of performance rather than checks on procedure. It is essential for these indices to be true measures of performance; indices taken in isolation can often work to the overall detriment of service.

The maintainers. What, one may ask, has systems maintenance got to do with implementation? The answer is a good deal, simply because many of the problems that occur later in modifying the system are the same as those that occur in implementation. The basic questions are therefore those of systems design, and five key elements are needed.

1. Close contact with the systems analysts, manager, and operators involved in the plan.
2. A set of diagnostic procedures.
3. A set of predictive simulations that can forecast the effects of change.
4. A well documented basic program structured to allow for change.
5. Above all, an implementation plan that is known to all and that can be modified by those responsible for operating the system.

The importance of the first and last of these cannot be overstressed. A man/computer system is a dynamic organism that does not behave in detail as it is designed, but neither does it behave in detail in the way that those within it say it does. The maintainer needs to be able to analyze and interpret what is happening; thus, a systems analyst needs to be involved, not just a computer programmer.

The controller. This executive is centrally involved in implementing the new system. He is committed to installing it—probably more strongly than anyone else, because it does a job he sees the need for doing; however, he also has to accept responsibility for its cost, and, should it come to a bad end, for its failure. He also has the task of resolving a host of minor conflicts between his staff and the systems designers. He has to decide on where flexibility may be allowed and where new procedures are enforced in detail. He must discuss departures from the plan, and the effect they will have, not only on his staff, but also on his customers. Above all, he must satisfy himself that he is getting what he wants; and, beyond that, whether the specification he agreed to actually meets his needs.

This last point is important: who can blame the system's designer for doing what was agreed upon, even if the agreement should not have been reached in the first place? In truth, there is no excuse—it is the designer's responsibility to see that what the customer says he wants is really what he needs. It is remarkable how often this point is overlooked when new organizational systems are established. In the provisioning case, for example, it is usually assumed that the prime purpose is to ensure that the stock ordering, storage, and movement activities minimize overall costs. If this is the sole purpose, the whole process becomes a mechanical operation, the controller can go home, and the computer can take over. He knows, however, that he cannot go home. If his organization faces a severe cash shortage, he must reduce stocks even if it means that overall costs go up. If he is in conflict with suppliers, or must balance certainty of supply against average lead time, or if he is negotiating discounts, he must have a system he can control. He must know the consequences of his actions, and he must be in control.

The design of a system that enables the controller to cut overall stocks in the best way is different from one that assumes overall costs always to be minimized; it is no more difficult, just different. It becomes difficult only when one tries to use the system for something it was not designed for. Thus, care is needed at the preimplementation phase.

The controller's next problem is control. How does he assure himself that the system is working properly and efficiently? The designer must bear in mind that several features of the new system will be new and that the controller will not have an instinctive understanding of what values new indices should take. (Do not underrate the importance of instinct to a senior manager; it is often the reason he has risen in the hierarchy.) Most of his indicators are internal—costs, quantities, staff, and others—and he has estimates from the systems designer he can use for comparisons. However, it is necessary to make two warnings. In the first place, almost by definition no system with an external purpose can be judged adequately from internal evidence; external indicators must also be introduced, and to be effective there must be data so that comparisons can be made before and after implementation. Second, it is also necessary to ensure that no problems are being pushed to one side in the course of implementation. Neglected problems can cause backlogs that lead later to serious deterioration in performance. Indicators that some problem has been overlooked may be nervous distress in the staff, or steady or increasing overtime. At the implementation phase, no disturbance is too small for study.

Implementation Involving Multiple Organizations

So far in this section the examples we have used have all involved implementation procedures under the umbrella of a single organization (although, of course, involving many of its subdivisions). This simplified setting—chosen entirely for the purpose of avoiding complications in the discussion—is not typical of systems analysis; in the usual large-scale systems problem many organizations are involved, and often they are quite independent administratively. Thus, while the general principles for the analyst discussed above for the simpler situation carry over, there are some additional ones that should be mentioned here.

Two of the examples described in Chapter 3 involve situations involving many organizations and interests: protecting an estuary from flooding and supplying global energy needs.

The analysis dealing with the problem of protecting the Oosterschelde estuary from flooding was done by a team from The Rand Corporation as part of a larger effort by the Netherlands Rijkswaterstraat. While its aim was to present the issues clearly to the Netherlands Cabinet and Parliament, it was also clear that there were many other interests affected by the results, and they would have to be dealt with in a constructive manner and whoever had these dealings would have to use material arising from the analysis. These facts dictated the scorecard method for presenting results.

In due course the Cabinet and Parliament arrived at the decision to adopt the storm-surge barrier plan. However, while this decision was based on the general properties of this option, and the compromises it represented, the need for analysis did not cease. A series of post-decision analyses was conducted to fix the engineering details and operating doctrines for this option, an activity that also involved the Rand analysts [for the results of one of these studies, see Catlett et al. (1979)].

Since the IIASA global energy analysis looking 50 years into the future could not be done for world decisionmakers (since such persons do not exist), implementation might seem at first glance not to be an issue. However, there are hundreds of enterprises and government agencies involved in energy policies and operations, and thousands of industrial executives and public officials with relevant responsibilities; for all of these this analysis offers useful insights, and for many it suggests local analyses that can be done against the backdrop of the global findings. The IIASA analysis team has helped such organizations and people in a variety of ways: by interpreting data, by adapting models, by extending analyses, by consultation, and other activities, all of which can be thought of as implementation [for one such example, see Sassin et al. (1983)].

A third hypothetical example suggests some sorts of issues that arise when a large-scale problem affecting many interests is being dealt with. Consider a systems analysis dealing with the problem of improving public transportation for a city, and suppose that it considered these primary alternatives:

improving the present bus and expressway systems,

introducing a surface streetcar system,

introducing an elevated rapid transit system, and

introducing a subway system.

Additional alternatives were formed by making various combinations of these primary alternatives.

Further, suppose that a high-quality system study has been completed in accordance with the highest standards suggested by the previous discussion, and that the various constituencies affected have agreed with the decision based on the study to introduce a subway system as a supplement to the current bus and road system, with careful coordination to be worked out. What are some of the issues and difficulties that will arise in implementing this decision?

For one thing, the current city transport authority, having handled only automobile and bus traffic, will have had no experience with subway construction or with the operation of an underground electric railway. Consequently, the authority will have to be augmented and possibly reorganized. Managers with seniority and political connections may have to be passed over. New staff with special experience and perhaps higher salaries will have to be added. The known difficulties with organizational decisionmaking will arise (March, 1965; March and Simon, 1958; Cyert and March, 1963; and Allison, 1971, p. 146).

For another, the systems study on which the decision to introduce a subway was partially based, while it may have been detailed enough to enable the decisionmakers to discriminate among the surface, elevated, and subway supplements to the current system, was very likely not detailed enough to answer many questions regarding implementation. For instance, for comparison purposes, it was probably not necessary to investigate whether the subway station nearest city hall should be on the corner of First and Main or Second and Market streets. For implementation purposes this has to be investigated and decided; after the decision the merchants at one location will profit and the losers will protest. Bus routes and schedules will have to be rearranged to connect with those of the subway; people who lose service will fight to regain it. Parking lots will need to be set up in the vicinity of stations in the suburbs at which commuters can leave their cars; some neighborhoods may object to these lots; some people will be glad to sell the required land, some of the property may have to be acquired through legal proceedings. Therefore the transit authority (in addition to being concerned with management, financial control, regulations, inspection and surveillance during construction, providing permits and clearances, and relations with other agencies) will be beset with people (i.e., political) problems. No potential supplier of any of the necessary services is likely to cooperate unless it is to his, or his organization's, interest to do so. Some who interact with the program will not be clear where their interests lie, and will add to the confusion and delay.

The original study may shed light on some of these matters, but some may call for additional study, in most cases by extensions of the original work; others should be handled as purely administrative and political concerns. However, throughout the process of implementation, analysts—either members of the original team or new ones familiar with their work—should be available to consult with the administrators involved, and to do the additional work that may become desirable.

Concluding Remarks

The important lessons of these examples are that implementation is as various as the problem settings themselves, that it is an important (indeed, essential) part of the systems analysis activity, and that it deserves careful thought, meticulous planning, and energetic effort—all guided by considerable diplomacy.

Throughout the discussion we have emphasized the need for the analysis team to be familiar with the existing situation, and we have distinguished between alternatives that can be implemented within an existing organization and those that may need new organizational structures. However, this focus should not be construed as a necessary constraint on the substance of the analysis or its findings. Indeed, it can be argued that important innovative policies and programs cannot be implemented without significant changes in organizations, and often creating new ones. Certainly it is not a rule of systems analysis—or bureaucratic life—that existing institutions and their present forms are facts to which study and decision must conform. Rather, one of the highest goals of systems analysis can, and should, be to help all concerned rise above parochial bureaucratic concerns and limitations. In sum, systems analysis should not look for alternatives just within the realm of the presently possible, but should explore broadly with a view to making the most desirable course possible.

Therefore, the advice to the analyst to become and remain thoroughly familiar with the existing situation during his work is not intended to be a constraint, but rather to give him the information base on which to build a view of the organizational innovations that various options may imply—and to consider the difficulties and costs of these innovations as part of his analysis.

If, during the course of an analysis, it becomes clear that a program or course of action cannot be implemented successfully, then it should never be recommended to the decisionmaker for his choice. This does not mean it should not be investigated, or even that it should not be called to his attention. In large institutions it is often clear from the start that the policy that will bring the most significant improvement in a given situation is not politically feasible and cannot be implemented. Such policies should often be studied nevertheless, for otherwise there may be no way to learn the costs of current political constraints—and thus prompt their critical reconsideration.

9.4. Some Additional Issues and Difficulties

For most issues, the alternatives competing for choice by the decisionmakers will differ in the ease with which they can be implemented. To the extent possible, the probability of unsuccessful implementation should be taken into account in the comparison. If alternative A is chosen and it is discovered later that implementation cannot be carried out successfully, resources will have been expended and possibly other costs generated. Alternative B or some inferior modification of A may then have to be implemented instead. Thus, in examining the benefits and costs for the various alternatives, the probability of failure during implementation ought to be estimated for each

Section 9.4. Some Additional Issues and Difficulties

alternative and the expected costs thereby incurred taken into account (Peterson and Seo, 1972).

Similarly, before implementation has started, the decisionmaker must make sure that the necessary resources, financial and otherwise, are available; the analysis, if done properly, will have determined the requirements.

The wastepaper baskets of the world are full of sound proposals never carried out because the resources were not available to act on them. It may not be the whole resource that is lacking, but only one small, nearly trivial, element. Nevertheless, once the opportunity has been lost, it seldom returns. Accordingly, it is essential for any recommendation arising out of a project directed toward a single decision to be matched to the prospective resources—financial, material, and human.

The first resource that must be considered is, of course, money. In most organizations, the financial resources are limited either by the funds that can be raised or by rules laid down by a higher level of management [for an interesting example illustrating the latter point, see de Neufville (1970)]. Thus, the project must be not only attractive in itself but also relatively attractive in connection with other proposals that management may be considering. Clearly, it is essential for the analyst to be aware of the system in which financial decisions are made, what the criteria are, and, if possible, what rival projects may be competing.

Physical resources and other costs must also be considered. A decision to implement that requires unobtainable equipment or unavailable land, or gives rise to environmental consequences that may be unacceptable, will inevitably be rejected, even though it may be highly desirable without these physical limitations. It can never be argued by a systems analyst that such factors are not his concern.

It can be argued that the importance of financial and physical resources is self-evident, that any competent systems analyst will automatically take full account of them in the course of his work. Moreover, it is easy to see how this can be done, and easy to check that it has been done. However, the problem of the human resources is altogether more difficult. Clearly, the human consequences of the proposals should be included in the systems analysis, along with the financial and physical ones, but the problems of doing this are more subtle. The proposal may call for more or fewer people working in an installation; it may require them to do different work. Some will gain in influence and power, others lose. The good manager is also concerned not only with the direct consequences but the secondary consequences. What effect will such a change have on the attitudes and efficiencies of those working with him? Is the proposal so against their opinions and prejudices that they will adopt it reluctantly? Will this reluctance reduce their efficiency or the quality of the advice he will receive on other matters? The good manager is not simply looking at this one decision. He must have peripheral vision that enables him to sense all the other consequences. If the advantages to be derived from a proposal that his staff will find difficult to accept are very great, he may still decide to go ahead. If, however, they are relatively small, he may well decide that the incidental cost to him of monitoring the implementation outweighs its apparent advantages. Thus, in translating proposals into reality, it is essential to make a careful study of the manager's human resources.

By examining a number of attempts to implement social policy decisions in the United States—policies striving to do such things as creating jobs for the hard-core unemployed, building new towns, getting teachers to act in a different mode, or protecting the civil liberties of persons alleged to be mentally ill—researchers have found such programs to be characterized by underachievement of objectives, delay, and excessive financial cost. Bardach (1977) attributes many of the difficulties to the domination of the implementation process "by many actors all maneuvering with and against each other both for end results and for strategic advantages." He terms these maneuvers "games."

One such maneuver is the attempt to divert resources, especially money, which ought to be used to enhance the program's objectives, to other, often equally worthy, purposes. Another "game" or maneuver is to deflect the goals of the effort, for instance, by what Bardach (1980, pp. 146–147) calls "piling on":

> If a new program enjoys certain initial successes, it naturally expands its political support. It then becomes a target for interests who may have only minimal commitment to the program's objectives but who wish to capitalize on its growing political assets. Such a program is vulnerable to Piling On in much the same way that a cash-rich corporation is vulnerable to being taken over by another firm through a merger or a tender offer to shareholders. By the time the Piling On process is over, the original program goal may have become greatly submerged and/or the supporting coalition may have collapsed under the weight of the new interests. For example, the concept of "affirmative action" in the United States once meant a commitment to give preferential treatment to job applicants from racial minorities when in other respects they were "equal" to applicants from nonminority backgrounds. Over the course of the last ten or fifteen years, however, the concept has come to mean quotas and a deemphasis on the "equality-in-other-respects" criterion. Many traditional liberals who supported the more restricted "affirmative action" concept have become resentful and frightened at its maximalist redefinition and, in effect, have withdrawn energy and attention even from the initial goals.

Other maneuvers attempt to negate the effect of a new policy by installing non-sympathizers high up in the enforcement agency, or by writing regulations and rules that condone existing practices and lighten the penalty for violations, or by setting a high threshold for violations and then putting the entire burden of proof on the implementing agency. Still another maneuver is to resist efforts to control behavior administratively by tokenism or procrastination. For others, see Bardach (1977).

It is not only the lower, operating, levels that cause difficulties with implementation. The higher, policymaking, levels can cause problems. No manager, good or bad, will forget that these levels exist or be unaware of their possible reactions to a decision that he may make. The same applies to committee chairmen and to the members of committees who may be reporting to superiors whose objectives are by no means in agreement with those of the committee. Of course, if a proposal has been well worked out and its implementation adheres completely to plan, the decisionmaker need have no fears, but in real life things seldom happen this way. There is always something that does not work according to plan—conditions may not be precisely those predicted, other changes may occur to alter how the proposal is put into practice. Almost invariably some part of the objective will not be achieved, or achieved in a different way from the proposal. Here is where the difficulty arises. More often than not those at higher levels in the hierarchy are more aware of departures from plan than they are of its overall successes. If these shortcomings are in areas in which they have particular interests, they are apt to react strongly. Consequently, most managers are sensitive to any departure from plan. They adopt a fail-safe policy. They are either looking for something with no risk, or something that avoids certain areas of risk. This makes it essential for the systems analyst to have not only a good idea of the robustness of his solution but also of the entire "political" situation, including all the actors involved, and the pressure falling on the decisionmaker from higher levels of control.

9.5. Coping With Implementation Prior to Decision

Matters of Good Practice

How can the implementation process be structured so as to increase the possibility that what is decided will be carried out and the objectives attained? Sabatier and Mazmanian (1979, pp. 484–485) contend that these five conditions are sufficient to insure successful implementation:

1. The program is based on a sound theory relating changes in target group behavior to the achievement of the desired end-state (objectives).
2. The statute (or other basic policy decision) contains unambiguous policy and structures the implementation process so as to maximize the likelihood that target groups will perform as desired.
3. The leaders of the implementing agencies possess substantial managerial and political skill and are committed to statutory goals.
4. The program is actively supported by organized constituency groups and by a few key legislators (or by the chief executive) throughout the implementation process, with the courts being neutral or supportive.
5. The relative priority of statutory objectives is not significantly under-

mined over time by the emergence of conflicting public policies or by changes in relevant socioeconomic conditions that undermine the statute's "technical" theory or political support.

This last condition, of course, can not be known in advance. While the analyst cannot ensure that conditions such as these exist, he can help a great deal in bringing about 1 and 2. He does this by formulating clear objectives, by suggesting sound alternatives, by identifying possible objections to their implementation, and by finding ways to overcome them before the implementation program is planned.

First, if the alternatives proposed to the decisionmakers are not directed toward clear objectives or are not based on sound analytic principles, the decision may be a poor one and not suited to the issue to be resolved. The program that is implemented is then not likely to be successful. To quote Bardach (1980, p. 153):

> the basic social, economic, and political theory behind the policy must be reasonable and sophisticated: it will not do, for instance, to pretend that most people do not act most of the time in accord with a rather restricted notion of their self-interest; nor will it do to ignore inconvenient features of the world like the sparse supply of managerial and technical competence or the enormous variety of local circumstances which policies must serve or the immense difficulty of coordinating large-scale activities on the basis of plans and promises rather than market signals.

Second, a basic administrative strategy for implementation should be designed. Such a strategy should be simple, placing as little reliance on bureaucratic processes as possible (Pressman and Wildavsky, 1973; Levine, 1972; Kneese and Schultze, 1975). It should include an estimate of the financial resources required by the implementing organization to hire staff, administer the program, monitor the changes, and to carry out any further analysis necessary. For each policy alternative, who has to do what, when, and how must be investigated. If the implementing organization exists, the analysts need to pay attention to the effects of the program to be implemented on the organization itself. Such effects may seem trivial but can have serious consequences. A decision to change the pattern of garbage collection in New York City was seriously delayed because it disrupted car pools (Beltrami, 1977). Sometimes incentives can be designed that will increase cooperation.

In any event, the analyst should work with his client's staff, involving them in the research if possible. This means not merely providing data and assumptions but questioning forecasts and hypotheses, proposing alternatives, and pointing out where the difficulties in implementation may lie.

Third, obviously the analyst must try to anticipate as many of the problems to be faced during implementation as possible. To do this, he may consider the list of program elements and their source and support, such things as regulations and guidelines, financial accountability mechanisms, goods and services needed, the participation by various agencies and bureaus, sources of funds, and so on. Next, he can ask: "What can go wrong?" "What can be done about it?" A systematic way to approach these questions is through developing a scenario.

Implementation Scenarios

The development of scenarios is one of the most useful devices for anticipating the future where uncertainty is large (Sections 4.5 and 7.3; Brown, 1968; Helmer, 1966). Preparing a set of hypothetical "future histories" of a proposed program forces the program designer to think seriously about the stresses and strains to which his proposed program may be subjected if implemented. Bardach (1977, pp. 254–255) observes:

> It is no easy task for the designer to predict, and following prediction to readjust, the outcomes of such dynamic and complex processes as are involved in a loose system of implementation games. In fact, the system is so complicated that it thoroughly defies analysis by means of even the most complex models known to any of the social or behavioral sciences. It must be approached through what has come to be known as "scenario writing." This latter method simply involves an imaginative construction of future sequences of actions—consequent conditions—actions—consequent conditions. It is inventing a plausible story about "what will happen if . . . " or, more precisely, inventing several such stories. Telling these stories to oneself and one's professional peers helps to illuminate some of the implementation paths that the designer does not want taken. He or she is then in a position to redesign some features of the system of implementation games that permit him or her and his or her colleagues to tell stories with happier endings. Trial and error through successive iterations produce better and better endings.
>
> Obviously, scenario writing is an art. It requires imagination and intuition. One suspects there is not much that can be formalized or codified about how to do it well. This may be one of the reasons why scenario writing is, in fact, not very common even among the most experienced policy analysts and designers.

Bardach (1977, pp. 264–265) offers an outline for writing an implementation scenario. It suggests such steps as making an inventory of the program elements, paying attention to who controls them either directly or indirectly, and statements as to how management will deal with problems of social entropy, incompetence for instance. It also asks the scenario writer to show how the policy will deal with various dilemmas of administration such as tokenism, procrastination, massive resistance, diversion of resources, and others.

For certain problems special analyses directed toward questions of implementation may be desirable, for others an actual experiment may be called for before full-scale implementation is attempted.

Implementation Analysis

Many studies can and should be done in two stages: a first analysis to find out what type of action should be taken or what sort of alternative to recommend, and then a second analysis to specify the details of the designated alternative and of the program to implement it. Such analyses, leading to the translation of a policy decision into a specific program whose objective is to carry out the policy's intent, are termed implementation analyses.[2] As an example, consider the hypothetical public transportation study mentioned earlier. To evaluate the advantages of a streetcar system over a subway, the decisionmakers probably need not consider whether the tracks should be laid on 1st or on 2nd Street, or whether the cars should have 40 or 50 seats. But if a streetcar system is to be installed, these decisions will have to be made. Again, in the Oosterschelde flood-control study outlined in Section 3.4, after the decision was made to choose the flow-through dam with a gate that could be closed during a storm, further analysis had to be done to determine the most practical width for the gate, as well as how best to operate it.

Sometimes the analysis that takes into account the details of implementation can be postponed until after the primary decision; in other cases, it may have to be done earlier, at least in part, in order to set the ranking of the top two or three alternatives.

Social Experiments

Decisions (whether they are the results of analysis or not) taken to alleviate social problems are notorious for unsatisfactory consequences. Implementations have frequently failed to achieve their objectives, often resulting in exorbitant costs and inducing great social disruption. One possible way to find out in advance that a program may not work as intended and thus avoid wasting resources and political prestige may be to conduct a social experiment before starting a full-scale program.

> In practice, a social experiment is an organized attempt to pretest a particular innovative policy before committing vast resources to the solution of some large social problem. An example might be the experiment in New Jersey with income maintenance, undertaken before there was a national commitment to such a program. In this case, alternative programs were tested on sample populations in several other states. [Brewer, 1973, pp. 152–153.]

---

[2] The term implementation analysis is also used to refer to the study of why authoritative decisions do not lead to expected results (Berman 1978) or to how "specific nonmarket activities (e.g., public policies) can be expected to operate, and to depart in predictable ways from their costs and consequences as originally estimated" (Wolf 1979).

The housing experiment described in Section 1.2 is another such example. For further discussion of the use of social experiments see Archibald and Newhouse (1980), Riecken and Boruch (1974), and Section 7.6.

A major advantage of experimentation is that it reveals empirical information about the proposed large program. Clues to the possible activities of those who lose or gain from the program are obtained, and minor changes that ease the path to implementation without compromising the objectives may be discovered.

Social experimentation is not a panacea that guarantees successful implementation. There are frequently ethical, methodological, or political reasons why experimentation is unwise. Brewer (1973, pp. 155–156) mentions some of these ethical issues:

> How are different benefits received by experimental subjects reconciled and justified? At the conclusion of an experiment, how does one make restitution for an experimental alternative not finally chosen but upon which recipients have become dependent? What about confidentiality of data and other human problems associated with the conduct of the experiment? These and many other primarily ethical issues all come into play and must be accounted for by the social experimenter.

Methodological problems are often formidable. It is not easy to design a valid experiment. An experiment is not a mere demonstration or a small-scale trial implementation of a large program that is under consideration. Such exercises are often useful, but a good experiment requires a properly selected control group and careful analysis of the results. Davis and Salasin (1978) provide an excellent discussion of the sort of implementation problems that would be likely to arise with a full-scale program and that may not be detected in a small-scale demonstration.

9.6. Coping with Implementation After Decision

It should be clear that analysis before, or just after, a decision cannot ensure that the implementation will go smoothly. Circumstances change and the unexpected can happen, requiring modification in the program for implementation. Analysis is needed both to find satisfactory modifications and to monitor and evaluate what takes place. Usually, because the authorities responsible for overseeing the implementation program are not those who made the original decision, analysts other than those who did the original study are involved.

Other than through the use of analysis, the decisionmaker or the agent of the deciding authority has essentially two approaches to keeping implementation on the desired path: mediation and persuasion, and intervention using the power of the mandate.

Mediation and Persuasion

Organizational development. In this approach, a "change agent" enters into a collaborative relationship with the organization and attempts to produce the planned change. He attempts to change structure and processes within the organization; decisions are not viewed as being imposed from on high but rather decisionmaking is envisaged as a participatory process (K. A. Archibald, 1970). The organizational developer may be a systems analyst, but different training is required. The approach does run the risk, however, of legitimating large distortions of the policy goals (Bardach 1980, p. 150). The successful strategy, moreover, often depends critically on the special characteristics of the target organization. As an example, see R. W. Archibald (1979) on the problems of managing change in fire departments, organizations that are characteristically low in complexity but high in centralization and in formalization.

Negotiations. The negotiator's goal is to reduce the delays, the misunderstandings, and the confusion associated with implementation by communication, persuasion, and face-to-face bargaining (Fisher and Ury, 1981; Raiffa, 1982). The analyst can help by suggesting the ways to compromise that do the most to retain the policy goals. The negotiating process can create problems as well as solve them, however (Bardach 1977, pp. 221–224).

Using the Power of the Mandate

Project management. Project management has worked well for the U.S. Department of Defense in new submarine development and for NASA to carry out most space missions. Project managers are widely used in private industry for keeping a project on schedule and costs within preset limits. One individual controls the implementation. Traditionally, he uses systems analysis, computers, PERT (see Archibald and Villoria, 1967), and other "modern" management aids. This approach represents a way of overcoming the limitations of the usual functional separation of labor (into sales, production, and research, for instance) when the organization undertakes a large complex project by concentrating power and responsibility in one individual. How effective project management can be made for social programs is still a question.

Political control. A project manager is limited by lack of authority; he is an agent, not the originator of the policy mandate or its political trustee. He cannot stand against strong political opposition. In contrast, an influential legislator or top political appointee can keep a program on track by interesting himself in its progress, playing the role of a "fixer" (Bardach, 1977)—mediating, arbitrating, coaxing, bullying, using his political clout. Such a fixer cannot work alone; he needs a staff, including analysts, to handle the detailed work.

9.7. Concluding Remarks

To select an implementation strategy and to modify it when necessary to hold to its objectives are sometimes not considered analytic functions. But all the characteristic activities that analysis can assist are there; choices have to be made in the face of uncertainty, data have to be turned into information, analyzed, and communicated, tasks have to be delegated, and incentives established. Hence systems analysts have a role, not only in preparing for implementation, but also in carrying it out, and in evaluating and monitoring the results to determine whether the policy is performing as it should.

On the other hand, we have seen that each issue or problem subjected to systems analysis possesses its own peculiar properties, which impede the development of any sort of standardized approach to implementation. Rather, based on examples, the scattered literature, and our own experience, we have advanced general ideas that should inform a systems analyst's approach to implementation. Clearly the future experience of this professional community will modulate these ideas and introduce new ones, and to do so will be one of its most important tasks.

At the beginning of this handbook we observed that systems analysis may involve as many as nine kinds of activities (see Section 1.4), and the last one of these is "evaluate the results of implementing the chosen courses of action." This activity has been referred to in several places in this chapter as an important part of the implementation activities, but it has not received the independent emphasis that it deserves. The basic reason for this unhappy state of affairs is that systems analysis has not yet made program evaluation its own, so that it occupies the key place that it should at the end of the systems analysis process. Achieving this goal is an urgent prospective task for the community of systems analysts.

On the other hand, the important need to evaluate the worth of social programs has prompted the growth, largely from the social science community, of a community of researchers devoted to program evaluation (for programs, however, emerging from other sources than systems analyses). Currently there exist substantial experience and a considerable literature [for example, Guttentag and Struening (1975), Rossi and Wright (1977), Rossi, Freeman, and Wright (1979), and Struening and Brewer (1983)]. As the systems analysis community turns its attention to the urgent issue of evaluating the results of the programs emerging from its work, it must take advantage of the work of the community of evaluation researchers.

References

Allison, Graham T. (1971). *Essence of Decisions: Explaining the Cuban Missile Crisis.* Boston: Little, Brown.

Anthony, Robert N. (1965). *Planning and Control Systems: A Framework for Analysis.* Boston: Graduate School of Business Administration, Harvard University.

Archibald, K. A. (1970). Three views of the expert's role in policy making: Systems analysis, incrementalism, and the clinical approach. *Policy Sciences* 1, 73–86.

Archibald, Russell D., and Richard L. Villoria (1967). *Network–Based Management Systems (PERT/CPM).* New York: Wiley.

Archibald, R. W. (1979). Managing change in the fire department. In *Fire Department Deployment Analysis,* (W. E. Walker, J. M Chaiken, and E. J. Ignall, eds.). New York: North Holland, pp. 100–124.

_____ and J. P. Newhouse (1980). *Social Experimentation: Some Whys and How,* R-2479-HEW. Santa Monica, California: The Rand Corporation.

Bardach, Eugene (1977). *The Implementation Game: What Happens After a Bill Becomes Law.* Cambridge, Massachusetts: The MIT Press.

_____(1980). On designing implementable programs. In *Pitfalls of Analysis,* (G. Majone and E. S. Quade, eds.). Chichester, England: Wiley, pp. 138–158.

Beltrami, E. J. (1977). *Models for Public Systems Analysis.* New York: Academic.

Berman, Paul (1978). The study of macro and micro implementation. *Public Policy* 26, 157–184.

Brewer, G. D. (1973). Experimentation and the policy process. In *Rand: 25th Anniversary Volume.* Santa Monica, California: The Rand Corporation, pp. 151–165.

Brown, Seyom (1968). Scenarios in systems analysis. In *Systems Analysis and Policy Planning: Applications in Defense* (E. S. Quade and W I. Boucher eds.). New York: Elsevier.

Catlett, Louis, Sorrel Wildhorn, Richard Stanton, Ary Roos, and Jan Al (1979). *Controlling the Oosterschelde Storm-Surge Barrier—A Policy Analysis of Alternative Strategies. Vol. I: Summary Report,* R-2444/1-NETH. Santa Monica, California: The Rand Corporation.

Checkland, Peter (1981). *Systems Thinking, Systems Practice.* Chichester, England: Wiley.

Churchman, C. West (1978). Philosophical speculations on systems design. In *Handbook of Operations Research: Foundations and Fundamentals* (Joseph J. Moder and Salah E. Elmaghraby, eds.). New York: Van Nostrand Reinhold, pp. 25–39.

Cyert, R., and J. G. March (1963). *A Behaviorial Theory of the Firm.* Englewood Cliffs, New Jersey: Prentice–Hall.

Davis, H. R., and S. Salasin (1978). Strengthening the contribution of social R and D to policy making. In *Knowledge and Power: The Uncertain Connection* (L. E. Lynn, Jr., ed.). Washington, D. C.: National Research Council, pp. 93–125.

de Neufville, Richard (1970). Cost–effectiveness analysis of civil engineering systems: New York City's primary water supply. *Operations Research* 18, 785–804.

Doktor, R., R. L. Schultz, and D. P. Slevin (1979). *The Implementation of Management Science.* Amsterdam: North-Holland.

References

Fisher, Roger, and William Ury (1981). *Getting to Yes: Negotiating Agreement Without Giving In.* Boston: Houghton Mifflin.

Giauque, W. C., and R. E. D. Woolsey (1981). A totally new direction for management education: a modest proposal. *Interfaces* 11(4), 30–34.

Guttentag, Marcia, and Elmer L. Struening (1975). *Handbook of Evaluation Research.* Beverly Hills, California: Sage.

Gvishiani, Jermen M. (1981). World Problems: Interrelations and Interdependence. *IIASA Reports* 3, 13–18.

Haley, K. B., ed. (1979). *Operational Research '78: Proceedings of the Eighth IFORS International Conference on Operational Research.* Amsterdam: North-Holland.

Hammond, John S., III (1979). A practitioner-oriented framework for implementation. In *The Implementation of Management Science* (R. Doktor, R. L. Schultz, and D. P. Slevin, eds.). Amsterdam: North-Holland, pp. 35–61.

Hargrove, F. (1975). *The Missing Link: The Study of Implementation of Social Policy.* Washington D.C.: The Urban Institute.

Helmer, Olaf (1966). *Social Technology.* New York: Basic Books.

Hildebrandt, Steen (1977). Implementation of the operations research/management science process. *European Journal of Operational Research* 1, 289–294.

_____(1979). From manipulation to participation in the operations research process. In *Operational Research '78* (K. B. Haley, ed.). Amsterdam: North-Holland, pp. 163–180.

_____(1980). Implementation—the bottleneck of operations research: The state of the art. *European Journal of Operational Research* 6, 4–12.

Hoos, Ida R. (1972). *Systems Analysis in Public Policy: A Critique,* Berkeley, California: University of California Press.

Huysmans, Jan H. B. M. (1970). *The Implementation of Operations Research.* New York: Wiley.

Kneese, A. V., and C. L. Schultze (1975). *Pollution, Prices, and Public Policy.* Washington D. C.: The Brookings Institution.

Levine, R. A. (1972). *Public Planning.* New York: Basic Books.

Majone, G., and E. S. Quade (1980). *Pitfalls of Analysis.* Chichester, England: Wiley.

March, James (1965). *Handbook of Organizations,* Chicago: Rand McNally.

_____. and H. Simon (1958). *Organizations.* New York: Wiley.

Meltsner, Arnold J. (1976). *Policy Analysts in the Bureaucracy.* Berkeley, California: University of California Press.

Mintzberg, Henry (1979). Beyond implementation: An analysis of the resistance to policy analysis. In *Operational Research '78* (K. B. Haley, ed.). Amsterdam: North-Holland. pp. 106–162. Also published in shortened form in *INFOR* 18 (1980), 100–138.

Moder, Joseph J., and Salah E. Elmaghraby (1978). *Handbook of Operations Research: Foundations and Fundamentals.* New York: Van Nostrand Reinhold.

Peterson, R. E., and K. K. Seo (1972). Public administration planning in developing countries: A Bayesian decision theory approach. *Policy Sciences* 3, 371–378.

Pressman, J. L., and Aaron Wildavsky (1973). *Implementation.* Berkeley, California: University of California Press.

Rabinovitz, F., J. Pressman, and M. Rein, eds. (1976). Policy implementation: guidelines. *Policy Sciences* 7, 399–518.

Raiffa, Howard (1982). *The Art and Science of Negotiation.* Cambridge, Massachusetts: Harvard University Press.

Riecken, H. W., and R. F. Boruch (1974). *Social Experimentation: A Method for Planning and Evaluating Social Intervention.* New York: Academic.

Rossi, Peter H., Howard E. Freeman, and Sonia R. Wright (1979). *Evaluation: A Systematic Approach.* Beverly Hills, California: Sage.

―――and Sonia R. Wright (1977). Evaluation research: An assessment of theory, practice, and politics. *Evaluation Quarterly* 1, 5–52.

Sabatier, P., and D. Mazmanian (1979). The conditions of effective implementation: A guide to accomplishing policy objectives. *Policy Analysis* 5, 481–504.

Sassin, W., A. Hoelzl, H.-H. Rogner, and L. Schrattenholzer (1983). Fueling Europe in the future: The long-term energy problem in the EC countries, RR-83-9/EUR 8421–EN. Laxenburg, Austria: International Institute for Applied Systems Analysis.

Schultz, R. L., and D. P. Slevin (1975). *Implementing Operations Research/Management Science.* New York: Elsevier.

―――and ―――(1982). Implementation exchange: Implementing implementation research. *Interfaces* 12(5), 87–90.

Struening, Elmer L., and Marilynn B. Brewer, eds. (1983). *The University Edition of the Handbook of Evaluation Research.* Beverly Hills, California: Sage.

U. S. Senate, 90th Congress, 2nd Session (1968). *Specialists and Generalists*: A report of the Subcommittee on National Security and International Operations. Washington, D. C.: U. S. Government Printing Office.

Van Meter, D., and C. Van Horn (1974). The policy implementation process: A conceptual framework. *Administration and Society* 6, 445–488.

Walker, W. E., J. M. Chaiken, and E. J. Ignall, eds. (1979). *Fire Department Deployment Analysis.* New York: North-Holland.

Williams, W., and R. F. Elmore, eds. (1976). *Social Program Implementation.* New York: Academic.

Wolf, Charles, Jr. (1979). A theory of "non-market failure:" Framework for implementation analysis. *Journal of Law and Economics* 22, 107–139.

Chapter 10
The Practice of Systems Analysis

Hugh J. Miser

10.1. Introduction

The previous chapters of this handbook have described the context, nature, and use of systems analysis, sketched its history, given examples of good systems analysis studies, laid out the methods that such work exhibits, dealt with the content of a good systems analysis study and how it is evolved, and provided a perspective on the work of implementing its results. The purpose of this chapter is to discuss what experience has taught systems analysts about professional practice, that is, how to approach their work, and what relations they should have with the clients who may use its results.

Thus, while this chapter speaks primarily to analysts, it also speaks to clients by telling them what sort of professional conduct they may expect from systems analysts.

Most of the material in the earlier chapters presumes a situation in which the systems analysts work directly with officials with relevant responsibilities and authorities, whether the analysts are employed by the same organization or not. We make the same assumption in this chapter. In actual fact, the analysts may be employed by another organization, such as a consulting firm or independent institute, such as the International Institute for Applied Systems Analysis in Laxenburg, Austria. The precepts and principles of professional practice as we discuss them here remain the same for all of these cases; however, the difficulties of communication may change, depending on whether or not the decisionmakers and analysts work in a common administration or different ones, whether there are a few or many relevant officials, and so on. Since each situation has its own characteristic and highly varied properties, there is little general guidance to be offered, beyond the obvious fact that barriers to effective communication must be removed if systems analysis work is to have important effect, as discussed later in this chapter.

While there is literature dealing with the practice of systems analysis [see, for example, Agin (1978)], it tends to be scattered and somewhat incomplete. Thus, in writing this chapter I have relied not only on relevant literature but also my own experience, coupled with that of others relayed to me through personal contact. Since systems analysis is a young and rapidly spreading field, experience to come may well supplement and modify what is said here. However, the reader may rest assured that everything in this chapter has served analysts well in significant past experience.

10.2. The Organizational Context

The concept of decision runs through much of the literature of systems analysis, and, indeed, much of what has been said earlier in this *handbook*. However, this concept seems to imply that whatever needs improvement in a problem situation can be changed adequately at a single stroke—an oversimplification of real life that, while useful for discussion purposes, does not represent the reality that we live with, particularly with regard to the large-scale interactive problems that systems analysis is likely to address.

It is more realistic to consider a more general concept of change, and to think of systems analysis being called on when there is an appreciation somewhere that change may be desirable. Change may then be achieved by a single major decision, or it may occur as the result of a complex of smaller decisions made in a variety of places in a large institutional structure, but coordinated and informed by the findings of an intelligent, broad approach to the issue of change. The role of systems analysis then is to provide an important contribution to this approach.

Perhaps the most basic task of the analyst, on which he should gather information from the beginning and of which he should have a well developed appreciation early in his work, is to understand the structure in which change may take place. If no decisions leading to change are possible, the work may be of absorbing interest, but it will likely be in vain, unless the situation changes. If the decision setting presents open opportunities for change, how can the work best be related to this setting? There is no simple answer to this question, indeed, much of what this chapter has to say bears on it, but it is one the analyst must ask early, and keep in his mind throughout his work, as interactions with the client organization shed more and more light on it. The knowledge accumulated during the work, as relations with the client develop, can—and should—have a major influence on how the findings are formulated, presented, and followed up. R. W. Archibald (1979, p. 127), in writing about fire departments, such as the one in Wilmington, Delaware, discussed in Section 3.3, puts it this way:

> The perspective taken is that of a "change agent" (i.e., a manager of change). The introduction of analysis is expected to change the end product or service delivered by the fire department. Most likely this will also mean changes in

Section 10.2. The Organizational Context

structure (the organizational system) and in process (the various methods and procedures employed to deliver the services). In turn, these changes will require members within, and perhaps outside, the organization to change their behavior. The analyst must see the issue not only in terms of solving a particular technical problem, but more importantly as the creation of circumstances that will encourage people to change their behavior. In performing this task, the analyst becomes the change agent.

Archibald also (1979, p. 127)

stresses the importance of thinking about groups of people, their common motivations, their organizational positions, and their values as they influence decisionmaking. As the analyst moves from the model of the problem to the development of programs to achieve desired results, the importance of who makes the decisions and who influences the decisionmaking process cannot be overstated.

Sound analytical results should be able to stand alone but they do not. People who make decisions frequently find themselves in situations in which the analysis alone is not sufficient to guide decisionmaking. A broad political rationality is likely to guide an individual's decisions more often than a narrower technical rationality. If political and managerial views are to be meshed with the specific problem-solving perspective of the analyst, the analyst needs to have anticipated, understood and tried to accommodate the values and perspectives of decisionmakers and the pressures they face.

To this last point an even stronger one can be added: Sometimes it is necessary for the analyst to confront the decisionmaker with the inadequacy of his values and perspectives, and help him toward more adequate ones. While this will at best be a role calling for diplomatic tact based on careful thinking and appropriate evidence, or at worst impossible, it may turn out to be the most important contribution the analyst can make.

In any case, accounting for the decisionmaker's values and perspectives only at the end of the study, or during implementation, is too late, and may pose insurmountable difficulties.

Here are some basic questions about the decision setting on which the analyst should have clear answers, if possible, before he finishes formulating the problem and begins his work.

First, what is the nature of the decision setting? Is there a single strong decisionmaker? Or is the decision setting a pluralistic one, in which there are many decisionmakers with varying degrees of power and influence, all of whom must be addressed? If the study is done for an organization, is its span of responsibility and authority complete with respect to the problem situation being contemplated, or will the changes needed involve compromise or coalition with other organizations?

Second, what are the important properties of the decision setting? Organizations, for instance, have widely differing styles of management that usually have important effects on the styles of their approaches to change. The personalities of key persons frequently are major determinants of these styles. The analyst cannot change an organization's style in a single systems study—although an association involving effective work over a period can lead to changes in style—so he is well advised to adapt his work to it to a reasonable extent; he will have difficulty enough in promoting the changes that emerge from his work as desirable without assuming the added burden of trying to change the organization's style at a single stroke.

Third, what constraints does the decision setting offer? The most basic and frequently encountered one is time: Can the systems analysis be completed in time to inform the decisions leading to change? If it cannot, there is little point in embarking on it; if it can, but only on a simplified and reduced scale, the analyst and the executives involved must consider whether or not such a "quick-and-dirty" study can help (in my experience it usually can). Are there constraints such as customs, policies, laws, or regulations that will affect change? If so, they may have to be accepted, but surprisingly often they can be altered when good reasons appear. Thus, while the analyst must recognize such constraints, he would be unwise to accord them too sacred a status. It costs little to explore a constraint change in many cases, and such an inquiry can turn up information about constraints that may make eliminating them appear to be desirable.

Fourth, if, as is usually the case, the work is to be done for an organization, what is the appropriate administrative level at which the analysis team should report? There is no simple answer to this question; rather, the proper answer will differ for each case, depending on many factors, not the least of which is the personalities and powers of the executives who may be chosen to supply the main administrative tie during the analysis. Since a problem situation leading to the need for a systems analysis almost invariably cuts across organizational lines, both horizontally and vertically, the organization's choice of a sponsoring executive offers some pitfalls. If he is ambitious and grasping, he may suppress findings he does not like, or the rest of the organization may resist even obviously desirable findings to keep him from adding to his span of power and control; if he is weak and compliant, he may not give the analysis team enough support to allow them either access to possibly embarrassing information or the freedom to develop potentially unpopular findings.

Fifth, what is the appropriate relation of the analysis staff to the administrative staff that will have to respond to the study's findings? Can an analysis group inside the organization be the most effective? Or should an outside group be employed? Will administrative formalities encumber the work? Will the sources of support—administrative, financial, and policy—be strong and adequate? Will these sources of support guarantee the analysis team the free access to information that is essential to good analysis? Should members of the organization's staff join the analysis team? If so, who? Since the fact that systems analysis is being contemplated suggests that change may be called

Section 10.2. The Organizational Context

for, people in the organization are almost sure to have mixed feelings about the analysis and the analysts who are doing it; in the face of this fact, experience teaches that strong support from the top is essential to a successful outcome.

All of these considerations are embedded in the system structure involved with the problem situation; the character of this setting has basic importance for the analyst and how he thinks about the problems and their possible solutions. For example, R. W. Archibald (1979, p. 125) describes U.S. fire departments this way:

> Fire service organizations pose special problems and opportunities for the manager of change. For example, the quasimilitary bureaucratic organization of fire departments is a source of resistance to changes in authority structures, tasks, and procedures; but this same organizational form can help expedite compliance with changes that have been ordered by the chief executive. The traditional single entry level into the organization is often a source of resistance to recommendations of people who have not personally experienced firefighting. Knowledge derived from unfamiliar disciplines or distant cities is not readily accepted by fire service personnel.
>
> The change agent must also learn to deal with the crisis orientation of fire departments, which focuses rewards on action rather than on contemplation. The lengthy, sequential decisionmaking process of systems analysis contrasts sharply with the drama of decisionmaking by commanding officers at the scene of a fire. Moreover, because most fire departments have not experienced financial pressures until recent years, fire service personnel with budgeting and planning skills are few in number.
>
> The manager of change must understand how organizations operate, and be able to view the fire department as a collection of organizations interacting with other organizations. New policies that arise from deployment analysis are likely to have impacts on other organizations—such as labor unions and community groups—whose interests must be considered.

This summary makes it clear that the character of the administrative (as well as the social and political) structure involved in potential change is important. Therefore, the analyst may look for characterizations of such structures similar to the one quoted above—perhaps one for manufacturing companies, another for sales organizations, still another for public service institutions. However, experience tells us that this is too much to hope for: There are military organizations that are far more informal and unstructured than some business organizations, and more oriented to problem solution; by the same token, some businesses are managed by very rigid bureaucracies, while others have less formal structures easily adapted to change. In sum, the analyst must make his own observations about the nature of structure and authority for each organization he deals with, and factor this information into his work.

Much more could be written about how these basic questions about the organizational context relate to successful systems analysis, but experience is so varied that on most points it is not possible to be prescriptive. However, experience does tell us that the questions are important, and that the analyst must develop ties with the client organization that are close and continuous enough to enable him to formulate answers to them. These answers, combined with his experience and reasoned judgment, are then likely to help him find a path to effective work; if he cannot find this path, he has good reasons to stop his work before a lot of effort is wasted.

Underlying these assessments there should be a mature and realistic view of the interacting roles of the analyst and his client. While many elements of this view have been offered by the earlier chapters of this handbook, the next section turns to the foundation on which a realistic view of analyst and client roles can be built.

10.3. Developing a Professional Philosophy for Systems Analysis

The years since 1945 have seen tremendous advances for society based on science and technology and a concomitant growth of the associated professions. And yet, in the two decades since 1963 the professions have faced a growing crisis of confidence and legitimacy with the public. As Schön (1983, pp. 9–10) points out, "in these years, both professional and layman have suffered through public events which have undermined belief in the competence of expertise and brought the legitimacy of the professions into serious question. . . . The success of the space program seemed not to be replicable when the problems to be solved were tangled socio-techno-politico-economic predicaments of public life." Systems analysis works against the background of this growing crisis, and, indeed, in problem areas sensitive to its crosscurrents. It is thus particularly important for this relatively new field not to reproduce the shortcomings and inadequate philosophies of older professions, but to find a commonly accepted philosophical foundation not only appropriate for systems analysis, but also capable of being shared with other professions as they emerge from obsolescence into modern relevance and maturity.

While one must admit that the systems analysis profession has not yet evolved such a basis for its work, it must do so. Many points set forth in this handbook can contribute to such a basis, and Schön (1983) points out a very useful direction. This section sketches Schön's approach, the quotations not otherwise attributed being taken from his book.

Schön (1983, pp. 14–17) finds these elements in the background of the current crisis in the professions—all of them familiar to the systems analyst:

> In such fields as medicine, management, and engineering, for example, leading professionals speak of a new awareness of a complexity which resists the skills and techniques of traditional expertise. . . .
> The situations of practice are inherently unstable. Harvey Brooks, an

Section 10.3. Developing a Professional Philosophy for Systems Analysis 287

eminent engineer and educator, argues that the professions are now confronted with an "unprecedented requirement for adaptability." . . .
Practitioners are frequently embroiled in conflicts of values, goals, purposes, and interests.

He says also that the narrow view of professional activity requires that the professional restrict his activity to applying rigorously tested and widely accepted scientific knowledge. Thus, in this view, finding a problem means identifying in the problem situation facing the practitioner a difficulty to which such knowledge is relevant, and problem solving then consists of applying this scientific knowledge until the difficulty is overcome; the goals of this activity are identifying the difficulty and overcoming it. On the other hand, a much wider view of professional activity emphasizes problem setting, that is, considering the various relevant and disparate possible goals, the different collections of means that may be adapted to achieving them, and the decisions that need to be made along the way. Schön says: "If it is true that professional practice has at least as much to do with finding the problem as with solving the problem found, it is also true that problem setting is a recognized professional activity."

These elements in the current crisis in the professions contribute to their unease because of the outdated philosophy that traditionally lies behind them, the dominant epistemology of practice being based on what Schön (1983, p. 21) calls "Technical Rationality":

According to the model of Technical Rationality—the view of professional knowledge which has most powerfully shaped both our thinking about the professions and the institutional relations of research, education, and practice—professional activity consists in instrumental problem solving made rigorous by the application of scientific theory and technique.

This model had its origins in the history of Western ideas (Schön, 1983, p. 31):

. . . Technical Rationality is the heritage of Positivism, the powerful philosophical doctrine that grew up in the nineteenth century as an account of the rise of science and technology and as a social movement aimed at applying the achievements of science and technology to the well-being of mankind. Technical Rationality is the Positivist epistemology of practice.

However, this dominant epistemology and its origin in positivism present the professions—and particularly systems analysis—with difficulties:

First, technical rationality presumes that the sole basis for problem solving is the knowledge of science, and that therefore a professional practitioner must be able to map a problem he faces onto this knowledge. The result is to make the arts of practice—particularly those relating to problem setting—appear as puzzling anomalies. While admitting that practical knowledge exists, the positivist cannot fit it neatly into positivist categories. Thus, the arts of professional craft do not have natural places in technical rationality.

Schön (1983, pp. 39–41) states the second and third difficulties this way:

> From the perspective of Technical Rationality, professional practice is a process of problem *solving*. Problems of choice or decision are solved through the selection, from available means, of the one best suited to established ends. But with this emphasis on problem solving, we ignore problem *setting*, the process by which we define the decision to be made, the ends to be achieved, the means which may be chosen. In real-world practice, problems do not present themselves to the practitioner as givens. They must be constructed from the materials of problematic situations which are puzzling, troubling, and uncertain. . . . It is this sort of situation that professionals are coming increasingly to see as central to their practice. . . .
>
> Technical Rationality depends on agreement about ends. When ends are fixed and clear, then the decision to act can present itself as an instrumental problem. But when ends are confused and conflicting, there is as yet no "problem" to solve. [Italics in the original.]

Finally, technical rationality poses the dilemma of "rigor or relevance"—rigorous application of existing scientific knowledge to a problem distorted to fit the available knowledge, or relevant by being allowed to keep its real form to which no existing knowledge is exactly apposite. Schön (1983, p. 42) poses this dilemma in this way:

> . . . In the varied topography of professional practice, there is a high, hard ground where practitioners can make use of research-based theory and technique, and there is a swampy lowland where situations are confusing "messes" incapable of technical solution. The difficulty is that the problems of this high ground, however great their technical interest, are often relatively unimportant to clients or to the larger society, while in the swamp are the problems of greatest human concern. Shall the practitioner stay on the high, hard ground where he can practice rigorously, as he understands rigor, but where he is constrained to deal with problems of relatively little social importance? Or shall he descend to the swamp where he can engage the most important and challenging problems if he is willing to forsake technical rigor?

Computer modeling in operations research and managment science offers an interesting example illustrating this last point. Here the emphasis is on increasingly complex models: whereas early relatively modest models have been used successfully to solve many operating problems, the much larger models have proved to be much less satisfactory in yielding results about large-scale policy and operating difficulties, where the problems are much more complex. However, the strong impulse—particularly in academia—behind the ideal of rigor has given the construction of such large models a life of its own, increasingly divergent from real-world problems of practice.

Lest the reader—perhaps a practicing systems analyst—feel that the field of systems analysis is free from the dilemma of rigor or relevance, I can cite two first-hand experiences. One involved a paper submitted to a professional

Section 10.3. Developing a Professional Philosophy for Systems Analysis

journal, the other a doctoral thesis submitted to a professional department. In each cases the analyst considered a practical situation in which he faced difficulties, applied the arts of professional craft to problem setting, and then devised a novel algorithmic approach to achieving results that, when applied, clearly achieved better outcomes than had been possible previously. Relevance was clear and obvious in both cases, but disciples of rigor (in academia in both cases) interposed objections to publication on the ground that the algorithms had not been proved to converge in the infinite limit. Happily, these objections were overcome—and the published papers both won significant formal recognition for high professional quality.

To remove the limitations of technical rationality, and, incidentally, resolve the false dilemma of rigor or relevance, Schön proposes to focus attention on the day-to-day activities of practice during which professionals make many judgments and display many skills, what he calls "knowing-in-action"—and what this handbook calls the craft of systems analysis. Systematic inquiry into these activities of practice Schön calls "reflection-in-action." Then he points to the direction for developing an epistemology of practice:

> ... The dilemma of rigor or relevance may be dissolved if we can develop an epistemology of practice which places technical problem solving within a broader context of reflective inquiry, shows how reflection-in-action may be rigorous in its own right, and links the art of practice in uncertainty and uniqueness to the scientist's art of research. [Schön, 1983, p. 69.]

The goal then is a rigorously developed and extensively tested epistemology of practice—or craft—on which a "reflective practitioner" can base his work. However, to be successful this concept requires that the client also be reflective in much the same sense, but with respect to the body of material that makes up the basis for his everyday activities. With these complementary outlooks, when a reflective practitioner and a reflective client agree to cooperate on an inquiry, their relation is not the classical subservience of a client to a professional but rather a new form of partnership called a "reflective contract" (Schön, 1983, pp. 296–297):

> ... in a reflective contract between practitioner and client, the client does not agree to accept the practitioner's authority but to suspend disbelief in it. He agrees to join the practitioner in inquiring into the situation for which the client seeks help; to try to understand what he is experiencing and to make that understanding accessible to the practitioner; to confront the practitioner when he does not understand or agree; to test the practitioner's competence by observing his effectiveness and to make public his questions over what should be counted as effectiveness; to pay for services rendered and to appreciate competence demonstrated. The practitioner agrees to deliver competent performance to the limits of his capacity; to help the client understand the meaning of the professional's advice and the rationale for his actions, while at the same time he tries to learn the meanings his actions have for his client; to make himself confrontable by his client; and to reflect

on his own tacit understandings when he needs to do so in order to play his part in fulfilling the contract.

This form of partnership between analyst and client can be expected both to come to grips effectively with the realities of the situation at hand, and to move solutions smoothly and effectively into implementation.

Historically, systems analyses have occupied many positions on the line between the classical professional-client relation of client subservience and the reflective contract, and will, no doubt continue to do so, depending on the circumstances. In particular, the blood-management (Section 3.2) and fire-protection (Section 3.3) examples occupy such intermediate positions. And throughout this handbook, in spite of its emphasis on the technical issues facing the analyst, the values of moving toward the reflective contract have been stressed; for example, the emphasis on the craft of systems analysis (Section 1.9 and Chapters 2, 5, and 9) moves in the direction of the concept of the reflective practitioner.

Nevertheless, this handbook, since it must *a fortiori* reflect the current state of systems analysis, describes professional activity midway between the classical client subservience and the reflective contract, while emphasizing throughout that the ultimate responsibility and authority of the client impel the activity toward the reflective contract.

10.4. Awareness of the Problem Situation

As Section 5.1 points out, "the systems analyst, seeking to contribute to real-world decisions, always finds himself facing, not a well defined problem, but a problem area or situation; his problem turns out to be as nexus of problems, what the French call a 'problématique,' or what Ackoff . . . calls 'a mess.'" While the manager's view may be incomplete—or even wrong—it can be accepted as a recognition that all is not well, and that an unsatisfactory posture should be examined for possible change aimed at improvement.

One might conclude that the analyst should try to get the manager to sharpen his problem statement. However, experience tells us overwhelmingly that this is the opposite of what is desirable at the beginning: the analyst is well advised to keep the manager's appreciation of his problem as broad and general as possible, so that the analyst making early inquiries into the situation is free to formulate the problem (if indeed this is possible) without the inhibiting constraint of an authoritative misperception. In fact, in my experience, perhaps the worst thing that can happen is for the executive to write a memorandum stating what the problem is, particularly if he is a very strong and dominating personality; his statement then becomes a major deterrent to developing the realistic problem appreciation needed for good analysis, and makes it doubly hard to get this appreciation accepted. The moral is plain: At the beginning, keep the discussions and interactions as broad and

Section 10.4. Awareness of the Problem Situation

flexible as possible, to the end that the early fact finding and analysis can dominate how the problem is formulated.

In sum, there is considerable practical experience backing the view that a careful problem investigation and formulation effort is an essential beginning; Chapter 5 provides an approach that can be adapted to most situations. In fact, to skip or slight this step is to risk spending effort on the wrong problem. The unhappy cases where this has happened seldom make their way into the literature, but the oral tradition contains many tales of analysis gone wrong because the problem investigation was not thorough enough to discover the key difficulty. For example, Agin (1978, p. 42) describes one case where this could have happened:

> A manager asked for a study to examine the consolidation of three of his firm's plants into one. The new plant was to be constructed at a location separate from the three existing plants. A preliminary examination of the economies which would result from the consolidation indicated the plants had no operations in common and that the proposed plan could only result in an increase in costs. The executive should have known this so that prior to an investigation in detail it was decided to review with him what he expected to achieve from the study. Doing this involved several days of discussion. From this, it was discovered that the real issue was an inability for this executive and the union leader at one of the plants to work together. Once this was recognized, a Vice President of Industrial Relations was hired to deal with the union and the idea of consolidation dropped. The undertaking of a study with little or no chance for real success was avoided.

Where the initial awareness of the problem situation exists in the organization may make considerable difference to how the analysis team proceeds. If the awareness comes from a high executive, it may be much easier to get an analysis started than if the awareness comes from a subordinate official in an operating department. If the awareness is forced on the organization by outside pressures or interventions, the managers may resist change more strongly than if the perception originated inside. The analysis group itself may be the source of the perception, since its continuing work sharpens its views. Thus at the beginning the analyst may be involved in discussions aimed at persuading managers that they are facing a problem situation, rather than vice versa. Many analysts feel that this is one of their most important duties and opportunities. Certainly, experience tells us that the analysis team that only answers the doorbell is never as influential or useful as the one that takes a broader and more entrepreneurial view of its work. As Section 2.2 points out, this was among the earliest perceptions of the operations research community; as Blackett (1950, p. 5) said of the 1940–1945 British experience: "... one of the clearest lessons ... [is] that the really big successes of operational research groups are often achieved by the discovery of problems which had not hitherto been recognized as significant. In fact the most fertile tasks are often found by the groups themselves rather than given to them."

This view is heavily underlined by operations research and systems analysis experience in the ensuing four decades.

A systems analysis group may be asked to undertake rather mundane analysis tasks. If these formed the entire menu, the group's purpose would be completely vitiated. However, such tasks should not be shunned entirely: when accepted graciously (unless demonstrably unsuitable) and done well and promptly, they can often provide entry to larger and more important work of systems-analytic character, both by giving opportunities for insights and by establishing sympathetic relations with influential executives. Further, systems analysts must learn a great deal about the organizations they serve, and opportunities to further this process have value in their own right.

A newly formed systems analysis team is seldom well advised to plunge immediately into the broadest and most global problems of the organization it serves. Rather, it should build up its knowledge and the confidence of the organization through a series of smaller studies; properly chosen and organized, these can constitute the building blocks of a broad understanding that will support work on the global problems.

Almost anywhere on this scale, however, the analyst in search of challenging work looks for these three characteristics in a problem situation:

A responsible person recognizes a problem situation and wants help.

The prospective project is functionally interdisciplinary—that is, it involves more than a single narrow function of the organization.

The solutions, as well as the problem situation, appear likely to fall outside the responsibility of a single small staff organization.

These are not absolute criteria of choice (for example, a single executive may have a very interesting problem over which he has control that is well worth a systems analysis effort), but they do suggest properties of a situation that may be particularly challenging, and therefore particularly appropriate for systems analysis.

Finally, as part of the issue of problem awareness, experience offers some advice about the management/analyst interactions and initiatives at the beginning: Keep them informal and somewhat fluid, so that the analyst is free to consider a variety of possibilities; interact as widely as possible, with the aim of gaining a varied and comprehensive a picture of the problem situation before formal work begins. We have noted that it is generally undesirable for the sponsor to hand the analyst a memorandum stating the problem at the beginning of the first discussion; it is equally undesirable for the analyst, right after the first discussion, to retire to his study to prepare a problem statement in precise terms—he is almost sure to be wrong, and thus eventually to be embarrassed by his own words as the early fact-finding and analysis probe the problem situation.

10.5. Formulating the Problem

The first step to take after the conference with the official who is aware of the problem situation is to begin a widespread, comprehensive, first-hand, and, where possible, on-site survey—a thorough background investigation. Chapter 5 provides guidance on how to approach this activity systematically. This survey is essential to the analyst's understanding of the situation; the details he discovers here will give him the essential foundation for his later analysis. Of course, the executive most concerned can supply much information of this sort, but first-hand observation is far more useful than second-hand description. For example, the analysts who were asked to study the possibility of increasing the productivity of a Third-World steel mill, as described in Section 9.2, would have been well advised to watch all facets of the operation for a substantial period of time; they would not then have been embarrassed to discover that the operators were illiterate—and their approach to the problem could well have been much simpler, the evolution of a new approach much quicker, and the results as good as what was finally achieved. The analysts asked to consider the plant consolidation described in Section 10.4, on the other hand, got to the bottom of the problem, the personality conflict, and did not proceed to study the issues of the proposed consolidation, because they realized that this type of solution could not follow from the facts of the case.

Similarly, a bit of knowledge of fundamental importance and well known to the persons directly involved in an operation, but missed by the analysis team, can destroy the client's confidence in the findings of the analysis, *even if this fact has no bearing on the findings*! An analysis team studying the problem of efficient supply and dispatch of tank cars for a chemical company running a continuous-process plant missed the fact that the cars had to be steam cleaned before each use; while this fact had only a very minor effect on the proposed course of action—indeed, the adjustment was made in a few minutes—the executive for whom the study was done was telling strangers several years later that systems analysts were of dubious value. Had the team observed the operations of the railroad yard at the chemical plant carefully, they would not have overlooked this fact (of vital importance to chemists, since even traces of some chemicals can spoil chemical processes) that embarrassed the analysis team at the time it was presenting its results.

In addition to giving the analyst a well-rounded view of the problem situation, a careful initial survey may also allow him to discover aspects of it unknown to the responsible executives. It is commonplace for workers to conceal bad news from the boss, but share it with an outsider—a fact that presents the analyst with a problem: If he leaks this bad news to the executive, thus violating an implied confidentiality, his source of reliable information may be cut off, and other difficulties may arise; but if he ignores it in his work, he risks reaching conclusions sufficiently unrealistic as to vitiate his findings, or inhibit their acceptance. There is usually a path through this dilemma, but no general principle can be enunciated beyond one supported by a large body of experience: If the analyst should behave in any way that makes him look to the workers like an "inspector," valuable information and easy relations will be lost.

The opposite can also occur in the case where the executive is seeking some sort of evaluation aimed at organizational adjustment, when the workers may be quite uncooperative—with a similar dilemma for the analyst to avoid.

It is usually wise to check the information from this early survey with many persons involved, to be sure that early impressions are accurate; judgment will have to be exercised about how trustworthy views and opinions might be. However, the number and variety of contacts will serve as a useful and surprisingly effective screening device.

Note that we have been talking here about a somewhat informal survey and investigation, not the formal data-gathering that may ensue as the project gets launched in earnest. In fact, such a survey may be a useful prelude to a decision about whether or not to undertake a systems-analysis project.

With the results of this survey in his notebook and his head, the analyst is now ready to formulate an initial appreciation of the ramifications of the problem situation and the potential effects of change, at least in broad terms: Is it a tactical matter? Is it a strategic question? Does the situation appear to have short-term or long-term consequences? Whose interests are affected, just those of the official inviting in the analysis team, or many others? Is the problem situation confined to the organization seeking help, or is it more widespread? Is the impetus for the concern an internal one, or does it come from outside the organization? This initial appreciation must be tentative, of course, but to make it explicit is an important step nonetheless—and Chapter 5 provides important guidance on how to go about it.

Against this background, the analyst is ready to formulate his preliminary synthesis of the situation, perhaps leading to a tentative problem statement. He now has some idea of the nature of the problem, what its boundaries may be, what at least some potential responses might be, what information may be needed to pursue the analysis, what data-gathering work must be undertaken on a systematic basis, and, most important of all at this stage, what management help will be needed to make the work proceed smoothly to an effective conclusion.

Thus the analyst is now ready to prepare the analysis plan, a step often neglected, but one that in my view is absolutely essential to a successful project of large scale.

The skeptic may argue that, if research is exploring the unknown, how can the exploration be planned? The experienced systems analyst will respond that a well-developed plan is an invaluable guide to action, even when unforeseen events or difficulties arise, not the least because the plan shows

Section 10.5. Formulating the Problem

quickly what the effects of such unforeseen matters may have on schedules, resource needs, and so on.

Also, the team leader needs to have an estimate of time, resources, and support that he can put forward early; the more detail that underlies this estimate, the more reliable it is likely to be.

A good analysis plan will do at least these things:

1. Describe the context of the problem.
2. State the problem in the preliminary form developed in the initial survey.
3. List the other organizations with interests in the problem and its outcome, along with suitable descriptions, including any work they may be doing on the problem.
4. List the data and information needed to investigate the problem, and the activities needed to gather this information and process it for use in the analysis.
5. Lay out the analysis activities that are foreseen.
6. Project a schedule of key events in the progress of the analysis and in the reporting activities that will accompany and follow the analysis.
7. Envision the products of the analysis activity (reports, briefings, backup material, and so on).
8. Specify the resources needed to carry out the work, including the reporting and follow-up activities.
9. Stipulate the management interactions and assistance needed throughout the activity.
10. Lay out a schedule for reporting activities that will present the results of the analysis to all of the constituencies that may be affected by, or interested in, its findings.
11. Give at least a hint, if possible, of the sort of implementation activities that might be called for. (It may be difficult, perhaps impossible, to do this at a stage when the findings cannot be forecast—but it is not too early for the attention of both analysts and client to be drawn to this issue, at least generically.)

An analysis plan may be anything from a short memorandum for a small-scale study to a long document for a major inquiry. It has many uses:

It can be used as the basis for negotiating with the client for the support needed in the work.

It serves as a useful goad to the analysis team to get on with its work. (It is very easy, in the face of conflicting demands and interesting new options, to let a schedule slip drastically or to let the resources trickle away, particularly when the project is a major one over a long schedule.)

It is not only a useful check on progress; it also serves as the point of departure for adjustment when new events or unforeseen difficulties force changes on the work and its schedule.

When the analysis team consists of many persons, perhaps at different locations, the analysis plan can be an essential instrument for keeping their work coordinated, even though a series of continuing interactions with the team leader and other workers may be needed to perfect the coordination.

Candor compels me to admit that practicing systems analysts do not always prepare analysis plans for their work—indeed, the number who do may be in a minority; however, my own experience supports the worth of this step so strongly that I have no hesitation whatever in recommending it strongly to others. Such plans are a commonplace among analysts working in consulting firms seeking analysis engagements with large industrial or governmental clients (the plan is usually incorporated in the "proposal" to the client), but for groups working as part of large organizations it is less common, although perhaps more needed.

Finally, as part of the formulation process, the head of the analysis team must, as is implicit in the analysis plan, negotiate the administrative formalities that will be associated with the work: financial support, administrative cooperation (both in providing access to information and supplying management participants in the work), arrangements for periodic reporting and review, possible phasing (if the project will entail more than one phase), and a prospect of what the final reporting process will be (so that the client and the analysis team have a common expectation).

Experience has shown that the second of the points is particularly important: It is highly desirable that at least one member of the client organization participate in the analysis throughout in an appropriate way. This person can offer many benefits, including these:

> He can facilitate information-gathering through his knowledge of the organization; indeed, he may be able to supply much of what is needed from his own resources. However, knowing where to go and whom to see can save much time and effort.
>
> As a bridge between the analysis team and the management throughout the project, he can keep them informed about progress between the times when formal progress reports are rendered. In some cases, this person can even serve in an informal way to help sell unusual or unexpected findings before they are finally reported.
>
> Most contexts have hidden presumptions that everyone takes for granted, and which may escape the analyst, since everyone in the context thinks they do not need to be stated. If such ignorance persists until reporting time, it can have a fatal effect on the management's confidence in the team's mastery of the problem (as the example of the team doing the

chemical-plant analysis not knowing of the need to steam clean tank cars illustrates). However, the well-informed team member from the management virtually assures that this cannot happen.

The ensuing five sections of this chapter all deal with matters that, from a more technical standpoint, have been discussed earlier in this handbook. However, from the point of view of practice there are some points to be added that are important, and they will be taken up here.

10.6. Gathering Information

The inexperienced analyst may set out to assemble everything he can put his hands on, somewhat indiscriminately, with the result that he will have a huge pile of data with little information content. Rather, data relevant to the problem should be gathered on the basis of a carefully worked out plan (it may be the analysis plan itself, or an addendum thereto) that not only lists sources and describes how they are to be tapped, but also how the raw data are to be converted to useful information bearing on the problem (see Majone, 1980). Care in planning this work and carrying it out will ensure both relevance and focus, and may well achieve considerable economy.

It is well to focus on important phenomena from more than one perspective, in order for internal consistency to be checked and cross-checked, to the end that one has evidence to support one's trust in the information—or lack thereof. External sources may be especially important in this regard, if they can be tapped. It is especially important for operational and technical expertise to be incorporated in the available information; one of the best ways is to have such specialists as members of the interdisciplinary team, contributing their knowledge throughout the work.

The process of collecting information to support a systems study must have in mind the fundamental lesson of census taking; that a carefully controlled sample is almost always going to give better estimates than a poorly controlled attempt at complete enumeration. More important, perhaps, is the central lesson of my experience: that what one knows about the supporting evidence will play a very large role in how the findings of the analysis are interpreted. This point argues against using data already gathered unless absolutely necessary, and certainly against using them without knowing how they were gathered and—equally important—how they were processed. In many cases systems analysts cannot avoid using data gathered elsewhere for other purposes (such as population statistics, economic data, government-generated time series, and the like), but considerable effort should be devoted to learning how these data were developed, and what their strengths and weaknesses are, so that the findings of the analysis can take account of such knowledge. Perhaps one of the most important pitfalls of analysis is to put more credence in data than is warranted by the way they were developed.

Another pitfall is to gather too much material—thus consuming valuable time—rather than just the right amount. There is no simple rule to follow, except perhaps the truism that it is usually better to have a small amount of reliable information than to have a great deal in which one has little confidence.

10.7. Formulating Alternatives

Since Chapter 6 deals with this matter, we need not repeat the main points here. However, it is worth reemphasizing the central importance of dealing with this issue imaginatively and continually throughout the systems analysis study. It should never be too late to introduce a new alternative if ideas and consequences come together to generate a new concept with preferred properties.

Anyone who doubts the importance of generating and considering the most imaginative and promising alternatives should contemplate the poverty of a large-scale systems analysis—complete with the full panoply of computer runs, economic concepts, optimization models, and so on—that confines its attention to relatively simple and primitive alternatives. For example, if the IIASA study of future world energy supply and demand (described in Section 3.5 and discussed further in 6.1 and 6.3) had restricted itself to simple alternatives of oil, coal, water power, nuclear generation, and so on, it would not have been able to consider the contribution of the allothermal coal liquefaction and gasification process that uses heat from breeder reactors or from hydrogen and that therefore adds greatly to the potential life of the world's coal reserves.

On the borders of the process of formulating alternatives there are some issues of practice and professionalism that deserve mention, although little prescriptive guidance can be offered.

An alternative may be deemed impractical because it breaches established laws, customs, prejudices, or attitudes. This does not necessarily mean that the alternative should not be considered; rather, it means that, if it is considered, the analyst will have a much larger burden of persuasion at the end of his study if it turns out to be attractive on other grounds. At this point he may face the issue of whether or not to introduce these social issues into his work, or to leave them for the client to judge. There are fundamental difficulties here, as Churchman (1979) points out. However, wise counsel is one of courage on the one hand (the client may surprise you with a burst of venturesome advocacy for change), but prudence on the other (by having less radical proposals available, even though they may not be as attractive). "Impractical" alternatives have been known to become practical after being pushed by someone with influence.

Similarly, since a truly important issue worth a major systems analysis is bound to harbor political issues that will flower into debates when the findings emerge, political feasibility may be an issue to consider in formulating alternatives. Here again experience offers little advice, although it does give some encouragement to be venturesome, the analyst being left for the most part to his own best judgment, which he should develop in concert with his client.

It is here that the analyst may face two of the most important dilemmas of his profession:

> How can he balance his loyalty to science and the profession of systems analysis with the loyalty to his organization when they come into conflict?
>
> In the face of potentially negative responses to alternatives—some responses being possibly so strong as to threaten the analyst's survival in his post—how can he best exhibit the venturesome courage to design and explore controversial alternatives, and present them as preferred if they occupy this place in the findings?

The inexperienced analyst's first reaction to these dilemmas may be to seek simply to avoid them—perhaps by dealing only with problems in which they cannot occur. But this dooms him to relatively unimportant problems: it is almost axiomatic that the coin of importance has a reverse side of controversy. Indeed, the analyst should understand that controversy is an important ingredient in the change process, one that has the desirable property of forcing those involved to think about the issues and options. Thus, the price the analyst must pay if he is to deal with problems of large and central importance is that he will be involved in the dilemmas of loyalty and controversy.

How the analyst is to behave in the face of these dilemmas will be discussed later in Section 10.15.

10.8. Choosing Modes of Analysis

Systems analysis is driven by its problems, not its methods. Therefore, the analyst should allow the problem to rule his choice of method, and this choice should be taken from an eclectic menu. He should choose methods and techniques that are appropriate, avoiding the seduction of popular or convenient technologies that may seem to add "class" to the analysis, but that are essentially inappropriate. In the same vein, complexities appropriate to the problem are necessary, and must be incorporated into the analysis, but those introduced merely to add analytic glitter to the product are to be shunned.

Six positive principles may be enunciated. Choose analytic machinery that is:

1. Appropriate to the problem and the prospective solutions to it that may emerge.
2. Matched appropriately to the available information (since an attractive model that calls for nonexistent data cannot yield trustworthy results).
3. Internally consistent (the delicate analytic machinery of one part should not be bludgeoned by hazy speculation in another).

4. Balanced in detail and accuracy. (If one enters with order-of-magnitude estimates, one is seldom entitled to five-figure accuracy in the results, or, if accurate estimates are combined with very questionable estimates, this fact should be reflected in how the results are presented.)
5. Appropriately interdisciplinary in the light of the appreciation of the problem with which the work began and is being continued.
6. Appropriate, if at all possible, to the process of presenting the findings that will emerge at the end of the study. (The client will surely not want to poke into the details, but a realistic understanding of the main building blocks and key relations has persuasive value for many users of systems analysis results.)

This last point deserves further discussion. The complexities that must be represented by models in a systems analysis arise from the problem being treated, and therefore one may argue that the model complexities are intrinsic. However, in practice it not infrequently happens that the choice of a model is not so constrained as this remark would imply; for example, it may be possible to choose a series of relatively simple connected models rather than one very complicated comprehensive model, and yet get adequate results. When such a choice exists, there is some merit in making it at least partially in the light of how the results of the work will have to be presented to the client. If the model used also provides a simple line of argument that will be persuasive to a nontechnical person, this value should be weighed in making the choice.

Howard Raiffa, the distinguished mathematician and systems analyst who was the founding Director of the International Institute for Applied Systems Analysis in Laxenburg, Austria, describes his experience this way (Raiffa, 1982, p. 1):

> As an analyst I have participated in several policy studies; as a professor in a public policy program I have critiqued a host of such studies; and as a decisionmaker myself or as a consultant to decisionmakers I have seen how such policy studies are used or not used.

And, on the basis of this experience he offers this advice (loc. cit., p. 7):

> In modeling reality for policy guidance there are a host of options to consider. First of all, some advice: Beware of general-purpose, grandiose models that try to incorporate practically everything. Such models are difficult to validate, to interpret, to calibrate statistically, to manipulate, and most importantly to explain. You may be better off not with one big model but with a set of simpler models, starting off with simple deterministic ones and complicating the model in stages as sensitivity analysis shows the need for such complications. A model does not have to address all aspects of the problem. It should be designed to aid in understanding the dynamic interactions of some phase of your problem. Other models can address other phases.
>
> Time constraints, however, may not allow you the luxury of tailoring

models to fit your problem. You may have to choose a model off the shelf, so to speak, and fiddle with fitting it as well as possible to your problem. But in these cases my advice is even more cogent: Keep it simple.

10.9. Carrying out the Analysis

This issue has been discussed so thoroughly in earlier chapters that little needs saying here. However, five points deserve emphasis.

First, the issue of documentation should be kept in mind from the beginning. The work should be documented as it proceeds, so that, at its end, when attention is properly focused on communicating the findings and following up on them, it will not be necessary to return to the earlier work to reconstruct—perhaps with considerable difficulty—what was done. Documentation is as much a part of the professionalism of systems analysis as it is of pure science, and the need to have full and clear records at the end of the project should be recognized and responded to. The easiest way to achieve this essential standard is to keep it in mind throughout, and to do what is necessary at each step of the analysis to build the records that will allow others to see clearly what was done, and, if they should ever desire, to duplicate or extend the work.

Second, the work of the analysis should be done openly, so that the participating personnel from the decisionmaker's staff can understand, interpret, and report informally to their colleagues what is going on. This policy risks possible misinterpretation, but this risk is more than overcome by the benefits to be accrued. This openness should also extend to others who may have legitimate interests in what is being done.

Third, any systems analysis contains the results of major decisions about how to proceed and how to interpret evidence—but there are also smaller ones that the analyst must make from day to day as his work proceeds (Can we ignore this factor? Is this small-sample estimate adequate? Can this result from another study be relied on? Is this small effect apparently exhibited by the data a realistic representation? And so on). Controlling these secondary decisions so that they do not cumulatively vitiate the main thrust of the analysis is important, particularly in a large study with many parts and many analysts. There are no simple rules for doing this beyond the one that says the leaders of the project should keep careful watch over this issue day by day as the analysis develops. If they do this, they will assure that the decisions are consistent, and that the potential impact on the findings can be assessed and reported candidly; if they do not, serious flaws may seep into the work. Pursuant to the first point, it is also important to document these secondary decisions as carefully as the primary ones, together with estimates of their potential effects.

Fourth, after the analysis is complete, and the findings tentatively formulated, it is wise for the analysts to stand back and review their work. The background context may have shifted, key client personnel may have changed, the analysts themselves will have developed new perspectives arising from their involvement with the problem, and so on—and such factors may have shifted the perspective on what was done and should have been done. This review may prompt some change of focus—perhaps even the development of some new alternatives for last-minute investigation.

In addition, the review should assess key variables and their impacts, assure that the needed sensitivity analyses have been carried out, and perform the supplementary analyses that the analysts and their clients may need to round out a good understanding of why the results came out as they did, and what their implications are.

Finally, before taking the study's results to the client, the analysis team should consider the advantages of an additional review by a group of analysts and others who have not participated in the work. Experience shows that such a careful review before an essentially friendly but perceptive audience can do much to sharpen the final presentation to the client.

The analyst may argue that, with the work already behind schedule and with demanding reporting needs staring at him, there is no time for these reviews. However, if he skips them, he may deny his reporting the balanced current perspective that his client will find most persuasive.

10.10. Formulating the Findings

The scientist inexperienced in systems analysis may well wonder why this topic needs taking up at all, since the work was aimed at discovering results; when they emerge surely the analyst recognizes and understands them. However, the client may not, and it is *his* understanding that is the goal of the analysis. Therefore, the experienced analyst knows that formulating the findings properly and effectively is a key task in his work, and involves four matters that deserve his careful attention.

1. The first of these is the most important: The formulation must be based, not on the interests of the analysts, but those of the client officials.
2. The formulation should be balanced in terms of their needs and perspectives. Thus, matters of particular interest to them should be emphasized; others of minor interest should be passed over lightly, or even omitted entirely if time or space is limited.
3. Special attention must be given to important results that may run counter to intuitive beliefs of the client officials; if their outlooks are to be changed, the evidence aimed at changing them must be carefully thought through and effectively presented.
4. Care must be exercised in choosing the form of the argument—the flow of evidence and logic—that will persuade the client of the validity of the results (see Section 2.7 and Majone, 1980), for if the client does not

factor the findings into his thinking in an effective way, much of the value of the work may be lost.

In sum, while the findings of the analysis may present numerous matters of interest to the analysts, the items of value and interest to the clients should be formulated with special attention, an effort that should extend to how best to present them. The analysts dealing with the estuary-protection problem discussed in Section 3.4 faced this problem, and devised a special approach, as we saw there.

Generally, the approach to systems analysis presented in this handbook has advocated continuing reconsideration of the problem as the analysis proceeds; in fact, of the nine steps in systems analysis listed in Section 1.4, the fourth was this: "Reconsider the problem—and its possible reformulation—in the light of the knowledge accumulating during the analysis." Raiffa (1982, p. 19) argues the case even more strongly, urging that it is

> ... helpful occasionally for analytical groups, even in their early deliberations ... to dwell a bit on the big picture: From problem formulation to policy generation to analysis to conflict resolution to advocacy to implementation and to evaluation; to try to identify those crucial issues that are at the cutting edge of the policy arguments; to examine, all along the way and not only at the end of the analysis, how the separate pieces of analysis can be fused together into a holistic, balanced, coherent, realistic, acceptable, implementable policy recommendation.

In formulating the findings of the analysis the systems analyst has his last—and perhaps most important—opportunity to conduct a sweeping reconsideration of the problem and the analysis response to it in the full panoply of its surrounding circumstances. He must make good use of this opportunity.

The analysis plan that was prepared at the beginning of the work included a section on communicating the findings, and therefore on the sorts of communication instruments that would be needed. When the findings are being formulated it is time to review this section and evolve a more detailed plan for communicating them, especially since the analysis team has now grown much more familiar with the client organization and its people. This combination of knowledge of the results of the study and the needs and interests of the client will yield a changed and refined communication plan. The next section will discuss preparing items that may appear in such a plan.

10.11. Preparing the Communication Instruments

A major systems analysis study calls, not only for a variety of communication instruments aimed at the varied audiences who are—or should be—interested, but also great care in preparing them. Indeed, the analysts who conducted the forest-pest analysis described in Section 1.2 wrote (Holling 1978, p. 120): "Our experience is that at least as much effort must go into communication as goes into analysis"—and they cite other experience to confirm this judgment. While the amount of effort involved in preparing communication instruments varies from case to case, there can be no doubt that it is a very important step in the analysis activity, and one that deserves careful and creative thought.

While several forms of reporting involving a number of media may be called for, the written report usually lies at the core of the communication process. Not only is this document the central reference for all concerned, but also its preparation is the final testing ground for how the findings will be presented. It is the wellspring from which all of the other communication instruments flow. I will discuss this document first, although the actual order of work may differ; for example, pressure from the client frequently forces the presentation process to begin with a briefing based on or followed by a rough draft, with the finished final report following later.

The Systems Analysis Report

The report on the findings should contain three parts:

1. A summary (complete enough to tell the busy executive in a few minutes what the problem was, what ground the analysts covered in their work, what the findings were, and what courses of action are being proposed).
2. The main report (written entirely in the language of the client organization and containing the complete story of the work from a nontechnical point of view).
3. The appendixes or supporting technical reports (containing the complete technical presentation of the analysis, including a programmer's manual and a user's manual for any computer programs to be transferred to the client).

To provide perspective, such a report could have a main body of several hundred pages, a summary of about 25 pages, and perhaps more than a thousand pages of supporting material, perhaps available as separate documents. For a less comprehensive study, the summary might be ten pages long, the main body 80 pages, with 150 pages of appendixes containing the technical material. For example: The global analysis of energy supply and demand described in Section 3.5, which occupied an analysis team over a seven-year span, was supported by some 80 technical reports (which in turn rested on a vast literature); the technical report is a book of over 800 pages. This book and its supporting reports constitute for this case the third item in the list above. The "main report" is a book for the general reader of some 200 pages; the summary was published separately in a paperback report of about 60 pages. (See Energy Systems Program Group, 1981).

The audiences are important in deciding what to say and how to say it:

Section 10.11. Preparing the Communication Instruments 305

the summary is for busy officials who only want a quick view, the main body is for the officials and members of their staffs who want a full story in nontechnical terms, the appendixes are for technical experts who may want to review details, or perhaps even extend the work at a later time.

The academic scientist accustomed to the space exigencies of today's technical journals may be startled by the redundancy of this approach: the same story is told three times in differing versions, depending on the audience. However, experience shows that academic conciseness will fail to communicate with the key audiences, while this redundant form, if well executed, will be effective.

The other novelty of this outline is the order in which it should be filled in. The experienced analyst does not start at the beginning with the summary; rather, he starts with the appendix material, shaping it so that it will support the main body when it is written. This supporting material should be complete: data, assumption, models, results of calculations, rationales for interpretations, and so on. After completing this foundation, at least in draft form, the analyst proceeds to write the main body of the report, keeping careful watch that its text rests solidly on the supporting material and that it speaks to the client and the members of his staff. At the same time, he has an eye on the exigencies of the summary that will bring the writing to a close. In fact, if the main body is shaped properly, the summary will almost write itself—after the heavy labor that preceded, an unalloyed joy! For example, the reports describing the findings of the global energy analysis mentioned above were written in the sequence just described.

There is another piece of advice that comes from experience: throughout the process of preparing the written report, it is wise to keep in mind the other communication instruments to be used, such as briefings with charts, slide shows, computer demonstrations, and so on (Holling, 1978, Chapter 9, suggests some of the variety that has been useful in ecological work). Thus material such as illustrations, charts, and tables can be worked up early, since these will be useful later in the various media of communication that are adopted. Then the written outlines, structural elements, and carefully worded findings will be all that will need to be added later.

Let us now turn to a more detailed discussion of the content of the main report. It should contain:

Key aspects of the context surrounding the problem (while the audience for the report can be assumed to have a general knowledge of this context, it is usually the case that the appreciation of key aspects of it needs sharpening if the analysis and its findings are to be understood properly).

A statement of the problem as it was finally evolved during the analysis.

The principal facts and assumptions on which the analysis is based.

The alternatives considered (it is very important to take particular care with this section if, as is likely, any of the alternatives considered are novel or likely to be surprising to the client, or if it is necessary to explain why some "obvious" alternatives have not been dealt with).

The key elements in the chain of logic leading to the analysis results (this item is discussed further below).

The findings.

The implications of the findings (this section foreshadows the next one on courses of action).

Possible plans for implementation, their advantages, disadvantages, and consequences.

New demands posed by these plans: resources, reorganization, new outlooks, etc.

Recommendations, if the analysis warrants them.

A careful delineation of the ground covered by the analysis, and, even more important, the limits of the analysis and the ground not covered. (This last point is an essential item of good professional practice, since it marks out the area in which the systems analysis can help the client, as well as the area in which the client must continue to rely on his own judgment and such other information as he has; thus the analyst avoids the pitfall of appearing to have done more than he actually did.)

The scientist entering systems analysis from another field may be surprised that this outline contains only one passing reference to the center of much of his professional interest, the analytic machinery that produced the results, and this reference is in novel language ("the key elements in the chain of logic leading to the analysis results"). There is a good reason for this: Unless the client is very unusual, he is not interested in such details, nor will an attempt to educate him about them be anything but counterproductive. However, there may be a simplified chain of logic based on the analysis details that sheds light on why the results came out as they did; in fact, this is usually the case, at least partially. To present this logical chain will be helpful; it should be included.

The technical appendixes provide the support for the findings presented in the main body of the report; however, they need not repeat the peripheral material from the main body—although they should be full enough to stand pretty well alone. Here the analyst is talking to his professional colleagues, and may use any of the jargon, formulas, or other technical paraphernalia common in his field, although still there may need to be care over communication between colleagues of different basic expertises.

The summary is written for the busy executive, and thus it should be relatively short. However, it must contain a boiled down version of all of the important material in the main body of the report, so that this busy executive gets a rounded picture. Thus it cannot be too short (such as the length of

Section 10.11. Preparing the Communication Instruments

the usual technical-paper abstract), since it must be long enough to exhibit the problem formulation, the structure of the solution, the findings, and the recommendations. It should contain, not only the text needed to convey the central message of the study, but also figures and tables (very carefully chosen and prepared) that will illuminate this message. Careful preparation of this summary is also the best preparation for the oral briefings and discussions that will almost inevitably follow completion of the analysis. Under some circumstances, a summary of the summary may also have to be prepared.

With the written report prepared, the analysis team is ready to turn to other forms of presentation, such as oral briefings, slide shows, movies, articles, and so on. What needs to be done is dictated by the context of the study itself. However, the commonest form of presentation other than the written report is the oral briefing, to which we now turn.

Oral Presentation

The dominant constraint for the oral presentation is time. The scientist used to the leisurely fifty-minute academic lecture will, no doubt, experience considerable shock to find that client executives may expect the findings of a major systems study to be presented in half an hour—or perhaps even as little as 20 minutes! Such short allotments of time are not desirable, but they are not unknown—and the analysts should be prepared to use such brief openings to good effect. In any case, time will be limited, and the analyst who is the spokesman for the team must plan accordingly.

The scientist comfortable with the blackboard talk with chalk in hand, occasionally jotting a note or graph on the blackboard, may feel that this experience will carry over easily to this new situation—but he couldn't be more wrong. The goal is to squeeze as much hard information as possible into a very limited time: Therefore, techniques to achieve this goal are called for, and how to use them must be carefully planned. The central lesson of experience here is that a briefing built around carefully prepared visual aids can be made to meet the need. Such visual aids can be an outline of the main parts of the talk, lists of points, tables, graphs, maps, photographs, charts, and so on. The goal is to give the audience dual impressions of key points, oral and visual.

This visual material can employ a variety of media:

- Stiff chart-boards, set on easels, that the speaker can set down as he finishes with them.
- A large easel-mounted tablet whose pages can be turned by the speaker as he passes from one to the next.
- Transparent plastic sheets that are set horizontally on a projector that throws the images on a vertical screen (sometimes called a "viewgraph").

Slides projected on a screen, with an advancement trigger available to the speaker.

The first three are appropriate for small to medium-sized groups, but do not work very well for large groups, because it is difficult to make them large enough to be seen clearly from the back of the room. Slides are the best option for large groups, but they have the disadvantage that the room must be darkened for them to appear to best advantage; this fact makes them undesirable for smaller groups, where the other options are better (the transparency projector being perhaps the least desirable of the three possibilities). For anything less than the large group, the media list above is in the order of effectiveness and preference.

Chart-boards or tablets set on easels offer another advantage that can be captured simply, and which can be quite important when a complicated story is to be told: It is easy to have two or three easels in use simultaneously. For example, one can be used for an outline of the presentation that remains in view throughout, a device that is helpful for persons not used to keeping a series of logical steps in mind; more importantly, it can also serve to keep the logical pattern of the study before the audience throughout the briefing. When geography, sophisticated technology, or some other element calling for pictorial treatment is involved, an easel can be dedicated to such pictures, which can be in view throughout the portion of the briefing making relevant points. It is easy for the speaker, who has his hands free, to deal with these materials himself—and this procedure has some advantages: it gives the speaker occasional purposeful motion, it allows him to produce the supporting visual evidence at just the moment of its greatest effectiveness, and it allows him to vary the order simply and without complicated instructions to a helper when a question from the audience or some other matter suggests that a variation would be helpful to effectiveness. The analyst with a well-developed set of points to make will find that appropriate ways to use the multiple-easel devise will come to mind easily.

The general idea of multiple easels can be adapted to viewgraph and slide presentations, but it usually calls for more equipment and arrangements than are likely to be available in the usual business or bureaucratic meeting room. However, when the equipment and assistance are available, the device can be effective in these cases.

Before proceeding to discuss the briefing and its charts further, there are three pitfalls that are so common that they must be mentioned here.

The visual material is not legible, particularly to persons sitting at the back. This pitfall produces a doubly negative effect: the persons at the back will not get the message fully, and they will not respect the sense of reality of anyone who ignores so simple a problem. The principle is simple: The visual material must be clearly legible to everyone in the room, and this visibility should be carefully checked before and after the visuals are prepared.

Section 10.11. Preparing the Communication Instruments

The visual material is so crowded with words and other information as to force the audience to make a choice of listening to the speaker or mastering the details of the visuals. This also detracts from the audience's ability to appreciate the message, and reduces their receptivity to it by producing a strain on their attention. The principle again is simple: Keep the visual material simple enough to be comprehended at a glance. In a list of points do not write whole sentences; put down two or three key words that will be explained by what you say. In a table, do not display several dozen numbers that the audience cannot analyze; show in a reduced table the few that are significant to your point. Keep graphs simple, but be sure to label the axes and units clearly.

The speaker prepares a complete text of what he has to say and then drones through it (with the visuals not always well coordinated with the text). The speaker plunged into this pitfall fails to establish the appearance of smooth competence, and distracts the audience by drawing its attention to mechanics.

There are various ways to avoid the last pitfall: The man with a good memory that works well while he is on his feet can leave the manuscript in the file and do splendidly; most, however, hesitate to rely on memory at so crucial a time, and want props to be sure that all points are covered in the right order. For these persons there are three possibilities: (1) if the visuals include enough points—and a well-prepared set usually will—they will serve alone to keep the speaker on his chosen path, allowing him to keep his hands free and giving the audience the feeling of relaxed discipline that makes the best impression; (2) if there are points that must be made that are not on the visuals, and the speaker has chosen to use either board charts or tablet pages, these points can be penciled lightly on the edges of the visuals so as to be clearly visible to the speaker but invisible to the audience; and (3) some inconspicuous papers or cards can be laid on the stand in front of the speaker. These possibilities are listed in order of effectiveness and preference.

These remarks about the oral presentation of the study results may appear to suggest that this is the most difficult part of all—but this lies counter to my experience. One has only to remember that the study has been done, the report and its summary written, and the material developed there available both in hard copy and the team leader's mind to realize that the job is merely one of selecting and shaping; indeed, it is one of the most pleasurable of the systems analyst's tasks, provided he takes pains to learn to do it well.

The project spokesman prepares a careful outline for his briefing, assembles the relevant graphs and charts, identifies the points to be made with each, and goes over the combination several times to establish continuity and completeness to his satisfaction. He is then ready for the final steps of preparation. Here there is a fact from experience that may seem at odds with all of the foregoing admonitions: to achieve a good effect the visual material does not have to be prepared by commercial artists or engineering draftsmen. In fact, many analysts with modest drafting and lettering skills can prepare their own, especially when time is severely limited (as is often the case). Felt pens, which are available in many colors, used on paper that shows a dim set of straight guidelines directly or through from a sheet below, produce effective visuals even in amateur hands when some care is taken. If the speaker prepares his own, he inevitably finds some further refinements emerging from the rethinking forced on him by the preparation process.

Next, with the briefing and its visuals prepared, it is essential to have a practice run in front of a friendly audience—the rest of the analysis team and perhaps others close to the work are the choice. This "dry run" will yield many benefits, not the least of which will be the speaker's confidence in what he is saying and how he has chosen to say it—and how long it will take.

Finally, there are some points to be made about time. If the manager has allotted 30 minutes for the meeting, it would be imprudent to prepare a 30-minute briefing for it. Schedules often do not hold exactly; most meetings spend at least a few minutes on introductions, pleasantries, and orienting remarks; and even a single question from an interested official will ruin so tight a schedule. Thus, the formal talk should be planned to fill only a portion of the time; how much should be left for questions, discussion, and delay is a judgment best left to persons familiar with the administrative setting involved.

If the study deals with an important problem and has reached challenging results, there will be lots of questions and discussion. The speaker can answer some points, but his team should be there to expand on them and to answer ones on which their knowledge is more thorough. It is also well to have some additional charts available that can be used to discuss such questions. Even though one cannot be sure just what questions will be asked, his knowledge of the subject allows him to make some shrewd and accurate predictions, and, if there is material ready to help respond to a significant number of them, the impression of the analysis team's care and thoroughness is greatly enhanced.

If the study deals with an important issue in which many people are involved, an effective first presentation will inevitably call for further briefings—perhaps even dozens of them. Each must be tailored to the group being addressed—and here is where many of the charts that may have been backup for the original audience will come into play, as the special interests of various groups are discussed. The context of the study will suggest what possibilities may emerge—and it will be well to capture their opportunities promptly by having most of the needed material ready, or nearly so, so that the peak of interest prompted by the initial reaction will not be lost before the followup briefings are given.

Concluding Remarks

There are other forms of presentation that may emerge from a major systems study, such as slide shows, movies, articles for the nontechnical press, and so on, but they will not be discussed here, since they are likely to involve experts who can bring appropriate standards to bear on them.

Throughout these processes of preparing the communication instruments, there are key charts and tables that play central roles. Thus the beginning, when technical discussions for the appendix are being prepared, is the time to think about and prepare them. The result will be that they—or simplified versions—will carry through the main body of the report, its summary, and the briefings. Preparing them early will help tie all of the versions together; indeed, all of the later versions can be built around these carefully prepared charts and tables worked out during the preparation of the most technical version of the report.

Finally, throughout the process of preparing the communication instruments, the audience should be uppermost in the minds of the analysis team, and the language and mode of argument should be appropriate to this audience (or, as may be the case, these audiences). This does not mean talking down to these people—they differ from the analysts only in background and training, not in intelligence—but rather using their vocabulary whenever possible, and taking care to define and illustrate the new terms that must be introduced into the explanations. The most important thing to do is to present a line of evidence and logic that will be persuasive to the audience, and that will build their confidence in the reliability and acceptability of the findings; the concepts and language must be the ones appropriate to this purpose, even if they present difficulties to the audience. Thus, our warning here is not against difficulty, but only against difficulty that is not needed for this purpose.

10.12. Additional Analysis

While any thorough systems analysis will have explored its problem area carefully, and performed a variety of analyses, including those to explore the sensitivities of the results, time is always limited and not everything possible will have been done. Thus, during the communication process there will inevitably arise questions that call for additional analysis. The team should anticipate this need, and be prepared to respond to it.

10.13. The Communication Campaign

When the problem dealt with by a systems analysis is relatively simple and there is only one decisionmaker with relevant responsibility and authority, the naive view may be correct: the analyst completes his work, reports its findings to this official in the form most appropriate for him, observes this decisionmaker choose the desirable course of action, and then retires in satisfaction to a well-earned period of relaxation, with congratulations echoing in his ears. Regrettably, life is seldom this simple, particularly when a large-scale problem is in hand and many interests are affected.

Here the analyst cannot just prepare a communication instrument and use it once; rather, he must plan a comprehensive communication campaign. One of the most basic reasons is that in large organizations decisions can be made widely and at many levels of responsibility—and for a major course of action to be effective all of these decisions must be coordinated by being based on a common understanding, not only of what course has been chosen but also of the factors affecting it and how subordinate actions and decisions fit into the scheme. Thus, the analyst will in all probability find that they have many people to communicate with on many levels; instead of one briefing, they may find themselves involved in many, supplemented by a large number of private consultations. This campaign must be planned and resources allotted to it, so that it can proceed effectively.

Two examples will serve to offer some insight; the first, based on a personal experience not documented in the literature, was a systems analysis that occupied a small team about three months and that led to a well defined decision by a high-level advisory committee; the second deals with the study of world energy supply and demand that was mentioned earlier in this chapter (see Section 10.11) and that has been described elsewhere in this handbook (especially Section 3.5).

An Example: Space Surveillance

It is a regrettable fact that the space around the earth contains many pieces of junk—fragments of various sorts from various activities in space—orbiting the earth at various altitudes and in various planes at angles with respect to the plane of the equator. Thus, if one wishes to keep careful watch on some vehicle, either one's own or someone else's, it must be discriminated from other items, a process that makes it necessary to keep careful track of everything.

This need dictates that surveillance instruments be placed about the earth so as to keep watch, and to feed the information from the watch into a central place where it can be sorted, identified, and tracked. A number of years ago the responsible U.S. officials were considering four new potential alternatives for maintaining this surveillance, and a high-level advisory committee was expected to make a recommendation within about 90 days. To support this recommendation, the committee asked a systems analysis team to study the feasibility, operating properties, and costs of the four possibilities, with one of the important costs being the trained manpower that would be required for each alternative.

A team of some eight experts in the major contributing technologies assembled under my leadership to undertake the work. Fortunately, all were familiar with the problem setting, so that the exploratory phases of the analysis were not so time-consuming as is usually the case. This enabled the team to

Section 10.13. The Communication Campaign 313

reach a consensus on the problem outline early, and obtain the agreement with the committee secretariat that work responding to this outline was what would respond to the request. Then, based on this consensus, the analysis plan was laid out. However, owing to the very short time allowed for the work, each expert had to work separately, relying on the team leader for coordination, and each prepared what became a chapter in the appendix to the final report. As these drafts came to the team leader for review, he was able to abstract from them the material needed for the main body of the report, while at the same time preparing visual material and tables that would be used, not only in the main report, but also in its summary and the oral presentation of the results that had already been scheduled for the end of the analysis period.

Thus, in a final interval of only two or three weeks, all of the basic material was completed: the technical appendixes, the text of the main report, the summary, and the visual material for the oral presentation. The whole consisted of some 300 pages, about two thirds of which was technical appendixes, about 75 pages the main report, and about 25 pages of summary. The team leader gave the oral presentation to the advisory committee on schedule, some 40 minutes having been allotted. After about 20 minutes of discussion, the committee agreed on recommendations and sent them forward within a few days.

Some of the good impression created by this analysis was the analysis team's candor, not only about the analysis that had been done and the results achieved, but also about the limitations of the work and the technical problems (there were several) that it had not been able to solve.

To the best of my knowledge, the members of the advisory committee never read the analysis report. However, it served two vital functions: writing it enforced the discipline of getting the results and testing them carefully before presenting them, and later it allowed a number of technical specialists elsewhere to check the work for adequacy before incorporating its findings into their own ongoing investigations.

In this relatively simple case, the time allotted was short, the number of people involved directly was less than ten (although quite a few others were consulted or made small contributions), and the advisory committee acted essentially as a single decisionmaker. During the first half of the analysis period, the team leader was primarily concerned with setting the problem, assembling the analysis team, laying out the analysis plan, and getting the work started; during the latter half of the analysis period, much of his effort was devoted to coordinating, focusing, and carrying out the communications work (working with the team members to improve the appendixes, preparing material for the main report and then the report itself, writing the summary, and preparing the briefing material), these activities also serving to bring the analytic work to a well-defined closure focused sharply on the needs of the client.

An Example: Providing Energy for the Future

This study was conducted at the International Institute for Applied Systems Analysis, Laxenburg, Austria, and began in the summer of 1973. The team leader, Wolf Haefele, summarizes the phases of the study this way: "The study . . . focused for the first two years on understanding and conceptualizing the energy problem. This led to the design of a set of energy models that were subsequently used for developing two scenarios—the principal tool in our quantitative analysis. A preliminary draft of our findings was completed in 1978 and sent out for review. The widespread substantive comments received on this draft were carefully considered in finalizing our report. This book, which was completed in December 1979, reflects our work up to this date" (Energy Systems Program Group, 1981, volume 2, p. xiii). In the meantime, although the team at work at any one time was never very large, some 140 people from more than 20 nations had been involved in the work over a period of seven years. While the volume Haefele refers to here (the 800-page technical report mentioned earlier in Section 10.11) was being given final review and being prepared for the press, work on the 200-page book that occupies the place of the main report was going forward. Both books appeared in the spring of 1981, followed shortly thereafter by the 60-page summary.

In the meantime, other forms of communication had begun with speeches (see, for example, Haefele and Basile, 1979), summary articles (for example, Haefele, 1980), and many consultations, followed by a major communication program with industry and government groups and individuals, involving dozens of oral presentations and hundreds of hours of consultations and cooperative work with teams wishing to incorporate facets of the IIASA findings into their own work—in sum, a communication program too widespread and various to be susceptible of easy summary here. The point, however, is clear: the analytic work has had to be followed up with a major communication campaign leading to activities in implementation, and to changes in perspective, as described in Section 9.3.

Concluding Remarks

This discussion has been intended to underline the importance of having an appropriate communication plan, assigning the effort to carry it out, and pursuing it with the same vigor and attention that was devoted to the analysis. Indeed, such an effort is an essential complement to doing the analytical work; it may consist of writing the report and giving a single oral presentation, as in the space surveillance example, or it may demand the effort of several people over an extended period, as in the case of the IIASA energy study—but without it the work may be wasted.

A communication plan depends so intrinsically on the problem and its administrative setting that there is little guidance of a general sort that can be given beyond urging that it get careful attention and adequate effort.

However, it is important that the analysts preserve a balanced, objective posture throughout. They must appreciate and accept, not only the analysis findings and their implications, but also the concerns of the many persons potentially affected by the new course of action and the additional matters that they must consider.

In the earlier chapters of this handbook, especially Chapter 9, we have stressed the importance of following up in the implementation phase after a course of action has been chosen. Thus, there is little to add here, except to affirm the importance of planning for this work, at least tentatively, so that in the happy event it should have to be done, all will be ready. It may involve additional analyses to respond to new conditions or unforeseen problems, as well as fairly comprehensive consultation interactions as the course of action is pursued.

10.14. Systems Analysis as an Agent of Change

Systems analysis is intrinsically an approach to solving real sociotechnical problems. As Section 2.7 argues, it

... is concerned with theorizing, choosing, and acting. Hence its character is threefold: descriptive (scientific), prescriptive (advisory), and persuasive (argumentative-interactive). In fact, if we look at the fine structure of analytic arguments we see a complex blend of factual statements, methodological choices, evaluations, recommendations, and persuasive definitions and communications. An even more complex structure emerges when we look at the interactions taking place between analysts and different audiences of sponsors, policy makers, evaluators, and interested publics. Moreover, descriptive propositions, prescriptions, and persuasion are intertwined in a way that rules out the possibility of applying a unique set of evaluative criteria, let alone proving or refuting an argument conclusively.

Further, as this handbook shows, and as Section 2.7 states, systems analysis "is a craft. The systems analyst as craftsman is a producer of data, information, and arguments, but also a social change agent. He must influence some people to accept his proposals, and other people to carry them out; he is expected to take some responsibility for implementation." In sum, to use Boothroyd's (1978) suggestive phrase, he is engaged in "articulate intervention" into the activities of sociotechnical programs.

However, the matter goes even deeper: The systems analysis team cannot stand aside from the organizational structure whose problems it is investigating; rather, it is both easy and realistic to argue that the team is itself a substructure in this larger structure—a state of affairs that faces the analyst with deep and important philosophical questions, as well as more practical ones of standards of professional behavior and ethical choice. Such problems of philosophy and ethics as they relate to systems analysis have been explored [notably by Churchman (1978, 1979)], but remain in a sufficiently restless state to make summarizing them inappropriate for this handbook. However, this is not to say that they are not important, or that we should not put discussions of the common views in a leading position if they existed; rather, it is to say that the stream of thinking has not as yet, unfortunately, permeated the community of systems analysts to an extent sufficient to allow us to state a view that represents the center of gravity of this community's outlook. Few would question that problems of philosophy and ethics, as they relate to systems analysis, are very important; they deserve more investigation and wider recognition than they have as yet received.

On the other hand, issues of professional behavior have been given some attention by the systems analysis community, and they are discussed in the next section.

10.15. Guidelines for Professional Behavior

A systems analysis can be judged by its outcome—that is, by whether or not its implemented results improve the operation of the structure that has been subjected to study. By this criterion, the investigation of improving blood availability and utilization described in Section 3.2 can be judged to have been successful, since the new system of managing the supply showed properties that were substantially improved over what was experienced before it was installed.

On the other hand, many system studies deal with problems and issues where the outcome test will be intrinsically denied. For example, the IIASA study of how best to supply the demand for energy for the next 50 years cannot be judged by testing its outcomes as in the blood-supply case. Even if world energy leaders adopt and implement some of its findings, the outcome test will in all probability not be possible, as experience with alternative courses will not be available for comparison. Here we must base our judgment of the quality of the work on criteria relating to the process by which the results were achieved.

Thus, the professional behavior of a systems analyst can be judged by standards internal to his work (relating to the process by which the results are obtained) or external to it (by judging both its outcomes and the analyst's relations to society).

Internal Evaluation

The previous section reminds us that systems analysis must be viewed as a craft. Majone (1980, pp. 26–27) carries the argument forward in this way:

> The systems analyst as craftsman goes through essentially the same operations that the scientist performs; and both scientist and analyst replicate on

an abstract conceptual level what the traditional craftsman or artisan does with material objects and physical tools. The artisan applies his tools to certain materials in order to produce an object fulfilling a given function. The intellectual craftsman (analyst or scientist) works on abstract materials (data, concepts, theories) using different tools and methods (mathematical, logical, "hardware") in order to produce an argument supporting certain conclusions and/or recommendations . . .

The notion of craft is intimately related to that of quality standards. Indeed, the main function of the master craftsman (and also, to some extent, of the patrons and connoisseurs of the craft) is creating standards of quality for the other practitioners. These standards usually remain inarticulate (they are taught more by example than by preaching), but they are nonetheless quite effective in guiding and controlling the work of the craftsmen. Scientific leaders fulfill similar functions for their disciplines, with the support of institutional mechanisms like professional organizations, refereed journals, and academies.

. . . the profession [of systems analysis] is beginning to understand that quality control (in the case of [systems analysis] . . . as of all other intellectual activities) is intimately related to a sophisticated understanding of process.

One of the main purposes of this handbook has been to make quality standards of the craft of systems analysis explicit, and much of the discussion in the previous chapters serves this purpose. It is also useful to examine the pitfalls into which unwary analysts have stumbled, and some of these have been described at appropriate places; Majone and Quade (1980) have compiled a large and very useful collection, together with leads to other literature on this important subject.

Systems analysis is still relatively young, and its standards are still developing. Thus, both the producer and user of systems analysis results would do well to conduct a continuing examination of such work as it emerges in order to refine their understanding and application of such standards.

External Evaluation

Whenever possible, the most important external standard of evaluation for systems analysis results is to compare their implemented outcomes with earlier experience. In fact, in Section 1.4 the list of nine possible steps in a systems analysis study has as its last one "evaluate the results of implementing the chosen courses of action." Thus, from the beginning we have considered this form of external evaluation to be an important step in systems analysis itself, even though it is the step that is so far the least well developed.

Relations with Society

However, society, whose future may well be affected by systems analysis results, has other concerns about systems analysis. Since society is not, in general, well equipped, either to judge whether or not craft standards have been met or to evaluate fully the efficacy of outcomes (particularly when no relatively simple comparisons can be made), it expects this new profession to hew to high standards of professional behavior. Such standards could be imposed by society from outside the profession, or they could be established by the profession itself. And, of course, society's chief concern with such standards is how they might govern the profession's relations to society.

So far, while there have been scattered expressions of concern about such standards by persons not in the profession [see, for example, Miser (1973), which mentions some examples], there has been no movement to impose such standards from without. However, there have been some efforts within the profession, although it cannot yet be said that a consensus has been reached. Thus, all that can be done here is to sketch some of the key strands of thought that have appeared in the writings on this subject by professional leaders in systems analysis.

The need for standards of professional behavior was recognized early: the constitution of the Operations Research Society of America adopted in 1952 stated that one of the objects of the Society was "the establishment and maintenance of professional standards" and in 1954 the Society's second president called for professional and ethical standards (Rinehart, 1954), as did the eleventh president nine years later (Miser, 1963). However, as Section 2.6 describes, the issue lay dormant until 1971, when the Society proposed a tentative set of "guidelines" (Caywood et al., 1971), which failed, however, to achieve a position of authority in the profession. Since then, there has been no effort by a professional group of systems analysts to promulgate standards aimed at acceptance by the profession as a whole, although in the United States there has been a growing, more general concern about the relations of science and technology to society, and, in particular, the appropriate ways for scientists to affect public policies (Chalk, Frankel, and Chafer, 1980). However, some writers have addressed the subject, and several threads have been fairly widely accepted as important.

Openness. Section 10.9 declares that "documentation is as much a part of the professionalism of systems analysis as it is of pure science, and the need to have full and clear records at the end of the project should be recognized and responded to." However, this principle extends beyond the written reports (which were the context in which this statement was made) to other forms of communication and discussion. The systems analyst should be as candid about the weaknesses, arbitrary judgments, and limitations of his work as he is about its findings and their strengths. Curiously, in my experience this does not weaken his case (as the inexperienced might expect); rather, it strengthens his authority as an analyst who knows what he knows, and, more importantly, knows what he does not know. The space-surveillance example of Section 10.13 illustrates the point: "Some of the good impression created by this analysis was the analysis team's candor, not only about the analysis that had been done and the results achieved, but also about the limitations of the work and the technical problems (there were several) that it had not been able to solve." Thus, the professional principle of openness is an inviting one, rather than painful and forbidding.

Sugden and Williams (1978) say that "The analyst must owe some allegiance to intellectual honesty," a loyalty that is almost certainly supported by the principle of openness.

Similarly, a number of writers call in various ways for objectivity—an elusive property hard both to define and achieve. However, candor about one's work and its background can move the communication firmly in this direction, even though the difficulties are severe, as Quade (1982, p. 345) points out:

> It is rarely possible to carry out an analysis of a public issue in such a way that all those who hold various views of the issue involved will consider it fair and objective. Generally, this is unavoidable owing to the nature of the issues, uncertainty and differing views of values . . .
> . . . Openmindedness, willingness to follow evidence wherever it may lead, and readiness to reconsider conclusions when doubts arise are supposedly the marks of a scientist, including the policy scientist. But these are more ideals than marks. Policy analysts are people like anybody else.

The obligations of a profession. Professions stake out claims with society and bind themselves to address classes of problems appropriate to their knowledge and skills; for example, medicine addresses problems of health, law problems of social regulation, systems analysis the operating and policy problems of government and industry and their interaction with society and the environment. In return, society accords these groups certain rights, privileges, and respect—usually including setting standards of training, behavior, and self-regulation. The implication is that society will be better off as a consequence of the intervention of the professions, and that, in turn, the professions will be suitably supported. In sum, there is a mutual obligation.

But this view places a burden on the individual members of the profession; they must not only be loyal to their employers (for the systems analysts, their decisionmaking clients) but also to their profession and, through this profession, to the society that supports it and accords it its privileges. Sugden and Williams (1978, pp. 240–241) present the argument in the context of cost–benefit analysis, but it applies equally well to systems analysis:

> An ethical justification for the decision-making approach to cost–benefit analysis must start from beliefs about how a political system ought to operate. Given particular beliefs of this kind, one can argue that in a democratic community the use of cost–benefit analysis contributes to the good of society; cost–benefit analysis *ought* to be used. The argument begins from the assertion that the role of the analyst is to assist, not simply a decision-maker,

but a decision-making process that has the assent of the community as a whole. In this process the community, as well as the decision-maker and the analyst, is involved. The decision-maker is responsible for making a decision, according to his own lights, but he is responsible to the community. His right to decide stems from the consent of the community, expressed through the political system. The community, then, ought to have the right to call upon the decision-maker to account for his decisions.

In this framework, cost–benefit analysis has a dual function. It assists the decision-maker to pursue objectives that are, by virtue of the community's assent to the decision-making process, social objectives. And by making explicit what these objectives are, it makes the decision-maker more accountable to the community.

This view of cost–benefit analysis, unlike the narrower value-free interpretation of the decision-making approach, provides a justification for cost–benefit analysis that is independent of the preferences of the analyst's immediate client. An important consequence of this is that the role of the analyst is not completely subservient to that of the decision-maker. Because the analyst has some responsibility to principles over and above those held by the decision-maker, he may have to ask questions that the decision-maker would prefer not to answer, and which expose to debate conflicts of judgment and of interest that might otherwise comfortably have been concealed. [Italics in the original.]

Forms of intervention. This handbook has dealt from first page to last with the intervention of systems analysts (scientists from a variety of disciplines) in operations, plans, and policies—and the emphasis throughout has been on careful study, documented as fully as possible and reported as openly as feasible. However, social history of the last two decades has seen scientists (including some calling themselves systems analysts) widely involved in public advocacy in a variety of ways.

Milton Katz of the faculty of the Harvard University Law School has provided the US National Academy of Sciences an illuminating discussion of how this problem has been dealt with by the profession of law (Katz, 1972, pp. 4–5):

When the expert speaks within the scope of his expertise, he may justly claim—and be accorded—a degree of special authority for his opinion. When he speaks as a citizen on a question of general policy, he is entitled—no more and no less than any other citizen—to have his views considered fairly and objectively on the basis of such merit as they may be found to contain. If he should purport to speak as an expert on matters outside the sphere of his special knowledge and skill, he would be assuming a false mantle of authority . . .

. . . The legal profession has had its own difficulties with this . . . problem. It has tried to protect itself—and others—by formalizing the distinction between a legal opinion and a legal brief. When a lawyer renders a legal opinion, he is expected to give a coldly analytical objective opinion, letting the chips fall where they may. When he presents a brief, it is understood that he is making the best argument that he can make under the circumstances, whatever his objective analysis may be. When the stakes are high or when energy, patience and time are short, the distinction may become blurred; but the lawyer's code of professional conduct enjoins him to keep it clear. When he is at his best, he does so.

I do not intimate that the form of the lawyer's distinctions between legal opinion and a statement of policy or between a legal opinion and a legal brief should be adopted by the National Academy of Sciences . . . or its members. I do venture to suggest that the substance of the distinctions may usefully be adapted to the situation of the Academy . . . and its members if and when they address themselves to societal problems and seek to feed their insights into the legislative process or the processes of the executive branch. Such an adaptation would import the gradual evolution and refinement of an accepted practice under which the Academy . . . and its members would regularly take pains to sort out, recognize, and identify the mode in which they are proceeding: whether they are rendering an objective assessment or advocating a cause, and whether they are speaking as experts within their field of special knowledge and competence or as citizens concerning a question of general public policy. Under such a practice, there would be no suggestion that they must restrict themselves to any one mode. But they would be expected to be clear themselves and to make clear to others which mode they were choosing; and they would be expected to recognize the different implications of the respective modes.

If, following Katz, we speak of a "scientific opinion," which states what science knows and (equally important) what it does not know relating to an issue or problem, and a "technical brief," which presents technical evidence aimed at making the most persuasive case for certain conclusions and recommendations, then we can by extension speak of a "systems analysis opinion" and a "technical brief," the latter perhaps containing some of the sort of work that would be considered as systems analysis. With this terminology in mind, it is clear that what we have been talking about throughout this handbook is the systems analysis opinion, as Katz puts it, "a coldly analytical objective opinion, letting the chips fall where they may," even though we recognize the difficulty of reaching so high a standard, as the quotation from Quade above suggests.

This is not to suggest that the systems analyst should not be willing from time to time to help his client with a technical brief; rather, it is to suggest that he and his client should be clear that this is what he is doing—and, most important of all, that the recipients be told clearly that what they are being given is a technical brief.

Alvin Weinberg has introduced the concept of "trans-science" (Weinberg, 1972a) and has summarized his thesis about this concept as follows (Weinberg, 1972b, p. 211):

Many of the questions that lie at the interface between science and politics involve questions that can be stated in scientific terms but that are in principle beyond the proficiency of science to answer. . . . I [have] proposed the term trans-scientific for such questions . . . For example, the biological effect on humans of very low level radiation . . . will probably never be fully ascertained, simply because [of] the huge number of animals required to demonstrate an unequivocal effect . . .

Scientific truth is established by the traditional methods of peer review: only what has value in the intellectual marketplace survives. By contrast, where trans-science is involved, wisdom (rather than truth) must be arrived at by some other mechanisms . .

Society faces many problems involving trans-scientific components, as Weinberg points out, and the experienced systems analyst has not infrequently had to wrestle with how to handle such components in his work, as well as how to report on them.

These considerations led me some time ago to these conclusions for scientists (Miser, 1973, pp. 107–108), equally applicable to systems analysts:

1. The objective scientific opinion—as I have defined it—is the best tool for most situations, be they consultations or studies related to possible courses of action, participation in adversary proceedings, or involvement in trans-scientific debate. In this last category, they can play the fundamentally important roles of defining what is known and what is not, estimating the uncertainties of possible projections, mapping the boundary between science and trans-science, and clarifying the central issues.
2. The role one is playing should be clear; if it is the scientist's role, the norms for this role should be so scrupulously observed as to be obvious; if it is the advocate's role, then the technical brief should make this disclaimer forcefully clear, both when the debate is an adversary one and when it deals with trans-scientific issues.
3. While all agree that the scientist is a citizen, and can participate freely in advocacy and rough-and-tumble debate, nevertheless society will never allow him to divest himself completely of his responsibility as a scientist, and will, fairly or unfairly, allow its judgement of his behavior in these roles to reflect on his dignity as a scientist, and even on the dignity of all scientists. The man who would enjoy the freedom and pleasure of science must pay the tax for this simple fact of life, some of it incurred by his own conduct, some by the conduct of colleagues over whom he has no control.
4. Thus, it is in the long-term best interests of all, of science and for the scientific community as a whole, to try to evolve standards of proper practice for giving advice and advocating public courses of action and for participating in trans-scientific debate. The price of failure could well be a significantly reduced confidence in, and support for, all of science.

The need for standards of professional behavior. The last conclusion just stated about the need for standards of professional behavior for systems analysis work, *ipso facto* aimed at decisions and policies affecting the public

Section 10.15. Guidelines for Professional Behavior

interest, is only part of a much wider recognition by the science and technology communities (Chalk et al., 1980). While some of these communities have made considerable progress, others, including systems analysts, have scarcely begun to think seriously about this matter. However, it is clear that this is one of the important professional issues facing the community of systems analysts today. So far, society has been willing for this community to undertake to regulate itself; however, if it postpones rising to this responsibility for too long, society could well impose regulation from without.

This view raises the question of what the content of such regulation should be—on which there is no agreement presently. It could consist of some principles governing the internal behavior of systems analysts (such as many that are discussed in this handbook), or it could deal with the relations of the profession to society, or perhaps it could contain elements of both. Dror (1971, p. 119) has suggested a challenging set of principles to govern the analyst's relations with his client (although written in the language of policy science, it can be understood to apply to the virtually synonymous systems analysis):

1. A policy scientist should not work for a client whose goals and values, in the opinion of the policy scientist, contradict basic values of democracy and human rights.
2. When the goals and values of a particular client contradict basic beliefs of the policy scientist, the policy scientist should resign rather than help in the realization of goals and values with which he intensely and fundamentally disagrees.
3. The purpose of policy sciences is to help in better policymaking, and not to displace legitimate policymakers and decisionmakers with policy scientists who become "gray eminences." Therefore, policy scientists shall try to preserve and increase the choice opportunities for their clientele, e.g., by always presenting a number of alternatives. In particular, a policy scientist should not hide an alternative because it contradicts his own personal values and preferences.
4. Policy scientists should explicate assumptions and should present clear value-sensitivity analyses, so as further to increase the judgment opportunities for their clientele.
5. A policy scientist should refuse to prepare studies, the sole purpose of which is to provide a supporting brief to an alternative already finally decided upon for other reasons and considerations by his client.
6. Policy scientists should not work for clients who do not provide necessary access to information and opportunities for presentation of studies and their findings.
7. All forms of conflict of interest should be avoided, including utilization of information for private and presentation of recommendations in respect to subject matters in which a policy scientist has a personal and private interest.

However, the experienced analyst will recognize quickly that a code cannot be applied to real situations in simple black-and-white terms. Suppose, for example, that an analyst has completed a major study as a member of a large bureaucratic staff with the support and cooperation of many members of this staff, only to find that the superiors ignore his findings and decide on a course not recommended for reasons that are offensive to the analyst's principles. Under Dror's second ethical principle, should the analyst resign, thus honoring his principles but depriving himself of any chance of effective further influence? Or should he continue in his post, recognizing that, in any large bureaucracy, persistent effort may well effect ultimate change in its direction? Meltsner (1976, p. 288), who has studied the experience of systems analysts in large U.S. Federal government establishments, says that

> ... Persistence does pay, but evidently it is the quality of the persistence that counts. Unfortunately, the quality that is desired is hard to capture in words, but I do know policy analysts who have acquired it.... Staying in the bureaucracy and learning from it can enhance the value of persistence.

There is no simple answer to these questions. Rather, the analyst, using his personal outlooks, knowledge of the situation and its future possibilities, and perhaps taking account of the advice of more experienced analysts, must himself work out the answer most satisfying to him.

There is little help here, however, for the fledgling analysts, who, as Meltsner (1976, p. 282) says:

> ... After their liberal education and professional training, analysts generally start off their careers with a respect for data, norms of openness, objectivity, and full disclosure and with a sense of loyalty to the client.

What the professional of systems analysis is saying to the beginner is that it cannot yet hand him a code of ethics and good practice as a comprehensive guide, and that he must rely to some extent on his own background of ethical training to guide him as he works out solutions to these dilemmas for himself. However, it can offer him the challenge of contributing constructively to the common experience of the profession that will lead to an appropriate code of ethics and good practice, together with a body of experience to illuminate it, that will guide analysts in the future. The scattered beams of light in this handbook will help him in meeting this challenge, perhaps, but the major contributions are yet to be made.

The systems analyst as citizen. A systems analyst is a citizen, and nothing we have said so far should be construed as limiting his rights to exercise the roles of a citizen. However, whether he likes it or not, his public behavior can, and will, reflect on the standing of his colleagues, as my third conclusion above brings out.

The nub of the matter has been put well by Don K. Price (1978, pp. 88–89):

Scientists are citizens too, and ought to be encouraged to participate fully in politics, to which they may make a unique contribution as long as they make clear the limits of their competence as scientists to answer unscientific questions.

10.16. Conclusion

Throughout this handbook we have been at pains to be not only descriptive and illustrative but also, wherever possible, prescriptive and normative whenever the state of the systems analysis art allows us to do so. However, the reader must not carry away the impression that the field has a rigidly prescribed paradigm, either overall or in any of its parts, that must be followed if the work is to be judged by systems analysts as correct and of high quality. Rather, the problem and what is appropriate to it must rule. What is presented here is much of the available menu of possibilities; in the face of the problem situation the analyst must exercise his judgment in choosing what is effective. The worst pitfall of all would be to adhere slavishly to a preconceived outline of work or arbitrarily restricted menu of technical choices.

The material presented in this handbook offers a varied set of possibilities and examples, pointing to challenging directions in which the systems analysis profession may go. This view of where the profession is now thus provides a basis for its continued growth in scope and effectiveness.

References

Agin, Norman I. (1978). The conduct of operations research studies. In *Handbook of Operations Research: Foundations and Fundamentals*. (J. J. Moder and S. E. Elmaghraby, eds.). New York: Van Nostrand Reinhold.

Archibald, R. W. (1979). Managing change in the fire department. In *Fire Department Deployment Analysis: A Public Policy Analysis Case Study*. (Warren E. Walker, Jan M. Chaiken, and Edward J. Ignall, eds.). New York: North-Holland.

Blackett, P. M. S. (1950). Operational research. *Operational Research Quarterly* 1, 3–6.

Boothroyd, Hylton (1978). *Articulate Intervention*. London: Taylor and Francis.

Caywood, Thomas E., et al. (1971). Guidelines for the practice of operations research. *Operations Research* 19, 1123–1258.

Chalk, Rosemary, Mark S. Frankel, and Sallie B. Chafer (1980). *Professional Ethics Activities in the Scientific and Engineering Societies*. Washington, D.C.: American Association for the Advancement of Science.

Churchman, C. West (1978). Philosophical speculations on systems design. In *Handbook of Operations Research: Foundations and Fundamentals*. (J. J. Moder and S. E. Elmaghraby, eds.). New York: Van Nostrand Reinhold.

———(1979). *The Systems Approach and its Enemies*. New York: Basic Books.

Dror, Yehezkel (1971). *Design for Policy Sciences*. New York Elsevier.

Dror, Yehezkel (1971). *Design for Policy Sciences.* New York Elsevier.

Energy Systems Program Group of the International Institute for Applied Systems Analysis, Wolf Haefele, Program Leader (1981). *Energy in a Finite World: Volume 1. Paths to a Sustainable Future; Volume 2. A Global Systems Analysis.* Cambridge, Massachusetts: Ballinger. Also: *Energy in a Finite World: Executive Summary.* Laxenburg, Austria: International Institute for Applied Systems Analysis. [The technical report mentioned in the text is Volume 2, the main report is Volume 1, and the summary is the report published by IIASA.]

Haefele, Wolf (1980). A global and long-range picture of energy developments. *Science* 209, 174–182.

———and Paul Basile (1979). Modeling of long-range energy strategies with a global perspective. In *Operational Research '78.* (K. B. Haley, ed.). Amsterdam: North-Holland.

Holling, C. S. (1978). *Adaptive Environmental Assessment and Management.* Chichester, England: Wiley.

Katz, Milton (1972). Quoted in *News Report* of the National Academy of Sciences, Washington, D.C., 22(6), 4–5.

Majone, Giandomenico (1980). *The Craft of Applied Systems Analysis,* WP-80-73. Laxenburg, Austria: International Institute for Applied Systems Analysis.

———and Edward S. Quade (1980). *Pitfalls of Analysis.* Chichester, England: Wiley.

Meltsner, Arnold J. (1976). *Policy Analysts in the Bureaucracy.* Berkeley, California: University of California Press.

Miser, Hugh J. (1963). Operations research in perspective. *Operations Research* 11, 69–677.

———(1973). The scientist as adviser: The relevance of the early operations research experience. *Minerva* 11, 95–108.

Price, Don K. (1978). Endless frontier or bureaucratic morass? *Daedalus* 107(2), 75–92.

Quade, E. S. (1982). *Analysis for Public Decisions,* 2nd Ed. New York: North-Holland.

Raiffa, Howard (1982). *Policy Analysis: A Checklist of Concerns,* PP-82-2. Laxenburg, Austria: International Institute for Applied Systems Analysis.

Rinehart, Robert F. (1954). Threats to the growth of operations research in business and industry. *Operations Research* 2, 229–248.

Schön, Donald A. (1983). *The Reflective Practitioner: How Professionals Think in Action.* New York: Basic Books.

Sugden, Robert, and Alan Williams (1978). *The Principles of Practical Cost–Benefit Analysis.* Oxford, England: Oxford University Press.

Weinberg, Alvin M. (1972a). Science and trans-science. *Minerva* 10, 209–222.

———(1972b). Science and trans-science. *Science* 177 (21 July 1972), 211.

A Selected Bibliography

There is a diverse and widely scattered literature of systems analysis, as the lists of references for the chapters of this book show, and these lists can help a conscientious scholar to explore the knowledge of and experience with systems analysis. However, a reader who wants an indication of the core literature, or who wishes to make a less ambitious exploration, needs a more focused and limited list that will lead to important, interesting, and useful literature. The short list of books that follows aims to meet this need.

For the purpose of this list, systems analysis is taken to include policy analysis, policy science, and the systems approach.

This bibliography does not list books dealing with the techniques and methods developed by the sciences that contribute to systems analysis; to trace this literature, one can consult the textbooks and standard treatises of these sciences. The second volume of this handbook contains references to the literature dealing with craft issues and procedural choices in systems analysis.

General

Dror, Yehezkel (1968). *Public Policymaking Reexamined.* Scranton, Pennsylvania: Chandler. An early classic overview that advocates a rational approach to policymaking.

Dunn, W, N, (1981). *Public Policy Analysis.* Englewood Cliffs, New Jersey: Prentice-Hall. A structured presentation of the methodology of policy analysis.

House, Peter W. (1982). *The Art of Public Policy Analysis: The Arena of Regulations and Resources.* Beverly Hills, California: Sage. A systematic account of lessons and attitudes emerging from the author's experience in the U.S. federal government.

McKean, Roland N. (1958). *Efficiency in Government Through Systems Analysis.* New York: Wiley. An early description of the systems-analysis approach.

Mood, Alexander M. (1983). *An Introduction to Policy Analysis.* New York: North-Holland. An introductory textbook.

Quade, Edward S. (1982). *Analysis for Public Decisions,* 2nd edition. New York: North-Holland. An updated version of the 1975 classic introduction to systems analysis.

——and W. I. Boucher, editors (1968). *Systems Analysis and Policy Planning: Applications in Defense.* New York: American Elsevier. An early overview of systems analysis, with applications to military planning issues.

Stokey, Elizabeth, and Richard Zeckhauser (1978). *A Primer for Policy Analysis.* New York: W. W. Norton. An introductory overview.

Tribe, Laurence H., Corinne S. Schelling, and John Voss, editors (1976). *When Values Conflict: Essays on Environmental Analysis, Discourse, and Decision.* Cambridge, Massachusetts: Ballinger. An inquiry into environmental issues in systems analysis.

Wildavsky, Aaron (1979). *Speaking Truth to Power: The Art and Craft of Policy Analysis.* Boston: Little, Brown. An overview of the qualitative aspects of policy analysis; includes a number of case descriptions.

Cost–Benefit Analysis

Sassone, Peter G., and William S. Schaffer (1978). *Cost–Benefit Analysis: A Handbook.* New York: Academic Press. An overview for both producers and users of cost-benefit analyses.

Sugden, Robert, and Alan Williams (1978). *The Principles of Practical Cost–Benefit Analysis.* Oxford, England: Oxford University Press. A conscientious introductory textbook.

Thompson, Mark S. (1980). *Benefit–Cost Analysis for Program Evaluation.* Beverly Hills, California: Sage. An introductory overview for both analyst and interested lay reader.

Cases

Allison, Graham T. (1971). *Essence of Decisions: Explaining the Cuban Missile Crisis.* Boston: Little, Brown. An exploration of a governmental decisionmaking process in the light of three conceptual models: The rational actor model, the organizational process model, and the governmental (bureaucratic) political model.

Drake, A. W., R. L. Keeney, and P. M. Morse, editors (1972). *Analysis of Public Systems.* Cambridge, Massachusetts: The MIT Press. A symposium centering its attention on brief accounts of cases.

Energy Systems Program Group of IIASA, Wolf Häfele, Program Leader (1981). *Energy in a Finite World: Vol. 1. Paths to a Sustainable Future; Vol. 2. A Global Systems Analysis.* Cambridge, Massachusetts: Ballinger. Extended discussions of the case described in Chapters 1 and 3 of this handbook.

——(1981). *Energy in a Finite World: Executive Summary.* Laxenburg, Austria: International Institute for Applied Systems Analysis. A conscientious and reasonably comprehensive but brief summary of the findings of the case described in the previous reference and discussed in Chapters 1 and 3 of this handbook.

Goeller, B. F., et al. (1977). *Protecting an Estuary from Floods—A Policy Analysis of the Oosterschelde: Vol. 1. Summary Report,* R-2121/1-NETH. Santa Monica, California: The Rand Corporation. A detailed overview of the findings of the case discussed in Chapters 1 and 3 of this handbook.

———(1983). *Policy Analysis of Water Management for the Netherlands: Vol. 1. Summary Report*, R-2500/1-NETH. Santa Monica, California: The Rand Corporation. A detailed overview of the findings of a major systems analysis study.

Hitch, Charles J., and Roland N. McKean (1960). *The Economics of Defense in the Nuclear Age*. Cambridge, Massachusetts: Harvard University Press. A landmark description of an approach to solving large-scale resource-allocation problems that makes important use of systems analysis.

Holling, C. S., editor (1978). *Adaptive Environmental Assessment and Management*. Chichester, England: Wiley. This book describes a systems analysis approach to managing forests and other ecological systems; it includes an extended description of a case discussed in Chapter 1 of this handbook.

Hopkins, David S. P., and William F. Massy (1981). *Planning Models for Colleges and Universities*. Stanford, California: Stanford University Press. Describes a six-year program of systems-analysis support for planning and decisionmaking at Stanford University, including both the models and the administrative processes that used results from them.

Walker, Warren E., Jan M. Chaiken, and Edward J. Ignall, editors (1979). *Fire Department Deployment Analysis: A Public Policy Analysis Case Study*. New York: North-Holland. Systems analysis applied to fire-response operations; background for the case described in Chapters 1 and 3 of this handbook.

Implementation

Bardach, Eugene (1977). *The Implementation Game: What Happens After a Bill Becomes Law*. Cambridge, Massachusetts: The MIT Press. Taking a case as a point of departure, this book presents an analytical framework for considering the organizational and political realities of implementing a program and achieving its goals.

Doktor, R., R. L. Schultz, and D. P. Slevin, editors (1979). *The Implementation of Management Science*. Amsterdam: North-Holland. A useful collection of essays.

Meltsner, Arnold J., and Christopher Bellavita (1983). *The Policy Organization*. Beverly Hills, California: Sage. Using an actual case as a point of departure, this book deals with how a policy can be implemented in a large organization.

Pressman, J. L., and Aaron B. Wildavsky (1973). *Implementation: How Great Expectations in Washington Are Dashed in Oakland*. Berkeley, California: University of California Press. A study of the difficulties encountered in implementing a policy.

Schultz, R. L., and D. P. Slevin, editors (1975). *Implementing Operations Research/ Management Science*. New York: American Elsevier. A collection of essays.

The Craft of Systems Analysis

Majone, Giandomenico (to appear). *The Uses of Policy Analysis*. New Haven, Connecticut: Yale University Press. This book brings together into a unified conceptual structure a number of strands of thought whose importance for policy and systems analysis is becoming increasingly clear, but which have seldom been discussed together.

———and Edward S. Quade, editors (1980). *Pitfalls of Analysis*. Chichester, England: Wiley. A critical discussion of a variety of errors to be avoided in systems analysis.

Schön, Donald A. (1983). *The Reflective Practitioner: How Professionals Think in Action.* New York: Basic Books. An exploration of the relation between practitioner and client and how it should be structured.

Background in Philosophy

Boothroyd, Hylton (1978). *Articulate Intervention.* London: Taylor and Francis. A philosophy for the practice of systems analysis.

Churchman, C. West (1968). *The Systems Approach.* New York: Dell. An early exploration of the context for systems analysis.

——(1979). *The Systems Approach and Its Enemies.* New York: Basic Books. An exploration of the systems approach to human affairs in contrast to four other powerful approaches (that the author calls its "enemies"): politics, morality, religion, and aesthetics.

Tomlinson, Rolfe C., and István Kiss, editors (1984). *Rethinking the Process of Operational Research and Systems Analysis.* Oxford, England: Pergamon. Selected essays from a symposium.

Critical Assessments

Feiveson, Harold A., Frank W. Sinden, and Robert W. Socolow (1976). *Boundaries of Analysis: An Inquiry into the Tocks Island Dam Controversy.* Cambridge, Massachusetts: Ballinger. A penetrating review of a celebrated case.

Greenberger, Martin, M. A. Crenson, and B. L. Crissey (1976). *Models in the Policy Process: Public Decision Making in the Computer Era.* New York: Russell Sage Foundation. A critical review based on several case histories.

Meadows, Donella, and J. M. Robinson (1984). *The Electronic Oracle: Computer Models and Social Decisions.* Chichester, England: Wiley. A critical review of nine large-scale models and the findings based on them.

Meltsner, Arnold J. (1976). *Policy Analysis in the Bureaucracy.* Berkeley, California: University of California Press. A penetrating review of the activities of policy analysts in the U.S. federal government.

White, Michael J., Michael Radnor, and David A. Tansik, editors (1975). *Management and Policy Science in American Government: Problems and Prospects.* Lexington, Massachusetts: Lexington Books. A useful collection of essays.

Extensions to Organizational Problems

Checkland, Peter (1981). *Systems Thinking, Systems Practice.* Chichester, England: Wiley. After a compact but conscientious survey of the historical development of systems analysis, this book presents, based on substantial practical experience, a highly interactive approach to problems in organizations.

Eden, Colin, Sue Jones, and David Sims (1983). *Messing about in Problems: An Informal Structured Approach to their Identification and Management.* Oxford, England: Pergamon. Another approach, also based on practical experience, to the interactive solution of organizational problems.

History

Blackett, P. M. S. (1962). *Studies of War.* New York: Hill and Wang. This book contains early memoranda on the role of operations research and interesting accounts of World War II experience.

Enthoven, Alain C., and K. Wayne Smith (1971). *How Much Is Enough? Shaping the Defense Program 1961–1969.* New York: Harper and Row. This book describes how systems analysis was used in the U.S. Defense Department.

Morse, Philip M. (1977). *In at the Beginnings: A Physicist's Life.* Cambridge, Massachusetts: The MIT Press. Chapter 7 describes the beginnings of operations research in the United States.

Smith, Bruce L. R. (1966). *The Rand Corporation.* Cambridge, Massachusetts: Harvard University Press. A history of the earliest large research institution that made substantial use of systems analysis; it includes a description of an important early case involving defense policy.

Waddington, C. H. (1973). *OR in World War 2: Operational Research Against the U-Boat.* London: Elek Science. A historical and analytical account of how operations research was used during the second world war.

Miscellaneous

Helmer, Olaf (1983). *Looking Forward: A Guide to Futures Research.* Beverly Hills, California: Sage. An introduction and overview.

Lynn, Laurence E., Jr., editor (1978). *Knowledge and Policy: The Uncertain Connection.* Washington, D. C.: National Academy of Sciences. Essays on the relation of social research to government policy.

Raiffa, Howard (1982). *The Art and Science of Negotiation.* Cambridge, Massachusetts: Harvard University Press. A structured exploration illustrated with many examples.

Rossi, Peter H., and Howard E. Freeman (1982). *Evaluation: A Systematic Approach,* 2nd edition. Beverly Hills, California: Sage. An introductory textbook.

Struening, Elmer L., and Marilynn B. Brewer (1983). *The University Edition of the Handbook of Evaluation Research.* Beverly Hills, California: Sage. An exposition of key ideas and knowledge in its field.

Author Index

A

Abrahamse, A. F., 89, 96, 115, 246
Ackoff, R. L., 53, 55, 55n, 64, 121, 128, 147, 152, 169, 187, 188
Aesop, 251
Agin, N. I., 282, 291, 325
Al, J., 278
Allison, G. T., 118, 147, 242, 243, 245, 267, 278, 328
Anderson, P. 151
Anthony, R. N., 255, 262, 278
Archibald, K. A., 252, 276, 278
Archibald, R. D., 276, 277
Archibald, R. W., 213, 216, 274, 276, 278, 282–283, 285, 325
Aristotle, 37
Arnoff, E. L., 55, 55n, 64
Arrow, K. J., 44, 64, 179, 188
Attaway, L. D., 228, 245

B

Bardach, E., 250, 252, 271, 272, 273, 277, 278, 329
Basile, P., 314, 326
Bellavita, C., 329
Beltrami, E. J., 272, 278
Berman, P., 252, 274n, 275, 278
Bigelow, J. H., 89, 96, 100, 102, 115, 116, 246
Blackett, P. M. S., 35–40, 41, 57, 58, 64, 291–292, 325, 330
Blum, E., 203, 205, 217

Bolten, J. G., 89, 96, 100, 102, 115, 116, 246
Bonder, S., 54n, 64
Boothroyd, H., 34, 41, 64, 213, 216, 220, 245, 315, 325, 330
Boruch, R. F., 275, 279
Boucher, W. I., 56, 66, 148, 218, 245, 246, 278, 328
Bowen, K. C., xvi, 197, 198, 211, 212, 216, 217, 218, 219ff, 230, 234, 235, 245, 247
Braybrooke, D., 48, 64
Brewer, G. D., 197, 200, 217, 218, 274, 278
Brewer, M. B., 277, 280, 331
Brill, E. D., Jr., 187, 188
Brodheim, E., 70, 71, 72, 73, 116
Brooks, H., 31, 49, 64
Brown, K., 170
Brown, S., 202, 217, 273, 278
Bruckmann, G., 192, 193, 218
Bullock, A., 165, 169
Bush, R. P., 206, 217

C

Catlett, L., 109, 116, 266, 278
Caywood, T. E., 318, 325; *see also* ORSA Ad Hoc Committee on Professional Standards
Chafer, S. B., 318, 325
Chaiken, J. M., 80, 84, 85, 116, 174, 176, 189, 203, 204–205, 218, 278, 280, 325, 329
Chalk, R., 318, 323, 325
Chang, S., 187, 188

Author Index

Checkland, P. B., xvi, 12, 31, 121, 147, 151*ff*, 154, 162, 165, 169, 171, 182, 194, 200, 217, 245, 245*n*, 250, 278, 330
Chesler, L. G., 98, 116
Churchman, C. W., 55, 55*n*, 64, 152, 154, 159, 169–170, 255, 278, 298, 316, 325, 330
Cook, R. I., 165, 170
Cooke, M. 39
Crenson, M., 194, 195, 214, 217, 330
Crissey, B., 194, 195, 214, 217, 330
Cyert, R. M., 242, 243, 245, 267, 278

D

Dalkey, N. C., 24, 31
Dantzig, G. B., 40–41
Davis, H. R., 275, 278
de Ferranti, D. M., 89, 96, 116, 246
DeHaven, J. C., 89, 96, 100, 102, 115, 116, 246
de Neufville, R., 269, 278
DeWeerd, H. A., 202, 217
Dewey, J., 161, 170
Doktor, R., 278, 279, 329
Dorfman, R., 41, 64
Drake, A. W., 195, 217, 328
Dror, Y., 27, 31, 47, 64, 179, 188, 224, 238, 239, 245, 323, 324, 325, 327
Dunn, W. N., 130, 147, 173, 188, 225, 239, 245, 327

E

Eden, C., 245, 245*n*, 330
Edie, L. C., 40, 41, 64
Eilon, S., 133, 147, 179, 188
Einstein, A., 19
Elmaghraby, S. E., xiii, 65, 195, 218, 278, 279, 325
Elmore, R. F., 252, 280
Emerson, D. E., 212, 217
Energy Systems Program Group, 7, 31, 110, 111, 114, 115, 116, 184, 188, 200, 202, 217, 304, 314, 326, 328
Enthoven, A. C., 39*n*, 331

F

Fairley, W. B., 64
Feiveson, H. A., 330
Feldstein, M. S., 43, 64
Feyerabend, P., 62, 64
Findeisen, W., xvi, 117*ff*
Fischhoff, B., 142, 148, 227, 245
Fisher, G. H., 225, 245
Fisher, R., 276, 279
Forrester, J. W., 96, 116, 206
Frankel, M. S., 318, 325
Freeman, H. E., 277, 280, 331

G

Gass, S. I., 145, 148
George, A. L., 242, 245
Giauque, W. C., 253–254, 279
Goeller, B. F., 89, 90, 93, 94, 95, 96, 98, 103, 105, 106, 116, 120, 148, 211, 214*n*, 214–216, 217, 220, 231, 245, 246, 328, 329
Gorham, W., 56, 64
Greenberger, M., 194, 195, 214, 217, 330
Guttentag, M., 277, 279
Gvishiani, J. M., 249, 279

H

Haefele, W., 31, 314, 326; *see also* Energy Systems Program Group
Haley, K. B., 31, 279
Hall, A. D., 160, 170
Hammond, J. S., 258, 279
Hammond, K. R., 165, 170, 235, 246
Hanika, F. de P., 169
Hargrove, F., 252, 279
Hatry, H. P., 177, 188, 242, 246
Hedersterna, A., 240, 246
Helmer, O., 31, 194, 198, 199, 200–201, 202, 217, 273, 279, 331
Heuer, F. J. P., 89, 96, 116
Hildebrandt, S., 18, 31, 250, 251, 252, 279
Hitch, C. J. 39*n*, 42–43, 43*n*, 56, 64, 142, 148, 158, 170, 181, 188, 213, 217, 220, 221, 223, 227, 246, 329
Hoag, M. W., 44, 64
Hoelzl, A., 247, 280
Holling, C. S., 11, 12, 14, 31, 191, 194, 200, 207, 211, 217, 220, 233–238, 246, 303–304, 305, 326, 329
Hoos, I. R., 27, 31, 166, 170, 252, 279
Hopkins, D. S. P., 329
Hopkins, L. D., 187, 188
House, P. W., 145, 148, 214*n*, 217, 327
Hovey, H. A., 173, 188
Hume, D., 63
Huysmans, J. H. B. M., 250, 279

I

Ignall, E. J., 80, 84, 85, 116, 174, 179, 189, 203, 204–205, 207, 217, 278, 280, 325, 329
Inbar, M., 242, 246

J

Jenkins, G. M., 156, 162, 169, 170
Jennergren, L. P., 227, 241, 246
Jones, S., 245, 245*n*, 330

Author Index

K
Kahn, H., 40, 65, 155, 156, 158, 170, 184, 188
Kaplan, M. F., 246
Katz, M., 320-321, 326
Keen, P. G. W., 242, 243, 246
Keeney, R. L., 129, 143, 144, 148, 179, 188, 195, 217, 221, 227, 230, 241, 246, 328
Kemeny, J. G., 19, 31
Kicker, W. J. M., 242, 246
Kimball, G. E., 37, 38n, 40, 40n, 55, 59, 65
Kirkwood, T. F., 116, 246
Kiss, I., xvi, 219ff, 330
Klitz, J. K., 165, 170
Kneese, A. V., 272, 279
Koestler, A., 151, 170
Kolesar, P., 203, 205, 207, 217
Koopman, B. O., 37, 40, 40n, 65
Koopmans, T. C., 41, 65

L
Lanchester Prize Committee, 65
Larson, M. S., 36, 39, 65
Lasswell, H. D., 200
Levien, R. E., 49n, 65, 170
Levine, R. A., 272, 279
Lindblom, C. E., 48, 62n, 64, 65, 242, 243, 246
Linstone, H. A., 201, 218
Lowry, I. S., 10, 31
Luft, H. J., 226, 246
Lynn, L. E., Jr., 27, 31, 118, 148, 244, 246, 278, 331

M
Madansky, A., 240, 246
Majone G., xvi, 27, 31, 33ff, 34, 37, 47, 60n, 63, 65, 122, 132, 139, 148, 170, 181, 189, 196, 205, 207, 218, 243, 246, 278, 279, 297, 302, 316-317, 317, 326, 329
Mann, I., 40, 65, 184, 188
Manne, A. S., 51n, 52, 62, 65
March, J. G., 242, 243, 245, 267, 278, 279
Massy, W. F., 329
Mazmanian, D., 271, 280
McCloskey, J. F., 65
McKean, R. N., 39n, 43n, 45, 56, 64, 65, 142, 148, 181, 188, 221, 227, 246, 327, 329
McLeod, J., 145, 148, 214n, 217
Meadows, D., 145, 148, 192, 193-194, 195, 211, 212, 218, 330
Medawar, P. B., 162, 170
Meltsner, A. J., 253, 279, 324, 326, 329, 330
Mintzberg, H., 118, 148, 252, 279
Miser, H. J., xv, 1ff, 16, 31, 53, 65, 249ff, 281ff, 318, 322, 326

Mishan, E. J., 142, 148, 225, 246
Mitroff, I. I., 60, 60n, 65
Moder, J. J., xiii, 65, 195, 218, 278, 279, 325
Mood, A. M., 38, 38n, 65, 120, 129, 141, 148, 195, 218, 230, 246, 328
Morse, P. M., 37, 38n, 40, 40n, 41, 53, 55, 58, 59n, 65, 195, 217, 328, 331
Mosteller, F., 38, 64, 65, 206, 217

N
Nagel, S. S., 65, 178, 189, 212, 218
Neef, M., 178, 189, 212, 218
Newhouse, J. P., 213, 216, 275, 278

O
Olson, M. L., 239, 247
Optner, S. L., 159, 170
ORSA Ad Hoc Committee on Professional Standards, 60, 66, 318

P
Paxson, E. W., 211, 216, 218
Peterson, R. E., 268, 279
Petruschell, R. L., 116, 246
Pindyck, J., 69
Pogson, C. H., 156, 170
Pollock, S. M., 166, 170
Popper, K. R., 207, 218
Prastacos, G. P., 70, 71, 72, 73, 116
Pressman, J. L., 252, 272, 280, 329
Prest, A. R., 45, 66
Price, D. K., 324, 326

Q
Quade, E. S., xv, 1ff, 26, 31, 56, 66, 67ff, 117ff, 139, 148, 154, 156, 160, 164, 165, 169, 170, 171ff, 189, 191ff, 196, 198, 218, 219ff, 223, 245, 246, 247, 249ff, 278, 279, 317, 319, 321, 326, 328, 329

R
Rabinovitz, F., 252, 280
Radnor, M., 330
Raiffa, H., 129, 143, 144, 148, 154, 170, 177, 179, 188, 189, 211, 218, 221, 230, 246, 247, 276, 280, 300, 303, 326, 331
Rakhmankulov, V., 170
Rapoport, A., 154, 170
Ravetz, J. R., 35n, 66
Rein, M., 118, 148, 239, 247, 280
Richardson, J., 192, 193, 218
Richels, R. G., 51n, 52, 62, 65

Riecken, H. W., 138, 148, 275, 280
Rijkswaterstaat, 109, 116
Rinehart, R. F., 318, 326
Robinson, J. M., 145, 148, 193-194, 195, 211, 212, 218, 330
Rogner, H.-H., 247, 280
Roos, A., 278
Rossi, P. H., 277, 280, 331
Rowen, H. S., 27, 32

S

Sabatier, P., 271, 280
Salasin, S., 275, 278
Samuelson, P. A., 41, 64
Sassin, W., 219, 247, 266, 280
Sassone, P. G., 328
Schaffer, W. S., 328
Schelling, C. S., 31, 32, 66, 328
Schlaifer, R., 211, 218
Schön, D. A., 18, 32, 286-290, 326, 329
Schrattenholzer, L., 247, 280
Schultz, R. L., 250, 252, 278, 279, 280, 329
Schultze, C. L., 272, 279
Schwartz, S., 246
Schwarz, B., xvi, 202, 218, 219*ff*
Sen, A. K., 97, 116
Seo, K. K., 268, 279
Shakespeare, W., 249
Shakun, M. F., 118, 148
Shils, E., 125, 148
Shubik, M., 197, 200, 217, 218
Simon, H., 181, 189, 222, 242, 243, 247, 267, 279
Sims, D., 245, 245n, 330
Sinden, F. W., 330
Singleton, D. W., 79, 80, 83, 86, 87, 89, 116
Slevin, D. P., 250, 252, 278, 279, 280,
Smith, B. L. R., 54, 56, 66, 79, 80, 83, 86, 89, 116, 331
Smith, K. W., 331
Socolow, R. W., 330
Soderbaum, P., 237, 247
Solow, R., 41, 64
Specht, R. D., 194, 218
Stallybrass, O., 165, 169
Stanton, R., 278
Starling, G., 239, 247
Starr, M. K., 246
Stokey, E., 148, 328
Stone, L. D., 40n, 66
Struening, E. L., 277, 279, 280, 331
Sugden, R., 45n, 66, 142, 148, 172, 173, 182, 189, 221, 225, 247, 319, 319-320, 326, 328
Svedin, U., 218
Szilard, L., 37n

T

Tansik, D. A., 330
Taylor, F. W., 38n, 39
Thomas, M. A., 198, 218
Thompson, M. S., 328
Thornethwaite, C. W., 41, 66
Tomlinson, R., xvi, 249*ff*, 330
Toulmin, S., 33, 34, 37n, 53, 55, 66, 207, 218
Trappl, R., 169
Trefethen, F. N., 65
Tribe, L. H., 27, 31, 32, 66, 230, 247, 328
Tukey, J. W., 37, 66
Turoff, M., 201, 218
Turvey, R., 45, 66

U

Ury, W., 276, 279
U. S. Senate, 251, 280

V

Van Horn, C., 252, 280
Van Meter, D., 252, 280
Veen, M. A., 133, 149, 187, 189
Vickers, G., 160, 165, 170
Villoria, R. L., 276, 278
Voss, J., 31, 32, 66, 328

W

Waddington, C. J., 37, 41, 58, 66, 331
Wagner, H. M., xiii, 55, 55n, 60, 60n, 63, 66
Walker, W. E., 79, 80, 81, 83, 84, 85, 86, 87, 116, 125, 133, 149, 174, 176, 187, 189, 203, 204-205, 207, 217, 218, 242, 244, 247, 278, 280, 325, 329
Weehuizen, J. W., 89, 96
Weinberg, A. M., 321-322, 326
Weyant, J. P., 51n, 52, 62, 65
White, D. J., 29, 32, 118, 149, 211, 218, 230, 247
White, M. J., 330
Wildavsky, A., 47n, 66, 252, 272, 279, 328, 329
Wildhorn, S., 278
Williams, A., 45, 45n, 47, 66, 142, 148, 172, 173, 182, 189, 221, 225, 247, 319, 319-320, 326, 328
Williams, W., 252, 280
Wittrock, B., 218
Wohlstetter, A., 54, 174, 189
Wolf, C., Jr., 252, 274n, 280
Woolsey, R. E. D., Jr., 253-254, 279
Wright, S. R., 277, 280

Z

Zeckhauser, R., 148, 328
Zeleny, M., 246
Zuckerman, S., 166-167, 170

Subject Index

A

Agent of change, *see* Change agent
Alternatives, 16, 119, 120–123, 126, 127, 129, 132–133, 140–145, 158, 161, 165, 169, 171–189, 196, 221, 238, 242, 252, 272, 298–299, 302, 305–306
  availability of resources for, 269
  chosen by satisficing, 222–223
  comparing, *see* Ranking
  consequences of, 208–212, 224
  controversial, 299
  decision on, 219
  designing, 182–188, 298–299
  desirable properties of, 185–186
  displayed on scorecards, 231–236; *see also* Scorecards
  feasible, 171, 226, 252, 268, 298, 299
  fine tuning, 187
  for flood protection, 6, 89–92
  for forest-pest control, 11, 234–237
  for future energy, 8, 113–114
  for housing assistance, 9
  generating, 186–187
  impractical, 298
  in cost–benefit analysis, 224–227
  in cost-effectiveness analysis, 227–229
  in decision analysis, 229–230
  screening, xiii, 93, 122, 123, 124, 126, 133, 187, 222–223, 226, 230
  step-by-step rejection of, 187–188
Analysis, *see also* Systems analysis
  a fortiori, 39–40, 187, 239
  contingency, *see* Contingency analysis
  cost–benefit, *see* Cost–benefit
  cost-effectiveness, *see* Cost-effectiveness
  cross-impact, 199–200
  quick-and-dirty, 284
  sensitivity, *see* Sensitivity analysis
Analyst, systems, *see* Systems analysis
Apprehension, 243
Architecture, social, 151
Attributes, 119; *see also* Consequences

B

BARCON (Barrier Control Project), 109
Behavior, professional, *see* Guidelines
Benefit–cost, *see* Cost–benefit
Blood
  availability rate for, 71–72
  demand for, 71, 72–73
  distribution system for, 4, 76–77
  implementing distribution system for, 75–79, 255–256
  long-dated inventories of, 76, 77
  objective for distribution of, 174, 179–180, 182
  outdate rate for, 3, 4, 69, 180
  penalty cost for shortage of, 74
  retention units of, 73
  rotation units of, 73
  scheduling factor for, 73
  shortage rate for, 3
  short-dated inventories of, 76, 77
  stock-dated inventories of, 76, 77

338　　Subject Index

Blood (cont.)
　supply and use, 2–4, 12–13, 17, 29, 67–68, 68–79, 146, 174, 175, 179–180, 182, 184, 196, 213, 255–256, 257, 290, 316
　transferable distribution system for, 256
　usage of, 71, 72, 73
　utilization rates for, 4, 69, 72–74, 78
Boundaries, 122–123, 137, 152, 153, 159, 160
Brief
　legal, 320–321
　systems-analysis technical, 321, 323
　technical, 321, 322
British Columbia, University of, 11
Brookings Institution, The, 56

C

Calibration, see Models, calibrating
Capta, 164
Cases, xiii–xiv, 2–12, 67–116, 257–265
　bibliography of, 328–329
　blood supply, 2–4, 68–69; see also Blood, supply and use
　coal-mine transport, 257–259
　energy demand and supply, 7–8, 109–115; see also Energy for the future
　fire protection, 4–6, 79–89; see also Fire protection
　flood control, 6–7, 89–109; see also Flood protection
　forest-pest control, 11–12; see also Forest-pest control
　housing assistance, 8–10; see also Housing assistance
　plant consolidation, 291, 293
　provisioning spare parts, 260–265
　space surveillance, 312–313, 318–319
　steel mill operations, 253–254, 293
　tank-car dispatch 293, 297
CBA, see Cost–benefit analysis
Change, systems analysis as contributor to, 282
Change agent, 63
　in fire-protection organizations, 285
　in implementation, 275–276
　systems analyst as, 62–64, 282–283, 315–316
Citizen
　scientist as, 322
　systems analyst as 324
Clients, 16, 156, 158–159, 161, 162, 166, 167; see also Decisionmakers
　reflective, 289–290
Climate of situation, 157
Coal-mine transport, 257–259
　computer program for, 258–259
Committee as source of advice, 28, 194, 199–200; see also Delphi

Communicating, 281; see also Scorecards
　aid to, 244
　briefings for, 307–310
　campaign for, 311–315
　candor in, 313
　during analysis, 123, 124, 125–126, 296–297
　findings, 16, 122–123, 126, 243–245, 295–296, 300, 302–303, 303–315
　instruments for, 303–315
　limits of analysis, 306, 313
　media for, 304, 305, 307
　plan for, 314–315; see also Plan, analysis
　reporting experiences in, 244–245
　reports as media for, 304–307
　results of blood supply and use analysis, 76
　results of energy-supply analysis, 304, 314
　results of flood-protection analysis, 96–107
Comparing alternatives, see Ranking
Computer modules
　for blood-distribution system, 78, 256
Computer systems, 259–265
　control in, 260, 262, 264–265
　human elements in, 260–265
　inversion principle for, 260
Computer use, see Cases, Models, computer
Conflict of interest, 323
Consequences, 119, 122–123, 126, 127, 130, 133, 135–140, 171, 173, 185, 187, 221; see also Attributes, Effects, Impacts, Indicators, Measures of performance, Outcomes, Results
　displayed on scorecards, 231–236
　in cost–benefit analysis, 224
　models as predictors of, 120, 122–123, 136–137, 185, 191–194, 196, 207, 210–211
　predicting, 208–212, 213, 226
Constraints, 63, 122–123, 124, 125, 127, 131–132, 160–161, 164, 168, 171–189, 238, 284,
　by converting objectives, 179, 222
　environmental, 159
　feasible, 131
　in energy-system analysis, 110–111, 113
　in decision setting, 284
　political, 47–48, 110, 268
　role as objectives of, 171, 181
　to control side effects, 241
Contexts, 2–12, 16, 33, 122–123, 126, 137, 156, 208–210, 295, 305; see also Environment, Decision situation
　establishing, 208–210
　organizational, 282–286
Contingency analysis, 211; see also Sensitivity analysis

Subject Index

Contract
  reflective, 289–290
Controller in a computer system, 261, 264–265
Controversy, 299
Coordinator, 159
Cost–benefit, *see also* Cost-effectiveness
  analysis, 21, 36, 44–46, 96–97, 141–142, 143, 179, 182–183, 224–227, 229, 319–320
  bibliography, 328
  comparison, 210
  criteria, 220, 221, 224–227, 233, 238
  measures, 142, 144
  objections to, 225–226, 239
Cost-effectiveness, 154, 179; *see also* Cost-benefit
  analysis, 23, 36–37, 44, 141–142, 227–229
  as measure of value, 228–229
  criteria, 221, 227, 238
  measures, 142, 144
  objections to, 228–229
  scale of effort in, 228–229
  tradeoffs, 177
Costs, xiii, 135, 154, 169
  as foregone opportunities, 135
  displayed on scorecards, 231–236
  opportunity, 181
Craft
  and technical rationality, 287–288
  in data analysis, 205
  in operations research, 37, 40, 59, 60–61
  of systems analysis, xiii–xiv, 2, 20, 29–30, 54, 60–61, 63, 67, 122, 145–146, 289, 290, 315, 316–317, 329–330
  standards, *see* Guidelines 208
Criteria, 119, 122–123, 127, 130–131, 140, 142, 154, 220–222, 223–224, 230, 243
  cost–benefit, 224
  cost-effectiveness, 227
  defined, 220
  multiple, 243
  tied to objectives, 222

D

Data, 161, 163, 164, 178, 205, 324
  analysis, 123
  collection, 123, 164, 297–298
  for conversion to information, 205, 297
  for forecasting, 134, 209
  rough, 37–38
Decision, *see also* Decisionmakers
  as simplification for change, 282
  embedded in process, 254–255
  guidance for, 219–245
  processes, 241–242
  setting, *see* Decision situation
  single or dispersed, 282

Decision analysis, 143–144, 229–230; *see also* Systems analysis, partial
  disadvantages of, 230
Decisionmakers, xii, 1–2, 117–118, 127, 132–133, 143–144, 156, 158–159, 161, 162, 166, 167, 171, 173, 196, 213–214, 230; *see also* Decisionmaking
  as problem givers, 153
  as rational actors, 118, 243
  as suboptimizers, 223
  for flood protection, 93
  formulating findings for, 302–303
  guidance for, 219–245
  in continuum of problems, 254
  in Delphi, 200
  in gaming, 199
  internal, 199
  loyalty to, 324
  model orientation for, 216
  multiple, xii, 13, 18, 45–46, 118, 141, 144, 146–147, 178, 199, 219, 220, 282, 312
  obligations to society of, 319–320
  perspectives of, 283
  problem appreciations of, 290–291
  properties desired by, 185–186, 230
  relations with, 16, 58–59, 123–126, 128, 212, 215, 227, 243–245, 258–259, 272, 282, 284–285, 289–290, 292, 295, 301, 323
  role in blood distribution, 256
  role in decision analysis, 229–230
  role in fire protection, 84–85
  role in implementation, 253, 255–268
  role in problem formulation, 152
  role of, 159
  secondary, 239
  use of scorecards by, 232
  values of, 122, 130–131, 143, 220, 229, 236–239, 283, 323
  value judgements of, 177, 243
  value sensitivity of, 179
Decisionmaking, *see also* Decisionmakers
  as weighing benefits against costs, 224
  process, 255, 283
Decision seminar, 200
Decision situation, *see also* Contexts
  apprehensive-man view of, 243
  basic questions about, 283–286
  constraints in, 284
  influences in, 283
  nature of, 283
  organization-process view of, 243
  pluralistic, *see* Decisionmakers, multiple
  political paradigm for, 243
  process-oriented view of, 243
  properties of, 283–284
  rational-actor model for, 118, 243

Decision theory, 44, 211, 240
Delphi, 199, 200–201, 209
DFL (Dutch guilders), 99n
Discount rate in cost benefit analysis, 225
Documentation, 20, 27–28, 145, 162, 301, 318
 in modeling, 206
Dominance, 187, 192
Dry run, 310

E

Effects, 119, see also Consequences
 distributional, 225, 229
 side, 169, 241
 spillover, 135, 169, 225, 229, 231–236
Eisenhower, D. E., 166
Energy for the future, 7–8, 13, 17, 68, 109–115, 146–147, 175, 182, 183–184, 184–185, 200, 202, 209, 209–210, 219, 238, 242, 265–266, 298, 314, 316
 analysis of, 113–114
 assumptions about, 110–111
 conclusions about, 112–113, 114–115
 constraints on, 182
 demand for, 112, 114
 further studies of, 266
 in European Communities, 219
 judgments models for, 200
 objectives for, 175–176
 scenarios for, 202, 209–210, 238, 314
 supply of, 112–113
Engineering, 19–20
 artifacts in systems analysis, 20
Environment, 156, 159–161, 169; see also Contexts
 appreciative, 160
 legislative, 160
 management, 200, 233
Equity, xiii, 24, 130, 212
Ethics
 code of, see Guidelines, for ethical choice
 issues in social experiments, see Experiments, ethical issues in
Evaluation, 17, 277, 331
 external, 316, 317
 internal, 316–317
 of implementation results, 123, 125, 145, 277
 program, 242, 277
 research, 277
Evidence, 61
Examples of systems analysis, see Cases, Systems analysis, applications of
Exogenous factors, 137, 140
Experiments, 193
 as part of the modeling process, 137–138
 by computer modeling, 194
 ethical issues in, 275
 in implementation, 274–275
 methodological problems in, 275
 pseudo, 196
 social, 8–10, 137–138, 178, 212–213, 274–275

F

Feasibility, 120–121, 122
 implementation, 238–239
 political, xiii, 236–239, 268
Figure of merit, 141; see also Indicator
Fire protection, 4–6, 17, 68, 79–89, 146, 174, 174–175, 176, 193, 196, 213, 257, 290
 firehouse-site evaluation model for, 85
 implementation of results for, 86–88, 257
 measures of performance for, 81
 objectives of, 174, 174–175
 organizations for, 285
 parametic allocation model for, 84–85
 proxy measures of performance for, 81, 175, 176
 recommendations in Wilmington for, 85–86
 travel distances for, 82–84; see also Square-root law
 travel times for, 81–84, 175
Flexibility, 186
 in computer-system design, 262, 263
 of an implementation program, 257
Flood protection, 6–7, 17, 68, 89–109, 130, 141, 146, 175, 176, 177–178, 183, 193, 208, 212, 213, 265–266, 274, 303
 alternatives for, 89–92
 analysis stages for, 92–96
 conclusions on, 104, 105–108
 decisionmakers for, 93
 decision on, 108–109
 designing cases for, 93
 impacts of alternatives for, 92, 93–96, 99–107, 177–178
 models for, 96
 objectives in, 175, 176
 post-decision analyses for, 266, 274
Forecasting, xiii, 133–135, 137, 208–210, 215; see also Contexts
 approaches, 134–135
 by computer models, 193–194
Forest-pest control, 11–12, 13, 14, 17, 233–237, 303–304
Forums of competition, 34

G

Games, 137; see also Gaming
 operational, 197
 political, 270

Subject Index

Gaming, 135, 194, 195, 197–199, 200; *see also* Games
  described, 197
  example of, 198
  genesis of, 197–198
GDP (Gross Domestic Product), 178
Genealogy of issues, 33–35
Goals, 128, 165, 169, 181; *see also* Objectives
  unclear, 14, 155
GYNBP (Greater New York Blood Program), 69; *see also* Blood
Guidelines
  for ethical choice, xiii, 315–316, 324
  for professional behavior, 59–62, 315–325

H

Hard systems, *see* Problem, hard
Harvard University Law School, 320
HBB (Hospital Blood Bank), 3, 69; *see also* Blood
Honesty
  intellectual, 319
Housing assistance, 8–10, 17, 212; *see also* Experiments, social
  experimental results for, 9–10
  judgments about program extension for, 10
HUD (U. S. Department of Housing and Urban Development), 8, 80

I

IFORS, *see* International Federation of Operational Research Societies
IIASA, *see* International Institute for Applied Systems Analysis
Impacts, 16, 126, 171, 216, 231; *see also* Consequences
  community, 231
  of flood-control alternatives, 6, 92, 93–96, 99–107
Implementation, 16–17, 117, 125, 144–145, 186, 187, 236, 242, 243, 249–277, 290, 315
  activities, 295
  administrative strategy for, 272
  analysis, 273–274
  as missing link, 252
  bibliography for, 329
  concerns, 253–255
  consequences of, 208
  coping after decision with, 275–276
  cost–benefit analysis in, 226
  defined, 249, 250–251
  difficulties in, 268–271
  feasibility of, 238–239, 268
  for blood management, 4, 75–79, 255–256
  for coal-mine transport planning, 257–259
  for energy-analysis results, 266, 314
  for fire protection, 5–6, 86–88
  for flood control, 265–266
  for housing assistance, 9–10
  for parts provisioning, 260–265
  for public transport, 266–267
  games, 270, 273
  good practice in, 271–272
  in business firms, 250
  involving multiple organizations, 265–267
  negotiations in, 276
  planning, 215, 216, 254, 264, 306
  scenarios for, 273
  social experiments in, 274–275
Index, 141, 143, 221, 232, 262–263, 265; *see also* Indicators
  ratio, 221
Indicators, 141, 143, 221, 265; *see also* Consequences
  combined into index, 221
  of forest-pest control policies, 11, 233–237
Industrial engineering, 35, 38, 53
Information gathering, 297–298; *see also* Data, collection
Insensitivity, 185–186
Institute of Management Sciences, The, 53, 54
Interfaces, 54
International Federation of Operational Research Societies, 58
International Institute for Applied Systems Analysis, xv–xvi, 7, 11, 56, 109, 146–147, 175, 182, 183, 184, 185, 219, 238, 242, 266, 281, 298, 300, 314, 316
Intervention
  articulate, 34, 315
  forms of, 320–322
Issue papers, 163, 164, 168–169
  format for, 168–169
Iteration, 121, 123–125, 137, 152–153, 161, 162–163, 172
  between analysts and decisionmakers, 215
  in cost–benefit analysis, 226
  in Delphi, 201

J

Journal of the Operational Research Society, 53
Judgment, *see also* Models, judgmental
  expert, 201
  group, 195
  in cost–benefit analysis, 226
  individual, 200
  in forecasting, 209

K
Knowing-in-action, 289–290

L
Lanchester Prize, 40, 55
  committee, 41, 59
Laws, 160
LIBS (Long Island Blood Services), 75, 256; see also Blood
Limits, see Constraints
Liquefacation
  allothermal, 113, 182, 183, 184, 298
  autothermal, 113, 183–184
Logistics, 186

M
Maintainers, 261, 263–264
Maintenance, 186
Management, see Decisionmakers, Project management
Management science, 51, 62, 251, 288; see also Operations research
Management Science, 51
Managers, see Decisionmakers
  in computer system, 261, 263
Mandate in implementation, 276
Markov chain, 71, 73
Mathematics, applied, 22
Maximin, 240
Measures of performance, 164, 169, 176–178, 187, 196, 227; see also Consequences
  faulty, 177
  for blood management, 3–4, 69, 72, 74, 78–79
  for fire protection, 4–5, 81–82
  for housing assistance, 10
  proxy, 176–177
Measuring effectiveness, 176–178; see also Measures of performance
Mess, 152, 288, 290
Modeling, 166, 191–218; see also Models
  contrasted with systems analysis, 22
  craft in, 29
  documentation in, 206
  in systems analysis, 44, 191–218
  mathematical, 200
  premises for, 214–216
  simplifications in, 205–206
  techniques, 194–202
Models, 19, 119–120, 122, 123, 127, 136–140, 161, 165, 185, 191–218, 243; see also Modeling
  analytic, 194–196
  as theories, 19
  as uncertain predictors, 139–140, 219–220
  calibrating, 207–208
  categories of, 194
  characteristics of, 214
  choice of, 300–301
  computer, 191, 193–194, 195, 211, 288
  descriptive, 196
  experiments as, 138
  for blood management, 3, 72–75
  for energy projections, 7–8, 114
  for fire protection, 5, 82–85
  for flood protection, 96
  for forest-pest control, 12
  gaming, see Gaming
  implementation planning, 215
  improving, 206–207
  in fine-tuning alternatives, 187
  informative, 196
  in science, 192–193
  in suboptimizations, 224
  interactive, 199
  judgmental, 199, 199–202, 205; see also Judgment
  large vs. small, 211
  man–machine, 194, 199
  mathematical, 200, 219–220
  mental, 192, 193–194; see also Models, judgmental
  monolithic, 215
  need for, 192–194
  planning, 216
  policy analysis, 215
  predictive, see Consequences, models as predictors of
  prescriptive, 21, 196
  quantitative, 195
  role-playing, 199
  simulation, see Simulation
  toolkit approach to, 215–216
  use in screening, 187, 192
  using, 138–139
  validity of, xiii, 137, 138, 207–208, 300
  verifying, 207
  what they give us, 213–216
Modes of analysis, 299–301
Monte Carlo method, 211–212, 239
Muddling through, 28

N
National Academy of Sciences, U. S., 320, 321
National Health Service, British, 43
Negotiator in implementation, 276
New York City–Rand Institute, The, 80–81
NYBS (New York Blood Services), 77; see also Blood

Subject Index

O

Objective function, 141, 238; *see also* Indicators
Objectives, 118, 121–123, 125, 127, 128–129, 158–159, 161, 164, 169, 171–189, 223–224, 227, 238, 272
　and criteria, 221–222
　competing, 13, 178–180, 219
　compromise among, 180
　conflicting, 158
　conversion to constraints, 179, 222–223
　hierarchy of, 128–129
　high-level, 173–174, 179, 223–224
　in cost–benefit analysis, 46
　in systems analysis, 154, 171–189
　low-level, 173–174, 179, 223–224
　multiple, 129, 178–180, 229, 243
　of blood management, 3, 174
　of energy-supply systems, 175
　of fire protection, 4, 174, 174–175
　of flood protection, 6, 175–176
　of housing assistance, 8–9
　role as constraints of, 181
　shifting, 14
　tentative, 171
　tradeoffs among, 179
　unclear, 14, 172
　unique group, 179
Objectivity, 319, 324
Obligations
　of profession, 319–320
　to society, 322
Oosterschelde, 89–90
　analysis, *see* Flood protection
Openness, *see* Systems analysis, openness in
Operational research, *see* Operations research
Operational Research Club, 53
Operational Research Quarterly, 53
Operational Research Society, 53, 58
Operations analysis, xii; *see also* Operations research
Operations research, xi, xii, xiii, 20, 21, 33, 35–44, 49–52, 57–62, 196, 213, 250–252, 259, 291
　aims of, 50
　applications of, 50
　as systems analysis, 51
　as art of suboptimizing, 213
　characteristic features of, 50
　computer modeling in, 288
　craft skills in, 37, 40, 59, 60–61
　criteria of quality and effectiveness for, 57–62
　criterion problems in, 43*n*
　development of, 35–44, 50
　economic viewpoint in, 43–44
　economists in, 42
　evaluation criteria for, 50
　guidelines for practice of, 60, 61
　implementation in, 250, 251
　professional development of, 52–57
　roles of analysts in, 58–59
　suboptimization in, 42–43
　systems in, 44
　technical viewpoint in, 43
　textbooks in, 54–55
Operations Research, 51, 53
Operations Research Group, 40
Operations Research Society of America, 42, 53, 54, 55, 57–58, 60, 220, 318
　Ad Hoc Committee on Professional Standards, 60, 318
Operators in computer system, 261–263
Opinion
　legal, 320–321
　scientific, 321, 322
　systems analysis, 321
Optimization, 155, 166, 179, 196, 199, 219–220; *see also* Suboptimization
OR, *see* Operations research
Oral presentation, *see* Communicating, briefings for
ORSA, *see* Operations Research Society of America
Outcomes, 119, 317, 318; *see also* Consequences
Outdate rate, 3, 4, 69; *see also* Blood
Outline
　study, 161; *see also* Plan, analysis

P

Pareto improvement, 221
　defined, 221
PBDS (Programmed Blood Distribution System), 4, 76–78; *see also* Blood
PERT (Program Evaluation Review Technique), 276
Perturbation, 216; *see also* Sensitivity analysis
Philosophy, *see* Systems analysis, philosophy for
Piling on, 270
Pitfalls
　of adherence to menu of choices, 325
　of adherence to paradigm, 325
　of analysis, 25, 26, 27, 317
　of appearing to do more than is done, 306
　of communication, 244
　of data analysis, 205
　of data belief, 297
　of data gathering, 298
　of forecasting, 134
　of modeling, 139
　of oral presentation, 308–309
　of problem formulation, 152
Plan
　analysis, 294–296, 303, 313

Poisson distribution, 72
POLANO (Policy Analysis of the
    Oosterschelde), 89; see also Flood
    protection
Policy advisor, 28
Policy analysis, xii, 21, 24, 44–49, 50–52,
    215, 327; see also Systems analysis
  aims of, 50
  applications of, 50
  as systems analysis, 51
  characteristic features of, 50
  evaluation criteria for, 50
  principles for, 323
Policy Analysis, 51, 54
Policymaker, see Decisionmaker
Policy science, see Policy analysis
Policy Sciences, 51, 54
Population growth, 111
Positivism, 37, 287
Practice, xiv, 281–326
  dilemmas of, 299
  epistemology of, 30, 287, 289
  good, 20, 306, 324
  in implementation, 271–272
Practitioner, see also Craft, Decisionmakers,
    relations with, Practice, Systems
    analysis
  reflective, 289–290
Prediction, see Consequences, predicting,
    Forecasting
Preference structure in decision analysis,
    229–230
Present value, 225
Presentation
  oral, 231–232
Problem, 1–2, 22–24, 305
  appreciation, 290–292
  as a subproblem, 223
  context, see Contexts
  criterion, 230
  environment, see Environment
  formulation, 122, 123, 124, 126, 127–132,
    151–170, 173, 236, 290–292, 293–297

  formulation activities, 161–164
  formulation concepts, 153–156
  giver, 153
  hard, 154, 155–156, 158, 161, 166
  in cost–benefit analysis, 44–45
  in nexus of problems, 254, 290
  in policy analysis, 48
  in systems analysis, 117
  perceptions, 156–157
  posers, 164, 167
  setting, 254, 287, 288, 313; see also
    Problem, situation
  situation, 17, 152, 156–157, 159–160, 162,
    167–168, 288, 290–292; see also
    Problem, setting
  soft, 154, 161, 166, 168, 173
  solver, 153
  solving, 165, 287–288; see also Problem-
    solving system
  structure, 157
Problématique, 152, 153, 159, 290
Problem-content system, 153–154, 156, 161,
    162–164, 167–168
Problem-solving system, 153–154, 156, 158,
    162–163, 167–168
Process, 157
Professional practice, see Practice
Professions
  crisis in, 286–287
Program budgeting, 34
Programming, 40–41
  linear, 185–196
Project management in implementation, 276
Proposals, 296
Provisioning spare parts, 260–265
Proxy
  measure of blood–supply cost, 180
  measure of effectiveness, 176–177
  measure of value, 228–229
  measures of fire protection, 5, 68, 81
  objectives, 129, 175, 179

Q
Quick-and-dirty study, 284

R
Ranking, 121–123, 127, 130, 140–145, 169,
    196, 210–211, 229, 238, 242
  by decision analysis, 229–230
  criteria for, 220–222, 238
  in cost–benefit analysis, 224–225
Rand Corporation, The, 6, 8, 54, 56, 89, 92,
    93, 98, 101n, 108–109, 146, 154, 183,
    265, 266
Rate of return
  internal 225
Ratio criteria, 221, 227–228
Rational actor model, see Decisionmaker, as
    rational actor
RBC (Regional Blood Center), 3, 69; see also
    Blood
Reflection-in-action, 289–290
Relevance, see Rigor or relevance
Reliability, 186
Report, see Systems analysis, report
Resources, 269–270
  financial, 269
  human, 269–270
  physical, 269
Resources for the Future, 56
Results, 119; see also Consequences
Rigor or relevance, 288–289
Rijkswaterstaat, 6–7, 89, 96, 99n, 100, 108–
    109, 146, 265
Risk, 241
  as cost, 224

Subject Index

assessment, 241
 displayed on scorecards, 231–236
 estimation, 241
 evaluation, 241
Risk–benefit analysis, 227
Robustness, 185–186
 in computer-system design, 263
 of implementation program, 257, 271
Role playing, 137
Root definition, 165
RWS, *see* Rijkswaterstaat

S

Satisficing, xiii, 62, 158, 179, 222–223
 defined, 179
Scale of effort, 228–229
Scenarios, 199, 201–202, 208, 209, 215, 216
 for forecasting, 134, 202
 for implementation, 273
 in energy analysis, 113–114, 202, 209, 209–210
Science, 18–20, 321–322
 defined, 19
 documentation in, 301
 in professional practice, 286–290
 method of, 19, 37
 models in, 192–193
 relation to systems analysis of, 18–20, 58–63, 151–152, 155
Scientific management, 38–39
Scorecards, 93, 98, 141, 142–143, 144, 227, 231–236
 advantages of, 232–233
 disadvantage of, 233
 for flood-protection alternatives, 93–107, 141
Screening, *see* Alternatives, screening
Search theory, 40, 40*n*
Sensitivity
 analysis, 138, 141, 211–212, 215, 239, 300, 302, 311, 323
 displayed on scorecards, 232
 of flood-protection alternatives, 93–94, 108
Shortage rate, 3; *see also* Blood
Simplifications, *see* Modeling, simplifications in
Simulation, 166, 194, 195, 196–197, 200, 201
 computer, 196–197
 defined, 196
 in coal-mine transport design, 258–259
 interactive, *see* Gaming
 man–machine, 137
 stochastic, 139
Social systems, *see also* Systems
 resistance to change in, 15
Société Française de Recherche Opérationnelle, 53
Society
 relations with, 317–325

Soft systems, *see* Problem, soft
Spillovers, *see* Effects, spillover
Square-root law for average travel distance, 83–84, 196, 203–204, 206
SSB (Storm-Surge Barrier), 89; *see also* Flood protection
Standards, *see* Guidelines
Stanford Research Institute, 56
Structure, *see* Problem, structure
Suboptimization, 42–43, 45, 46–47, 213, 220, 223–224, 228; *see also* Optimization
Subproblems, 223
Systems, xi
 appreciative, 165
 associated with problems, 12
 complexity in, 15
 environments for, *see* Environment
 illustrated, 1
 in operations research, 44
 in systems analysis, 44
 man–machine operating, xi, 20
 phenomena, 20
 regular behavior in, 1
Systems analysis, xi–xiv, 1–30, 50–52, 57–64, 117–147
 activities in, 16–17, 122–127, 251
 adaptive, 255
 additional, 311
 a fortiori analysis in, 39–40, 187
 aims of, 16, 33, 50, 153, 155, 215, 244, 323
 applications of, 22–24, 50; *see also* Cases
 as articulate intervention, 34
 as change agent, 62–64, 282–283, 315–316
 as discipline, 35–52
 as procedural basis, 49
 as process, xiii–xiv; *see also* Systems analysis, as social process
 as profession, 35, 52–64
 as social process, 18, 48, 62; *see also* Systems analysis, as process
 as tool of advocacy, 24, 34
 as guidance for decision, 219–245
 as meant here and elsewhere, 21–22
 as part of larger process, 255
 as policy analysis, 44–49, 51
 bibliography for, 327–331
 briefing, 307–310
 books on, 56–57; *see also* Systems analysis, bibliography
 carrying out, 301–302
 characteristics of, 15–18, 21
 client participation in, 296–297
 consistency in, 45–46
 contrasted with science, 20
 craft of, *see* Craft
 criteria of quality for, 54, 57–62
 criticisms of, 26–27, 166, 330
 defined, 2, 15–16, 20, 30
 descendent problems in, 35

Systems analysis (*cont.*)
  development of, 33–66, 252
  difficulties in, 14–15
  disciplinary criticism in, 34
  evaluation criteria for, 50
  explicitness in, 45
  focusing findings of, 243–245
  formulating findings of, 302–303
  framework for, 121–127
  genesis of, 20–21, 33–66; *see also* Systems analysis, history of
  goals of, 7, 11, 268; *see also* Systems analysis, aims of
  hard, *see* Problem, hard
  history of, 20, 33–66, 330–331
  implementation in, *see* Implementation
  innovative, 255
  language of, 62–64
  limitations of, 26
  limits of, 306, 313
  methods of, 33
  methodology of, 16–18, 117–147
  misuses of, 25
  modes of analysis in, 299–301
  nature of problems for, 12–15, 17
  objectives of, *see* Systems analysis, goals of
  obligations to society of, 319–320
  openness in, 301, 318–320, 324
  organizational design for, 56–57
  paradigm for, 325
  partial, 126–127
  phases of, 123, 124, 126
  philosophy for, 154, 286–290, 315–316, 330
  plan for, 295–296
  principles for, 323
  professional development of, 52–57
  quick-response, 126
  related to other specialties, 18–22
  report, 304–307
  reporting level for, 284
  rigor or relevance in, 289
  role in contributing to change of, 282; *see also* Systems analysis, as change agent
  role in implementation of, 255–268
  rough data in, 37–38
  secondary decisions in, 301
  soft, *see* Problem, soft
  support for, 295–296
  systems in, 44
  tools of, 16
  unifying role of, 18
  value of, 24–25, 25–26, 28, 30–31
  variational methods in, 39
Systems engineering, 20, 50, 51, 53, 154, 187
Systems research, xii; *see also* Systems analysis

T
Target, 128, 129; *see also* Objectives
Technical rationality, 287
  difficulties caused by, 287–289
Technology contrasted to systems analysis, 151–152
Terawatt, 112
Theories, *see* Models
Time horizon, 136
TIMS, *see* Institute of Management Sciences, The
Toolkit, 215–216, 232
Trans-science, 322
Triangular distribution, 72
TWyr (terawatt-year), 112

U
Uncertainties, 13, 155, 239–241, 243
  about future conditions, 219
User of systems analysis, *see* Decisionmakers
Utility
  analysis, 221
  functions, 143–144, 179

V
Validation, *see* Models, validity of
Value, 228–229; *see also* Judgment
  analysis, 236–239
  clarification, 173
  critique, 173
  function, 143–144, 179, 230
  function, multiattribute, 143–144
  in decision analysis, 229
  preferences, 241
  theory of, 199
Values, 154, 155, 164, 165, 229, 238; *see also* Decisionmakers, values of
  distinguished from facts, 238
  legitimate judges of, 238, 241
  monetary, *see* Present value
  societal, 232
Verification, *see* Models, verifying
Visual aids, 307–310; *see also* Scorecards
Vulnerability, 186

W
Wilmington, Delaware, *see* Fire protection
Workbook for problem formulation, 162–164, 167–168